The Politics of Education

Monographs in German History

Volume 1

Osthandel and Ostpolitik: German Foreign Trade Policies in Eastern Europe from Bismarck to Adenauer
Mark Spaulding

Volume 2

A Question of Priorities: Democratic Reform and Economic Recovery in Postwar Germany
Rebecca Boehling

Volume 3

From Recovery to Catastrophe: Municipal Stabilization and Political Crisis in Weimar Germany
Ben Lieberman

Volume 4

Nazism in Central Germany: The Brownshirts in 'Red' Saxony
Christian W. Szejnmann

Volume 5

Citizens and Aliens: Foreigners and the Law in Britain and the German States 1789–1870
Andreas Fahrmeir

Volume 6

Poems in Steel: National Socialism and the Politics of Inventing from Weimar to Bonn
Kees Gispen

Volume 7

"Aryanisation" in Hamburg
Frank Bajohr

Volume 8

The Politics of Education: Teachers and School Reform in Weimar Germany
Marjorie Lamberti

Volume 9

The Ambivalent Alliance: Konrad Adenauer, the CDU/CSU, and the West, 1949–1966
Ronald J. Granieri

THE POLITICS OF EDUCATION

Teachers and School Reform in
Weimar Germany

Marjorie Lamberti

Berghahn Books
NEW YORK · OXFORD

First published in 2002 by

Berghahn Books

www.berghahnbooks.com

First paperback edition published in 2004

© 2002, 2004 Marjorie Lamberti

All rights reserved.
Except for the quotation of short passages
for the purposes of criticism and review, no part of this book
may be reproduced in any form or by any means, electronic or
mechanical, including photocopying, recording, or any information
storage and retrieval system now known or to be invented,
without written permission of the publisher.

Library of Congress Cataloging-in-Publication Data

Lamberti, Marjorie, 1937–
 The politics of education : teachers and school reform in Weimar Germany / Marjorie Lamberti
   p. cm. (Monographs in German history ; v. 8)
 Includes bibliographical references and index.
 ISBN 1-57181-298-9 (cl. : alk. paper)— ISBN 1-57181-299-7 (pbk. : alk. paper)
   I. Title. II. Series.

LC93.G3 L36 2002
370'.943—dc21   2001043574

British Library Cataloguing in Publication Data

A catalogue record for this book is available from
the British Library.

Printed in Canada on acid-free paper

To my sister Alice

Contents

Acknowledgments	viii
Introduction	1
Chapter 1: The Avant-Garde of the School Reform Movement in Imperial Germany	11
Chapter 2: The November Revolution and the Opening of a New Era for School Reforms	44
Chapter 3: Pedagogues and Pastors in the Political Conflicts over the School	69
Chapter 4: Educational Reformers and the Modern School in the Republican State	105
Chapter 5: The Culture Wars over the Schools in the Weimar Era	151
Chapter 6: Schoolteachers and the Nazi Movement during the Crisis of the Republic	196
Conclusion	245
Bibliography	253
Index	267

Acknowledgments

The completion of this book would not have been possible without the cooperation and help of a large number of archives, libraries, and research institutes in Germany and the United States. A special debt of thanks is due to the librarians and archivists whose competent and efficient service and personal kindness made the labor of historical research become an adventurous and pleasurable experience at the Geheimes Staatsarchiv Preussischer Kulturbesitz, Abteilung Merseburg (the depository is now located in Berlin-Dahlem), the Sächsisches Hauptstaatsarchiv in Dresden, the Bundesarchiv in Potsdam, the Staatsbibliothek Preussischer Kulturbesitz and the Bibliothek für Bildungsgeschichtliche Forschung in Berlin, the Sächsische Landesbibliothek in Dresden, and the Deutsche Bücherei and the Universitätsbibliothek in Leipzig. For a scholar living in a town in rural Vermont, the use of the rich and extensive collection at the Sterling Memorial Library of Yale University has been essential for every one of my research projects, and I am deeply grateful for the library privileges granted to me over many years. Closer to home, Fleur Laslocky and the interloan library staff at the Starr Library at Middlebury College have always been cheerfully helpful whenever I submitted requests for books.

Middlebury College has a generous sabbatical program and professional development fund for its faculty, and this financial support has made it possible for me to work in Germany for extended periods of time and to fulfill my aspiration to be both a teacher and an active scholar, while living in the glorious setting of the Green Mountains of Vermont. Working on this project in two research centers afforded me the advantage of presenting my historical findings and testing out my interpretations and conclusions in a community of scholars. I would like to express my appreciation to the Institute for Advanced Study in Princeton, New Jersey, for a fellowship in 1992–93, and to the Woodrow Wilson International Center for Scholars in Washington, D.C., for a fellowship in 1997–98. At both research centers I found not only superb facilities and an ideal environment for research and writing, but also a very congenial community of scholars with whom I discussed my work in progress in formal seminar settings and informally over lunch. I benefited immensely from the wise advice that Peter Paret gave me at a time when my project was taking a clearer shape. For their interest in my research, probing questions, and insights, I would like to thank Arnulf Baring, Ernst Falzeder, Albert Hirschman, Michael Katz, Peter Katzenstein, Doris Kaufmann, Harold Mah, Franz Georg Maier, Richard King, Peter Schäfer, George Stocking, and Martin Wiener.

I received very helpful critical comments from Roger Chickering and Andreas Daum when I presented a paper at a meeting of the Standing Seminar in German History at the Center for German and European Studies at Georgetown University in 1998. I was greatly encouraged by the appreciative remarks of Margaret Anderson and Claudia Koonz when I presented a second paper at the annual meeting of the German Studies Association in 1999. Both papers were published as articles in *History of Education Quarterly* and *Central European History*. James Albisetti, Konrad Jarausch, and Kenneth Barkin made informed critical comments on sections of my work, and their rigorous questioning led me to clarify and strengthen my analysis and argument. Fritz Ringer was kind enough to read the entire manuscript promptly and to provide me with valuable suggestions and astute advice for the task of revision. David Blackbourn, Roger Chickering, William Hagen, Konrad Jarausch, James Melton, and James Sheehan gave me strong support when I requested their help, and I remain deeply grateful to them for their encouragement and confidence in my successful completion of this project. Finally, I want to express my thanks to Marion Berghahn for adding my book to her distinguished list of publications and to Shawn Kendrick for her meticulous editorial work and for shepherding my manuscript through the publication process.

Introduction

The "crisis of education" was a catchword in the polemical discourse of many conservative and Nazi opponents of the Weimar Republic in the early 1930s. Widely discussed in circles of the educated elite and among rural and small-town teachers was a spate of articles in the press on the loss of public confidence in the elementary schools. Neoconservative ideologues in *Die Tat*, for example, lambasted progressive education in the schools of Germany's postwar democracy, and declared that the pedagogues had alienated many sections of society by advocating reforms that were similar to the school program of the Social Democratic Party.[1] As this critique of the school reforms introduced by the Social Democrats and German Democrats after the revolution of 1918 indicates, *Kulturpolitik* played a significant role in the right-wing assault on the republican state. Notwithstanding postwar Germany's economic distress and political instability, the Weimar years were a time of exuberant pedagogical innovation and optimistic plans to reform the stratified educational system in the name of democracy and social justice. Forged in the culture wars over the schools in the 1920s was a coalition of traditionalists, including clergymen and educators in the secondary schools, who opposed the reforms and who could count on the political muscle of the Catholic Center Party and bourgeois conservative parties. Their prime target were the pedagogues in the elementary schools who were organized in the German Teachers' Association (Deutscher Lehrerverein), the most active advocacy group for educational reform in the country since the turn of the century.

Many individuals espoused the cause of educational reform in Weimar Germany, but the activists of the German Teachers' Association can undisputedly claim the central place in a historical account of the school reform movement since 1900. This professional society was the biggest organization of teachers in Germany with a membership of 132,043 in 1922. Its members included two-thirds of the 195,946 full-time teachers who instructed the more than 8,890,000 children in the German elementary schools at that time.[2] After the November Revolution, elementary schoolteachers were among the "new middle class" of civil servants who joined or actively supported the German Democratic and Social Democratic Parties. These members of the teachers' association fought for school reforms in public life with an investment of time and energy that was matched by no other organization in or outside of their profession. Its elected leaders knew and had access to officials in the Reich Interior Ministry and in the education ministries of the states of the Reich. Several of its members were elected to the German National Assembly and state parliaments in 1919, and many more of them were appointed to offices in the school administration. In comparison, the League of Resolute School Reformers (Bund entschiedener Schulreformer), organized by Paul Oestreich and other secondary schoolteachers on the political left in September 1919, was a small coterie of cultural socialists that never became a significant presence in the public debates on educational reform or school legislation. Turning a blind eye to his own ineffectiveness, Oestreich belittled the fight for school reforms waged by the "liberal elementary schoolteachers."[3]

The role of elementary schoolteachers in the educational reform movement has been obscured or underestimated in much of the historical literature on the teaching profession and the reform pedagogy in the Weimar years. Historical studies of the thinking of the German educational reformers have given little attention to the institutional basis of the reform movement and the connection between culture and politics. In some of these works, the founders of a few small, experimental private schools and the professors who taught philosophy of education in the universities have a more prominent place than do the pedagogues in the public elementary schools.[4] Research on elementary schoolteachers in the Weimar Republic has concentrated on the history of their professional associations and the question of their attraction to the ideology of National Socialism.[5] In view of this line of historical inquiry, it should come as no surprise that numerous studies of Weimar culture have overlooked the educational reform movement—and the conservative mobilization against it—in their discussions of cultural modernity in the 1920s.[6]

The movement for educational reform was born in the *Kaiserreich*, and its earliest supporters were predominantly left-wing liberals who taught in the elementary schools in the big cities. Chapter 1 provides a social and political profile of the avant-garde of the school reform movement. Of particular interest here is the intriguing question of why these pedagogues, recruited to a large extent from the lower strata of the bourgeoisie, became the most vocal critics of Germany's rigidly stratified school system, which was patterned after the class structure of society, and began the fight for a more democratic educational system during the imperial monarchy. Although the German reformers were contemporaries of John Dewey, the American philosopher of education who is often referred to as the "father of progressive education," they were stimulated more by the theories of child development and the learning process formed in the field of psychology in their own country than by Dewey's writings, and became exponents of the *neue Pädagogik*, as progressive education was called in Germany after the turn of the century.

The reformers' proposals for change contested the legitimacy of the traditional structures of public education in Imperial Germany. They demanded the removal of the barriers that limited access to the institutions of secondary and higher education. Invoking the principle of equality of rights and opportunity, they proposed reforms that would allow all youths, irrespective of the wealth and class status of their parents, to attain a level of education commensurate with their abilities. In a nation sharply divided into social classes and Catholic and Protestant sociocultural milieus, the reformers believed that public education should be used as a means to promote social reconciliation and cultural integration and to foster a civic identity that transcended group solidarities. They called for the closing of the socially exclusive public preparatory schools (*Vorschulen*), the elimination of confessional segmentation in the elementary school system, and the legal establishment of the common school (the *allgemeine Volksschule* or *gemeinsame Grundschule*) for children of all social classes and religious faiths.

With soaring expectations of school reforms, members of the German Teachers' Association welcomed the founding of the Weimar Republic and the assumption of governmental power by the Social Democratic and left-liberal German Democratic Parties in Prussia, Saxony, and other states in the German Reich. And yet, as chapter 2 shows, the biggest hurdle for the reformers arose shortly after the revolution of 1918, when governmental decrees related to catechism instruction, prayers, and the observance of religious holidays in the schools provoked massive protests, and the issues of the relation of church and school and religious instruction in the schools were thrust onto the center stage of party politics. The future of religious education in the elementary schools became the most contentious and ideologically polarizing question in the politics of culture.

The question of religious instruction in the schools and the claims of the Christian churches to the right to supervise it could not be resolved as quickly in Germany as it had been in France under the Third Republic. The secularization of the French public school system in the 1880s made *laïcité* a test of republican allegiance that few politicians would fail to meet by the 1920s. Freedom of education in France gave parents who wanted a religious education for their children an exit out of the state's school system, and the Catholic Church there developed an extensive system of private schools.[7] In Germany, on the other hand, the state's monopoly of education, preserved throughout the nineteenth century by the practice of making accommodations to the interests of the Christian churches, was a historical legacy that was viewed as an encumbrance by some left-liberal reformers in the 1920s.[8] Religious instruction, based on the confessional beliefs of the Catholic and Protestant faiths, was a subject in the public elementary schools. The system of confessional schooling that prevailed in most states in the German Reich had many disadvantages for the Jewish minority and for parents and teachers who no longer believed in the doctrines of Christian orthodoxy. In the interests of promoting community, tolerance, and freedom of conscience in a diverse society, the Social Democrats in the school reform movement advocated the exclusion of religious instruction from the curriculum. The German Democrats represented the views of a larger number of schoolteachers when they took into account the significant place of religion in the cultural heritage of the German people and the deep feelings aroused by the issue of religion in the schools. These left-liberal reformers adopted a mediating position with the hope of settling the school question by a consensus that would avoid any violation of freedom of conscience and yet open the way to an integrated elementary school system.

It is tempting to see the political conflicts over the schools in the Weimar Republic as a bipolar struggle between the parties of the "unbelieving" left and the Christian churches. To reconstruct and interpret these controversies as an assault of anticlerical socialists on the churches is an oversimplification.[9] The three parties of the Weimar coalition in the German National Assembly, the Center, German Democrats, and Social Democrats, negotiated a compromise on the fundamental principles for a national school law that were inscribed in the school articles of the Reich Constitution of 1919. The account of the political battles over the schools in chapters 3 and 5 explains how and why public discourse on the school question became polarized after the framers of the Constitution completed their work. Standing as defenders of the parents' right to choose the kind of public school that their children would attend, Catholic and Protestant churchmen built up and led massive parents' organizations to fight the reformers and preserve confessional schools. The effectiveness with which the Catholic School Organization (Katholische Schulorganisation) and Protestant Parents' League (Evangelischer Elternbund) mobilized millions of parents at the grassroots set an example that left-wing socialists sought to emulate in the Ruhr and other industrial areas with large working-class populations. Although the traditionalists perceived this radical agitation as a major threat, the extent to which these socialists actually succeeded in organizing a powerful secular school movement must be examined. In view of the activism of clergymen in school politics throughout the Weimar period, the neglect of this subject in the historical literature on the Protestant Church during the republic is striking and inexplicable.[10] Political historians, too, have failed to note the centrality of the school issue in Weimar's public life and parliamentary politics.

"Hostility to religion"—a charge hurled at the Social Democrats and the progressivist pedagogues alike by clergymen and politicians in the Center and German Nationalist Parties—neither does justice to the complexity of the issues nor explains the intentions and motives of those Germans who fought for school reforms. In 1921–22 and 1927, members of the German Teachers' Association lobbied deputies in the Reichstag and mobilized public opposition to defeat school bills whose concessions to the demands of Catholic and Protestant church leaders violated the letter and spirit of the school articles of the Constitution. By incorporating the teachers in this story, my book not only provides a more complete analysis of the culture wars but also disentangles the fundamental issues from the propaganda slogans.

Some aspects of these polemical exchanges are still alive today because the issues of contention are similar to those questions concerning public education that have preoccupied citizens in many democratic and culturally diverse societies in modern times.[11] The traditionalists and progressivist pedagogues in Weimar Germany had different perspectives on how the purposes of public education should be defined and drew different conclusions about the consequences of cultural pluralism for public educational institutions. They were not of one mind on the employment of the mechanism of public schooling to enhance commonality in the civic community, on the assessment of the extent of the rights of parents and the power of the state as the representative of the whole social community in the sphere of public education, and on the place of religious education in the public schools. In their defense of confessional public schools, churchmen and other conservatives, who had mourned the fall of the imperial monarchy and the old authoritarian order in November 1918, became adept at framing their arguments with references to the nature of a "true democracy," the constitutional rights of parents, freedom of conscience, and tolerance.

Although the workings of parliamentary democracy and governing coalitions gave the Center Party tremendous leverage in *Kulturpolitik*, and the progressivist pedagogues experienced some disappointments, the Weimar years can rightly be seen as "a great age of educational reform," as Detlev Peukert wrote.[12] During the deliberations of the German National Assembly in 1919, the leaders of the German Teachers' Association lobbied vigorously to persuade the parties to add fundamental principles related to public education to the future constitution. The school articles of the Weimar Constitution actually incorporated many of the reformers' demands and aspirations. Chapter 4 examines the factors that facilitated the implementation of school reforms and the transformation of traditional school life in many cities through the introduction of the new pedagogy. The founding of the republic infused the progressivist pedagogues with a new sense of purpose. Republicans by conviction and affective loyalty, they now related the methods of progressive education in the active-learning school to the development of the child as well as to the requirements of civic education in the democratic state.

The account of educational reform in Weimar Germany in this book has a broad societal perspective and discusses the reception of these innovations within society and the mobilization of political opposition to them.

The traditionalists were a coalition of Catholic and Protestant churchmen, political right-wingers in the German Secondary Schoolteachers' Association (Deutscher Philologenverband), and splinter groups of disgruntled, antirepublican principals and teachers in the elementary schools, whose voices in the public debates on the schools were enhanced by their connection to specific parties in parliamentary politics. In explaining the social and cultural conflicts in Weimar Germany, historians frequently point to the fragmentation of political culture and the problems of national unity and consensus in a sharply divided society.[13] My narrative of the culture wars over the schools probes beneath this macroanalysis of German society to capture the specificity of voices, aspirations, and events, and to ground explanations more closely in human decisions and actions.

This study of the educational reformers and the politics of culture moves from the metropolis to the provinces and examines closely developments in two states in the German Reich. Apart from the fact that public education during the Weimar period continued to be a matter of state regulation and administration, my research revealed the importance of doing regional studies and seeing the differences among schoolteachers in the cities and in small towns and villages in order to arrive at a more nuanced assessment of the extension of the reforms and to understand the cultural backlash against them. The pedagogical innovations widened the chasm separating teachers in the modern school in the cities and the traditional schoolhouse in the countryside. Saxony was the hub of progressive education in Germany, and the reformers and experimental schools in Leipzig, Dresden, and Chemnitz in the 1920s played a significant role in the training of teachers in the new methods. In comparison with the predominantly Protestant population of industrial Saxony, Prussia, the largest state in the Reich, embodied the religious diversity of German society and was the home of 59 percent of the Catholics and 71 percent of the Jews living in Germany in 1925.[14]

Historians have recently begun to explore in more detail the links between the backlash against cultural modernity and the political destabilization of the Weimar Republic. Research on the Fighting League for German Culture (Kampfbund für deutsche Kultur) documents the readiness of cultural conservatives to collaborate with this Nazi front organization in its war against modernism in the arts.[15] Studies of Thuringia in the Weimar years, when the Social Democrats in the state government carried out sweeping social and educational reforms, reveals how *völkisch*-nationalist and Nazi groupings found optimum conditions for development in this political landscape.[16] The last chapter in this book uncovers another facet of this relationship by examining the traditionalists' critique of the modern school and their longing for a right-wing reorientation in school politics and also the susceptibility of certain sections of the teaching profession to the ideology of National Socialism at the time of crisis in the republican state. The Nazi movement's success in winning the support of elementary school principals and teachers, a minority in the profession prior to 1933, lay in the field of *Kulturpolitik* to a greater extent than historians have recognized.[17] At the same time, the presence of many steadfast republicans in the German Teachers' Association and their defense of the democratic state vis-à-vis the threat of National Socialism underscores the necessity of viewing schoolteachers as a politically differentiated profession when examining the erosion of support for liberal democracy among them.[18]

To ensure a clear understanding of the intentions of the reformers discussed in this book, some remarks should be made about the gender-inclusive language in the discourse of male and female elementary schoolteachers in the progressive education movement. The progressivist pedagogues spoke about children (*Kinder*) and persons (*Menschen*) and the child's nature and needs without making distinctions between boys and girls. The progressivist pedagogues, men and women alike, wrote about the instruction of arithmetic and natural science without expressing any assumptions or normative expectations in regard to gender-differentiated capacities for learning in these subjects. In the modern schools in which they taught during the Weimar era, gymnastics and other sports that promoted physical fitness and self-confidence were part of the curriculum for girls and boys alike. The school reformers sought to develop the intellectual potential and creative powers of both girls and boys and to cultivate in them a sense of freedom and moral responsibility as well as the capacity to act on their own initiative and to think independently.

Notes

1. Horst Grueneberg, "Schulreform mit falschem Ziel," *Die Tat* 23 (April 1931): 1–17; idem, "Was wird aus der Schule?" *Die Tat* 23 (September 1931): 460–79.
2. *Vierteljahrshefte zur Statistik des Deutschen Reichs.* Vol. 39, Ergänzungsheft 5: *Das Schulwesen im Deutschen Reich 1926-27* (Berlin, 1931), p. 3.
3. Paul Oestreich, *Der deutsche Schulkampf im zwanzigsten Jahrhundert* (Frankenhausen, 1925), pp. 9–10; Winfried Böhm, "Lehrer zwischen Kulturkritik und Gemeinschaftsutopie. Der Bund entschiedener Schulreformer," in *Der Lehrer und seine Organisation*, ed. Manfred Heinemann (Stuttgart, 1977), pp. 191–200.
4. Heinz-Elmar Tenorth, "Pädagogisches Denken," in *Handbuch der deutschen Bildungsgeschichte.* Vol. 5: *1918-1945*, ed. Dieter Langewiesche and Heinz-Elmar Tenorth (Munich, 1989), pp. 111–48; Wolfgang Scheibe, *Die Reformpädagogische Bewegung 1900-1932. Eine einführende Darstellung* (Weinheim, 1969); Jürgen Oelkers, *Reformpädagogik. Eine kritische Dogmengeschichte* (Weinheim, 1989); Ulrich Herrmann, "Pädagogisches Denken und Anfänge der Reformpädagogik," in *Handbuch der deutschen Bildungsgeschichte.* Vol. 4: *1870-1918*, ed. Christa Berg (Munich, 1991), pp. 147–78; H. J. Hahn, *Education and Society in Germany* (Oxford and New York, 1998), chap. 3. A well-researched account of the politics of school reform in Hamburg can be found in Hildegard Milberg, *Schulpolitik in der*

pluralistischen Gesellschaft. Die politischen und sozialen Aspekte der Schulreform in Hamburg 1890–1935 (Hamburg, 1970). Two other works end their examination of developments in Bremen and Saxony in the early years of the Weimar Republic. Dirk Hagener, *Radikale Schulreform zwischen Programmatik und Realität. Die schulpolitischen Kämpfe in Bremen vor dem Ersten Weltkrieg und in der Entstehungsphase der Weimarer Republik* (Bremen, 1973); Burkehard Poste, *Schulreform in Sachsen 1918–1923. Eine vergessene Tradition deutscher Schulgeschichte* (Frankfurt am Main, 1993).

5. Rainer Bölling, *Volksschullehrer und Politik. Der Deutsche Lehrerverein 1918–1933* (Göttingen, 1978); Ernst Cloer, *Sozialgeschichte, Schulpolitik und Lehrerfortbildung der Katholischen Lehrerverbände im Kaiserreich und in der Weimarer Republik* (Ratingen, 1975); Wilfried Breyvogel, *Die soziale Lage und das politische Bewusstsein des Volksschullehrer 1927–1933* (Königstein, 1978); Heinrich Küppers, *Der Katholische Lehrerverband in der Übergangszeit von der Weimarer Republik zur Hitler-Diktatur* (Mainz, 1975).

6. Manfred Gangl and Gérard Raulet, eds., *Intellektuellendiskurse in der Weimarer Republik. Zur politischen Kultur einer Gemengelage* (Frankfurt am Main, 1994); Jost Herand and Frank Trommler, *Die Kultur der Weimarer Republik* (Munich, 1978); Walter Laqueur, *Weimar: A Cultural History* (New York, 1974); Peter Gay, *Weimar Culture: The Outsider as Insider* (New York, 1968).

7. Antoine Prost, *Histoire de l'Enseignement en France 1800–1967* (Paris, 1968); John Talbott, *The Politics of Educational Reform in France, 1918–1940* (Princeton, 1969).

8. Johannes Tews, *Elternrecht und Staatsrecht auf dem Schulgebiete* (Langensalza, 1924), pp. 10ff.

9. See Frank J. Gordon, "The German Evangelical Churches and the Struggle for the Schools in the Weimar Republic," *Church History* 49 (1980): 47–61, and idem, "Protestantism and Socialism in the Weimar Republic," *German Studies Review* 11 (1988): 423–46.

10. Jochen Jacke, *Kirche zwischen Monarchie und Republik. Der preussische Protestantismus nach dem Zusammenbruch von 1918* (Hamburg, 1976); Kurt Nowak, *Evangelische Kirche und Weimarer Republik. Zum politischen Weg des deutschen Protestantismus zwischen 1918 und 1932* (Göttingen, 1981); Wolfram Pyta, *Dorfgemeinschaft und Parteipolitik 1918–1933. Die Verschränkung von Milieu und Parteien in den protestantischen Landgebieten Deutschlands in der Weimarer Republik* (Düsseldorf, 1996).

11. Walter Feinberg, *Common Schools/Uncommon Identities: National Unity and Cultural Difference* (New Haven, 1998); Amy Gutmann, *Democratic Education* (Princeton, 1987); David Paris, *Ideology and Educational Reform: Themes and Theories in Public Education* (Boulder, 1995).

12. Detlev Peukert, *The Weimar Republic: The Crisis of Classical Modernity*, trans. Richard Deveson (London, 1991), pp. 142–43. In Peukert's general discussion of educational reforms, the statement that "the educational reformers looked to the youth movement and the progressive rural boarding schools for models" is disputable. For another interpretation, see Marjorie Lamberti, "Radical Schoolteachers and the Origins of the Progressive Education Movement in Germany, 1900–1914," *History of Education Quarterly* 40 (2000): 22–48.

13. Peukert, *The Weimar Republic*, chap. 12; Heinrich August Winkler, *Weimar 1918–1933. Die Geschichte der ersten deutschen Demokratie* (Munich, 1993), chap. 10; Detlef Lehnert and Klaus Megerle, "Problems of Identity and Consensus in a Fragmented Society: The Weimar Republic," in *Political Culture in Germany*, ed. Dirk Berg-Schlosser and Ralf Rythlewski (New York, 1993), pp. 43–59; Siegfried Weichlein, *Sozialmilieu und politische Kultur in der Weimarer Republik. Lebenswelt, Vereinskultur, Politik in Hessen* (Göttingen, 1996).

14. *Statistisches Jahrbuch für das Deutsche Reich* (Berlin, 1929), vol. 48, p. 16.

15. Alan Steinweis, "Conservatism, National Socialism, and the Cultural Crisis of the Weimar Republic," in *Between Reform and Resistance: Studies in the History of German Conservatism from 1789 to 1945*, ed. Larry Eugene Jones and James Retallack (Providence and Oxford, 1993), p. 343.

16. Jürgen John, "'Weimar' als regionales, intellektuelles Reform- und Experimentierfeld," in *Die Weimarer Republik zwischen Metropole und Provinz*, ed. Wolfgang Bialas and Burkhard Stenzel (Weimar, 1996), pp. 17–20.

17. Hans Schemm's propaganda strategy and activities in seeking the support of cultural conservatives in the teaching profession and the Protestant Church are overlooked in the narrowly conceived history of the National Socialist Teachers' League in Willi Feiten, *Der Nationalsozialistische Lehrerbund. Entwicklung und Organisation. Ein Beitrag zum Aufbau und zur Organisationsstruktur des nationalsozialistischen Herrschaftssystems* (Weinheim, 1981).

18. For the alienation of *Gymnasium* teachers from the ideology of liberalism and the republican state, see Konrad Jarausch, *The Unfree Professions: German Lawyers, Teachers, and Engineers, 1900–1950* (New York, 1990); idem, "The Decline of Liberal Professionalism: Reflections on the Social Erosion of German Liberalism, 1867–1933," in *In Search of a Liberal Germany: Studies in the History of German Liberalism from 1789 to the Present*, ed. Konrad Jarausch and Larry Eugene Jones (New York and Oxford, 1990), pp. 261–86.

Chapter 1

THE AVANT-GARDE OF THE SCHOOL REFORM MOVEMENT IN IMPERIAL GERMANY

*E*lementary schoolteachers in the big cities of Germany were highly visible in public life as advocates of school reform many years before the Weimar Republic provided the political conditions for the fulfillment of their aspirations and goals. From the 1890s on, proposals for the reform of the traditional pedagogy and the stratified educational system in the states of the German Empire were widely discussed in the meetings and newspapers of the professional associations of elementary schoolteachers. At their national congress in 1892, representatives of the chapters of the German Teachers' Association adopted a resolution calling for the abolition of the preparatory elementary schools (*Vorschulen*), which charged a tuition and were attended by a privileged minority of upper- and middle-class children before entering secondary school. They demanded the reorganization of the elementary educational system based on the concept of a common school for the children of all social classes and religious confessions.
Educational reform became an organized movement from 1908 on, with the founding of the League for School Reform and the creation of an office within the German Teachers' Association for the promotion of the *neue Pädagogik*, as progressive education was called at that time. The avant-gardists of this movement—pedagogues in the big cities who were predominantly Protestant and left-wing liberals—were a small part of the elementary school teaching profession, but they exercised an influence in their professional society out of proportion to their numbers. Why did these schoolteachers take up the political fight for democratic school reforms and become exponents of the "new pedagogy" and the *Arbeitsschule*, as Germany's child-centered and active-learning school was called?

From the perspective of the social milieu from which the majority of German elementary schoolteachers were recruited, one would not expect members of this profession to be intensely engaged in public life for the cause of progressive educational reforms. Male elementary schoolteachers came from the lower strata of the bourgeoisie and from small towns and rural villages. Generally, it was the brightest sons of small farmers, artisans, and shopkeepers as well as the sons of subaltern civil servants who entered the seminaries that trained schoolteachers (Lehrerseminare). Protestant women teachers were often the daughters of university-educated civil servants and professionals, but the family backgrounds of Catholic women teachers were similar to those of their male colleagues.[1] Members of this profession came predominantly from a social milieu that was known to be distrustful of and defensive toward the social changes and cultural values of modernity. It would be mistaken to attribute too much influence to their class origins.[2] Many urban schoolteachers acquired a critical perspective on the old structures of political power and social privilege and the traditional educational system. They became proponents of the theories and practices of progressive education through their professional experiences and grievances, their political-ideological outlook, and their discovery of the "new" science of psychology.

Although women were appointed to teaching positions in increasing numbers from the late 1880s on, male teachers continued to outnumber them and sought to guard the profession against feminization. In 1905, women constituted only 15.4 percent of the teachers in the elementary schools in Prussia, 18.2 percent in Bavaria, 10.3 percent in Baden, and 3.9 percent in Saxony. Most of the women teachers in Prussia taught in the heavily Catholic regions of the Rhine Province and Westphalia.[3] The resistance of male teachers to the increasing entry of women in the profession strained the relations between the separate organizations of men and women teachers. Manifestations of male prejudice in the discussion of this issue at the national congress of the German Teachers' Association in 1906 offended and piqued women teachers. Although the tradition of gender differentiation in the associational life of the teachers did not end during the Weimar Republic, the German Teachers' Association respected the civic equality of women guaranteed in the Constitution of 1919 and welcomed into its membership 12,000 women by 1930.[4]

From the 1890s on, an increasing number of urban and younger schoolteachers altered the social profile of the profession. The school administrations in the states of the German Empire created many new teaching positions in response to the pressures of demographic growth and urbanization. By 1913, one-third of the male teachers worked in heavily populated cities, and more than half of the men in the profession were thirty-five years of age and younger.[5] Freed from the constraints of rural society, the control of Conservative landowners, and the close oversight of the parish pastors, teachers in the cities became actively involved in political life and more outspoken in their criticism of social institutions, caste privilege, and injustices. Most of the teachers working in Berlin had migrated from the provinces of Pomerania, Silesia, and Saxony. It was the most ambitious and independent-minded teachers who moved to Berlin; they had been unhappy in the parochial and inhibiting environment of the village and small town, where they were often suspected of being politically too progressive. A similar freethinking spirit characterized teachers in other big cities, such as Bremen, Hamburg, and Leipzig, where teachers of the younger generation were often city-bred.[6]

The *Lehrerseminare* that trained elementary schoolteachers did not confer on them the professional status and social prestige possessed by Germans who attended secondary schools leading up to the examination for the *Abitur* that allowed them to matriculate to the universities. After 1890, elementary school pedagogues protested with greater indignation the social prejudices that blocked them from professional advancement, the degrading nature of their subordination to clergymen who served as part-time local and county school inspectors, and the big disparity in the salaries paid to teachers in the *Volksschule* and the *Gymnasium*. Because elementary schoolteachers were paid a salary that was lower than the earnings of subaltern civil servants in the postal and railway systems, they fought constantly to attain a ranking in the salary scale for state civil servants that was commensurate with their professional training and the value of their work. For decades teachers had opposed the supervision of the elementary schools by churchmen and demanded the professionalization of the school inspectorate. They were bitterly disappointed when the Prussian Ministry of Education after 1890 slowly increased the number of full-time county school inspectors and recruited young, university-educated theologians and secondary schoolteachers for these offices. The ministry's preference for applicants who had studied theology and philology at the universities seemed to them to be a deliberate policy of discrimination. The teachers sought to attain greater professional stature by upgrading teacher education and making it an academic course of study pursued within the universities.[7]

Left Liberals and the Cause of School Reform

To a far greater extent than other members of their profession, pedagogues who belonged to the German Teachers' Association stood in the forefront of the educational reform movement in Imperial Germany. Founded in 1871 and led by an executive board located in Berlin, the Deutscher Lehrerverein provided elementary school educators with a public space and an associational life that were independent of state control. By 1912, it could boast of a membership of more than 125,000 Protestant and Catholic male teachers, organized into 2,905 chapters.[8] Associational life afforded the progressivist pedagogues an invaluable means of disseminating their ideas of school reform within the profession. In addition to the local chapter meetings, the national association and each of its state branches held imposing congresses, where all the important issues related to the profession and the schools were debated and put to a vote. The association's newspapers published articles on the new pedagogy and reports on the activities of the societies and institutes founded for the study of educational psychology.

Within the much smaller German Women Teachers' Association (Deutscher Lehrerinnenverein), Elisabeth Morgenstern in Dresden, Magda Böttner in Bremen, and Eva Kulke and Elfriede Schäfer in Berlin, and other members embraced the cause of pedagogical reform and disseminated the ideas of the movement. However, their professional society uniting elementary and secondary schoolteachers and private tutors had a relatively low profile in school politics.[9] Two years after the association law of 1908 permitted women to become members of political organizations, Gertrud Bäumer, a secondary schoolteacher and feminist leader who had joined the left-liberal Progressive People's Party, deplored how many women in her profession frowned upon party activity. She thought that male teachers with "a half century [of experience] as a profession and as political citizens before them" reacted more constructively to the influence of politics in the sphere of public education than women teachers generally did. Urging women teachers to emulate the political engagement of their male colleagues, Bäumer pointed out how effectively the German Teachers' Association worked to enhance the public's understanding of the importance of the schools for civic culture and to acquire a political voice for the profession.[10]

Teachers who joined the Catholic Teachers' Association of Germany (Katholischer Lehrerverband des Deutschen Reiches) observed the development of the school reform movement from a distance, with a certain wariness and distrust. This organization, which was founded in 1889 to unite Catholic educators and to put up a wall against the interconfessional and liberal-leaning German Teachers' Association, was more successful in recruiting members in the western provinces of Prussia than elsewhere in Germany. It had a membership of 18,000 in 1909, when about 51,000 Catholic teachers were working in Germany's elementary schools. In the eyes of many Catholic teachers in Baden, Bavaria, and Württemberg, this organization seemed to be "a creature" of the Center Party, whose leadership included an influential contingent of Catholic churchmen. The Catholic Teachers' Association handled the thorny issue of the appointment of clergymen as school inspectors at its annual congress with extreme reluctance and in a timid and anxious manner in sessions closed to the public. In 1913 a Catholic teacher chided the executive board for treating the teachers' demand for the professionalization of the school inspectorate as a "forbidden question."[11] A resolute defender of the confessional public school, the Catholic Teachers' Association viewed the advocates of the active-learning school as political radicals with "anticlerical and irreligious tendencies." Franz Weigl warned in 1912 that if the principles of experiential learning and learning as an activity of the self were "pushed too far," the active-learning school could pose a danger to a Christian education.[12]

Besides its defense of the material and professional interests of its members, the German Teachers' Association became the foremost advocacy group for school reform in the nation after the turn of the century. The organization's weekly newspaper, published under the title *Pädagogische Zeitung* before 1919, disputed the prevailing view in the state administration that teachers, who had the status of public servants, should not embroil themselves in party politics and should cast their ballots for the right-wing parties that supported the government's policies.[13] The campaign for the reform of the school system was politicized in Prussia in 1905-6 and in Saxony in 1908-12, when the state parliaments debated school bills proposed by the governments. The school authorities issued formal admonitions to five teachers in Dresden for attending Social Democratic public meetings and to another teacher in Leipzig for criticizing the abuse of authority by conservative school principals. Teachers in Dresden and Leipzig challenged the legality of these official sanctions and defended their civil liberties and their right to criticize public institutions.[14]

The leadership and most active members of the German Teachers' Association supported the two left-liberal parties that merged in 1910 under the name of the Progressive People's Party. Some of these educators were highly visible in civic life, sitting on the executive committees of the local party clubs and campaigning for Progressive candidates in parliamentary elections. Teachers constituted 10.1 percent of the delegates at the party's national congress in 1912. As the editor of the *Pädagogische Zeitung* remarked, elementary schoolteachers had good reason to see the Progressives as "old, tried-and-tested friends." In 1913 a teacher in Halle observed that the Progressives had given them a voice in the Prussian Landtag as no other party had done. Four members of the elementary school teaching profession sat in the party's parliamentary delegation and seized the opportunity of the annual debates on the education budget to expose the deficiencies of the elementary school system and to speak out for the reforms demanded by the German Teachers' Association.[15]

Many politically active members of the German Teachers' Association, including Gustav Menzel, Otto Pautsch, and Johannes Tews in Berlin, were attracted to the circle of Progressives around Heinrich Rickert, Theodor Barth, and Friedrich Naumann, whose liberal ideology was imbued with a strong sense of social responsibility and a commitment to social justice. They attributed their own affinity for "social liberalism" to their profession as educators "in the service of the broad masses of people."[16] Their political outlook was more radical than the laissez-faire liberalism of the commercial bourgeoisie; they had a deeper social consciousness than did the liberals who defined their ultimate ideal in terms of political liberty. As Tews stated: "Freedom in itself has value only for the strong. A person who does not uplift the weak does not make him strong." He contended: "The educational system does not belong to those secondary matters in which one may acquiesce in inequalities and injustices. School education is one of the most essential earthly possessions in which no person may suffer harm without having his entire future affected most severely."[17] Left liberals in the German Teachers' Association were the most vocal critics of the rigidly stratified educational system in their country. In comparison, the reformers of secondary education within circles of the university-educated elite concentrated on issues related to the curriculums and parity of the neohumanist *Gymnasium* and the newer, "modern" types of secondary schools (*Realgymnasium* and *Oberrealschule*), and their discussions never assumed a socially radical character.[18]

In Imperial Germany Johannes Tews did more than any other left liberal to put school reform on the agenda of national politics. Born in the Prussian province of Pomerania in 1860, Tews moved to Berlin in 1883 after the completion of his professional training for schoolteaching. In 1891 Tews was appointed general secretary of the Society for the Spread of Adult Education (Gesellschaft für Verbreitung von Volksbildung), which was founded in the 1870s by liberals who hoped to foster the cultural integration of the German people in the new national state and to solve the "social question" by means of education. Permitted by the school administration to reduce his teaching hours and then to take a two-year leave of absence in 1904-6, Tews became increasingly active in school politics. Through his public speeches and articles in the *Berliner Tageblatt* and other liberal newspapers, he acquired a certain notoriety in circles of the political right as a radical critic of the state's school policies and the church's influence in the elementary school system.[19] Twice he ran unsuccessfully as a Progressive candidate for the Landtag in an electoral district in Berlin. His defeat in the 1913 election brought to an end his ambitions for a parliamentary seat, but up to the end of the 1920s, he remained a prominent publicist in school politics.

To the vexation of officials in the Prussian Ministry of Education, Tews's untiring campaign for improvements in the elementary schools put the public spotlight on the large number of overcrowded classrooms, the decrepit condition of rural schools, and the comparatively low public investment in popular education. Tews deplored how anxiety over the growing electoral strength of the Social Democratic Party as well as the belief that the schooling of the working class served merely to expand its ranks had made Conservative agrarians and sections of the bourgeoisie unsympathetic to the interests of the elementary schools. He criticized the isolation of the *Volksschule* from the elitist institutions of secondary education in Prussia. Convinced that the social stratification and barriers within the school system were a reflection of the powerful influence of the aristocracy in the state government and the marked caste consciousness in society, he supported the reform of the three-class franchise in Prussia.[20]

Tews played a leading role in the Progressives' fight against the Prussian school bill in 1905-6 and articulated boldly the demands of a growing number of elementary schoolteachers for the end of the "subordination" of the *Volksschule* to the church. His political activism aroused the ire of the school administration, which ordered him to return to full-time teaching or to resign his tenured school office. He chose to give up the security of his employment as a civil servant. Tews opposed the division of the elementary school system along confessional lines and the immense influence exercised by churchmen in their roles as school inspectors, chairmen of the school boards, and directors of the *Lehrerseminare*. From his experiences in school politics, Tews became an advocate of the separation of church and state and a strong critic of the Catholic Center Party, whose defense of confessional schooling and clerical supervision over the schools was unbending. As he observed, Protestant churchmen had become "less resolute and less unanimous" in school politics after the turn of the century. Conservatives in the Protestant Church continued to assail the demands of left-liberal teachers for the autonomy of the school as "un-Christian" and "a grave threatening danger for the state, the church, and the Christian family." However, "Protestant clergymen in the left wing" had come to see that "the complete separation of the church and school alone shall lead to a satisfactory relationship between both institutions." These pastors understood that the teachers' opposition to clerical school inspection was a matter of professional dignity and self-esteem. Tews thought that an agreement with the Protestant Church on this issue would be "possible," but the school reformers would prevail over the Catholic clergy "only by means of political power."[21]

Apart from these emancipatory goals, Tews and other school reformers proposed a reorganization of the educational system to eliminate the injustices and impediments suffered by children in the lower classes. In the 1890s Tews began to campaign for the abolition of the public preparatory schools (*Vorschulen*) that required the payment of a fee. He advocated the establishment of a common elementary school (*allgemeine Volksschule* or *gemeinsame Grundschule*) for the instruction of children of all social classes and religious confessions and the elimination of secondary school tuitions. To integrate the elementary and secondary schools into a unified educational system (*Einheitsschule*), he proposed that the first four grades of the common school provide the foundation of learning for admission to all types of secondary schools. This plan for a reorganization of the school system was based on Tews's commitment to the principle of equality of rights and educational opportunity and his belief that the best political system was a state in which this principle achieved its fullest realization. As he saw it, the state had an obligation not only to provide elementary schooling for all citizens but also to introduce measures so that no student would face any barriers in acquiring the highest level of formal education to which he or she had the capacity and will to attain. Tews envisioned an educational system with greater social mobility and more paths leading from the elementary school to secondary education. Pupils who were educated in the elementary school up to the age of fourteen were barred from entering a secondary school. Before 1914, Tews and other left liberals in the German Teachers' Association focused on reforms in elementary education. It was not until the years of World War I that they argued for the creation of two new kinds of secondary schools—the *Aufbauschule*, which would admit pupils who had been taught in the upper level of the elementary school, and the *deutsche Oberschule*, whose curriculum would emphasize the geography, history, and cultural heritage of Germany in contrast to the cult of classical antiquity in the neohumanist *Gymnasium*.[22]

The proposals of the educational reformers amounted to an ambitious vision of social change in Imperial Germany. The historical development of educational institutions in the nineteenth century left the public schools as the predominant provider of elementary and secondary education. An extensive system of Catholic parochial schools or private schools for the progeny of the governing class and business elite did not emerge to challenge the state's monopoly of education. The state made accommodations to the interests of the Catholic and Protestant religious communities and to the status-consciousness and social ambitions of the propertied and educated bourgeoisie by maintaining a confessionally segmented system of elementary schooling and a socially stratified structure of public education with different curriculums for pupils of diverse social backgrounds. The social position of a child's family determined which school he or she attended and the kind of education he or she received. The public educational system reflected and helped to perpetuate the sharp class distinctions and confessional cleavages in German society.

Children entered the secondary-school track—a decision with significant consequences for their entire life—after they passed an examination in the fourth year of elementary school. In many cities in northern Germany, educated and propertied bourgeois parents paid tuition fees to send their children to public *Vorschulen*, whose curriculum was specifically designed to prepare pupils for entrance to a secondary school in three years. Children in these preparatory schools enjoyed the privilege of being admitted to a secondary school without having to take an entrance examination. Exclusiveness in the early schooling of upper-class children gained momentum after the 1870s. The opening of preparatory schools spread rapidly in Hamburg, Berlin, and the cities in Prussia's eastern provinces. In other states such as Saxony, a differentiated system of public elementary schooling, created by a scale of school fees, had the effect of separating the children of the "better" families in the middle and higher *Bürgerschulen* from the offspring of the working class in the *Volksschule*. Elementary schoolteachers criticized the preparatory schools as "a nursery of caste consciousness" and thought that only "a false social pride" led wealthy parents to enroll their children there. They rejected the negative image of the *Volksschule* as an inferior school for the poor, a perception of the ruling class that had dire consequences for school funding and facilities. While elementary schools were overcrowded with fifty to sixty pupils in one classroom, public preparatory schools in Berlin, Königsberg, and Magdeburg had classes with thirty pupils or less.[23]

In 1892 the congress of the German Teachers' Association adopted a resolution calling for the reorganization of the elementary educational system on the basis of the common school for all children. The sociopolitical aims that motivated the reformers were expressed in a speech delivered by Heinrich Scherer before the representatives of the chapters voted on this resolution. Scherer argued that the schooling of children together without any distinctions based on social class, up to the age when differentiation became appropriate out of consideration for later professional education, would help to diminish class hostilities and nurture bonds of mutual caring and respect. A socially integrated school system would remove a cause and symptom of the estrangement between the classes and contribute thereby to the solution of the "social question."[24]

In the following years, left liberals in the teaching profession augmented this argument for school reforms by putting more emphasis on the principle of the equality of rights of all citizens. Tews contended that the common school was "the only form of schooling that can pass the test of our political and social conscience" because it fulfilled the principle of equal rights for all and offered the same blessings of culture to all children irrespective of the status and income of the parents. If "access to all public educational institutions should be open to all citizens," the elementary schools had "to be brought into an organic connection with the secondary schools" so that the passage up the educational ladder would be open and free of impediments. The "logical consequence" of this idea was that the schools should "not be divided according to social ranks and classes" but only according to educational goals and levels. Tews had optimistic expectations of "the social benefits of the common school." Young people in their formative years would learn to live and work together and come to see that intellectual merit and moral virtues were not bound to a specific social class or level of wealth: "The recollection that often the poorest boy was the most gifted pupil would restrain intense class consciousness later in life, open a person's mind to an understanding for many of the demands of the underprivileged, and lead to a willingness to accommodate their just demands."[25] On 2 June 1914 the national congress of the German Teachers' Association voted for a resolution calling for a unified educational system that would "provide for each child the level of education to which he makes a claim on the basis of ability."

The progressivist pedagogues challenged the traditional practice of determining the educational path of schoolchildren at an early age and criticized the curriculum and methods of teaching in the preparatory schools. On the basis of research conducted by the statistical office of the German

Teachers' Association in 1912, the reformers pointed out that hundreds of children admitted to the secondary schools at the age of nine performed poorly and flunked out. These pupils, whose abilities were not suited to the study of classical languages, would have had a better learning experience in another kind of school. The reformers criticized the preparatory schools for ignoring the development of the child and for drilling children from the ages of six to nine in the subject of grammar in order to prepare them for the study of Latin and Greek in the *Gymnasium*. A teacher in Breslau stated that the pupils in the preparatory schools were often anxious and tense because they were "burdened with learning material" to which their abilities were not yet equal. "How many children are thwarted in their development in this way? How many are cheated of the most beautiful time of their life?" he asked.[26]

In many cities in Prussia, elementary schoolteachers fought for the closing of the public preparatory schools, and their sociopolitical and pedagogical arguments informed the position taken by many left-liberal deputies in the debates on this issue in the city councils. In Frankfurt am Main, the Democrats, Progressives, and Social Democrats in the city council voted in 1905 for a resolution that requested the magistrates to introduce a bill for the abolition of the preparatory school classes in the city's secondary schools. The magistrates rejected this proposal with the explanation that it would only lead to the opening of private schools and the subsequent loss of tuition fees for the public secondary schools. The reformers criticized this decision and pointed to the example of Bavaria, which had neither public nor private preparatory schools. One city councilman retorted that the reformers did not know Frankfurt society well. He stated that class-consciousness was stronger in Prussia than in Bavaria and that the upper crust in Frankfurt would never allow their children to sit on the same school bench with working-class children. The Frankfurt teachers' association and deputies in the city council revived the campaign to close down the preparatory schools in 1912–13. A second resolution, which declared that the common elementary school and tuition-free secondary education for pupils with little financial means were "a corollary of the modern idea of the state based on the principle of equal rights for all," won the support of a large majority in the city council. Once again, the magistrates turned down this demand.[27]

The school conflict in Frankfurt am Main and the discussion of educational reform in the newspapers and meetings of the German Teachers' Association aroused the apprehensions of secondary schoolteachers and other conservatives, who saw in the reformers' proposals a grave threat to elite education and the existing social order. The traditionalists feared that the common school would promote social mobility and that children of the lower classes would compete with young people in the middle and upper classes for admission to the institutions of higher learning and for employment in the civil service and the professions. Secondary schoolteachers who leaped into the fray contended that instruction in the common school would not provide the rigorous training in grammar that would enable pupils to study classical languages successfully in the *Gymnasium*. Their defense of class privilege and their ambivalence about the social consequences of the principle of merit were unmasked when they contested a process of selection based exclusively on ability and grades, invoking the right of parents of certain family traditions and social standing to enroll their sons in a secondary school. An association of university-educated teachers in Frankfurt defended the preparatory schools and praised the city's government for protecting the citizens' "freedom of choice between the diverse types of schools." They underscored the anxiety of middle-class parents who had expressed concerns about "the threatening moral dangers to which children from better-situated families are exposed in a common school with children from the poorer classes."[28]

Secondary school educators accused the reformers in the German Teachers' Association of opposing the preparatory schools out of sheer self-interest, to improve their social status and salaries by eliminating the social distance between the *Volksschule* and the prestigious secondary schools. The director of a secondary school scorned the "fanaticism, vague theory, and pure doctrinairism" of the enemies of the preparatory schools, "marshaled in the democratic camp." In the elementary schools, the overwhelming majority of children came from circles of society that had "different moral values and a different style of life than the children raised in the homes of the educated middle class." Another ploy of the traditionalists was to link the goals of the pedagogical reformers with the platform of the Social Democratic Party. "The ideological foundation, upon which the theory of the unified school system [*Einheitsschule*] rests, consists of socialist utopias that aim at a mechanistic leveling of the social differences existing in the world today," Otto Hesse wrote.[29]

The Most Difficult Hurdle for the School Reformers

The common school advocated by the progressivist pedagogues was a radical challenge to the tradition of having Catholic and Protestant children taught separately in the elementary school system by teachers of their own religious faith. The policy of confessional schooling was carried out extensively in most German states and was facilitated by the geographic distribution and settlement of Catholics and Protestants in regionally concentrated masses. Striving to push back Catholic clerical influence in public life in the 1860s and 1870s, the governments in Baden and Hesse—with the support of the liberal parties in the state parliaments—introduced a system of interconfessional schools (*Simultanschulen*) in which children of all faiths were instructed together, while separated by confession only for the subject of religion. During the *Kulturkampf* launched by Bismarck against the Catholic Church and Center Party in the 1870s, National Liberals in the Prussian school administration who were avid political crusaders against confessional particularism created interconfessional schools in the predominantly Catholic Rhineland and the Polish-speaking areas in the provinces of Poznan and West Prussia. The strong resistance put up by the Catholic clergy and laity to the opening of these schools and the opposition of the Protestant Church to this policy blocked the extension of interconfessional schooling to other parts of the state.[30]

Confessional schooling remained the form of elementary education for a vast majority of Catholic and Protestant schoolchildren in Germany, despite the advance of industrial capitalism and the migration to the cities that produced a greater confessional mixture in the population of many areas. In Prussia in 1906, with an enrollment of more than 6.1 million pupils, 97.5 percent of the Protestants, 90.6 percent of the Catholics, and 27.3 percent of the Jews attending the public elementary schools were taught in schools of their own confession. Among the other Jewish children, 5,006 attended the interconfessional schools that were opened in Berlin, Frankfurt am Main, and a few other cities; 8,219 attended Protestant schools; and 2,921 attended Catholic schools and were exempted from religious instruction there. Religious instruction was provided for these Jewish children in the after-school hours by the synagogue congregations out of their own tax levy. The disadvantageous position and discriminatory treatment of the Jewish minority in this school system led Jewish community leaders to collaborate with the left-liberal parties in the fight for the interconfessional school.[31] The amendments sponsored by the Progressives were voted down in the deliberations on the government's school bill in the Prussian Landtag in 1906. The new school law kept intact the system of confessional schooling and stipulated that schoolchildren should receive instruction, as a rule, from teachers of their own confession and that teachers of one and the same faith should be appointed to a school.[32]

The deep divisions within the German Teachers' Association over the issue of religion in the public schools early in the century pointed already to the intractability of this problem in the politics of culture during the Weimar Republic. The conflicting opinions were aired with an unprecedented boldness in 1906, when the national congress discussed the school question. From the recent political debate on the school bill in Prussia, the executive committee knew how cunningly the opponents of educational reform in the churches and the Conservative and Center Parties had used this issue. To give the public a clear statement of the teachers' position, the officers presented a set of propositions to the delegates for a vote. They invited Gärtner, a school principal in Munich, to speak for their theses in support of the interconfessional school and Lütgemeier, a Protestant teacher in a rural village in Lippe, to state the argument for the opposing side.

It is indicative of the strained relations between devout Protestant schoolteachers and the parish pastors in many small towns and villages that Lütgemeier distinguished his defense of the confessional school from the standpoint of its "clerical supporters," who sought to preserve the clergy's authority as school inspectors and envisioned "a church school that downgraded secular knowledge and practical skills." He believed that religious instruction should have a central place in the elementary school and that the significance of the school to society would diminish if it ceased to be an institution of moral and religious education. He contended that Catholics and Protestants had a different understanding of the Reformation and other historical epochs. The requirements of parity in an interconfessional school would impose constraints on the teachers and prevent them from teaching history with any feeling lest they offended the other religious community. He emphasized the value of the "unified wholeness" of the educational experience in a school in which children of one and the same confession were instructed by teachers of that faith.[33]

In a society segmented into Protestant and Catholic cultural milieus and political camps, Gärtner championed the interconfessional school as a means of attenuating the consciousness of religious antagonisms and separateness, promoting a heightened appreciation of a shared national cultural heritage, and nurturing a common civic identity that transcended group solidarities. Apart from these social purposes, he pointed out the instructional advantages of interconfessional schooling in a country with countless confessionally mixed school districts. The confessional school had many drawbacks for the children of the religious minority in the school district, who were often taught in a small school without separate classrooms for each grade. Gärtner deplored the rhetoric used by opponents of the interconfessional school, and stated that parents would raise no objections if clerical politicians did not instigate them. "Church interests stubbornly defend the confessional separation [of the schoolchildren]," he declared, "not for educational reasons as much as for the purpose of preserving clerical school supervision, isolating the adherents of each religious faith in their youth, and keeping at a distance those influences that are undesirable from a narrow-minded, clerical perspective." From his own experience in Munich, Gärtner sought to dispel the fear that interconfessional schools, which instructed children of all religious faiths together and separated them only for the religion lesson, would harm the religious and moral education of the youth. He disputed the claims of Catholic and orthodox-Protestant defenders of confessional schooling that religious instruction should form the core of the curriculum and radiate outward, penetrating the instruction of the other subjects. At the center of a modern education in the German elementary school, "especially in the present age of technology and science," should be the subjects of German language and literature, history, geography, and science.[34]

Tews was aware of the grievances of Jewish citizens from their discussion of the school question at meetings of his party (Freisinnige Vereinigung) in Berlin. Sensitive to the inequitable arrangements for the schooling of Jewish children, he brought out the injustice of the confessional school system for a religious minority. He argued that every citizen had the same right to a school maintained by public funds without any difference in respect to religion. With confessional schooling, this right was not respected: "If the children of a religious minority attend the school of another confession, the national cultural heritage is transmitted to them with the coloring of a confession that is perhaps opposed to their own. The parents must put up with the fact that their children grow up in an intellectual atmosphere and are nourished with an intellectual fare that are contrary to their own religious faith." If confessional separate schools were built for children of a religious minority, the parents would have to be content with a poorly equipped small school. Tews thought that a confessional school was justified only as a private school. By maintaining confessional public schools, the state was making the same concession to "the narrow interests" of the church as it did to "caste privilege" by supporting special preparatory schools.[35]

In the discussion at the 1906 congress, a small faction of philosophically freethinking and politically radical teachers from Bremen and Hamburg provoked a heated exchange of opinion on the issue of religion in the schools. The executive committee's moderately worded proposal demanded that school legislation place interconfessional and confessional schools on an equal footing and permit the free development of interconfessional schools in localities with a mixed population. The supporters of this position constituted a sizable majority among the more than 4,400 delegates who attended the congress. Several delegates from Bremen and Hamburg introduced an alternative proposal for the removal of religious instruction from the school curriculum and the secularization of the elementary school system.

Wilhelm Holzmeier, the spokesman for the radicals, belonged to a small circle of covert Social Democrats in the teaching profession in Bremen. In 1905 Holzmeier had followed closely the proceedings of the Social Democratic Party's congress held in Bremen and was deeply impressed by the speeches delivered by Heinrich Schulz and Clara Zetkin in support of the secular school. At the teachers' congress a year later, he argued, as the Social Democrats had done, that religious instruction should be left up to the church and that the church should not use the power of the state to preserve its influence in society through the public school. The Prussian House of Deputies, elected on the basis of an undemocratic three-class franchise, did not represent the thinking of the people during its deliberations on the "reactionary" school bill. The Social Democrats, the largest party in Germany, had placed the demand for secular schools in their political platform. "We have the obligation to give help to [the realization of] this goal, to demonstrate its feasibility," Holzmeier stated. Strong outcries of disapprobation were made when he proclaimed: "The Bible is not the source of the moral instruction that we need in our time, for it bears the traces of antiquity. Much wrong has been done in the name of Christianity."[36]

Several left-liberal reformers from Berlin rose to defend their moderate position on this controversial issue. Carl Louis Pretzel argued that the secularization of the schools would be a political blunder because the churches would demand and exercise their freedom to open private schools. The Germans should learn a lesson from the outcome of a similar radical reform in Holland, where the state's secular schools "lost out to the private confessional schools" in the number of enrollments. Otto Pautsch was irritated at Holzmeier and predicted grimly that the remarks of the pedagogues in Bremen and Hamburg would expose the German Teachers' Association to attacks in the right-wing press. A delegate from Augsburg stated that if the congress did not disclaim the views of these mavericks, the organization's members in small towns and villages would "face much hostility." In fact, after the 1906 congress, politicians and newspapers affiliated with the Conservative and Center Parties began to stir up a public hysteria by spreading suspicion that the German Teachers' Association was harboring covert Social Democrats and was "a stepping stone to Social Democracy."[37]

At the same time, a statement made by another teacher from Munich, who was more circumspect than Holzmeier, indicated that dissatisfaction with religious instruction, as it was then taught in the elementary schools, was not confined to Bremen and Hamburg. He praised the "courage" of the teachers there and observed that their views had been propounded for years by the German Society for Ethical Culture. He confessed that two years earlier at a meeting of his chapter, he, too, had expressed the conviction that "the secular school with ethical instruction rather than confessional religious instruction is a corollary of freedom of conscience."[38] No vote was taken on the proposal in favor of the exclusion of religious instruction from the schools because the theses defended by Gärtner were brought to a vote first and adopted.

From 1905–6, the issue of religious instruction in the public schools was discussed with frankness and fearlessness by a radical wing of the German Teachers' Association. Although Johannes Tews maintained that the doctrinal contents of the catechism were too abstract for the comprehension of schoolchildren and called for the reform of religious instruction as early as the 1896 congress,[39] other school reformers in Prussia were reluctant to roll out this explosive issue. Such considerations of expediency carried more weight in Prussia, where the state branch of the German Teachers' Association had a sizable Catholic membership and had to fend off the challenge of a small splinter group of conservative rural teachers, than in Saxony, Bremen, or Hamburg. The predominantly Protestant working-class population in the industrial cities of Saxony created a political milieu that made teachers there more willing to take the risk of bringing the issue of religious instruction in the schools before the public.[40]

The congress of the Saxon Teachers' Association in 1905 decided that in the next two years the local chapters would hold discussions and draft proposals for the reform of religious instruction. As a school principal in Chemnitz explained, the consciousness of "living in times of a religious crisis"—manifested "in the tensions between the church and modern culture, in the irreconcilable contradiction between old religious views and modern knowledge of the world"—made teachers in Saxony "feel obliged to work for the solution of this burning question." The requirement to give religious instruction based on church doctrines was regarded by a number of teachers in Dresden and Leipzig as "a coercion and an oppression of their consciences." Arthur Arzt, who later became a Social Democratic propagandist for the secular school, complained that teachers did not have any freedom in this instruction and had "to teach doctrines, which they do not believe and which modern scholarship has called into question."[41]

In 1908 the executive committee of the Saxon Teachers' Association drafted a set of propositions on the reform of religious instruction that would be discussed and put to a vote at the upcoming congress in the city of Zwickau. This issue engrossed teachers in Saxony so intensely that close to 3,500 members came to this meeting. The so-called Zwickau *Thesen*, adopted by an overwhelming majority of the delegates, stated that religious instruction as "an autonomous activity of the elementary school" should be free of any church supervision. The curriculum and form of instruction should "correspond to the psychological development of the child." The Zwickau theses emphasized the application of "psychological-pedagogical principles" in the selection of the instruction material. Because confessional doctrines were full of abstract concepts beyond a child's experience and understanding, the Zwickau theses rejected the use of the catechism as the foundation for religious education in the school. Instead, the life and teachings of Jesus were to form the core of religious instruction for Christian children of elementary school age.[42] In contrast to the radical pedagogues in Bremen and Hamburg who agitated for the exclusion of religious instruction from the schools, the Saxon Teachers' Association supported a more moderate reform in 1908.

For most German pedagogical reformers at this time, "emancipation from the church" did not mean the secularization of the schools. The problems of teaching religion in the public schools were clearly apparent to Tews. Conflicts between pedagogues and pastors arose over the interpretation of religious texts. The situation became "more difficult" if the teachers were "set to the task of bringing the pupils to faith through [religious] instruction." He queried, "Who should determine what and how much must be believed and when doubt may begin? Should the school stop criticism? Should it suppress doubt? That contradicts its methods in all other subjects of instruction." Unlike the Social Democrats, Tews did not see the exclusion of religious instruction from the schools as a way out of this dilemma. He was too impressed by the place of religion in the culture of the German people and the importance of religious thought and feeling in the life and moral education of human beings. In a speech delivered in Berlin, he declared that the elementary school would restrict its sphere of influence if it gave up the instruction of religion. In his plan for educational reform, the public schools would teach the subject "in complete freedom," covering only the great personalities and texts in the religious literature of the Christian confessions and Judaism. Tews had still another reason for rejecting the secular school. He contended: "The radical parties make one of the most dangerous mistakes when they believe that they can press the church to the wall by the exercise of authority. Any such struggle against institutions that are rooted in popular life is not only without prospect but is also ruinous for those who are waging the fight. A party in school politics that wants to have a future must formulate its position on the claims of the church in the educational system on the basis of facts."[43]

Conservative political circles observed the discussions of the reformers in the German Teachers' Association with dismay and disapproval. The *Reichsbote*, a conservative newspaper with close ties to the Protestant Church, detected "an antipathy or hostility to Christianity" in the ideas of these pedagogues. The interconfessional school pushed religion as a mere subject to the periphery of school life and signified "the first step to the irreligious school [and] the beginning of the end of the German *Volksschule* as a Christian educational institution and of the German people as a Christian nation." After "the liberal teachers" eliminated the influence of religion in the rest of the instruction, they would then "strive to get rid of the religion lessons." To attain this objective, the newspaper wrote, "they will say: the school is a state institution; only if the school is irreligious can we make it into a national educational institution." The Social Democrats were "totally candid" in demanding the complete exclusion of religious instruction from the schools. The *Reichsbote* chastised the bourgeois liberals in the school reform movement for failing to see how they were ultimately promoting Social Democratic changes in society and the state.[44]

In June 1909 the executive committee of the Association for the Preservation of the Protestant Elementary School (Verein zur Erhaltung der evangelischen Volksschule) decided to launch an agitational campaign against the German Teachers' Association. The general synod of the Protestant Church in Prussia adopted a resolution denouncing the ideas expressed at the teachers' congresses as a threat to Christian religious education and the Protestant elementary school. In the following year, August Grünweller, a school principal and orthodox-Protestant firebrand, wrote a tract that was circulated to all church superintendents and provincial synods in Prussia. Grünweller assailed Johannes Tews and the teachers in Saxony as "enemies of the church" and characterized their proposals for the reform of religious education in the schools as "a fight against Christianity."[45] When Protestant Church officials in Saxony assembled at a conference in Meissen in 1909, an ultra-orthodox theologian charged that "radical elements" in the Leipzig teachers' association had fallen astray into atheism. Copies of the church officials' remonstrance against the Zwickau theses were distributed to church parishes throughout Saxony, and parish councils were urged to inundate the Ministry of Education with similar protests.[46]

The Pioneers of Progressive Education in Wilhelmine Germany

The reformers' objections to religious-doctrinal instruction in the schools were one aspect of a broader critique of teaching practices in the *Lernschule*, as they dubbed the traditional elementary school. The educational reformers in Bremen and Hamburg were among the severest critics of the old pedagogy, and their satirical descriptions soon turned the traditional school into an object of scorn. "The center of gravity" in the old school, they observed, lay "not in the child, but in the teacher, the teaching material, and the lesson plan." "Didactic materialism" and "mechanistic didacticism" in the traditional method of instruction placed too much emphasis on learning by rote and the child's knowledge of the subject matter transmitted by the teacher. Questioning the effectiveness of this kind of instruction, these pedagogues pointed out that the pupils did not assimilate the material deeply by working through it themselves. Learning was fleeting because schoolchildren were compelled to possess knowledge of things that they hardly encountered in their lives and in which they could have no interest. School instruction did not nurture the child's imagination, creativity, and sensibilities, or the capacity to act independently. Johannes Gläser called the traditional school "an obstacle to the development of the whole person" because its objectives were "the formation of submissive subjects and a useful army of laborers." "Our school suffers from the hypertrophy of the intellect and the atrophy of the imagination and heart," wrote Wilhelm Reese.[47]

The pedagogical reformers in the elementary schools in Wilhelmine Germany were contemporaries of the American philosopher John Dewey, whose writings on education at the turn of the century laid the foundations for the progressive education movement in the United States. Two German pedagogues, Paul Vogel in Leipzig and Otto Schmidt in Berlin, were familiar with John Dewey's early work on progressive education, *The School and Society*, which was published in 1899 in the United States. From reading the reports of educators who visited America, they thought that the views on experiential learning and child development propounded by the great Swiss and German educational reformers, Johann Heinrich Pestalozzi and Friedrich

Froebel, had had a greater impact on schools on the other side of the Atlantic than in Germany.[48] On the other hand, Joseph Mayer Rice, an American who studied at the universities in Jena and Leipzig, thought that schoolteachers in Germany had a livelier interest in the application of the science of psychology to pedagogy than in his own country.[49] What stimulated the progressivist pedagogues in Imperial Germany were new developments in their own country and their appreciation of a heritage of educational reform theory going back to Friedrich Diesterweg and Karl Wander, two German disciples of Pestalozzi in the first half of the nineteenth century.

The progressive education movement in Germany in the early 1900s was a collection of individuals and local circles. Several reformers such as Paul Geheeb and Gustav Wyneken founded experimental country boarding schools, but these small private schools were too unconventional to provide a model for the public schools.[50] Among the public school educators, the most radical reformers were associated with the journals *Roland* in Bremen and *Pädagogische Reform* in Hamburg.[51] Less extreme and dogmatic in their theory and practice were the progressivist pedagogues in the Leipzig teachers' association. Fritz Gansberg and Heinrich Scharrelmann in Bremen and Johannes Gläser and Heinrich Wolgast in Hamburg took pride in playing a pioneering role in the conception of the "pedagogy from the perspective of the child" (*Pädagogik vom Kinde aus*) and the child-centered school. When the dissemination of progressive educational thought in the elementary school teaching profession is studied closely, however, the work of the reformers in Leipzig becomes indisputably more significant.

After 1900, Leipzig emerged as a major center of experimentation and innovation in the pedagogical world. Saxony was far ahead of other German states in permitting elementary school teachers, who were not educated in a secondary school leading to the *Abitur*, to enroll at the University of Leipzig. An impressive number of teachers in Saxony took advantage of this opportunity to attend the university and to acquire a more sophisticated knowledge of the psychology of education than they had received in their *Lehrerseminar* training. In 1900, the Leipzig teachers' association created a section for the science of pedagogy for those members who were interested in the new field of child psychology. From the research of Wilhelm August Lay, Ernst Meumann, and other psychologists on child development and the effectiveness of teaching and learning methods, the teachers in this circle acquired an appreciation of psychology as an aid to pedagogy.[52] In 1906 they founded the Institute for Experimental Pedagogy and Psychology to promote the study of the psychology of education more widely in their profession. The Leipzig teachers' association gave the institute the space and funds to undertake research projects and to offer courses on educational psychology taught by Max Brahn, a lecturer at the University of Leipzig.[53] Hugo Gaudig, the director of a girls' secondary school in Leipzig, collaborated with Meumann in the publication of the *Zeitschrift für*

Pädagogische Psychologie und Experimentelle Pädagogik and wrote extensively on the reform of pedagogical practices.[54]

The proponents of the new pedagogy were very conscious of the way in which modern ideas were bringing ferment to and unsettling the world of education, and they felt the excitement of departing from the past and moving in new directions. They admitted that the principles of learning from experience and learning as an activity of the self were not new and could be traced back to the great educational reformers of the past, but they thought that the pedagogical reform movement of the twentieth century gave a deeper theoretical underpinning and a more developed form to the idea of the active-learning school (*Arbeitsschule*). Much that was "new and original" in the reform movement, they said, could be found in "the connections" between education, the principles of child development, knowledge in the field of psychology, and a cluster of cultural trends of the late nineteenth century that crystallized in a yearning for the unity of human nature and in the desire to overcome an excessive intellectualism and to cultivate the emotional, imaginative, sensory, and creative capacities of the human being.[55]

The theories of progressive education that gained widespread acceptance among big-city schoolteachers were articulated in *Die Arbeitsschule*, a manual published by the reformers in Leipzig. "The rule and law for all education" in the active-learning school, they declared, was the development of the child rather than the ideological purposes of the state or church. Education should release the potential and develop the particular innate gifts of each child. The progressivist pedagogues often defined their educational goals concisely by speaking of "education in the service of developing the whole person." Such an individual possessed attitudes of openness and questioning, a capacity for independent thought and a will to act, and a sense of freedom and moral responsibility. The reformers saw no conflict between the life of the larger social community and an education emphasizing the development of the individual and free self-expression. They conceived of the development of the child also in the sense of socialization, the growing up into one's social world and cultural surroundings, and placed a high value on the task of the school in transmitting the cultural heritage of the nation. In the *Arbeitsschule*, as in John Dewey's school ideal, the pupils in each class formed an embryonic community, which accustomed them to work together cooperatively, to be tolerant and respectful of one another, and to put themselves in the service of the community. The school cultivated the civic virtues needed for self-government.[56]

This model for the school of the future was outlined without reference to the question of coeducation. The progressivist pedagogues who taught boys and girls in separate public elementary schools seldom disputed the custom of separating schoolchildren by gender as it was practiced in the cities of Germany at this time. The secondary educational system was, in fact, the real battleground where the fight over the education of women in coeducational or girls' schools was waged. After the turn of the century, some radical middle-class feminists began to call for coeducation in the secondary schools as a means of widening the opportunities of women for secondary education and matriculation in the universities. "But most women teachers and almost all Catholic educators," as James Albisetti points out, "continued to favor separate schools where women could exercise a strong influence on girls."[57]

In the elementary schools, the instruction of boys and girls together was very common in the countryside and in small towns, where schoolhouses had one to three classrooms. Coeducational classes were sometimes introduced as a practical measure in medium-sized cities in order to ensure that the confessional public schools would have individual classes for each grade. In cities with a large school-age population, boys and girls were customarily taught in separate schools. In Prussia in 1901, about two-thirds of the boys and girls in the elementary schools were instructed in coeducational classes. Close to one-half of the pupils in Saxony in 1904 were taught in coeducational classes.[58] In a public forum in 1906, Johannes Tews gave a spirited argument against the separation of boys and girls in elementary school education. He thought that the Catholics' strong support for this practice exercised a considerable influence within the school administration. Protestant parents, too, showed a high preference for the separation of children by gender in the big-city school systems.[59] After coeducational classes were introduced in the experimental schools in Berlin, Chemnitz, and other large cities during the Weimar era, pedagogues in these schools could report that the innovation had benefited both sexes.[60]

The central principle of the new pedagogy was learning as an activity of the self, learning from experience and by doing. Knowledge was acquired by schoolchildren more effectively, the progressivist pedagogues thought, through their own observations and activity than through the transmission of the subject matter by the teacher. The pedagogues' concept of work and the name *Arbeitsschule*—meaning, literally, a working school—were often misconstrued in the early years of the movement. Traditionalists claimed that the active-learning school would empty education of its intellectual content and emphasize the cultivation of manual skills. Hugo Gaudig and other reformers in Leipzig tried to dispel these false perceptions in many public forums. School teachers and administrators soon learned to distinguish the Leipzig conception of the active-learning school from the politically utilitarian and vocationally oriented school envisioned by Georg Kerschensteiner, a school reformer in Munich, who first popularized the idea of the *Arbeitsschule*. Kerschensteiner's ideas for the education of "useful state citizens," through the addition of manual arts instruction and civics to the curriculum, had a greater appeal for the National Liberals in the upper strata of the bourgeoisie than for the pedagogues.[61] The Leipzig reformers conceived of work in the active-learning school primarily as the activity of the mind and the senses. The manual arts were pursued only insofar as they served the development of the imaginative, creative, and constructive faculties of the child.

Teaching from the perspective of the child, another fundamental principle of the modern pedagogy, required a radical reorientation in the methods and self-identity of the pedagogue. The educational reformers saw themselves as guides and helpers in the development of the child rather than as figures of authority controlling the child's behavior. They viewed childhood as a phase of life with its own particular psychological characteristics. The natural interests and abilities of children at each stage in their development, they counseled, should determine the selection and handling of the instruction material. Children in the early years of schooling were more drawn to what they could see and touch. Their visual sense was stronger than their ability to grasp abstract concepts and to draw generalizations and conclusions. School instruction was not efficient when it made "premature" demands and required pupils to learn what was beyond their comprehension. Learning was faster and better when children could work under their own motive power and out of an interest coming from within themselves.[62]

The importance of observation and experience in the learning process led the progressivist pedagogues to the principle of "proceeding from the *Heimat*," from the world that was familiar to the child. The spiral of learning proceeded from the actual surroundings of the pupils, and experiential instruction formed the core of education in the early grades. The new pedagogy added the subjects of *Naturkunde* and *Heimatkunde*—the natural world and the geography of the home region—to the curriculum and extended the classroom to the outdoors so that pupils could observe the physical and social environment of their native land and could learn about plants and animals in schoolyard gardens, farms, and woods. This conception of *Heimatkunde* tied to experiential instruction was very different from the political-ideological use of this subject after World War I. The right-wing ideologues, who organized the National League for the Heimatschule in 1920 and advocated the introduction of a school curriculum and pedagogy that would cultivate nationalist sentiments and values, criticized the progressivist pedagogues for having "a narrowly intellectualistic and didactical approach" to this subject.[63]

In comparison with the reformers in Leipzig, the proponents of progressive education in Bremen and Hamburg were more radical and uncompromising in the conclusions that they drew from their pedagogical principles. The reformers in the two Hanseatic cities were inclined to see irreconcilable polarities and contradictions between freedom and compulsion in education, between the development of the child and learning-achievement goals, and between pedagogy from the perspective of the child and instruction according to a lesson plan. Heinrich Scharrelmann's high-spirited articles on the modern pedagogy in *Roland*, a monthly journal founded by a circle of radical teachers in Bremen in 1905, provoked considerable controversy. Conservatives in the teaching profession seized upon his flamboyant and ironical statements as evidence of the "dangers" of the new movement.[64] Scharrelmann considered discipline and restraint to be harmful to the development of the child and derided the prevailing practice of maintaining order in school. "From the first to the last day of school, the child is surrounded by a thorny hedge of petit-bourgeois, pedantic, and senseless rules," he wrote. Pedagogues should have "the courage to dare to escort our sham ideal of order out the school door and to come without discipline before the class so that the children can create for themselves an independent, free, new, and genuine order."[65]

If the radical reformers of Bremen and Hamburg had been the sole advocates of progressive education in Germany, it would not have won over a significant section of the elementary school teaching profession. Much in Scharrelmann's writings "provokes dissent or rejection, much also laughter and the shrug of one's shoulders," wrote Robert Rissmann in the *Deutsche Schule*, the journal of the German Teachers' Association devoted to pedagogical issues. Observing the "chaos of opinions" and the presence of "many a zealous reformer" with "utopian ideas" in the pedagogical world, Rissmann wrote in 1909 that it would be a mistake to dismiss the reform movement with contempt during this "interregnum" on the way to a "new era of pedagogy." There were "earnestly conceived efforts at reform" besides the "half-true and long-winded" articles written by the Bremen and Hamburg radicals in "the superficial *Feuilleton* style." The contrast that they drew between the traditional and active-learning schools, he thought, was too exaggerated and could easily be misunderstood to mean that the new pedagogy placed no value on the pupil's acquisition of knowledge. He disapproved of their disdain for "system" and instructional planning. On the important question of the relationship of compulsion and freedom in education, he chided them for finding a "facile answer" in the rejection of compulsion and in an "idealized" view of the natural development of the child.[66]

Beginning in 1908, pedagogical reformers in Berlin, Leipzig, Munich, and other cities formed an organized movement and acquired a clearer collective identity. The executive board of the German Teachers' Association gave a big boost to the cause of educational reform when its chairman, Gustav Röhl, joined a group of pedagogues who assembled in Berlin on 13 April for the purpose of founding the League for School Reform. In a public announcement, the organizers of the League for School Reform stated that the *neue Pädagogik* had already won a following among German elementary schoolteachers. Bound to the lesson plans prescribed by the school administration, they were unable to apply modern psychological and pedagogical principles in their classroom teaching. They thought that the reforms should not be confined to the private boarding schools founded by Hermann Lietz, Paul Geheeb, and Gustav Wyneken, which were attended by a small number of youths from families of wealth and cultural sophistication. The aim of the new organization was to persuade the state authorities to permit teachers to use the methods of progressive education in the public schools and to open model experimental schools.[67] Also in the spring of 1908, reformers at the congress of the German Teachers' Association lobbied to make their professional society a more dynamic force in the progressive education movement. The executive board set up an office within the association (Pädagogische Zentralstelle) to publicize the work of the reformers to wide circles of society and to influence the thinking of officials in the school administration so that they would "open the way for the implementation of the less controversial reforms on a trial basis."[68] Chosen to head this public relations office was Carl Louis Pretzel, a school principal in Berlin of considerable intellectual power and self-assurance.

Following the model of the Institute for Experimental Pedagogy and Psychology in Leipzig, the teachers' associations in Berlin, Breslau, Chemnitz, Dortmund, Dresden, Hamburg, Munich, and other cities provided funds for the creation of institutes and centers for the study of educational psychology and the promotion of pedagogical reform.[69] Teachers who participated in these programs of continuing education became convinced that the principles and practices of pedagogy should be based on modern psychological knowledge. "Psychology has taken the work of education out of dilettantism and has given it the character of a science as well as an art," wrote Ernst Weber, a progressivist pedagogue in Munich. Oskar Hübner conveyed the atmosphere in the Berlin teachers' association at this time, when he wrote: "The idea of the active-learning school continues its triumphal march, greeted everywhere with jubilation. Today it is no longer a question of whether we should create the active-learning school but only how it is to be created."[70]

In assessing the strength of the pedagogical reform movement during these early years, it should be noted first that the institutional basis for the study of educational psychology in Germany on the eve of World War I was "relatively well developed, certainly better in comparison with most European countries."[71] Between 1880 and 1914, 21 journals and 28 associations devoted to child psychology and pedagogy were founded in Germany. The constituency of the movement resided in the big cities and in several medium-sized cities such as Magdeburg. The participation of elementary schoolteachers in the pedagogical reform workshops was striking as well as intense. The active membership of the Institute for Experimental Pedagogy and Psychology in Leipzig grew from 30 in 1906 to 195 in 1912. The courses offered by the Institute for Educational Psychology in Munich had impressive enrollments of 123 and 185 teachers in the winter and summer semesters of 1911–12, and enrollments of 126 and 248 teachers in 1912–13.[72] The executive boards of the state and Prussian provincial organizations within the German Teachers' Association were located in cities, so that the leadership was to a large extent in the hands of urban school principals and teachers, many of whom were left liberals and supported the educational reform movement. Although the advocates of the new pedagogy were a minority in their profession before 1914, they exercised an influence on it out of proportion to their numbers. Their criticism of the traditional school shook up settled beliefs and fostered an openness to change and new ideas.

When the leadership of the German Teachers' Association placed the question of the new pedagogy on the agenda of the national congress in May 1912, the principles of progressive education were familiar to wide circles in the profession. Progressivist pedagogues thought that the time had come for their professional society to take an official position, and Ernst Weber, a member of the Pädagogische Zentralstelle and a school principal in Munich, drafted a resolution endorsing the active-learning school. More than 8,000 teachers from all parts of Germany came to the congress as delegates representing the local chapters and as spectators. Well-organized and smoothly running, the congress of 1912, held in a massive auditorium in Berlin, gave the public an imposing picture of the association's strength and dignity. In his speech, which opened the debate on the resolution, Weber made a conscious effort to distance himself from the more radical proponents of progressive education and to create a consensus anchored in the middle. He presented the principles of the new pedagogy in terms of a series of "balances" in the relationship between freedom and compulsion in education and in the cultivation of the mental, imaginative, aesthetic, and manual faculties of the whole person.[73]

An overwhelming majority of the delegates voted for Weber's resolution, with the result that the German Teachers' Association officially endorsed the new pedagogy and added the active-learning school to its program of educational reforms. In the debate prior to this vote, two delegates assailed the active-learning school without any reference to Weber's disarmingly moderate statements. Heinrich Wigge, a temperamental school principal from Thuringia, cried out that this movement was having "the regrettable effect of pushing the big goals [in school politics] in the background." Why didn't the congress respond to his call to "put an end to the entire active-learning school movement?"[74] Since 1908, pedagogues who avoided extreme conclusions had gained leadership of this movement. A school principal from Leipzig underscored this point in the debate when he stated that the new pedagogical principles were not revolutionary ideas and that the teachers could "unite on the basis of Weber's moderate approach." The pedagogical reform movement won followers in the German Teachers' Association because the active-learning school was, in fact, associated with the fundamental aims of the teachers, with their yearning for autonomy in the practice of their profession.

The progressive education movement reached another milestone when teachers in Saxony were successful in persuading the school boards of several cities to open experimental school classes. The school board and magistracy of Leipzig decided to create 24 experimental classes in 21 public schools in the spring of 1911. The minister of education gave his approval to the experiment for two years on the condition that only with the consent of their parents would children be placed in these classes. In spite of attempts to instigate the parents against the experiment, in almost all of these schools in Leipzig the registration of the children for the "reform classes" was higher (about 1,400 boys and girls) than the number that could be accepted. In the spring of 1912, the minister authorized the opening of 7 experimental school classes in Chemnitz, 15 in Dresden, and 3 in Ölsnitz. Some of the district school inspectors, who were laymen in Saxony, were not predisposed against the new pedagogy and were eager to observe it in the experimental school classes. Their reports reveal that the teachers in these classes were mostly between the ages of thirty and thirty-six, and were dedicated, earnest, and competent.[75]

Conservative school principals in Leipzig who were hostile to the principles of the active-learning school bitterly contested the experiment. In 1913 they advised the minister of education against the continuation of the experimental school classes. Sensitive to their criticism, the minister granted authorization for only 10 experimental school classes in Leipzig for the next two years. Saxony's early experiment with progressive education was interrupted by the world war. After the teachers were inducted into military service, instruction in these classes returned to the old methods.[76]

The opposition of the traditionalists in the teaching profession to the active-learning school was a forecast of the culture wars during the Weimar Republic. Fears about freedom and the loss of order and authority in the schools loom large in the school principals' reports sent to the Saxon minister of education. Many of the principals could not conceive of a school without the traditional discipline of enforced quiet and uniformity. The lively activity in the classroom and the spontaneous and joyful interactions of the pupils and teacher struck them as "chaos" and "anarchy." Describing contemptuously the new methods of teaching as the "pedagogy of coddling," one principal said: "To eliminate all requirement and compulsion from education and to take only the child's inclination as the guide and standard are tantamount to proclaiming the sovereignty of the child." The principals claimed that the new pedagogy was not training children to fulfill duties conscientiously or accustoming them to discipline and order.[77]

In the Last Years of the Old Political Order

By 1914, left liberals in the German Teachers' Association had framed a program of school reform and were actively working for change. The question of religious instruction in the schools, the problem that would trouble them throughout the Weimar years, already appeared as a dark cloud hovering over the reform movement. Pedagogues in Bremen and Hamburg who had Social Democratic leanings spoke out for the secularization of the schools. The reformers in Saxony achieved unity with a compromise in the Zwickau theses, which proposed changes that would make religious education in the school an autonomous activity of the pedagogue, free of clerical supervision. Tews and others reformers in Prussia thought that the demand for a secular school system was "a dangerous political mistake." It was politically more pragmatic, they counseled, to support an integrated school system in which the subject of religion alone would be taught to the pupils separated by confession. Tews contended that Catholic and Protestant clergymen remained uncompromising on the issue of religious instruction in the schools. He saw no prospect of success in an all-out fight against the churches. The Christian churches had deep roots in the life of the people, and the reform movement would be harmed if it started a war with them. These circumstances led him to concede that the churches had "a natural right to participate in popular education," but he did not define how this right would be exercised.[78]

On the prospects for achieving a more democratic educational system, the reformers oscillated from a somber view of the state of school politics to optimistic hopes. They were keenly aware of their isolation. Elitist educators in the secondary schools felt threatened by the proposal for a unified educational system, and the relationship between teachers in the elementary and secondary schools became contentious after 1906.[79] The new populist movements of the lower middle class and the agrarian Conservatives were alike "in their hostility to popular education," lamented Tews. Social mobility and the rising educational level of the working class were disturbing changes to social groups that clung to old methods of work and to the traditional relations between employer and worker. Tews did not expect reforms in the foreseeable future in "a state as little democratic as Prussia." As long as "its political institutions bore the stamp of feudalism," the elementary school would "be kept in a condition of bondage." The highest offices in the state administration were held by members of a small caste, whose children were not educated in the *Volksschule* and who had no interest in improving the education of the masses. Gustav Menzel, a teacher and close observer of political life in Berlin, bitterly criticized the Prussian Ministry of Education for repeatedly turning down the petitions submitted by the German Teachers' Association. The discussions in the education committee of the Prussian Landtag in December 1912, he reported, showed "how little teachers could count on the ministry's help in eliminating old conditions and opening the way for even the most modest measures of reform in the sphere of our professional and school politics."[80]

And yet left liberals in the teaching profession, who saw school reform as a matter of political power as well as enlightening the public, participated actively in civic life and aspired to positions of public influence.

Although Tews was defeated in his bid for election to the Prussian Landtag in 1913, four other members of the German Teachers' Association were successful Progressive Party candidates. The participation of urban schoolteachers in political life, as many contemporaries noted in 1912 and 1913, was strikingly intense. Politically active teachers in the big chapters in Berlin, Breslau, Chemnitz, Dresden, Halle, Leipzig, Stettin, and other cities formed associations (Vereinigungen für Schulpolitik) to observe the activities of the political parties and the deliberations of the state parliaments related to school affairs and to work in election campaigns on behalf of candidates who supported their program of school reform. The Social Democratic Party with a mass electoral constituency had adopted a large part of their reform agenda. Statements made by some reformers at the congresses and in the press of the German Teachers' Association indicate that they pinned their hopes on the growing electoral strength of the Social Democrats.[81]

Notes

1. "Die persönlichen Verhältnisse der Lehrer und Lehrerinnen in Preussen," *Schulstatistische Blätter. Beilage zur Pädagogischen Zeitung*, 20 November 1913: 102–3; *Die Lehrerin in Schule und Haus*, 26 June 1909: 1125–26; Rudolf Fischer, *Beiträge zu einer Statistik der deutschen Lehrerschaft. Ergebnisse der von der Statistischen Zentralstelle des Deutschen Lehrervereins am 1. April 1913 veranstalteten Erhebung* (Leipzig, 1916), pp. 12–16.
2. Attributing too much influence to their class background and their relation to the state as civil servants, historians for a long time overlooked or downplayed the liberal political ideology of urban schoolteachers and their commitment to educational reform and stressed instead the conservative values and social ambitions that bound the profession to the existing social and political order of Imperial Germany. See, for example, Folkert Meyer, *Schule der Untertanen. Lehrer und Politik in Preussen 1848–1900* (Hamburg, 1976), pp. 117ff; Hans-Günther Thien, *Schule, Staat und Lehrerschaft. Zur historischen Genese bürgerlicher Erziehung in Deutschland und England 1790–1918* (Frankfurt am Main, 1984), pp. 216–24.
3. *Die Lehrerin in Schule und Haus*, 11 November 1905: 192; *Schulstatistische Blätter. Beilage zur Pädagogischen Zeitung*, 17 April 1913: 45.
4. On the discrimination against women in the teaching profession, see *Bericht über die Deutsche Lehrerversammlung in München am 4. bis 7. Juni 1906* (Leipzig, 1906), pp. 40–83; *Die Lehrerin*, 1 July 1906: 1077–91. On the German Women Teachers' Association in the years before 1914, see James Albisetti, *Schooling German Girls and Women: Secondary and Higher Education in the Nineteenth Century* (Princeton, 1988), pp. 169ff; Helmut Beilner, *Die Emanzipation der bayerischen Lehrerin—aufgezeigt an der Arbeit des bayerischen Lehrerinnenvereins 1898–1933* (Munich, 1971), pp. 51ff.
5. Fischer, *Beiträge zu einer Statistik der deutschen Lehrerschaft*, pp. 6, 18.
6. Johannes Tews, *Berliner Lehrer* (Leipzig, 1907), pp. 16–17; idem, *Der preussische Volksschullehrerstand* (Bielefeld, 1894), pp. 13–15; Hagener, *Radikale Schulreform*, pp. 21–22. On the big-city teachers in Saxony, see Karl Trinks, *Die Sozialgestalt des Volksschullehrers* (1933; reprint, Stuttgart, 1980), pp. 25–27.

7. Jakob Beyhl, *Wir fordern unser Recht! Ein Wort zur wirtschaftlichen Befreiung der Volksschullehrer* (Würzburg, 1913), pp. 26-29; *Pädagogische Zeitung*, 11 February 1909: 116; ibid., 8 April 1909: 308-9; ibid., 26 August 1909: 760; ibid., 6 February 1913: 93-96; A.G. [Albin Günther], "Die hauptamtlichen Kreisschulinspektoren in Preussen," *Schulstatistische Blätter. Beilage zur Pädagogischen Zeitung*, February 1910: 9-11. On the traditional role of churchmen in the supervision of the elementary schools, see Marjorie Lamberti, *State, Society, and the Elementary School in Imperial Germany* (New York, 1989), pp. 15-16, 89-93.
8. Carl Louis Albert Pretzel, *Geschichte des Deutschen Lehrervereins in den ersten fünfzig Jahren seines Bestehens* (Leipzig, 1921), pp. 109-10; Bölling, *Volksschullehrer und Politik*, pp. 33-36. See also Rainer Bölling, *Sozialgeschichte der deutschen Lehrer. Ein Überblick von 1800 bis zur Gegenwart* (Göttingen, 1983).
9. On the women teachers who supported the new pedagogy in their professional society, see *Die Lehrerin*, 17 November 1906: 213-14; ibid., 2 February 1907: 510-12; ibid., 25 July 1908: 1231-37; ibid., 23 January 1909: 478-82. According to a survey of 14,892 working members of the German Women Teachers' Association conducted in 1908, 54.5 percent taught in the elementary schools, 20.5 percent taught in the secondary schools, and the rest taught in private schools or were private tutors. See ibid., 24 July 1909: 1232-40.
10. *Die Lehrerin*, 24 September 1910: 201-2. See also a similar observation of Franziska Ohnesorge, a teacher in Dresden, in ibid., 18 May 1907: 921-22. Ohnesorge stated that the passionate debates over the reform of the instruction of religion among male teachers in Bremen and at the national congress of the German Teachers' Association in 1906 "have passed many of us by without any effect."
11. *Pädagogische Zeitung*, 1 May 1913: 345, 350-55. On the history of the Catholic Teachers' Association before 1914, see Cloer, *Sozialgeschichte, Schulpolitik und Lehrerfortbildung der Katholischen Lehrerverbände*; Josef Tymister, *Die Entstehung der Berufsvereine der katholischen Lehrerschaft in Deutschland* (Cologne, 1965).
12. Otto Kley, *Die deutsche Schulreform der Zukunft* (Cologne, 1917), pp. 16-17, 92, 123; Franz Weigl, *Wesen und Gestaltung der Arbeitsschule* (Paderborn, 1921), pp. 9-10, 19ff.
13. *Pädagogische Zeitung*, 14 September 1893: 517-18; ibid., 16 June 1898: 386.
14. Ernst Beyer, *Fünfundzwanzig Jahre Sächsischer Lehrerverein. Zur Geschichte des Sächsischen Lehrervereins in den Jahren von 1898 bis 1923* (Leipzig, 1923), pp. 7-9, 25ff; *Die Lehrermassregelungen in Sachsen in den Jahren 1911-1912* (Leipzig, n.d.), pp. 5ff.
15. *Pädagogische Zeitung*, 27 February 1896: 137-38; Emil Saupe, *Die politischen Parteien und die preussische Volksschule* (Spandau, 1913), pp. 76-77; Manfred Hettling, *Politische Bürgerlichkeit. Der Bürger zwischen Individualität und Vergesellschaft in Deutschland und der Schweiz von 1860 bis 1918* (Göttingen, 1999), pp. 126-28.
16. *Pädagogische Zeitung*, 19 January 1893: 34-35. On the political activities of left-wing liberal teachers in Berlin, see Erich Leonhardt, *50 Jahre Berliner Lehrerverein 1880-1930* (Berlin, 1930); Johannes Tews, *Aus Arbeit und Leben. Erinnerungen und Rückblicke* (Berlin, 1921), pp. 126-28, 156-73.
17. Tews, *Berliner Lehrer*, pp. 73-74; Johannes Tews, *Die gemeinsame Elementarschule* (Bielefeld, 1896), p. 1.
18. For the reform of the secondary schools, see James Albisetti, *Secondary School Reform in Imperial Germany* (Princeton, 1983); James Albisetti and Peter Lundgreen, "Höhere Knabenschulen," in *Handbuch der deutschen Bildungsgeschichte*, ed. Berg, vol. 4, pp. 228-66.
19. See Tews's autobiography, *Aus Arbeit und Leben*, pp. 156ff.
20. Johannes Tews, *Schulkämpfe der Gegenwart. Vorträge gehalten in der Humboldt-Akademie in Berlin zum Kampf um die Volksschule in Preussen* (1906; 2nd ed., Leipzig, 1911), pp. 17-18, 44-46.
21. Ibid., pp. 67-70.
22. Tews, *Die gemeinsame Elementarschule*, pp. 3ff; idem, *Schulkämpfe der Gegenwart*, pp. 120ff; Johannes Tews, *Die deutsche Einheitsschule. Freie Bahn jedem Tüchtigen* (Leipzig, 1916), pp. 5ff;

Sächsischer Lehrerverein, *Grundforderungen der Sächsischen Volksschullehrer zur Reform des Volksschulgesetzes* (Dresden, 1909), pp. 12ff.
23. Johannes Tews, "Zur Vorschulfrage," *Schulstatistische Blätter. Beilage zur Pädagogischen Zeitung*, 18 April 1912: 39-48; idem, *Schulkämpfe der Gegenwart*, pp. 17-19; idem, *Die gemeinsame Elementarschule*, p. 6; *Pädagogische Zeitung*, 20 March 1913: 221-22; ibid., 2 October 1913: 717-19. On the different types of elementary schools and the social class of the pupils, see Frank-Michael Kuhlemann, "Niedere Schulen," in *Handbuch der deutschen Bildungsgeschichte*, ed. Berg, vol. 4, pp. 196ff.
24. For a stenographic report of the congress, see *Allgemeine Deutsche Lehrerzeitung*, 26 June 1892: 252-56.
25. Tews, *Die gemeinsame Elementarschule*, pp. 3-6, 12.
26. *Schulstatistische Blätter. Beilage zur Pädagogischen Zeitung*, 18 April 1912: 46-48; *Pädagogische Zeitung*, 20 March 1913: 221-22; ibid., 2 October 1913: 717-19.
27. *Pädagogisches Jahrbuch. Rundschau auf dem Gebiete des Volksschulwesens 1905* (Berlin, 1906), pp. 81-82; *Pädagogische Zeitung*, 20 March 1913: 221-22; ibid., 4 December 1913: 910. See also Kurt Schäfer, *Schulen und Schulpolitik in Frankfurt am Main 1900-1945* (Frankfurt am Main, 1994), pp. 83-93.
28. See the report of their opposition in *Pädagogische Zeitung*, 20 March 1913: 221-22.
29. Prahl, "Die arme Vorschule," *Preussische Jahrbücher*, August 1912: 299-302; Otto Hesse, "Vorschulen," in ibid., 307. See also the criticism of the decision of the 1914 congress of the German Teachers' Association in Hans Delbrück, "Das demokratische Zukunftsideal und die Schule," *Preussische Jahrbücher*, July 1914: 169-74.
30. Lamberti, *State, Society, and the Elementary School*, pp. 62ff, 93-97.
31. *Preussische Statistik*. Vol. 209: *Das gesamte niedere Schulwesen im Preussischen Staate im Jahre 1906* (Berlin, 1908), Teil I, p. 64. On the discrimination against the Jews in public elementary education, see Marjorie Lamberti, *Jewish Activism in Imperial Germany: The Struggle for Civil Equality* (New Haven, 1978), chap. 7.
32. On the political battle over the Prussian school bill, see Lamberti, *State, Society, and the Elementary School*, pp. 197ff.
33. *Bericht über die Deutsche Lehrerversammlung am 4. bis 7. Juni 1906*, pp. 101ff.
34. Ibid., pp. 88ff.
35. Tews, *Aus Arbeit und Leben*, p. 126; Tews, *Schulkämpfe der Gegenwart*, pp. 140-43.
36. *Bericht über die Deutsche Lehrerversammlung*, pp. 120-22. On the elementary schoolteachers in Bremen and Hamburg who were sympathetic to Social Democracy, see Hagener, *Radikale Schulreform*, pp. 74-75, 80-81; Milberg, *Schulpolitik in der pluralistischen Gesellschaft*, pp. 66-73.
37. Marjorie Lamberti, "Elementary School Teachers and the Struggle against Social Democracy in Wilhelmine Germany," *History of Education Quarterly* 32 (Spring 1992): 92-94.
38. On this debate, see *Bericht über die Deutsche Lehrerversammlung*, pp. 131ff.
39. For a stenographic report of the congress, see *Pädagogische Zeitung*, 25 June 1896: 425; ibid., 9 July 1896: 462.
40. Karsten Rudolph, "Das 'rote Königreich': Die sächsische Sozialdemokratie im Wilhelminischen Deutschland," in *Sachsen im Kaiserreich. Politik, Wirtschaft und Gesellschaft im Umbruch*, ed. Simone Lässig and Karl Heinrich Pohl (Weimar, 1997), pp. 87-99.
41. From the stenographic report of the Zwickau congress in Sächsischer Lehrerverein, *Die Umgestaltung des Religionsunterrichts in den sächsischen Volksschulen* (Leipzig, 1908), pp. 3-4, 72-73. See also Arzt's views in the *Sächsische Schulzeitung*, 20 November 1908: 822-24.
42. *Die Umgestaltung des Religionsunterrichts*, p. 79. See also Otto Hertel, *Der Leipziger Lehrerverein in den Jahren 1896-1920* (Leipzig, 1921), pp. 37-39; *Hundert Jahre Chemnitzer Lehrerverein 1831-1931* (Chemnitz, 1931), pp. 44-45.
43. Tews, *Schulkämpfe der Gegenwart*, pp. 24-27, 70; see also Carl Pretzel's similar argument in *Bericht über die Deutsche Lehrerversammlung*, pp. 131-32.
44. Quoted in *Pädagogisches Jahrbuch 1906*, pp. 137-38.

45. For a report of this attack, see *Pädagogische Zeitung*, 7 July 1910: 671–73.
46. For an account of this conflict in Saxony, see Hertel, *Leipziger Lehrerverein*, pp. 37–44.
47. See Wilhelm Reese's and Johannes Gläser's essays in *'Pädagogik vom Kinde aus.' Aufsätze Hamburger Lehrer*, ed. Theo Gläss (Weinheim, n.d.), pp. 33–56; Fritz Gansberg's essay in *Die Pädagogische Bewegung 'Vom Kinde Aus'*, ed. Theo Dietrich (Bad Heilbrunn, 1967), pp. 109–11.
48. Leipziger Lehrerverein, *Die Arbeitsschule. Beiträge aus Theorie und Praxis* (Leipzig, 1909), p. 10; *Pädagogische Zeitung*, 11 March 1909: 205. On the slow growth of the kindergarten movement in the country of Friedrich Froebel's origins, see Ann Taylor Allen, "'Let Us Live With Our Children': Kindergarten Movements in Germany and the United States, 1840–1914," *History of Education Quarterly* 28 (1988): 23–48.
49. See the account of a visiting school principal from Indiana in *Pädagogische Zeitung*, 27 May 1909: 476–78, and Rice's comment cited in Arthur Wirth, *John Dewey as Educator: His Design for Work in Education 1894–1904* (Lanham, Md., 1989), p. 32. Lawrence Cremin's *The Transformation of the School: Progressivism in American Education, 1876–1957* (New York, 1961) still remains a valuable introduction to the educational philosophy of John Dewey and the work of his followers. On progressive education as an international movement, see Hermann Röhrs and Volker Lenhart, eds., *Progressive Education Across the Continents* (Frankfurt am Main, 1995).
50. On the pedagogical ideas and the innovative private country board school opened by Paul Geheeb in 1910, see Dennis Shirley, *The Politics of Progressive Education: The Odenwaldschule in Nazi Germany* (Cambridge, Mass., 1992). Shirley writes (p. 41): "Each morning began with 'air baths,' or exercises done outside in the nude by students. These exercises reflected *Zeitgeist* currents in the youth movement and back-to-nature 'life reform' movements, which criticized modern society for increasingly separating individuals from contact with nature." For a general survey of the pedagogical thought of the leading reformers, see Jürgen Oelkers' valuable analysis in *Reformpädagogik. Eine kritische Dogmengeschichte* (Weinheim, 1989) and Ulrich Herrmann, "Pädagogisches Denken und Anfänge der Reformpädagogik," in *Handbuch der deutschen Bildungsgeschichte*, ed. Berg, vol. 4, pp. 147–78.
51. On the pedagogical reformers in Bremen and Hamburg, see Johannes Hein, "Die Entwicklung der Hamburger Reformbewegung," in *Die neuen Schulen in Deutschland*, ed. Fritz Karsen (Langensalza, 1924), pp. 9–23; Hagener, *Radikale Schulreform*, pp. 24ff; Milberg, *Schulpolitik*, pp. 66ff.
52. Max Brahn, "Ernst Meumann und die Organisationen zur Pflege der wissenschaftlichen Pädagogik," *Zeitschrift für Pädagogische Psychologie und Experimentelle Pädagogik* 16 (1915): 227–32. See also Marc Depaepe, *Zum Wohl des Kindes? Pädalogie, pädagogische Psychologie und experimentelle Pädagogik in Europa und den USA, 1890–1940* (Weinheim, 1993), pp. 68ff, 225ff; Peter Dudek, *Jugend als Objekt der Wissenschaften. Geschichte der Jugendforschung in Deutschland und Österreich 1890–1933* (Opladen, 1990), pp. 90ff.
53. Hertel, *Leipziger Lehrerverein*, pp. 32ff; Otto Scheibner's report in *Zeitschrift für pädagogische Psychologie und Experimentelle Pädagogik* 12 (1911): 183–85. See also Andreas Pehnke, *Sächsische Reformpädagogik. Traditionen und Perspektiven* (Leipzig, 1998), pp. 20ff.
54. In some historical accounts of women's secondary education, Hugo Gaudig is seen primarily as an opponent of coeducation. See Elke Kleinau, "Gleichheit oder Differenz? Theorien zur höheren Mädchenbildung," in *Geschichte der Mädchen- und Frauenbildung*. Vol. 2: *Vom Vormärz bis zur Gegenwart*, ed. Elke Kleinau and Claudia Opitz (Frankfurt, 1996), pp. 119ff. Gaudig assumed that women had an innate nature different from that of men, and he defended an equally valuable but separate secondary education for girls. Most German women teachers at that time likewise favored separate schooling for girls. Gaudig's important contribution to pedagogical reform thought and practice should not be overlooked. Gender issues were not part of his writing on the new pedagogy in *Die Schule im Dienste der werdenden Persönlichkeit*, 2 vols. (Leipzig, 1917) or in "Die Arbeitsschule als

Reformschule," *Zeitschrift für Pädagogische Psychologie und Experimentelle Pädagogik* 12 (1911): 545–52.
55. *Pädagogische Zeitung*, 20 June 1912: 483; Ernst Weber, *Die Lehrerpersönlichkeit* (Leipzig, 1912), p. 1; Vogel's speech on the new pedagogy in *Bericht über die Vertreterversammlung und Hauptversammlung des Sächsischen Lehrervereins am 2. und 3. Oktober 1911 zu Leipzig* (Leipzig, n.d.), p. 33.
56. *Die Arbeitsschule*, pp. 15–18, 43. See also Max Brahn's public address, "Neue Ziele und Wege der Pädagogik," to an audience in Berlin, in *Pädagogische Zeitung*, 11 December 1913: 925–27; Robert Rissmann, *Volksschulreform, Herbartianismus, Sozialpädagogik, Persönlichkeitsbildung* (Leipzig, 1911), pp. 19–22, 65, 72; Gaudig, *Die Schule im Dienste der werdenden Persönlichkeit*, vol. 2, pp. 30–32.
57. Albisetti, *Schooling German Girls and Women*, p. 281; Marianne Horstkemper, "Die Koedukationsdebatte um die Jahrhundertwende," in *Geschichte der Mädchen- und Frauenbildung*, ed. Kleinau and Opitz, vol. 2, pp. 204–6.
58. *Preussische Statistik*. Vol. 176: *Das gesamte niedere Schulwesen im preussischen Staate im Jahre 1901* (Berlin, 1903), Teil II, pp. 8–9; *Fünfter Bericht über die gesamten Unterrichts- und Erziehungsanstalten im Königreiche Sachsen* (Dresden, 1905), p. 120.
59. Tews, *Schulkämpfe der Gegenwart*, pp. 145–49.
60. See, for example, Dora Petzold's statement in *Die Chemnitzer Versuchsschule: Ein kurzer Bericht über ihre Entwicklung und ihren derzeitigen Stand* (Dresden, 1928), pp. 26–28.
61. See Gaudig's famous debate with and criticism of Kerschensteiner in Bund für Schulreform, *Erster Deutscher Kongress für Jugendbildung und Jugendkunde zu Dresden am 6., 7., und 8. Oktober 1911* (Leipzig, 1912), pp. 13–14, 29–30. Georg Kerschensteiner, *Der Begriff der Arbeitsschule* (Leipzig, 1912). On Kerschensteiner's thought and work, see Derek Linton, *"Who Has the Youth, Has the Future": The Campaign to Save Young Workers in Imperial Germany* (Cambridge, 1991).
62. *Die Arbeitsschule*, pp. 20–27.
63. Quoted in Margarete Götz, *Die Heimatkunde im Spiegel der Lehrpläne der Weimarer Republik* (Frankfurt am Main, 1989), pp. 29–37.
64. Heinrich Wigge, *Die Gefahren der Arbeitsschulbewegung* (Langensalza, 1913), pp. 46–47; L. Mittenzweg, *Lernschule oder Arbeitsschule? Eine kritische Betrachtung* (Langensalza, 1910), pp. 33–34.
65. Heinrich Scharrelmann, "Heil'ge Ordnung," in *Erlebtes Pädagogik. Gesammelte Aufsätze und Unterrichtsproben* (Hamburg, 1912), pp. 29–34.
66. Rissmann, *Volksschulreform*, pp. 14–19, 65, 71–75, 91–92, 107–8.
67. *Pädagogische Zeitung*, 12 March 1908: 242. On the founding of the League for School Reform, see *Pädagogische Zeitung*, 7 May 1908: 422–23; *Die Lehrerin*, 20 June 1908: 1102–3.
68. *Pädagogische Zeitung*, 29 April 1909: 373–74. See the reports of the central commission's work in *Zeitschrift für Pädagogische Psychologie und Experimentelle Pädagogik* 13 (1912): 222–23; ibid., 14 (1913): 416–18; ibid., 15 (1914): 62–65.
69. *Pädagogische Zeitung*, 27 August 1908: 791; ibid., 2 September 1909: 783; ibid., 25 January 1912: 60–62. See Alois Fischer's report on the founding of the Pädagogisch-psychologisches Institut in Munich in *Zeitschrift für Pädagogische Psychologie und Experimentelle Pädagogik* 12 (1911): 67–70.
70. Weber, *Die Lehrerpersönlichkeit*, p. 56; *Pädagogische Zeitung*, 22 July 1909: 657–58. For the views of elementary schoolteachers on the contribution of the discipline of psychology to the new pedagogy, see *Pädagogische Zeitung*, 18 March 1909: 230; ibid., 15 December 1910: 1196–99.
71. Depaepe, *Zum Wohl des Kindes*, p. 73.
72. See the reports in *Zeitschrift für Pädagogische Psychologie und Experimentelle Pädagogik* 14 (1913): 63–66, 232–33; ibid., 15 (1914): 425–26.

73. For a stenographic report of this session at the congress, see *Pädagogische Zeitung*, 20 June 1912: 481-89.
74. For these arguments in the debate, see *Pädagogische Zeitung*, 27 June 1912: 511-12, 514-15.
75. Sächsisches Hauptstaatsarchiv Dresden [hereafter SHA], Nr. 13838, Blatt 2, 6, and 12, three reports of the district school inspector in Ölsnitz to the minister of education, 14 June 1911, 1 March 1913, and 25 March 1914; Bl. 15 and 23, district school inspector in Chemnitz to the minister, 10 February 1913 and 19 February 1914; Bl. 130, district school inspector in Leipzig to the minister, 30 June 1913. On the teachers' campaign for the opening of experimental schools in Saxony, see *Sächsische Schulzeitung*, 3 March 1911: 131-32; ibid., 8 September 1911: 531.
76. SHA, Nr. 13838, Bl. 43, district school inspector in Dresden to the minister of education, 3 May 1915; Bl. 113, district school inspector in Plauen to the minister, 19 July 1915; Bl. 141, district school inspector in Leipzig to the minister, 18 November 1915.
77. SHA, Nr. 13838, Bl. 138ff, Gesamtbericht über den Versuch einer 'Reform des Elementarunterrichtes' in Leipziger Volksschulen. Ostern 1911-Ostern 1913; Bl. 145ff, report on the experimental schools in Leipzig, written by School Principal Weigeldt for the conference of school principals and sent to the Ministry of Education by the school inspector on 18 November 1915.
78. Tews, *Schulkämpfe*, pp. 24, 70.
79. Karl Muthesius, *Die Einheit des deutschen Lehrerstandes* (Berlin, 1917), p. 28.
80. Tews, *Schulkämpfe*, pp. 4-6, 46-47, 85-87; *Pädagogische Zeitung*, 16 January 1913: 45.
81. *Pädagogische Zeitung*, 12 June 1913: 459. On the favorable view of the Social Democrats held by left-wing liberals in the profession during these years, see Lamberti, "Elementary School Teachers," pp. 89-90.

Chapter 2

THE NOVEMBER REVOLUTION AND THE OPENING OF A NEW ERA FOR SCHOOL REFORMS

The reformers in the teaching profession accepted the end of the old political order without sorrow when Philipp Scheidemann, the Social Democratic leader, announced the abdication of the Hohenzollern dynasty and the founding of the republic on 9 November 1918. Even before the outbreak of the revolution there was considerable unrest among elementary schoolteachers, who were radicalized by the decline in their real income and standard of living under the impact of wartime inflation. They took the initiative in organizing the demonstrations that civil servants staged in several cities in August and September 1918 to bring their grievances to the notice of the state authorities and the public.[1] In the conflict over war aims and peace negotiations, Saxon teachers who were now openly sympathetic to Social Democracy opposed the annexationist program of the right-wing nationalists in the Fatherland Party.[2] In 1917–18 the German Teachers' Association worked alongside the Progressive and Social Democratic Parties in making the democratization of the educational system an issue in domestic politics. In a wartime pamphlet, Johannes Tews struck a resonant chord when he exclaimed, "The unified school system shall come" since it has "received its charter in the trenches."[3] The progressivist pedagogues now related the enormous sacrifice of human life demanded by the state in the world war to its obligation to give all children, irrespective of the social rank and income of their parents, equal access to secondary and higher education. After this war "we may no longer drag class differences into educational questions in the future," a teacher in Dresden said.[4]

The School Reformers in the New Government

After the November Revolution, the educational reformers rallied to the support of the provisional governments formed by the Social Democrats in the

Reich and the states. When Social Democrats became the ministers of education in Prussia and Saxony, the progressivist pedagogues took satisfaction in knowing that the Social Democratic Party's school program "contained a substantial part of the demands drawn up by the German Teachers' Association, the latter for pedagogical reasons and the former for political reasons." With an idealistic and exuberant view of the young republic, they expected that school reforms would be carried out quickly. "As regrettable as the outcome of the world war is for Germany," a teacher in Breslau confessed, "without this circumstance the reforms that will be carried out now would not have come about. We teachers can observe the new developments calmly; they shall bring us the fulfillment of our old demands."[5]

These expectations seemed to be confirmed by the swiftness with which the new ministers of education began the "liberation" of the elementary school from the church. Instead of waiting for the election of the state parliaments and the passage of reform legislation, Konrad Haenisch and Adolf Hoffmann, who represented the Majority and Independent Social Democratic Parties in the Prussian Ministry of Education, swept away the inspection of the elementary schools conducted by the parish pastors by an edict on 27 November 1918. Another administrative order on 29 November prohibited celebrations of a religious nature in the schools and the recitation of prayer at the opening and closing of the school day. Teachers were released from the obligation to give religious instruction. Religion ceased to be a compulsory subject of instruction for all pupils; parents or guardians were free to exempt their children from this instruction at the time of school registration. Anticipating the objections that the clergy would raise, the two Social Democratic ministers stated that they did not intend to curtail the freedom of religious belief and worship. In the past, however, the churches had used the state's coercive power to uphold and spread their doctrines and had inflicted "a grave conflict of conscience on many teachers, who see themselves condemned day after day to impart to the youth doctrines that conflict with their own feeling and understanding and often do not correspond to the children's real capacity of comprehension." Minister of Education Wilhelm Buck in Saxony introduced similar changes expeditiously by edicts. In addition, his decree of 2 December excluded the catechism from the instruction of religion in the schools and reduced the time allotted for this subject from four to two hours weekly during the first four years of schooling.[6] Many pedagogues, who hailed these decrees, took care to reassure the pastors that they would continue to give religious instruction. They hoped that "a free collaboration" between teachers and clergymen would begin "on the basis of complete equality and mutual respect."[7]

The appointment of many reformers to offices in the school administration during the early years of the republic gave them an opportunity to influence policymaking and push for change. Gustav Menzel, a member of the executive board of the German Teachers' Association, became the councilor for elementary school affairs in the Prussian Ministry of Education. Menzel did not hesitate to call himself "a representative of the teachers in the school administration" and to assure the leadership of the teachers' association that they would "find an open door in the school administration at any time."[8] In appointing a councilor on school organization for the Saxon Ministry of Education, Buck selected Paul Häntzschel from the three individuals nominated for this post by the executive board of the Saxon Teachers' Association. Menzel and Häntzschel were among a number of elementary schoolteachers who joined the Social Democratic Party after the November Revolution, when the restrictions on the political affiliations of civil servants were lifted. The Saxon reformers called for the removal of the holdovers in the school inspectorate from the past and contended that these "pedantic and reactionary" bureaucrats would never reconcile themselves to the "new times" and "the idea of a free school." When Buck appointed Ernst Beyer, Max Brethfeld, and Alwin Wünsche as district school inspectors, the teachers' association warmly praised him for selecting men who had courageously and tenaciously led the fight for school reform before 1914.[9]

With the encouragement of their professional societies, male schoolteachers were very active in the election campaigns for the German National Assembly and the state constituent assemblies in the winter of 1918-19. The German Teachers' Association urged its members to join those parties whose platforms supported their goals in cultural politics. Only by working within the political parties, its leaders said, could teachers gain a strong voice on school issues in political life and participate in the big tasks of reorganizing the educational system.[10] Women teachers in Berlin, Leipzig, and other cities who embraced the cause of school reform began to join the local branches of the German Teachers' Association after 1918. Its revised statutes opened membership to women, and by 1923 about 10,000 female teachers had enlisted.[11] Some of these women may have been disappointed with the staid congress of the German Women Teachers' Association in 1919. As one member said afterwards, the program adopted there did not incorporate "the new demands that have spread beyond a small circle of radical male teachers in the wake of the revolution and have become the subject of widespread discussion in the pedagogical press."[12]

The intense political activity of elementary schoolteachers in these years can be gauged by the number of reformers in their profession who were elected to the German National Assembly and the state legislatures. These deputies in the National Assembly in Weimar included the Social Democrat Carl August Hellmann, a teacher in Hamburg, and two German Democrats, Richard Seyfert, the director of a *Lehrerseminar* in Saxony, and Karl Weiss, a teacher in Nuremberg. In the Prussian parliament, members of the elementary school teaching profession held four seats in the Social Democratic delegation and eight in the delegation of the German Democratic Party, the successor of the Progressive People's Party. Among these German Democrats were several leaders of the provincial branches of the Prussian Teachers' Association: Heinrich Kimpel in Hesse, Hermann Juds in Pomerania, and Reinhard Otto in Brandenburg. Two members of the Saxon Teachers' Association, the Social Democrat Arthur Arzt and the German Democrat Bernhard Claus, were among the six members of the teaching profession who were elected to the Saxon parliament.[13]

Although quantitative data is not available on the party affiliations of the mass of schoolteachers, a significant factor in their choice of a party was the issue of religion in the schools. Members of the Catholic Teachers' Association supported the Center Party, which made the defense of the confessional school a high priority in its political campaigns. They worked so wholeheartedly in the Center's election campaigns in the Rhineland that they demanded that the party allocate at least two secure parliamentary seats to teachers in the region's electoral districts.[14] Conservative school principals and teachers who had organized in small coalitions such as the League of German Protestant Teachers' Associations (Verband Deutscher Evangelischer Lehrer- und Lehrerinnen-Vereine) were attracted to the German National People's Party because its platform endorsed the confessional school that placed "character formation and national education based on a religious foundation at the center of its work." The German People's Party straddled the fence by expressing a preference for the interconfessional school (*Simultanschule*) and affirming the legal right to open confessional schools.[15]

Judging from the comments on the German Democratic Party's school program in the newspapers published by the state and provincial branches of the German Teachers' Association during the election campaigns, a sizable part of its membership, especially in the cities, can be counted among the "new middle class" of civil servants who supported the German Democrats.[16] This assessment is confirmed by an opinion poll of members of the Prussian Teachers' Association conducted in 1926, which shows that 44.8 percent of the respondents in big cities stood to the left of the center and on the left of the political spectrum. In medium-sized cities, small towns, and the countryside, 33.8 percent of the teachers placed themselves politically to the right of the center and on the right and far right, in comparison with 18.2 percent to the left of the center and on the left. Locating themselves in the political center were 39 percent of all respondents, who were "inclined toward the left despite some uncertainty," as the polltaker reported.[17] The German Democratic Party enhanced its image as a socially progressive party by adopting the "school demands" announced by the executive board of the German Teachers' Association on 17 November 1918. Its platform stressed the relationship between a democratic state, the principle of equality of opportunity, and the right of intelligent children to have an education corresponding to their ability and will to learn, irrespective of the wealth, class, and religious faith of their parents. The German

Democrats favored the continuation of religious education in the schools, but were not of one mind in respect as to whether this instruction should be confessional or more inclusively Biblical and ethical in nature.[18]

Teachers who crossed over to the Social Democratic camp in 1918–19 were a minority in the profession and within the German Teachers' Association, but they were numerous and highly vocal in Saxony, Bremen, Hamburg, and some sections of Prussia, such as Greater Berlin and the industrial centers of Silesia and Westphalia. The new allegiance of teachers who joined the Social Democratic Party was not an overnight change in political colors. As the *Sächsische Schulzeitung* stated, before 1914 these teachers were "democratic and social as a result of their profession." They lived among and knew working-class people and "had to recognize the justice of many of their demands." Notwithstanding their criticism of the capitalist system, these teachers were more likely to identify with the reformism of the Majority Social Democrats than with the extreme radicalism of the Independent Social Democrats, whose rhetoric of "class conflict" and "the dictatorship of the proletariat" alienated them.[19] What made the Social Democratic Party attractive to them was, above all, its resolute and unequivocal commitment to the secularization of the elementary schools, a principle enshrined in the party's Erfurt program of 1891. They read the party's official line that religion was "a private matter" as a commitment to freedom of conscience and the separation of church and school. The German Democratic Party's position on the issue of religious education in the schools, they thought, was rife with "contradictions and inconsistencies." It stood for the emancipation of the school from clerical supervision and yet did not want to remove religious instruction from the curriculum. Teachers who wanted "no compromise" but a complete separation of church and school believed that the Social Democrats offered a fundamental solution to this problem more than did the liberal Democrats.[20]

The affiliation of elementary schoolteachers with the Socialist parties was a startling phenomenon to Catholic and Protestant churchmen and other conservatives. In the winter of 1918–19, small groups of Social Democratic teachers were formed in several cities. On 21 April 1919 teachers who belonged to the Majority Social Democratic Party gathered at a conference in Berlin, organized by Heinrich Schulz, a former teacher in Bremen who had served as the party's leading spokesman in school politics for many years and who would soon become the head of the newly created Department for Cultural Affairs in the Reich Interior Ministry in June 1919. The Social Democratic leaders wanted to create a party-affiliated teachers' organization that would disseminate the ideas of Social Democracy within the profession, do propaganda work in public life, and provide help for the party's youth movement. The Association of Social Democratic Teachers (Arbeitsgemeinschaft sozialdemokratischer Lehrer und Lehrerinnen) was founded at this conference, and at a subsequent meeting the executive committee agreed that as "part of the Social Democratic Party," the new group would be "bound to its statutes and decisions."[21] Teachers who stood closer to the more radical Independent Social Democrats met in Berlin on 10–11 June to organize the Socialist Teachers' League (Verband sozialistischer Lehrer und Lehrerinnen), whose purpose was defined in its statutes as "the realization of Socialism in the realm of the entire educational system in the closest collaboration with the struggle of the class-conscious proletariat." The founders of this leftist organization boasted that they would not follow the "obsolete" tactics of the "old" German Teachers' Association but would fight for "the liberation of the school and the teaching profession" as "a revolutionary union."[22]

The Social Democratic teachers' organizations did not attract a large membership or drain the vitality of the German Teachers' Association. In 1919 the local groups in the "red" cities of Bremen and Hamburg counted 54 and 80 members respectively. Although 300 teachers from all parts of Upper Silesia attended a meeting organized by the Social Democratic Party's office in Gleiwitz on 2 March, only 50 signed up when the party's loyalists created a teachers' club in Upper Silesia a month later. By the spring of 1920, the Association of Social Democratic Teachers had recruited about 2,000 educators from all levels of the school system in Germany.[23] With 132,043 members organized in 2,563 chapters in 1922, the German Teachers' Association remained the profession's most significant presence in school politics. Its leadership disapproved of the founding of the "separate organizations" tied to political parties, and most of the elementary schoolteachers in Saxony and elsewhere who had Social Democratic sympathies chose to remain loyal to their professional society. As a teacher in Breslau explained, the formation of teachers' organizations exclusively on the basis of party affiliation and political ideology was not in the best interests of the schools and the teaching profession because "the danger" existed that "we will then formulate our school program no longer from the point of view of education but from that of party politics."[24]

While the reformers in the teaching profession greeted the ministerial decrees and the reforms that "fell in [their] laps as the fruit of the revolution,"[25] Catholic and Protestant clergymen and the political parties defending church interests protested "the cultural-political dictatorship" of the Social Democrats. With their emotional attachment to the monarchy, many churchmen reacted to the November Revolution and the founding of the republic with shock and despondency. They were soon aroused to action by the school decrees of the left-wing provisional governments. Catholic and Protestant churchmen condemned the edicts related to prayer, religious observances, and catechism instruction in the schools as an assault on religious freedom. In a pastoral letter to their dioceses on 20 December, the Catholic bishops in Prussia protested the attempt of the Social Democrats to impose a secular school system on the nation by ministerial edicts before the election of the National Assembly. In Saxony, Protestant pastors in the pulpit harangued against the Social Democratic government's "fight against the Christian religion." Their perception that the Social Democrats posed a threat to church life was reinforced by developments in other predominantly Protestant states. Edicts issued by the workers' and soldiers' councils in Hamburg abolished the instruction of religion in the schools as well as the church tax, and eased the official procedures for the disaffiliation of citizens from the churches.[26]

The issue of religion in the public schools played a major role in the election campaigns of the Center and German National People's Parties for the German National Assembly and the state assemblies in January 1919. The Center's campaign propaganda emphasized the defense of religious freedom and confessional schooling and the protection of the rights of the church and parents. Catholic teachers who worked as publicists for the Center Party characterized the school goals of the German Teachers' Association as "anticlerical," and accused its leadership of striving "to carry out a revolution in school politics."[27] Catholic politicians and pastors were highly successful in drawing voters to the polls with campaign slogans about the threat of Socialist school reforms and "a new *Kulturkampf*." The Center Party won ninety seats in the National Assembly and, as the second largest party, commanded considerable leverage when the Social Democrats and German Democrats had to build a governmental majority. Having accepted the democratic republic as the most effective way of bringing Germany out of political chaos, the Center's leadership was ready to join these two parties in governing coalitions in the Reich and in Prussia in order to protect Catholic Church interests and to keep their partners from moving further to the political left.[28]

Protestant pastors and theologians who saw the influence of the Christian churches in the state and in society threatened by the November Revolution found political shelter in the antirepublican and monarchist German National People's Party. Among the prominent Protestant clergymen who became politically active German Nationalists were church superintendents Otto Dibelius in Berlin and Franz Költzsch in Dresden, and Friedrich Winckler, the chairman of the executive committee of the general synod of the Protestant Church in Prussia. In the press and in political meetings during the election campaign, right-wing churchmen indicted the Social Democrats and "radical groups of teachers" for being "hostile to the Christian religion" and for striving to take Christian instruction away from schoolchildren. Recently enfranchised women were told that anyone who did not vote was strengthening "the enemies of the church." A leaflet circulated in Saxony condemned Buck's school decrees and warned parents that their children would no longer learn the Lord's Prayer and the Ten Commandments and would grow up without a knowledge of the Protestant faith. Eight of the thirty Protestant churchmen who ran as candidates on the

German Nationalist ticket were elected to the National Assembly, including the clerical firebrands Reinhard Mumm and Gottfried Traub. Four church superintendents and a pastor, all of whom campaigned as German Nationalists, won seats in the Prussian State Assembly. The agitation on the school issue did not subside after the elections. Since the newly elected legislative bodies would now make decisions about the character of the elementary schools, Protestant Church officials in Prussia decided to launch a petition-signing campaign to bring popular pressure to bear on the legislators. By June 1919, parish pastors and volunteers had collected the signatures of nearly seven million men and women throughout Germany on a petition demanding that "in the future as in the past our youth should receive an education based on the foundation of Christianity."[29]

Members of the German Teachers' Association criticized the tactics used by churchmen who claimed that religion and morality were in danger in the republican state, and who defamed the progressivist pedagogues by characterizing them as "hostile to religion." In the election campaign, observed Max Brethfeld in Dresden, clergymen often fought "with unscrupulous distortions of the truth." He reproached them for playing upon the emotions of the parents with "frightening" and "false" assertions about the school reforms. Another teacher in Königsberg lamented that clerical activists had aroused feelings that could "by no means promote a peaceful compromise of undeniably existing and deeply felt differences." Teachers in Magdeburg and other cities observed with astonishment how quickly thousands of people, including those who had voted for the German Democrats and Social Democrats, had signed the church's "innocuously worded" petition without discerning the intentions of its sponsors. The election campaigns awakened in some reformers an ambivalent attitude about the relationship of politics and the school. As one progressivist pedagogue wrote: "We must speak out for the greatest possible autonomy for the elementary school, for its organization solely according to pedagogical principles, and for the exclusion of all obstructive elements. The school must develop, if necessary, *against* family, commune, and church. The school can thrive and prosper only if the state withdraws the school from the influence of clerical and political parties and regulates its administration so that the voice of the elementary schoolteachers has a decisive importance."[30]

Progressivist Pedagogues and the Debate on Religion in the Schools

When the German National Assembly convened in the city of Weimar in February 1919 to begin its work on the constitution, the local chapters of the German Teachers' Association were already engrossed in a debate over the draft of a new school program. Primarily the work of German Democrats on the executive committee, Carl Louis Pretzel, Johannes Tews, and Georg Wolff, the draft school program set forth the following principles for a settlement of the problem of religious education in the schools. First, initiating children into the confessional beliefs of a church should not be the task of the public schools. The subject of religion should be taught "as a living cultural heritage" without coercion or the imposition of beliefs. Second, the churches should have no right to supervise religious instruction in the public schools. Third, to prevent any infringement of freedom of conscience, teachers should have the right to decline to give religious instruction without detriment to their professional employment, and pupils should be exempted from it if their parents or guardians should make such a request.[31] In the months before the congress of the German Teachers' Association convened to vote on the new school program, this issue stirred up intense feelings among its membership. Teachers attended the meetings of the big urban chapters in massive numbers when this section of the draft program was on the agenda, and the debates continued late into the night.

With their conception of a common school for all children in which the subject of religion would be taught in a nonconfessional form, the German Democratic reformers were not only striving to find a compromise but also acting on their own convictions. They firmly believed that it should not be the task of the schools in a secular state to cultivate confessional identity, proselytize and demonstrate the truth of one or another confession, and initiate children into church life. And yet they were no less convinced that religion was a significant part of the history and cultural life of Germany, and that the transmission of this religious-cultural heritage to the youth was an essential task of the school. They doubted that moral instruction, as it was taught in the secular schools of France, was as effective as religious instruction in imparting ethical norms and values. In their view, the appropriate form of religious instruction for schools (*religionsgeschichtlicher Unterricht*) would give pupils a historical knowledge of religion. The moral impact of this instruction would come from the children's encounters with the great figures in the Old and New Testaments and in church history. With this kind of religious instruction, the issue of the relation of the church to the school would be settled; there would be no reason for the church to play any supervisory role. As Georg Wolff stated, religious instruction would become "an independent activity of the state school." The pedagogues would devise the curriculum and decide on the methods of teaching. No longer would they be required to present material as "truth" that stood "in contradiction to the truths of natural science, history, and ethics."[32]

The mediating position taken by the German Democrats in the executive committee of the German Teachers' Association in the winter of 1918–19 satisfied neither the traditionalists nor the Social Democrats in the membership. August Kain, a defender of the confessional school, criticized the conceptualization of the school subject of religion as a cultural heritage. Religious instruction that did not initiate pupils into the faith and life of a specific church seemed worthless to him. "There is no faith without doctrine and no religion without confession," he exclaimed. Traditionalists harped on the rights of parents in the debate on the draft school program at the convention of the Prussian Teachers' Association on 30-31 May 1919. Impressed by the millions of signatures on the petitions circulated by the Protestant Church, Paul Diesener boasted that if a referendum were held, it would prove that a majority of people favored religious education in the schools. He warned the representatives of the chapters that their national organization was "heading into a conflict with the churches and the parents."[33]

The Social Democratic reformers criticized the "inconsistency" in the German Democratic argument for the continuation of religious instruction in the schools, and contended that the Catholic and Protestant Churches would never consent to the instruction of this subject without confessional doctrine and observances. At the time, these pedagogues believed that the Social Democratic Party had the political power to establish a secular school system in the republic. Oskar Hübner, a teacher in Berlin, called the secular school the logical corollary of the November Revolution and the establishment of the democratic state. Since the churches would give catechism instruction, the reform would "not deprive anyone of religious faith." "The Social Democrats are a tolerant party and are not denying anyone the right to maintain a religious life," he contended at the convention.[34] In these debates, Hübner and a few other left-wing teachers made remarks about the church that were grist for the mill of the clerical opposition to the school reforms. In an earlier crossfire of opinions at a meeting of the Berlin teachers' association, Hübner had contended that only people who were "devoted to capitalism" wanted "religious influence in the schools in order to have it serve their political interests." Heinrich Bahlke asserted that the church must assume some of the responsibility for "the moral bankruptcy" that ultimately led to the collapse of the empire.[35]

The majority of delegates at the congress of the Prussian Teachers' Association voted for a school program that followed the views of the German Democratic leadership. The reference to the "life of Jesus and his teachings" in the description of the subject of religious instruction was an attempt to reassure pedagogues with more traditional views and to achieve unity.[36] The stridency of some radicals in these debates deeply troubled the German Democrats. Otto Schulz appealed to the membership to stand on their "common ground, the science of pedagogy" and to discuss this question as "a purely pedagogical matter." He observed unhappily how "religious instruction as an ideological question" was being "passionately drawn into the political conflicts" of ideologies pitted against each other. He feared that the teachers would forfeit any possibility of influencing the deputies in the National Assembly and the wider public if they continued to wrangle over it.[37]

In the Saxon Teachers' Association, reformers who advocated the secularization of the schools in the Leipzig chapter quickly assumed a commanding position in the debate on religious instruction in the schools. They criticized the "timid position" adopted by Pretzel, Tews, and other German Democratic reformers in Prussia. "The Berlin leaders are making a grave mistake if they believe that they can placate the confessional zealots," wrote Kurt Wehner in the *Leipziger Lehrerzeitung*. Since January 1919, he pointed out, church officials in Prussia were conducting a "fight against 'the pedagogue who has fallen away from God' with all the ruthlessness, hostility, and unscrupulousness that the *ecclesia militan* alone can generate." The Social Democratic reformers in Saxony did not believe that church officials would relinquish their influence over the schools voluntarily and agree to the instruction of religion on the terms proposed by the progressivist pedagogues in Prussia. Voting for a resolution that was more radical than the Zwickau theses of 1908, teachers in the Leipzig chapter now declared that they would not give religious instruction based on church confession. The pupils should learn about religious culture through "an objective instruction of the history of religions."[38] Arthur Arzt and Kurt Wehner proposed the introduction of the subject of moral instruction into the school curriculum. *Moralunterricht* or *Lebenskunde*, as this subject was called, would show the pupils models of moral behavior in the history of humanity, cultivate a moral conscience and will in them, and prepare them for civic life.[39]

The delegates at the congress of the Saxon Teachers' Association on 29–30 March 1919 in Dresden heard arguments for and against the Leipzig proposal. After a lively debate lasting more than two hours, the defenders of religious instruction knew that they were in the minority and tried to postpone the vote without success. By a large majority the delegates accepted the Leipzig theses.[40] Why was the outcome of the debates on religious instruction within the state branches of the German Teachers' Association more radical in Saxony than in Prussia? Teachers who were Social Democrats were a strong presence in the debate in Saxony. They argued that the issue of religious instruction was "a political question" and that teachers would "never get away from the power of the church" if the schools continued to teach it. Impressed by the strong electoral vote for the two Socialist parties in Saxony, these reformers thought that political conditions following the November Revolution created the most favorable time for "a definitive solution" to the problem of the relation of church and school. They were determined not to let this opportunity go by. As they interpreted the outcome of the elections in Saxony, the massive votes for the Social Democrats showed "with irrefutable clarity" that the majority of parents held modern views that differed from the traditional religious education provided in the schools. The secularization of the schools would eliminate "the disharmony" between school instruction and the cultural environment of the home.[41]

Moreover, the personal attitudes of some Social Democratic teachers toward organized religion may have led them to underestimate the political power of the Christian churches. In these debates, remarks made by veterans indicated that their experiences in World War I had shaken their religious faith. Fritz Müller, a teacher in Chemnitz, stated that this conflagration meant "the complete collapse of organized religion" so that it could "no longer provide any foundation for morality." Likewise for Arthur Arzt, the war exposed "the bankruptcy of the Christian churches," and he looked to ethical socialism for the values that would spur the renewal of postwar Germany. Criticizing the pastors who served as army chaplains, he confessed: "I could not get through the war with the Gospel of Jesus. The sermons were hairsplitting and turned the Gospel upside down." Max Brethfeld recalled bitterly that many pastors were among "the most notorious war agitators," even when soldiers on the front knew that the war was lost.[42]

When the congress of the German Teachers' Association convened in Berlin on 10–12 June to vote on the draft school program proposed by the executive committee, the sharp division of opinion was registered as the delegates from Prussia sat together on the right side of the auditorium, and the other delegates went to the left side. To avoid a wearisome debate, amendments to the paragraph on religious instruction were referred to a subcommittee to formulate a compromise proposal that would secure the widest agreement. The subcommittee, chaired by Heinrich Scherer from Hesse and Daniel Winkle from Bavaria, recommended that "religious instruction as a discrete subject [should be] left up to the religious communities." The state should allow the Christian churches and Jewish synagogue congregations to use classrooms for the instruction of religion in after-school hours; teachers could choose to give it under a free contract with them. This proposal meant the exclusion of religious instruction from the school curriculum. Scherer and Winkle took this bold step because they were convinced that the Catholic Church and orthodox Protestants would never agree to any reform of the existing confessional instruction in the schools. They doubted, moreover, that it would be possible to teach religion in the schools without the supervision of the churches.[43]

Carl Louis Pretzel opposed the Scherer-Winkle proposal and reminded the delegates that political issues were to a great extent "questions of expediency, for which the right answers [could] not be given for all times, peoples, and states." Any solution to the issue of religion in the schools, he argued, would have to exclude any violation of freedom of conscience and offer the possibility of creating a consensus among people holding opposing views. The experience of other countries showed that the opening of private church schools increased wherever the state secularized the elementary schools. From the history of the interconfessional schools (*Simultanschulen*) in the states of Baden and Hesse, Pretzel and other German Democratic reformers believed that the Catholic Church would sooner or later reconcile itself to the common school if the subject of religion was taught to pupils separated by religious affiliation. They doubted that the Catholic Church would ever consent to an ecumenical instruction for all Christian confessions. Moral instruction and the history of religions as elementary school subjects did not seem to them to be pedagogically sound alternatives. The history of religions would have little connection to the child's feelings and world of experience, and moral instruction would "turn into a new kind of catechism instruction" and be "cold, boring, ineffective, and worthless."[44]

There was high suspense among the delegates when the vote on the Scherer-Winkle amendment was counted. Sixty delegates abstained, and by a close vote of 172 to 165 the amendment was accepted. This amendment, which became section 4 of the association's school program, did not bury the differences among its members. The advocates of the secular school hailed this decision at the national congress of 1919 as a momentous event. Richard Ballerstaedt in Hamburg stated that the school program marked a clear break from "the earlier caution and timidity of the German Teachers' Association on the question of religion" and "a turn toward the left." Most reformers in Prussia did not share his elation. A teacher in Breslau lamented that the delegates in the majority did not behave in a politically pragmatic and responsible manner. They were "wrong in believing that religion [was] no longer a force in the life of the state."[45] Johannes Tews refused to see the adoption of section 4 of the 1919 school program as a victory for the advocates of the secular school. He attributed the outcome of the debate to an accidental majority and pointed out that the coalition of delegates who voted for it acted out of diverse intentions.[46] Polls taken by several branches of the German Teachers' Association in the early 1920s confirm Tews's view that the majority of the membership supported the continuation of religious instruction, albeit without the catechism and confessional doctrines. In the culture wars of the Weimar years, the 1919 school program became something that the progressivist pedagogues had not envisioned. Catholic and Protestant opponents of educational reform used it to tar the German Teachers' Association with the label of being "hostile to religion."

Political Horse-Trading and the School Compromise of July 1919

After the elections in January, the reformers in the German Teachers' Association observed apprehensively the negotiations of the German Democratic, Social Democratic, and Center Parties for the formation of governing coalitions in the Reich and Prussian state. They did not know whether political logrolling and concessions to the Center's demands would make the school become "the bloody sacrificial lamb slaughtered on the altar of political fraternization." Their perception that the Prussian minister of education was retreating and softening his position in February and March 1919 added to their sense of uneasiness.[47] Konrad Haenisch, who was now serving in this office alone after Hoffmann's resignation, admitted that the provisional government had exceeded its mandate in issuing the school decrees in November 1918 before the election of a sovereign national assembly. He repealed the ministerial order that eliminated school inspection on the local level by the parish clergy. This issue was settled by the enactment of the law of 18 July 1919, which finally abolished the office of local school inspector. On 1 April, Haenisch annulled the ministry's regulation on prayer and the celebration of religious holidays in the schools. Participation was not obligatory, however, for those pupils who were exempted from the instruction of religion at the request of their parents. Haenisch's remarks in a public address on 3 February revealed his pragmatic assessment of the strength of the opposition to the Social Democratic school program and foreshadowed the path that the party's leadership would follow during the Weimar era. Reforms affecting the place of religion in school instruction, he counseled, should be "thought out carefully over time" and carried out "only organically." Turbulent years of revolution were "the most unsuitable time for bringing [Germany] to a solution of these extremely controversial and delicate questions." He confessed: "I am not such a philistine to want to press the richly diverse and widely segmented cultural life of our German people into the straitjacket of a doctrine held by a small party group."[48]

The Reich government's draft constitution, written by Hugo Preuss, had a short section related to the school system and showed little trace of the Social Democratic school program. Striving to avoid a conflict with their coalition partners, Social Democratic leaders in the cabinet decided to leave controversial questions concerning the schools up to the legislation of the states in the future.[49] The school reformers in the teaching profession and in the German Democratic and Social Democratic delegations in the National Assembly were unhappy with this strategy. They wanted to see their reform goals anchored as principles in the Reich constitution and the jurisdiction of the Reich extended to the educational sphere. In a petition on 16 February, the executive board of the German Teachers' Association urged the National Assembly to write the fundamental rules for the organization of the school system into the constitution.[50] This petition made a strong impression on some of the deputies. During the first reading of the draft constitution, Gustav Stresemann declared that the German People's Party considered "the demands in [the teachers' petition] to be justified." German Democratic and Social Democratic deputies complained that the draft constitution provided no guarantee for a unified school system.[51]

Many of the reform goals of the German Teachers' Association were incorporated in an amendment to the draft constitution proposed by Richard Seyfert and Karl Weiss. Under this German Democratic amendment, the elementary educational system would be organized on the basis of the common school for children of all religious confessions, and the regulation of religious instruction in the schools would be left to future state legislation. Seyfert and other German Democrats in the National Assembly were convinced that a large majority of Germans wanted religious education in the schools. Accordingly, they supported a common school in which Protestant, Catholic, and Jewish pupils were separated by faith only for the instruction of religion. Seyfert told the constitution committee that religious instruction in the schools should not cover confessional doctrines and should stand "only under the supervision of the state." He believed that the dissolution of the ties between church and school did not have to lead to an adversarial relationship; he hoped, instead, that "a kind of division of labor" in the religious education of the youth and "a peaceful coexistence" would follow. Material of a confessional nature would be taught by the churches and synagogue congregations, and the instruction of religion in the schools would be primarily the study of the Bible.[52]

The other two parties in the Weimar coalition did not accept the Seyfert-Weiss amendment. Social Democratic deputies such as Carl August Hellmann contended that the relation of church and school should be settled in the constitution by excluding religious instruction from the curriculum and granting the churches the right to open private schools. The Catholic bishops rejected the German Democrats' concept of the common school as an essentially secular school with the addition of religious instruction as a mere appendage. A fervent champion of federalism in the past, the Center Party now discerned the advantage of incorporating the principles for a national school law into the Reich constitution as a safeguard against laws that could be passed by Social Democratic majorities in Hamburg, Saxony, Thuringia, and other states. To pressure their coalition partners to make concessions, Joseph Mausbach, a professor of theology, and other deputies of the Center Party alluded to the *Kulturkampf* of the Bismarck era and the current separatist movement in the Rhineland. Catholic pressure for concessions gained more weight when the Versailles peace treaty provided for plebiscites in Masuria and Upper Silesia. Catholic politicians hinted that the boundaries of Germany could be adversely affected if a new *Kulturkampf* started.[53]

The school reformers became alarmed when the press reported on the efforts of Friedrich Naumann, a Protestant theologian and German Democratic deputy, to mediate the differences between the parties and to find the wording for an article on religious instruction that would be acceptable to both sides. On 4 April, a majority of deputies in the constitution committee voted for his amendment, which made religious instruction a subject taught in the schools "in agreement with the teachings and doctrines of the religious communities." Protesting this decision in another petition to the National Assembly, the executive officers of the German Teachers' Association stated that highly respected representatives of the science of pedagogy and a large number of teachers believed that the contents of religious instruction should not focus on what separated the various confessions but should emphasize instead what they shared in common.[54]

When the German Democrats declined to assume responsibility for the signing of the Versailles treaty and withdrew from the Weimar coalition in June, the Center Party's leadership took advantage of the governmental crisis to press harder for concessions on the school question in their negotiations with the Social Democrats on the formation of a new cabinet. In confidential talks, Heinrich Schulz, in his capacity as undersecretary of state in the Reich Interior Ministry, and representatives of the two parties devised a compromise agreement on the basis of "mutual tolerance," namely, to allow each of the three types of schools complete freedom for development. In effect, a victory for the Center Party, this compromise, adopted in the second reading of the draft constitution on 18 July, gave the confessional school (*konfessionelle Schule*) equal legal standing with the common school for children of all religious faiths (*gemeinsame Schule*) and the secular school (*weltliche Schule*). The will of the parents would determine the organization of the schools in each commune, or local administrative district. Except in the secular schools, religion would be a regular school subject and would be taught according to the teachings of the churches.[55]

Throughout the country, school administrators as well as teachers raised a loud outcry against this political deal. During the second reading of the draft constitution, Richard Seyfert bitterly accused the Social Democrats of trading off the unity of the school system for a constitutional guarantee of parental choice. He doubted that they would benefit from the provision for the opening of secular schools as much as they expected.[56] For a very small number of secular schools, the Social Democrats were "surrendering 90 percent or more of the schools to clerical influence." At their party's congress on 19–22 July, German Democratic school reformers argued that the most effective means of fighting the two-party compromise would be gained by reentering the governmental coalition.[57] After failing to prevent this compromise, Konrad Haenisch continued his resistance and organized a meeting of the education ministers of the large German states on 21 July. In a protest sent to Reich Interior Minister Eduard David on the following day, the state officials pointed out "the danger of an extensive splintering" of the school system and stated that the implementation of some of the proposed articles would create problems for the school administration. Especially disturbing to them was the prospect that the political fight over the elementary schools would be sharpened and perpetuated through the right of the parents to choose one of three school types.[58]

The leaders of the German Teachers' Association reproached the Social Democratic politicians in the National Assembly for sacrificing a unified school system in their political bargaining with the Center delegation. Far from fostering consensus, they contended, the school compromise moved the theater of conflict from the national and state parliaments to the communes.

In one bitter reaction, a teacher in Breslau said: "At a date every five or eight years the parents are to decide on the character of the school. Does anyone believe that such an election can be conducted without conflict, without the sharpening of confessional differences, without malicious and unkind remarks?"[59] Teachers in the Social Democratic rank and file openly rebuked their party's leadership for making a deal with Center politicians that would establish "the dominance of the confessions in the new republic." In a letter of protest, the Socialist Teachers' League called the school compromise "a flagrant betrayal of the Socialist ideology" and urged the Social Democrats in the National Assembly "to adhere unconditionally to a secular and unified school system in the last hour."[60]

After the German Democrats reentered the coalition government, the Social Democrats in the National Assembly reopened the negotiations on the school compromise, now with Richard Seyfert's participation. Shortly before the debate on the school articles in the final reading of the draft constitution on 31 July, the three parties agreed to a second compromise, which provided the wording for the provisions in the Reich Constitution of 11 August 1919. After haggling over more than a dozen differently worded versions of Article 146, the Center's representatives, Adolf Gröber and Joseph Mausbach, finally conceded to the German Democratic argument that the common school for all children should be the rule (*Regelschule*). Thereafter, the two Catholic negotiators stubbornly held the line. Although many Center politicians thought that the school compromise had taken a turn for the worse, Gröber and Mausbach retrieved some of the key points from the first agreement.[61]

The Weimar Constitution of 1919 had numerous provisions related to the schools—a testament to the significance of the contentious school issue in German society as well as to the perseverance of the reformers in the teaching profession in pressing for the incorporation of their goals in the republic's highest law. A Reich school law would set forth the principles according to which school legislation in the states would regulate specific matters. Article 143 stipulated that the training for elementary school teaching was to be regulated uniformly for the entire Reich according to the principles that applied for secondary schoolteachers. This article placed an obligation on the government to elevate teacher education to an academic course of study pursued in the universities. Besides affirming the principle of the state's supervision of the schools, Article 144 redressed an old grievance of elementary schoolteachers by stipulating that full-time school inspectors must be professionally trained educators. Article 145 guaranteed to the nation's youth that the instruction and learning supplies in the elementary schools would be free. The framing of Article 146, paragraph 1, showed clearly the influence of the reformers' concept of a unified educational system. It stated that the public school system was "to be organically built up" and that the secondary schools had to be "built upon a common basic school for all" young people (*eine für alle gemeinsame Grundschule*). Admission to any school on the secondary and higher levels of education was to be granted on the basis of the pupils' ability and motivation, irrespective of the wealth, social status, or religious confession of their parents. Public funds for educational grants (*Erziehungsbeihilfen*) would be available for qualified students whose parents had little means. A declaration on behalf of tolerance in Article 148 stated that care should be taken in public school instruction so that the sensibilities of persons of another conviction would not be violated. This same article added civic education (*Staatsbürgerkunde*) to the school curriculum and required the distribution of copies of the Reich Constitution to the pupils.

The ambiguous wording of the constitutional provisions related to school organization, parents' rights, and religious instruction and the likelihood of conflicting interpretations made many reformers in the teaching profession look to the future with disquiet. The German Democrats were relieved to see that Article 146, paragraph 1, gave the common school, which integrated children of all religious and social backgrounds, a position of precedence as the *Regelschule*. Confessional and secular schools could be established only under certain conditions as *Sonderschulen*. Article 146, paragraph 2, added that within the communes, at the request of parents and guardians, confessional and secular schools could be established "insofar as a proper school organization" would "not be adversely affected." The will of the parents and guardians was "to be considered as much as possible." In the making of the national school law, would the Constitution's criterion of "a proper school organization" for the opening of confessional schools be interpreted by the political parties as a school with an enrollment of pupils sufficiently large to have separate classrooms for each of the eight grades, as the reformers thought?[62] What did the clause on the will of the parents mean in actual practice? Did the requirements of a viable common school limit the extent to which the parents could exercise their right to request the opening of a confessional or secular *Sonderschule* in any locality?

Article 149 declared that religious instruction was "a regular school subject," except in the secular schools. Religious instruction in the schools had to be taught "in accordance with the tenets of the religious society (*Religionsgesellschaft*) concerned, without detriment to the state's power of supervision." Did the addition of the last clause in this sentence negate any future church claims to a right to supervise religious education in the schools? The school articles provided three safeguards for freedom of conscience. The Constitution granted to teachers the right to decline to give religious instruction, and to parents the freedom to decide whether their children would participate in religious instruction and the observance of religious holidays in the schools. Article 147 prohibited private preparatory schools of an elitist character, but allowed the opening of private schools if a public school did not exist in the commune for that minority of parents who wanted a confessional or secular school. Article 174 stipulated that up to the enactment of a Reich school law, the existing legal arrangements for the schools remained in effect. Frequently called the "embargo paragraph," this provision prevented the states from enacting new school laws before the Reichstag passed a framework school law for the entire nation.

Educational reformers were critical of the parties responsible for the political bargain that produced the inconsistencies in Article 146 of the Weimar Constitution. They were angry at the tough and unyielding stance of the Center Party and reproached its leaders for continuing to see the elementary school under the republic as "an institution assisting the church" and for emphasizing the rights of the parents "in a one-sided and extreme manner." Georg Wolff, the editor of the weekly newspaper published by the German Teachers' Association, reproached the Center Party's leaders for using their power in the formation of governmental coalitions to "stop the wheels of progress in the Prussian school system."[63] In a public statement, Oskar Gleissberg, the chairman of the executive board of the Saxon Teachers' Association, rebuked the parties in the Weimar coalition for failing to recognize the importance of cultural unity and consensus on fundamental values for the development of the democratic state. Secular schools would be opened mainly in big cities and for working-class children and would be "oases in the wilderness of confessional schooling," he predicted.[64]

Teachers in the Social Democratic rank and file were deeply disappointed that their party's delegation in the National Assembly had not handled the school question on the basis of principle but had subordinated the party's programmatic school goals to considerations of political expediency. They found little consolation in the explanations offered by spokesmen for the party, who pointed to the political constraints faced by the Social Democrats in the Reich cabinet owing to Germany's critical situation in foreign politics and the necessity of forming a coalition government. The Social Democrats were "compelled to make compromises," explained Richard Lohmann. They could "just as little expect to bridge the deep ideological divisions [on the school question] in the near future as contemplate the test of power of a *Kulturkampf*." Collaboration with the Center Party in the Weimar coalition would have broken down, Heinrich Schulz stated, if an agreement in "these difficult matters of conscience" had not been reached on the basis of "mutual tolerance" and freedom for the establishment of the three types of public schools.[65] Paul Oestreich, a secondary school educator and a Social Democratic member of the Berlin city council, chided the Social Democrats in Weimar for succumbing to the opportunistic tactics of the Center Party and entering negotiations on "epoch-making educational questions" with Catholic politicians, for whom "all political measures are only means for the purpose of stabilizing the domination of the church in society."[66] Max Brethfeld asked whether "parliaments in their present form" could "create a healthy educational and school system." In making school laws, he observed, deputies were guided "far more by church, party, and political-economic reasons" than by "the science of pedagogy and the experience of educators."[67]

Although the educational reformers were troubled by the possibility of an improper interpretation of Article 146 of the Constitution, they were not alienated from the new parliamentary state. Nor did they become resigned and cynical about political life. As politically mature citizens, they took into account that the Constitution had to be "a work of compromise" because none of the three parties had won enough votes to govern alone. Georg Wolff coupled his criticism of the founding fathers of the Weimar state with the acknowledgment that the coalition of the three parties was forged "just as much by the emphasis on the interests of democracy shared by them as by the clear recognition of political necessity." The parties in the Weimar coalition deserved the gratitude of the nation because they "incorporated in the work of the Constitution the great ideas of national unity, political freedom, and social justice."[68]

The articles of the Constitution contained the potential for comprehensive and democratic reforms in public education. These changes were to be given definition and substance in subsequent legislation and political action. The reformers in the German Teachers' Association saw clearly the tasks before them, first, to mount an active public relations campaign to ensure a correct interpretation of the school articles, and, second, to win over government officials, deputies in the national and state parliaments, and the wider public to their pedagogical point of view. Hermann Degenhardt, a teacher in Erfurt and a German Democratic deputy in the Prussian National Assembly, told a convention of the teachers' association in the province of Saxony: "The unfortunate aspect of school politics is that it is the sphere in which highly political questions can be settled by way of compromise at no cost. We cannot put an end to this [practice] completely. But we must do whatever we can to change these circumstances. We must declare that the reorganization of the school system is not merely a political question; it is much more a pedagogical question, and we who practice the science of pedagogy demand to be heard."[69] In 1919 the leaders of the German Teachers' Association started to publish a series of popular tracts on school politics "to put at the disposal of the republican state our special knowledge and experience in all school and educational questions as well as our will to build up and create a new system."[70]

The designation of the common school for all children as the *Regelschule* in the Constitution offered the possibility of settling the school question in Weimar Germany by compromise and consensus. After the work of the National Assembly was completed, however, neither the Center Party nor the Social Democrats adapted their school programs to the new constitutional reality. The Social Democrats continued to defend the secular school (*weltliche Schule*) instead of putting the greatest possible unity in the school system over the principle of secularization. Schulz and Lohmann claimed that the legal recognition of the secular school was the Social Democratic Party's major achievement in the school compromise. Its support for this agreement was interpreted as a vote for a gradual realization of a secular school system in tandem with the development of political culture and political-power relations in the republican state. In August 1919, Lohmann stated in the Social Democratic newspaper *Vorwärts* that "by constant propaganda work," the Social Democrats must "make secular schools out of the interconfessional schools so that finally the exception is changed into the rule." Shortly thereafter, he wrote: "The step from the interconfessional school to the secular school is very small, in any case much smaller than the step from the confessional school to the secular school. Wherever we can attain an interconfessional school in place of a previous confessional school, pioneering work is done for the secular school." He urged the Social Democrats to engage in an active propaganda campaign to win public support for the secular school and to persuade the parents to exempt their children from religious instruction at the time of school registration. The party must demand of teachers professing Socialist ideas that they decline to give religious instruction in the schools. When Social Democracy's electorate saw the value of treating religion as a private matter, there would be "a majority in the nation and the Reichstag for a revision of Article 146 of the Constitution."[71]

Center politicians and Protestant churchmen in the German National People's Party were even more confident of their prospects of making the confessional school (*konfessionelle Schule*) become the de facto rule through the mobilization of the parents. The Center politicians had rescued the confessional school in the final round of negotiations with the recognition of the parents' right to request a *Sonderschule*. The Center and German Nationalist Parties now construed the school compromise in Article 146 so that it signified "the peaceful competition for the achievement of a good school" and "the honest competition of the [ideological] forces" in cultural politics.[72] Viewing this political bargain also as a guarantee of freedom of conscience and religion, Catholics and conservative Protestants began to interpret Article 146 to mean that the parents in each school district had "the decisive word in educational questions." As a German Nationalist defender of the confessional school maintained, the school compromise made "the choice of the school and the type of school education a question of the consciences of the parents."[73]

Notes

1. On the economic hardships of teachers during the war, see *Pädagogische Zeitung*, 6 June 1918: 220; ibid., 1 August 1918: 291-92; ibid., 19 September 1918: 363; *Schulblatt der Provinz Sachsen*, 26 June 1918: 202; *Schlesische Schulzeitung*, 31 July 1918: 276; ibid., 14 August 1918: 293; ibid., 28 August 1918: 313; *Leipziger Lehrerzeitung*, 10 April 1918: 112; ibid., 28 August 1918: 253-55; ibid., 25 September 1918: 308-11; *Sächsische Schulzeitung*, 25 September 1918: 296-97.
2. *Sächsische Schulzeitung*, 2 January 1918: 1-3; ibid., 6 February 1918: 45-46.
3. Tews, *Die deutsche Einheitsschule*, p. 96.
4. *Sächsische Schulzeitung*, 26 June 1918: 217-18; Richard Seyfert and F. W. Foerster, *Für und wider die allgemeine Volksschule* (Leipzig, 1918), pp. 9, 13; *Leipziger Lehrerzeitung*, 4 September 1918: 270; *Schulblatt der Provinz Sachsen*, 16 October 1918: 327. On the impact of the war experience on the political outlook of elementary schoolteachers, see also Alfred Rennert, *Der Volksschullehrer im alten und im neuen Deutschland* (Düsseldorf, 1919), pp. 28-32.
5. *Schlesische Schulzeitung*, 11 December 1918: 449-51; ibid., 20 November 1918: 416; *Pädagogische Zeitung*, 28 November 1918: 477; *Sächsische Schulzeitung*, 20 November 1918: 373-74, 379; ibid., 27 November 1918: 387-88; *Leipziger Lehrerzeitung*, 13 November 1918: 393-94; ibid., 20 November 1918: 406; Johannes Tews, *Sozialdemokratie und öffentliches Bildungswesen* (Langensalza, 1919), pp. 58-59; Rudolf Irmer, *Der freie Lehrer im freien Volksstaate* (Berlin, 1919), pp. 6ff.
6. *Zentralblatt für die gesamte Unterrichtsverwaltung in Preussen*, December 1918, no. 12: 719-21, 757-58; *Verordnungsblatt des Sächsischen Ministeriums für Volksbildung*, January 1919, no. 1: 12-16.
7. *Schlesische Schulzeitung*, 11 December 1918: 454-55; ibid., 18 December 1918: 464; *Pädagogische Zeitung*, 5 December 1918: 497.
8. See Menzel's speech in *Stenographische Berichte über die Verhandlungen des Preussischen Lehrertages am 30.-31. Mai 1919* (Magdeburg, 1919), 5-6.
9. *Sächsische Schulzeitung*, 8 January 1919: 7; *Leipziger Lehrerzeitung*, 22 January 1919: 29; ibid., 26 February 1919: 99-100.
10. *Pädagogische Zeitung*, 19 December 1918: 526; *Schulblatt der Provinz Sachsen*, 15 January 1919: 24; ibid., 19 February 1919: 77.
11. *Die Lehrerin*, 15 December 1919: 138-39; *Zehn Jahre Lehrerverband Berlin 1920-1930* (Berlin, 1931), pp. 98-99, 138; *Leipziger Lehrerzeitung*, 25 February 1920: 150. Although the tradition of gender differentiation in the professional associations of teachers did not end during the Weimar era, the number of women who joined the German Teachers' Association had increased to 12,000 by 1930. In comparison, the German Women Teachers' Association had 18,000 elementary schoolteachers among its members. Representing 24 percent of the teachers in the elementary schools in Germany in 1926-27, women were very conscious of being a minority in their profession. Many women teachers opposed the merging of the two associations and stressed the advantages of a separate organization for female educators. See the argument in *Die Lehrerin*, 15 December 1919: 138-39; *Deutsche Lehrerinnenzeitung*, 1 February 1931: 37-38; ibid., 1 October 1932: 325-30. For the point of view of women who joined the German Teachers' Association, see the articles by Adelheid Schäfer in *Allgemeine Deutsche Lehrerzeitung*, 24 October 1929: 865-68; ibid., 18 December 1930: 968-69; ibid., 5 March 1931: 182-84.
12. *Die Lehrerin*, 15 July 1919: 59-60; ibid., 1 August 1919: 67. The presence of secondary school educators in the German Women Teachers' Association may well have affected its position on issues in school politics. It is striking that female as well as male educators in the secondary schools who were elected to the Prussian Landtag in the Weimar era belonged to a considerable extent to the right-wing German People's Party and German National People's Party. See also Doris Kampmann, "'Zolibat—ohne uns!'—die soziale

Situation und politische Einstellung der Lehrerinnen in der Weimarer Republik," in Frauengruppe Faschismusforschung, *Mutterkreuz und Arbeitsbuch. Zur Geschichte der Frauen in der Weimarer Republik und im Nationalsozialismus* (Frankfurt am Main, 1981), pp. 94-95, 98; Elizabeth Harvey, "The Failure of Feminism? Young Women and the Bourgeois Feminist Movement in Weimar Germany 1918-1933," *Central European History* 28 (1995): 1-28.
13. *Allgemeine Deutsche Lehrerzeitung*, 6 February 1919; 75, 77; ibid., 13 February 1919: 94. The organ of the German Teachers' Association was given this new title in 1919. *Sächsische Schulzeitung*, 26 February 1919: 89.
14. *Westdeutsche Lehrerzeitung*, 21 December 1918: 450; ibid., 4 January 1919: 4; ibid., 11 January 1919: 13; Adolf Gottwald, *Zentrumspolitik in Preussen. Das Zentrum und die Lehrer* (Berlin, 1920), p. 3.
15. Hans Hermann, *Die Schulpolitik der Vergangenheit und das Schulprogramm der Deutschnationalen Volkspartei* (Langensalza, 1919); Ludwig Richter, *Kirche und Schule in den Beratungen der Weimarer Nationalversammlung* (Düsseldorf, 1996), pp. 103-20. Bölling estimates (*Volksschullehrer und Politik*, pp. 39-40) that the membership of the League of German Protestant Teachers' Associations never exceeded 4,000 in the Weimar era.
16. On the social constituency of the German Democratic Party, see Larry Eugene Jones, *German Liberalism and the Dissolution of the Weimar Party System 1918-1933* (Chapel Hill, 1988), pp. 23-24; Lothar Albertin, *Liberalismus und Demokratie am Anfang der Weimarer Republik. Eine vergleichende Analyse der Deutschen Demokratischen Partei und Deutschen Volkspartei* (Düsseldorf, 1972), pp. 131ff.
17. Wilhelm Meyer-Dinkgräfe, *Der Lehrerstand. Berufspsychologische Erhebungen und Untersuchungen* (Göttingen, 1928), p. 190. On the party affiliation of the leadership, see also Bölling, *Volksschullehrer und Politik*, pp. 114ff.
18. Richard Seyfert, *Das schulpolitische Programm der Demokratie* (Leipzig, 1919), pp. 3ff; Paul Sommer, *Das deutschdemokratische Schulprogramm in seinem geschichtlichen Werden und in der Gegenwart* (Langensalza, 1919), pp. 13ff.
19. *Sächsische Schulzeitung*, 27 November 1918: 387; ibid., 4 December 1918: 398-99; ibid. 15 October 1919: 425; Otto Pautsch, *Der Lehrer im Volksstaat* (Langensalza, 1919), pp. 7, 26; Ewald Hiemann, *Die geistigen Strömmungen der Gegenwart und die Lehrerschaft* (Leipzig, 1921), pp. 13-16; *Die neue Erziehung*, no. 1, January 1919: 5.
20. *Schlesische Schulzeitung*, 11 December 1918: 454; ibid., Schulpolitische Beilage, June 1919: 6-7; *Leipziger Lehrerzeitung*, 22 January 1919: 31-32.
21. *Vorwärts*, 22 April 1919, no. 203; *Die neue Erziehung*, May/June 1919, no. 11: 398-400; ibid., June 1919, no. 12/13: 434-35.
22. *Die neue Erziehung*, May/June 1919, no. 11: 370-72.
23. *Schlesische Schulzeitung*, 26 March 1919: 137; ibid., 21 May 1919: 232-33; Wolfgang Stöhr, *Lehrer und Arbeiterbewegung. Entstehung und Politik der ersten Gewerkschaftsorganisation der Lehrer in Deutschland von 1920-1923* (Marburg, 1978), pp. 159-60, 186. See also Peter Lösche and Franz Walter, *Die SPD. Klassenpartei—Volkspartei—Quotenpartei. Zur Entwicklung der Sozialdemokratie von Weimar bis zur deutschen Vereinigung* (Darmstadt, 1992), pp. 37-40.
24. *Schlesische Schulzeitung*, Schulpolitische Beilage, June 1919: 8; *Allgemeine Deutsche Lehrerzeitung*, 6 February 1919: 75; *Sächsische Schulzeitung*, 3 December 1918: 398; *Leipziger Lehrerzeitung*, 15 January 1919: 20-21; Johannes Tews, *Parteipolitische Spaltungen im Lehrervereinswesen* (Langensalza, 1920), pp. 12-24.
25. *Sächsische Schulzeitung*, 8 January 1919: 2; *Leipziger Lehrerzeitung*, 8 January 1919: 3.
26. On this opposition within the Catholic and Protestant Churches, see Christoph Führ, *Zur Schulpolitik der Weimarer Republik* (Weinheim, 1970), pp. 32ff; Günther Grünthal, *Reichsschulgesetz und Zentrumspartei in der Weimarer Republik* (Düsseldorf, 1968), pp. 19ff; Richter, *Kirche und Schule*, pp. 26ff. On the hostility of Protestant churchmen to the republican state, see Jacke, *Kirche zwischen Monarchie und Republik*; Nowak, *Evangelische Kirche und Weimarer Republik*.
27. *Westdeutsche Lehrerzeitung*, 14 December 1918: 437-39.

28. Rudolf Morsey, *Die Deutsche Zentrumspartei 1917–1923* (Düsseldorf, 1966), pp. 110ff; Karsen Ruppert, "Die Deutsche Zentrumspartei in der Mitverantwortung für die Weimarer Republik. Selbstverständnis und politische Leitideen einer konfessionellen Mittelpartei," in *Die Minderheit als Mitte. Die Deutsche Zentrumspartei in der Innenpolitik des Reiches*, ed. Winfried Becker (Paderborn, 1986): 71–88.
29. Daniel Borg, *The Old Prussian Church and the Weimar Republic: A Study in Political Adjustment, 1917–1927* (Hanover, 1984), p. 80; Nowak, *Evangelische Kirche*, pp. 31–38; Jacke, *Kirche zwischen Monarchie und Republik*, pp. 85–118.
30. *Sächsische Schulzeitung*, 15 January 1919: 14–15; *Lehrerzeitung für Ost- und Westpreussen*, 25 January 1919: 40; ibid., 8 March 1919: 99; *Schulblatt der Provinz Sachsen*, 12 March 1919: 110.
31. *Pädagogische Zeitung*, 21 November 1918: 465; ibid., 12 December 1918: 509–11.
32. *Allgemeine Deutsche Lehrerzeitung*, 16 March 1919: 149–51; see also the address given by Kolrep, a principal in Magdeburg, in *Verhandlungen des Preussischen Lehrertages* (1919), pp. 24–25.
33. *Allgemeine Deutsche Lehrerzeitung*, 8 May 1919: 291; ibid., 16 March 1919: 153–54; *Verhandlungen des Preussischen Lehrertages* (1919), pp. 33–34.
34. *Verhandlungen des Preussischen Lehrertages* (1919), p. 27.
35. *Allgemeine Deutsche Lehrerzeitung*, 8 May 1919: 289–90.
36. *Verhandlungen des Preussischen Lehrertages* (1919), p. 179.
37. *Allgemeine Deutsche Lehrerzeitung*, 24 April 1919: 252.
38. *Leipziger Lehrerzeitung*, 19 February 1919: 81–82; ibid., 5 February 1919: 62.
39. *Leipziger Lehrerzeitung*, 26 February 1919: 98–99; *Sächsische Schulzeitung*, 19 March 1919: 122; Erich Viewheg, *Die sittliche Erziehung in der weltlichen Schule* (Leipzig, 1921), pp. 27ff.
40. *Sächsische Schulzeitung*, 9 April 1919: 160–62.
41. *Leipziger Lehrerzeitung*, 22 January 1919: 32; ibid., 12 March 1919: 117; *Sächsische Schulzeitung*, 12 February 1919: 69. On the Social Democrats in Saxony in the early Weimar years, see Karsten Rudolph, *Die sächsische Sozialdemokratie vom Kaiserreich zur Republik, 1871–1923* (Weimar, 1995), chaps. 5–6.
42. *Leipziger Lehrerzeitung*, 30 April 1919: 200–201; *Sächsische Schulzeitung*, 19 March 1919: 122; ibid. 15 January 1919: 15.
43. For the debate at the congress, see *Allgemeine Deutsche Lehrerzeitung*, 19 June 1919: 389–92.
44. Carl Louis Pretzel, *Die Frage des Religionsunterrichts* (Langensalza, 1919), pp. 3, 11, 32–39.
45. *Allgemeine Deutsche Lehrerzeitung*, 3 July 1919: 431; *Schlesische Schulzeitung*, 23 July 1919: 342.
46. See Tews's comments on the public's misinterpretation of the vote at the congress of 1919 in *Allgemeine Deutsche Lehrerzeitung*, 8 June 1923: 267.
47. *Allgemeine Deutsche Lehrerzeitung*, 6 March 1919: 139; ibid., 3 April 1919: 203.
48. Konrad Haenisch, *Kulturpolitische Aufgaben* (Berlin, 1919), pp. 8–11.
49. Wolfgang Wittwer, *Die sozialdemokratische Schulpolitik in der Weimarer Republik* (Berlin, 1980), pp. 85–86; Dirk Gentsch, *Zur Geschichte der sozialdemokratischen Schulpolitik in der Zeit der Weimarer Republik* (Frankfurt am Main, 1994). Wittwer contends (p. 76) that the course followed by the party's leadership in regard to school politics was not a matter of weakness or a betrayal of Social Democracy's old school demands. They found "no solution to the tension between the necessity for mutual tolerance as a result of the constraints of political collaboration [with the Center Party] and the representation of their own goal of secularization." On the framing of the Constitution, see Ernst R. Huber, *Deutsche Verfassungsgeschichte seit 1789*. Vol. 6: *Die Weimarer Reichsverfassung* (Stuttgart, 1981).
50. Text of the petition in *Allgemeine Deutsche Lehrerzeitung*, 27 February 1919: 121. See also the speech given by Otto Pautsch at a meeting of the Berlin chapter in ibid., 16 March 1919: 160–61.
51. *Verhandlungen der verfassunggebenden Deutschen Nationalversammlung. Stenographische Berichte* (Berlin, 1920), 28 February 1919, p. 376; ibid., 3 March 1919, pp. 461, 478; ibid., 4 March 1919, p. 496.

52. See Seyfert's report on the deliberations of the constitution committee in *Allgemeine Deutsche Lehrerzeitung*, 24 April 1919: 249-50; Seyfert, *Das schulpolitische Programm*, pp. 17, 31-33; Sommer, *Das deutschdemokratische Schulprogramm*, pp. 17-18.
53. Grünthal, *Reichsschulgesetz und Zentrumspartei*, pp. 37-39, 47-50.
54. *Allgemeine Deutsche Lehrerzeitung*, 24 April 1919: 250; for the petition to the National Assembly, ibid., 15 May 1919: 301-2.
55. Heinrich Schulz, *Der Leidensweg des Reichsschulgesetzes* (Berlin, 1926), pp. 33ff; Grünthal, *Reichsschulgesetz und Zentrumspartei*, pp. 53-57.
56. *Verhandlungen der Nationalversammlung*, 18 July 1919, pp. 1685-89.
57. *Bericht über die Verhandlungen des 1. Parteitags der Deutschen Demokratischen Partei abgehalten in Berlin vom 19. bis 22. Juli 1919* (Berlin, 1919), pp. 253-55, 279.
58. Quoted in Hermann Rosin, *Das Schulkompromiss* (Berlin, 1920), pp. 45-46.
59. *Allgemeine Deutsche Lehrerzeitung*, 10 July 1919: 454; ibid., 17 July 1919: 474-75; *Schlesische Schulzeitung*, 23 July 1919: 341; ibid., Schulpolitische Beilage, August 1919: 13; Rosin, *Das Schulkompromiss*, pp. 42-44.
60. *Die neue Erziehung*, no. 15/16, July/August 1919: 521-23; *Vorwärts*, no. 361, 17 July 1919.
61. Richter, *Kirche und Schule*, pp. 600ff, 623.
62. Rosin, *Das Schulkompromiss*, pp. 67-69.
63. *Allgemeine Deutsche Lehrerzeitung*, 28 August 1919: 547; Georg Wolff, *Die Schule in der Verfassung des Deutschen Reiches* (Langensalza, 1919), p. 41.
64. *Sächsische Schulzeitung*, 10 September 1919: 377.
65. Schulz, *Der Leidensweg*, pp. 34-35, 47; Richard Lohmann, *Das Schulprogramm der Sozialdemokratie und ihre Schulpolitik* (Stuttgart, 1921), pp. 14-16, 82-83. See also the articles by Schulz and Lohmann respectively in *Vorwärts*, 31 July 1919, no. 386; ibid., 8 August 1919, no. 402.
66. *Die neue Erziehung*, no. 15/16, July/August 1919: 497-503; see also *Leipziger Lehrerzeitung*, 20 August 1919: 390.
67. *Sächsische Schulzeitung*, 27 August 1919: 337-39.
68. Wolff, *Die Schule in der Verfassung*, p. 7.
69. *Schulblatt der Provinz Sachsen*, 22 October 1919: 312-15. See also *Leipziger Lehrerzeitung*, 3 September 1919: 433; Rosin, *Das Schulkompromiss*, pp. 75-76.
70. Georg Wolff, *Einführung in das Studium der Schulpolitik* (Langensalza, 1919), pp. 6-7.
71. *Vorwärts*, no. 402, 8 August 1919; Lohmann, *Das Schulprogramm*, pp. 24-27.
72. Quoted in Richter, *Kirche und Schule*, p. 625; Rosin, *Das Schulkompromiss*, p. 63. See also the discussion of Anton Rheinländer, an educator and Center politician, in *Westdeutsche Lehrerzeitung*, 13 September 1919: 341-42.
73. See the contention of August Grünweller, the head of the League of German Protestant Teachers' Associations, in *Deutsche Lehrerzeitung*, 16 August 1919: 364-65; Otto Kley, *Das Schulprogramm des Zentrums* (Langensalza, 1919), pp. 6, 13.

Chapter 3

PEDAGOGUES AND PASTORS IN THE POLITICAL CONFLICTS OVER THE SCHOOL

*E*arly in the 1920s the reorganization of the elementary school system emerged as one of the most contentious issues in the culture wars of Weimar Germany. The Constitution of 11 August 1919 provided the fundamental principles for the making of a national school law and gave preference to the common school for children of all religious affiliations and social classes as the *Regelschule* for elementary education. In this model of the common school, the subject of religion would be taught to Catholic, Protestant, and Jewish children according to the tenets of their faiths, except for those pupils who were exempted from it at the request of their parents. Before a school bill was introduced in the Reichstag in April 1921, Catholic and Protestant churchmen made preparations for a political battle to preserve confessional schooling by creating massive parents' organizations. They exploited a new democratic institution in the republic—elected parents' councils—as an instrument for fighting school reforms, and they resorted to school strikes to intimidate and put pressure on the school authorities. With strikingly less success, organizations formed by radical Socialists and freethinkers used similar tactics. The agitation that accompanied the mobilization of parents at the grassroots polarized popular opinion on the school issue in the new democratic state.

The Churches and the Mass Parents' Movements

After the Constitution went into effect, Catholic Church leaders and Center politicians began to give an interpretation to Article 146 that diverged from the understanding of the school compromise held by Adolf Gröber and Joseph Mausbach during the deliberations in the National Assembly in July 1919. Catholic defenders of the confessional school claimed that the school articles in the Constitution had to be implemented without curtailing the rights of the parents. Center politicians warned that the conditions for establishing a separate school should not be interpreted in a way that limited the right of a minority of parents in a school district to choose a confessional school. The new state could "not be called a genuine democracy if the majority forces its school type on the minority," argued Albert Lauschner, a Catholic theologian, in the Prussian State Assembly.[1]

In a pastoral letter sent to the parishes in their dioceses in 1919, Catholic bishops in Bavaria defended the primacy of the will of the parents in respect to the education of their children, which should not be restricted by the jurisdiction of the state or school legislation. There would be resistance, they warned the state authorities, "if school legislation lays down further tracks in the direction of the irreligious compulsory school and if the *Kulturkampf* continues." They threatened to tell parents in Bavaria that "no constitution, no law, no administrative order, can impose on the consciences of the parents the obligation to send their children to the public school if that school takes God away from these children and destroys what fathers and mothers have instilled in the children up to school age." If Catholics were pressed to the point of opening parochial schools, the parents would "assert their political rights and refuse to pay a double taxation"—taxes for the public school and tuition for a private Catholic school.[2]

Admiring the "fearlessness" and "consciousness of power" with which the Bavarian bishops issued their "declaration of war," the *Neues Sächsisches Kirchenblatt*, a right-wing Protestant newspaper in Saxony, urged clergymen to "learn from [the conduct of] the Catholic Church leadership" and to oppose the Transitional School Law of 22 July 1919 with greater defiance.[3] This legislation, which was passed by the two Socialist parties in the Saxon Volkskammer before the Reich Constitution was adopted, removed the subject of religious instruction from the school curriculum and established a secular school system for children of all religious faiths and social classes. At a meeting of the church synod in the fall of 1919, conservative clergymen and laymen were confident that the enactment of the national school law would nullify these provisions of the state's school law. Hugo Hickmann, a professor of theology in Leipzig, and Johannes Siegert, a secondary schoolteacher in Chemnitz, declared that the Constitution gave parents the possibility of rescuing the confessional school and that they must be mobilized for this battle. The synod issued an appeal to Christian parents reminding them of their duty to exercise their constitutional right to demand confessional schools.[4]

Unwittingly, the Social Democrats gave assistance to the conservatives' efforts to mobilize parents for the political battle over the schools by introducing elected parents' councils in several of the states in Germany after 1918. The Social Democrats expected that this democratic innovation would give parents a voice in school affairs and foster a cooperative working relationship between the home and the school. The order of 5 November 1919 issued by Minister of Education Haenisch in Prussia required the formation of parents' advisory councils (*Elternbeiräte*) in schools consisting of a minimum of five members or one member per fifty pupils in the school. Under this regulation, the elections of the parents' councils were held once every two years, and representation was based on the proportion of the vote won by each slate of candidates. In Saxony, the elected parents' councils were established by the Transitional School Law. Members of the parents' councils, which ranged in size from a minimum of three to a maximum of fifteen members, were elected on the basis of proportional representation for a three-year term.[5]

At this time the Social Democrats were inclined to dismiss the objections raised by members of the German Teachers' Association, who thought that the parents' councils elected on the basis of proportional representation would be manipulated by political and confessional coalitions and bring dissension to school life. Soon after the ministerial order of 5 November 1919 was issued, teachers in Prussia pleaded with Haenisch to alter the procedures for electing the parents' councils, so that the school system would "not become a battleground of political and confessional passions."[6] Defending this edict in the Prussian State Assembly in February 1920, the minister's spokesman declared that the electoral system of proportional representation had the advantage of ensuring that the minority would have a voice. He doubted that the elections of the parents' councils would be as combative as some teachers were predicting. In another rebuff to the critics of the minister's order, Richard Lohmann declared, "We must summon the courage to be a democracy."[7] Convinced that a majority of working-class parents supported the Social Democratic school program, he was confident that the elected parents' councils would ultimately become an instrument for educational reform. In 1919-20 this belief was widely held among the progressivist pedagogues in the cities of Saxony that had a large Social Democratic electorate.[8]

Founded by Wilhelm Marx and other Center politicians in 1911, the Catholic School Organization (Katholische Schulorganisation) built up a mass following during the Weimar Republic and became a dynamic force in school politics. Under the leadership of Wilhelm Böhler, a priest who served as its general secretary, the Catholic School Organization acquired a tight, hierarchical structure and became the Church's vehicle for marshaling the masses of Catholic parents into the political battle for the confessional school. Catholics within an individual parish or commune were organized in a parents' association, whose members elected a parents' committee. A parish priest usually sat on each committee and served as its chairman. On the regional level of the diocese, a parents' committee was formed with a seat reserved for a churchman who functioned as the bishop's deputy. The central office in Düsseldorf coordinated the Catholic School Organization's activities in school politics, directed its extensive press and publicity work, organized training courses for activists in the parents' committees, and maintained communications with the bishops and Center Party's leadership. The Catholic School Organization raised funds for its work through collections taken in every church parish on designated "school Sundays."[9]

From December 1919 onward, Catholic pastors worked intensively to organize local parents' associations and to make preparations for the first elections of the parents' councils in Prussia. The bishops assigned to the pastors the tasks of preparing the slates of candidates and mobilizing all parish clubs to do propaganda work in the election campaign. The Catholic School Organization wanted to be certain that the Catholics who were nominated and elected to the parents' councils belonged to its own local parents' committees and hewed to the Church's line in school politics. Election campaigns for the parents' councils were waged with vehemence in the industrial areas of the Rhineland and Westphalia, where the Social Democrats agitated for the opening of secular schools among the working classes. The Catholic School Organization also used these elections as a battleground for the ideological struggle over the future school law. At public meetings, Catholic priests and politicians delivered speeches condemning the Social Democratic and German Democratic proposals for a unified school system. They contended that the Social Democrats "in league with the forces of Freemasonry and the German Teachers' Association" wanted "to de-Christianize the school."[10]

Stimulated by the example of the Catholic subculture, Protestant churchmen in Prussia, Saxony, and other states started their own agitation to mobilize Protestant parents. Working together with the clergy in this propaganda campaign were traditionalists in the teaching profession, who were affiliated with the German National People's Party. Before the election of the parents' councils in the spring of 1920, Protestant clergymen, with the help of politically conservative laymen, organized Christian parents' associations in many localities. Following instructions from the consistories, pastors usually sat on the executive committees of the Christian parents' associations and made certain that the other members were active participants in church life and "independent of the teachers." Clerical influence in the League of Christian Parents' Associations (Verband der christlichen Elternvereine) on the state and national levels was very strong. Walter Geissler, a pastor in Dresden, served as the chairman of the league in Saxony, and three other clergymen sat on its executive committee. In 1922 Pastor August Hinderer, the director of the Protestant Church's press and public relations office in Berlin-Steglitz, took the initiative in uniting the parents' leagues in the German states into a national organization. By 1926 the national membership had risen to 1.5 million. Protestant clergymen devoted considerable time to the functions of the parents' associations and the election campaigns for the parents' councils. They were quick to perceive the possibility of using these elections as a quasi referendum to influence the

Reichstag's interpretation of the school articles of the Weimar Constitution in the making of the national school law.[11]

The Protestant parents' associations conducted a propaganda war against the school reformers in the German Teachers' Association and the Social Democratic and German Democratic Parties. In the elections for the parents' councils, they nominated candidates for the so-called "Christian-nonpartisan slates" and distributed propaganda leaflets. They kept a close watch on the progressivist pedagogues in the schools and worked to undercut the efforts of Social Democratic activists who were attempting to persuade parents to register their children out of religious instruction before the opening of a new school year. Conservative school principals and teachers volunteered to be speakers at the public meetings of the Protestant parents' associations. Their polemical propaganda blurred the distinction between the common school and the secular school that was made in the Weimar Constitution, and stamped the common school with the false label of "an irreligious school."[12]

Activists in the League of Christian Parents' Associations in Saxony had a profound distrust of the reformers in the Saxon Teachers' Association. Leaflets passed out to parents and manifestos posted in public places urged the parents to protect their children against teachers who were striving to banish religious instruction from the schools. Surveillance of the teachers became one of the prime tasks of the parents' associations in Saxony, as the statutes of the league drafted in May 1920 reveal. Members of the parents' associations were expected to report on the "infringements" committed by "radical teachers in their fight against Christian religious instruction." Reports were to be submitted whenever teachers delivered public speeches advocating moral education in place of confessional instruction or used evening meetings with the parents to influence them to sign a formal request for the withdrawal of their children from religious instruction. These complaints were to be handled by one person on the executive board in strict confidentiality so that the identity of the parents would not be disclosed to the teachers when the protests were sent to the Ministry of Education.[13]

The partisan political campaign for the election of the parents' advisory councils in some cities in the early 1920s confirmed the apprehensions of many teachers. The Catholic and Protestant defenders of the confessional school and the Social Democratic advocates of the secular school put up competing slates of candidates. In the political battle, the League of Christian Parents' Associations aroused anti-Socialist sentiment and the fears of the parents with distorted statements about political indoctrination, poor discipline, and the lack of moral training in the secular school. Leaflets handed out by the parents' league in Leipzig in 1922 appealed to the parents not to let "the immortal souls of children of the ages of six to fourteen be delivered to the state for pedagogical and Socialist experimental purposes in the secular school."[14] The tactics employed by the clerical defenders of the confessional school vexed the reformers in the German Teachers' Association. Propaganda about the "godlessness of radical teachers" put them on the defensive in their campaign for the reorganization of the school system. They were compelled to refute the accusations made by church officials and pastors in the *Reichsbote* and other right-wing newspapers.[15]

In the elections of the parents' councils in Prussia in 1920 and 1922, the clerical defenders of confessional schooling succeeded in reaching beyond the circle of devout middle-class churchgoers. As the elections in Berlin show, Protestant churchmen campaigned actively on the political terrain of the left-wing parties in working-class districts. Instructed by the Protestant High Church Council to bring out voters for the Christian-nonpartisan slates, parish pastors made visits to the homes of parents and distributed leaflets with the slogans "our children need religion" and "politics should not meddle in the schools." Shortly before the election on 25 January 1920, appeals were made to the parents to protect their children against those who wanted to deprive them of the Christian religion in the schools. The Christian-nonpartisan slates won 43.5 percent of the seats on the parents' councils in the city's schools.[16] Since the Majority and Independent Social Democratic Parties together had received 64 percent of the votes cast in Berlin in the elections for the National Assembly a year earlier, the clergymen who fought against the secular school could take satisfaction in the outcome of the first election of the parents' councils. In 1922 the Christian-nonpartisan slate won a decisive victory and captured 66 percent of the seats on the parents' councils in the schools of Greater Berlin. The outcome of the elections in the industrial area of the Rhineland and Westphalia gave the Christian-nonpartisan slates an even bigger margin of victory with more than 75 percent of the vote.[17]

In Saxony, the advocates of secular schooling and the League of Christian Parents' Associations waged a fierce political battle in the first election of the parents' councils in 1921. The reformers in the Saxon Teachers' Association observed unhappily the agitation of demagogic partisans in both camps. They criticized the bourgeois conservative press for spreading so-called "scandalous stories" about the progressivist pedagogues based on the unsubstantiated denunciations of informers working for the parents' league.[18] At the same time, they chided the Communists and Independent Social Democrats for inserting their party ideology into the campaign for the secular school. Even before the elections in Dresden and Leipzig were over, the leaders of the teachers' association realized that in the future they would have to work much harder to "raise the secular school above the conflict of the parties and make [it] into a purely educational question."[19]

The support for the Christian-nonpartisan slates in the elections of the parents' councils in the cities of Saxony in 1921 was heavier than many members of the Saxon Teachers' Association had expected. In Dresden and Leipzig, the Christian-nonpartisan slate won 48.7 percent and 53.1 percent of the vote respectively. The secular school slate in Chemnitz triumphed with 68.3 percent of the vote in 1921, but it lost this favorable margin in the election a year later. While the secular school slate held a slight advantage in the tight races in Leipzig in the years after 1921, the vote for the Christian-nonpartisan slate increased in the other two cities and had risen to 55.1 percent in Dresden and 61.1 percent in Chemnitz by 1924.[20] After the 1921 election, the newspaper published by the Saxon Teachers' Association conceded that the Protestant parents' league had been successful in giving large numbers of parents the impression that the secular school was an ideological product of the parties of the political left. In the future, school reformers would have "to make the neutral character of the slates for the secular school clear and unmistakable." From the experience of these elections, the Saxon pedagogues were now able to assess the strength of the Protestant conservative forces. Far from yielding ground, they steeled their will for the hard struggle ahead with the conviction that confessional religious instruction in the schools was "the root of all strife and conflict" and that the school system would "never achieve peace until the complete separation of school and church [was] carried out."[21]

The organization of a massive parents' movement enabled Catholic churchmen and politicians to employ school strikes as a weapon in the early 1920s. The school strikes staged by the Catholics were generally boycott actions against teachers who had disaffiliated from the church or who exercised their constitutional right to decline to teach the subject of religion. The refusal of the parents to send their children to school was used as a means of pressuring the school administration to suspend and dismiss these teachers. In Prussia up to 1921, only 1,146 teachers, less than 1 percent of all teachers in the elementary schools, chose not to give religious instruction; most of these teachers worked in Berlin and the industrial cities of the Rhineland and Westphalia.[22] One of these strike actions in the city of Herne in Westphalia lasted from 1 June to 15 July 1920 and kept more than 6,900 children out of the schools. Catholic parents demanded the dismissal of four teachers who decided not to teach religion because they no longer adhered to the Catholic faith. When the school administration refused to accede to this demand, the Center Party's press and clerical and lay activists of the Catholic School Organization incited the parents and justified the resort to a strike. Wilhelm Böhler contended that teachers who were Social Democrats and had disaffiliated from the church would use school instruction to alienate the pupils from their religious faith. Under these circumstances, the parents had a "moral obligation to protect their children from bad influence." A month later, to put more pressure on the minister of education to intervene, the Catholic School Organization's provincial committee threatened to extend the strike throughout Westphalia.

Officials in the Arnsberg district government and the Ministry of Education met with the leaders of the Catholic School Organization in July to negotiate an end to the strike. Haenisch's decision in the settlement of the school strike formed the basis for a provisional solution until the enactment of a national school law. Pupils who were registered out of religious instruction in Herne were assembled in separate classrooms as much as possible by grade. Secular schools under the name of *Sammelschulen* were created out of these classes. The four teachers who were the target of the protest strike would henceforth give instruction in classrooms to which schoolchildren exempted from religious instruction were assigned. The Catholic parents' committee in Herne was unhappy with the minister's mediation and thought that these teachers should have been dismissed for breach of contract. The school board in Herne doubted the legality of the minister's decision, but agreed to designate two separate classrooms for 102 pupils within the school building. On 15 July the parents' committee announced the end of the school strike.[23]

Members of the German Teachers' Association criticized the strike actions of the Catholic School Association against teachers who exercised their freedom to decline to give religious instruction for reasons of conscience. The school strike in Herne revealed the vulnerability of teachers who no longer concealed their dissenting views. The local chapter of the teachers' association was so disturbed by the intimidating tactics of the Catholic School Organization that they resolved to go on strike if their four colleagues were suspended from office. In the aftermath of the school strike, some teachers in Westphalia began to question the wisdom of the politically partisan system of electing parents' councils. "It is a clear sign of a flawed democracy or an ultrademocracy that the parties that fight democracy and are opponents of the Constitution enter the battle for their ideology always with the Reich Constitution as their shield," one teacher declared. He doubted that the health of a deeply divided nation could be restored by defining democracy in terms of parental rights in school life, and demanded that the Prussian government and parliament show firmness in the defense of the freedom and unity of the school system vis-à-vis the forces of confessional particularism.[24]

The Secular School Movement on the Political Left

The militant activism of the Catholic School Organization in the industrial centers of the Rhineland and Westphalia set an example that was soon followed by left-wing Socialists. Early in 1920, activists in the Socialist teachers' organizations launched a propaganda campaign to build up a working-class parents' movement. Their agitation was far less successful than they had expected. The parents' associations for secular schools (*freie Elternvereinigungen*) attracted only a small proportion of the most politically conscious workers. In 1920, 121 such groups with a membership of about

100,000 were united in the League of Free School Societies (Bund der Freien Schulgesellschaften Deutschlands). Its stronghold lay in Düsseldorf, Duisburg, and other industrial cities in the Rhineland and Westphalia, and its leadership cadre was drawn heavily from the circle of left-wing Socialist teachers who had disaffiliated from the church.[25] The secular school movement rode on the big wave of disaffiliation from the church in the early years of the Weimar Republic, when more than one million Protestants and about 200,000 Catholics broke their church ties.[26] Propagandists for the League of Free School Societies argued that the secular school alone fulfilled the requirements of genuine tolerance and Germany's new democracy because it ensured complete freedom of conscience and placed the integrating civic ideal of the republican state at the center of public education. A resolution adopted at its congress in 1921 declared that the confessional school had been a strong pillar of the alliance of throne and altar in the past and would "never earnestly work for the preservation and strengthening of the German republic." The confessional school stood now as before "in the service of those circles of society who are only interested in seeing that the great mass of the people are taught to be obedient subjects, humble believers, and cheap slave laborers."[27]

In 1920 the free school societies in many cities demanded the opening of secular schools for those pupils who were registered out of religious instruction. In Duisburg, Düsseldorf, Elberfeld, and Gelsenkirchen, Catholics and Protestant conservatives formed coalitions on the school boards and municipal councils to block the creation of secular schools.[28] They viewed secular schools, as the suffragan bishop of Paderborn described them in a polemical pamphlet, as schools in which "fanatics of the Socialist freethinking ideology" gave instruction and the children were "educated in neopaganism."[29] The Prussian minister of education tried at first to placate the dissident parents by referring to the enactment of a national school law in the near future. As a concession to them, he issued two directives to the school bureaucracy in April and May 1920, stating that children who were registered out of religious instruction should not be required to learn church hymns in the music lessons and that religious instruction should be given in the first or last hour of the school day out of consideration for these children.[30]

Radical secularists became impatient when the draft of a national school law was not introduced in the Reichstag in 1920. Parents who had registered their children out of religious instruction staged school strikes in Elberfeld and Gelsenhausen in October 1920. In Gelsenhausen, over the course of a long strike, from 7 October up to the Christmas recess, from 1,520 to 1,330 pupils stayed out of school. A big wave of school strikes broke out in April 1921. Parents in Düsseldorf remained defiant up to June and kept about 5,500 children out of school. In Hamborn, where the strike went on for many more months, from 1,600 to 1,700 pupils were kept out of school.[31]

Officials in the Prussian Ministry of Education experienced considerable frustration in their efforts to mediate these conflicts. They were concerned about the frequency with which confessional and freethinking groups resorted to school strikes, and the numerous days of school instruction that the pupils were losing. And yet they were reluctant to impose penalties on the parents because any forceful measure could appear as a repression of the consciences of the parents and create martyrs. When Minister of Education Carl Becker submitted a report on the school strikes to the Reich Interior Ministry in the fall of 1921, he stated that the present situation had become "untenable" and that the enactment of a national school law could not be delayed any longer. He expressed his concern about the "anarchy in the schools," and noted how difficult it was to negotiate a settlement of the strikes organized by parents demanding secular schools in the industrial regions of the Rhineland and Westphalia. Coalitions of Catholics and conservative Protestants in the city councils adamantly opposed any interim solution. Catholic parents in Merscheid and Ohligs in the Düsseldorf provincial district defiantly staged school strikes in the spring of 1921, when classrooms in the confessional schools were set aside as *Sammelklassen* for children who did not take religious instruction. Left-wing parents in one locality threatened to occupy a school building after an unsuccessful strike.[32]

The League of Free School Societies never developed into a mass movement as politically powerful as the Catholic or Protestant parents' movements. It suffered from internal dissension between factions with conflicting conceptions of the secular school. Pedagogues in the Saxon Teachers' Association envisioned the secular school as a community school for the children of all people, unencumbered by any dogma and devoted to free inquiry and objective knowledge. They disagreed with the left-wing Socialists in the league, who thought that the secular school should be an ideological school in the service of the struggle for the emancipation of the proletariat and for a classless society. This division between pedagogues and political ideologues kindled a lively debate at the league's national convention in Dortmund in 1925, when a majority of the representatives voted for a resolution that associated the direction, goals, and principles of the secular school movement with the Marxist working-class struggle.[33]

The difficulties experienced by the Social Democrats in mobilizing working-class parents can be seen in the outcome of the elections for the parents' councils and the comparatively low number of children whose parents registered them out of religious instruction. In the election for the parents' councils in 1922, the Independent and Majority Social Democrats and Communists in Greater Berlin formed a coalition to "fight against political and clerical reaction in the schools." Each of the three left-wing parties contributed one-third of the candidates to a common slate. This campaign was conducted with a political combativeness that dismayed many members of the Berlin teachers' association, who chastised the political parties for "misusing the parents' councils to propagate their own ideology." The results of the election were a humiliating defeat for the leftist coalition, which garnered 2,350 seats on the parents' councils in the city's schools while the Christian-nonpartisan list captured 4,256 seats.[34] Explaining the defeat of the Socialist slate, Fritz Ausländer, an activist in the Socialist Teachers' League, pointed out that the Christian-nonpartisan candidates had the benefit of funds from the right-wing parties and the service of the entire church apparatus. The advocates of the secular school, he added bitterly, had "not succeeded in shaking working-class parents out of their sleep and mobilizing them for this election campaign." Thus, the bourgeoisie could "conduct the fight this time under the mask of religion and thereby split the proletariat."[35]

Ausländer's remark about the apathy of the proletariat was an awkward attempt to come to terms with the fact that a large number of working-class parents, who voted for the Social Democratic Party in parliamentary elections, wanted to have their children receive religious instruction in school. In Prussia, the data collected for the massive statistical report of the school administration in November 1921 showed that only 2.2 percent of all elementary school pupils were registered out of religious instruction. Less than 1 percent of the teachers chose to exercise their constitutional right to decline to give religious instruction.[36] At the end of 1921 there were only 55 secular schools with an enrollment of 26,291 children: 11 in Berlin, 16 in the Arnsberg provincial district, 22 in the Düsseldorf provincial district, 5 in the Cologne provincial district, and 1 in a town in Silesia.[37] The agitation of the League of Free School Societies was never as grave a threat as the traditionalists maintained. What alarmed them was the league's radical rhetoric and the apparent intensity of its activism among working-class parents in several areas of the state—Greater Berlin, especially in the working-class districts of Moabit and Wedding, and in the Düsseldorf, Hanover, Höchst, Merseburg, and Ruhr industrial regions. In May 1920, 53,890 schoolchildren were registered out of religious instruction; by November 1921 the number had more than doubled and rose to 117,794.[38]

The Clash between the Pedagogues and Pastors in Saxony

The Constitution of 11 August 1919 did not end the political conflicts over religious education in the elementary schools of Saxony. Pedagogues and pastors fought over this issue more fiercely in Saxony than in other states in Weimar Germany. Article 2 of the Transitional School Law of 22 July 1919 banned the instruction of religion as a school subject in Saxony, beginning in April 1920.[39] In December 1919 Richard Seyfert, the minister of education at the time, announced in the state parliament that the government intended to introduce a bill to amend this law because a secular school system could not be reconciled with Article 149 of the Constitution, which made religious instruction according to the beliefs of the religious communities a subject in the common school. A German Democrat, Seyfert implored the parties on the political right and left not to split the school system into atoms by demanding confessional and secular *Sonderschulen.* "Concessions by both sides," he declared, would bring the school conflict to an end in the parliament and communes.[40]

Speaking for the Social Democratic delegation, Arthur Arzt declined this appeal for a compromise, and argued that such a revision of Saxony's new school law would "stop a development that was favored and hastened by the revolution." Owing to the Center Party's trumps, the churches secured "their powerful influence [over elementary school education] in the Reich Constitution." The Social Democrats now saw before them two options: either to "retreat before this clerical power" or "to have the courage to let a strictly educational point of view be decisive here." The Majority and Independent Social Democrats took refuge in the technical argument that the Transitional School Law was passed before the third and final reading of the school articles in the National Assembly on 31 July so that the secular school in Saxony was protected by the "embargo paragraph" of the Constitution.[41]

Among Protestant churchmen, the response to Seyfert's mediating efforts was intransigent in some quarters and conciliatory in others. Church leaders and pastors on the right decided not to give up their fight for confessional schooling, as Franz Rendtorff, a Protestant professor of theology in Leipzig and a German Nationalist deputy in the Volkskammer, indicated in his reply to Seyfert on 8 January 1920. He insisted that the Reich Constitution superseded state law, and pressed the Saxon government to issue an order requiring that religious instruction be taught as a confessional subject.[42] Superintendent Franz Költzsch of Dresden considered Seyfert's proposal for restoring peace in school affairs as "a temptation for our church." In a news bulletin for the church parishes in Dresden, he declared that "all threats and temptations from the state" would "not make the officials of the governing bodies of the Saxon church go astray in their fight for their legitimate right."[43]

Twenty-seven pastors signed a declaration pleading with church officials and parishes to support Seyfert's policy and to halt their campaign for confessional schooling so long as there existed the possibility that the state parliament would introduce the community school with religious instruction as a subject in the curriculum.[44] One of these pastors, Eduard Kruspe, was also a German Democratic deputy in the Volkskammer. Appealing to the parties on the political right and left to accept the minister's proposed settlement, Kruspe maintained that the organization of the school system on the basis of Article 146, paragraph 1, of the Weimar Constitution should be an acceptable compromise for both sides because it provided the possibility for the continuation of religious instruction without subjecting the schools to church authority. Religious instruction taught according to the Zwickau theses and "removed from the sphere of church power and dogmatic influence" would be a free activity of the schools. Kruspe criticized the unyielding position taken by the Saxon Teachers' Association at its recent congress. When Social Democratic teachers urged workers to disaffiliate from the church at party meetings and gave moral instruction in place of the subject of religion, he said sharply, Christian parents could not be blamed if they were mistrustful toward such schoolteaching. If the compromise was to succeed, he counseled, both sides must shed their suspicions, and teachers who were outspokenly critical of the churches should no longer teach this subject. He pointedly reminded the Social Democrats and members of the Saxon Teachers' Association that behind the defense of religious instruction in the schools was a mass of parents. Teachers should not see these Christians as "puppets" who were "led by clerical wire-pullers in the background."[45]

When the Socialist majority in the state parliament refused to support a government bill repealing Article 2 of the Transitional School Law, the Reich Interior Ministry, under pressure from the Center Party and German Nationalists, appealed to the Reich High Court in Leipzig to resolve the issue of whether and how the "embargo paragraph" of the Constitution applied to the school system in Saxony. In April 1920 Seyfert postponed the implementation of this provision of the law until the court gave its judgment. In the interval, schoolteachers were ordered to give religious instruction in accordance with the edict issued after the November Revolution, which eliminated the catechism and reduced the religion lessons per week to two hours of Bible instruction.[46]

The progressivist pedagogues in Saxony continued to fight obstinately and pursued a strategy of passive resistance. Before the opening of the new school year in the spring of 1920, some teachers in Leipzig announced that they would refuse to give religious instruction as a confessional subject. This right guaranteed to the teachers in the Constitution as a matter of freedom of conscience gave them an instrument for opposing confessional education in the schools, as Bernhard Claus, a teacher in Leipzig and a German Democratic deputy, hinted in his speech in the state parliament as early as January.[47] The congress of the Saxon Teachers' Association decided to hold a referendum on the issue of religious instruction in March so that the position of the teachers would be crystal clear to the government and church officials. At that time, the organization had a membership of 17,801, including 1,214 teachers in retirement. In the referendum, 13,344 active teachers returned their ballots. Only 370 of these teachers, 2.8 percent, stated in response to the first question that they were willing to give religious instruction according to the confessional teachings of the churches. On the other hand, 12,743 teachers, 95 percent of the ballots, gave a negative reply. The other teachers abstained or gave unclear responses. In the second question, 84.6 percent of the respondents were willing to teach the subject of religion as a cultural heritage. By an overwhelming majority, elementary schoolteachers in Saxony rejected the instruction of religion, as Article 149 of the Constitution prescribed it.[48]

How did the leaders of the Saxon Teachers' Association understand the purpose and meaning of the referendum? The referendum was not a poll on the religious faith of the schoolteachers, although part of the responses to the second question suggest that a small percentage of these teachers may have been freethinkers. As Erich Viehweg, a pedagogue who belonged to the Social Democratic Party, stated, the central issue in the referendum was "only the old problem of the church and school, religious instruction in the spirit of and under the commission of the church." Viehweg wrote that the decision for confessional instruction would mean that "the school and [teaching] profession would be bound once again to the church." Religious instruction given in accordance with the doctrines of the churches would "bring clerical supervision and the subservience of the teachers, no matter what 'new forms' are devised." Clerical activism in the parents' movement made Viehweg and other Saxon teachers all the more distrustful of the pastors. He stated that the supervision of the schools could become more vigilant and intrusive because the Protestant Church had created "in the parents' associations and parents' leagues a new instrument of influence over the schools." Churchmen with school-age children were generally the first to be nominated for election to the parents' councils.[49]

Religious education in the elementary schools of Saxony was thrown into disarray before the opening of the new school term in April 1920. Some teachers submitted statements to the district school inspectors in which they declined to give religious instruction for reasons of conscience and out of pedagogical considerations. Other teachers informed the school inspectors that they were giving religious instruction with an ethical and a historical orientation in the two hours allocated for this subject each week. In those cases in which the teachers filed their notices later in the spring, religious instruction ceased abruptly in their classes in the middle of the school term. In April and May the school inspectors sent reports to the Ministry of Education on the number of these teachers and the number of classes in the schools in which religion was no longer taught.[50]

The intrepid boldness of these teachers provoked a sharp reaction from the Protestant Church and parents' associations. Two church superintendents protested to Seyfert on 1 May that teachers in Leipzig were handling the subject of religion in a manner that could not be recognized as religious instruction, as it was understood in Article 149 of the Constitution. They demanded that the minister put a stop to "this attempt to make this paragraph of the Constitution null and void for Leipzig." A few days later, the magistrates there informed Seyfert that "a very large number of teachers" had declined to give religious instruction, and inquired whether the ministry would assign substitute teachers to fill in the gap.[51] Parents who expected no sympathy or help from Social Democratic school inspectors sent their complaints directly to the ministry. Municipal officials in Pirna filed a complaint against teachers in the local schools who told the children to give to their parents a leaflet announcing a public meeting at which Arthur Arzt delivered a speech advocating a secular school system.[52]

The behavior of the defiant pedagogues and some of the school inspectors appointed in Saxony under the republican government strengthened the clergymen's suspicions about instruction in the schools. The case of Clemens Max Wippler, a teacher and adherent of theosophy, reveals how this distrust took root in 1920. Wippler continued to give religious instruction after he formally gave up his affiliation with the Protestant Church in April. Church officials demanded that the school inspector of the district prohibit him from teaching the subject of religion. Declining to issue such a command, School Inspector Stenzel replied that religious instruction in the schools of Saxony did not stand under the church's supervision and was "not an entirely confessional, dogmatic instruction." Under certain circumstances, a teacher who had left the church could also give religious instruction. It depended on whether the teacher acted out of antireligious reasons or only for reasons related to the institutions of the church and the persons working in it. The school inspector added that there were "good Christians" who turned their backs on the church because their deep religious feeling found "no satisfaction in the church." Such people could be permitted to give religious instruction and would "probably teach religion better and more genuinely" than persons who were inwardly indifferent but had not made the inner break evident by cutting their external ties to the church. Angry at Stenzel's reply, church officials appealed to the minister and warned that parents would stage a boycott if Wippler were not prohibited from teaching religion in school. Seyfert showed a greater appreciation of the views and sensibilities of Protestant clergymen and parents than the tactless school inspector did, and ordered Wippler to relinquish the instruction of religion.[53]

In response to the protests from Protestant clergymen and parents, Seyfert issued a ministerial order on 15 May 1920 that indicated his own disapproval of the teachers' conduct. He stated that the instruction of religious history could "not be considered religious instruction in the sense of Article 149 of the Reich Constitution." When teachers refused to give religious instruction in their classes, and no other teacher in the school was able to provide it in their place, the school boards were obliged to appoint substitutes who were qualified to give such instruction on the basis of an examination.[54]

After Seyfert issued this order, the progressivist pedagogues had to make a choice—to teach religion as a confessional subject or to exercise their freedom to refuse. The executive board of the Saxon Teachers' Association tried to get around this dilemma by advising members in August 1920 to act according to their vote in the referendum; they should inform the school inspectors that they would not give religious instruction based on confessional doctrine but were willing to teach this subject with an ethical and a historical focus. In the following weeks, many members of the teachers' association sent such notices to the school inspectors of their district. In Leipzig alone as many as 1,553 teachers gave up confessional instruction.[55] Social Democratic school reformers in this city were hoping to advance the cause of secular schooling through this resolute action. They thought that church officials should no longer close their eyes to the "facts" that "the majority of people had abandoned the old doctrines of the church" and that the church had "lost the following of the masses."[56]

In the fall of 1920, religious education in the schools of Saxony was in a state of uncertainty and confusion. Local officials did not know whether religious instruction would be taught in all classes when the new school term began in October. In Leipzig, the small number of teachers who were willing to give religious instruction to their own schoolchildren would not always agree to cover for their colleagues in other classes. Teachers from neighboring elementary schools or from secondary schools who were willing to serve as religion teachers expected remuneration for this additional work. Citing financial constraints, local school boards were reluctant to hire substitute teachers until the state government assumed the costs for employing them. Some municipal officials such as the mayor of Nossen suspected that the teachers were acting "not for reasons of conscience" but were engaged in "a trial of strength against the government."[57] School boards in several towns in the Pirna inspection district found a quicker way out of this problem by declaring the local schools to be secular, a decision that exceeded their legal authority. Dissension arose in the industrial town of Einsiedel near Chemnitz when the Social Democratic club sent a questionnaire to the parents asking them to vote for or against the continuation of religious instruction. When the parents of 66 percent of the schoolchildren voted in the negative, the Social Democrats wanted to use the poll as a referendum for creating a secular school.[58]

Seyfert made another attempt to mediate the differences between the teachers and churchmen in a meeting with Pastor Kruspe and other Protestant clergymen in the city of Meissen. Pastors in the liberal wing of the church in Saxony were willing to accept the minister's view that religious instruction taught according to the Zwickau theses of 1908 would satisfy the language of Article 149 of the Constitution. In a speech in the state parliament on 25 October, Seyfert reiterated this view, and asserted that "Christian religious instruction of a Biblical-historical nature, in which dogma [would] recede far into the background," did not conflict with the teachings of the Protestant Church. He expressed the hope that this compromise would enable teachers to resume the instruction of religion.[59] In the following months, neither the consistory nor the synod of the Protestant Church of Saxony raised any objections to his point of view.[60] In November, the district school inspector in Leipzig reported that "a number of teachers" had expressed a willingness to give religious instruction on the basis of the Zwickau theses. Teachers in Glauchau informed the school board that they would continue to teach religion along these lines. The school inspector there reported in December that "wider and wider circles in the Protestant Church [were] coming around to the view" held by Seyfert.[61]

The report of the conference in Meissen did not soften the intransigence of the advocates of secular schooling in the Saxon Teachers' Association. They argued that the pastors at that meeting represented a minority position and could not speak for the powerful orthodox wing of the church. Repeatedly, they justified their inflexible position by stating that the clergy would always demand confessional instruction.[62] In reality, these Social Democrats in the teachers' association were themselves opposed to any compromise on the basis of the Zwickau theses and would not abandon their fight for the secular school. A deep-seated stubbornness was clearly evident in October 1920, when Arthur Arzt and other Social Democrats in the state parliament introduced a resolution demanding that the government issue an ordinance stating that religious instruction according to the Zwickau theses was not instruction as Article 149 of the Constitution required. Arzt's other intention was to block pastors from entering the schools to give confessional instruction in those classes in which the teachers had declined to do so. The motion stated that only people who had demonstrated evidence of adequate pedagogical training on the basis of a state examination should be recruited for the instruction of religion.[63] Alwin Wünsche, the newly appointed school inspector of the Löbau district, discouraged teachers from resuming the instruction of religion on the basis of the Zwickau theses. A pastor in Löbau complained to the ministry in November that when "a number of teachers" decided to give religious instruction again under this condition, Wünsche would not give his approval and stated that this practice would lead to protests from ultraconservative Protestant circles.[64]

The conduct of the Saxon teachers in the conflict over religious instruction alienated devout Protestants and was widely criticized. At a meeting of the church synod, Rendtorff upbraided the teachers in Leipzig and denounced the *Leipziger Lehrerzeitung* for instilling in them the defiance and daring to give moral instruction in the hours allocated for the subject of religion. The synod demanded that the minister of education put a stop to such arbitrary practices.[65] In another protest sent to Seyfert, the church superintendent in Leipzig objected to the efforts of "radical teachers" to mobilize left-wing Socialists in the parents' councils for the purpose of carrying out a referendum on the question of religious instruction.[66] Karl Rothe, the German Nationalist mayor of Leipzig, deplored the tension between the teachers and

Christian churchgoers at the parents' meetings and reproachfully counseled the teachers "to preserve peace in the schools." In a letter to the minister, he accused School Inspector Ernst Beyer, a former teacher and a Social Democrat, of failing to work hand in hand with the city magistracy as a "nonpartisan" school inspector should do. Beyer saw himself "expressly appointed as the representative of the teachers to protect their interests one-sidedly," the mayor wrote.[67] In a collective protest, the church parish boards in Leipzig called school conditions in the city intolerable and complained that the teachers were "proceeding arbitrarily" in the instruction of religion and that the parents were "kept completely in the dark" about what their children were being taught.[68]

Protestant clergymen and parents' associations objected to the efforts of some teachers to persuade the parents to withdraw their children from religious instruction and to request moral instruction in its place. August Hering, the chairman of the League of Christian Parents' Associations in Leipzig, complained to Seyfert that teachers were holding parents' meetings in the evenings for the "agitational purpose" of urging the parents to register their children out of religious instruction. The mayor of Eibenstock told the minister that parents were upset when teachers at the local school asked the pupils to obtain the signatures of their parents on printed registration forms for moral instruction. Parents in several towns objected to the "interference" of the teachers, "the misuse of the teachers' authority," and "the exploitation of the children" in other petitions to the minister.[69] A leaflet handed out by teachers in Gröba provoked the ire of the pastor and church parish board. The leaflet informed the parents that 24 of the 31 teachers in Gröba and the surrounding area could not reconcile confessional instruction with their pedagogical conscience. The teachers explained that religious instruction based on church dogma was not comprehensible to young pupils, and added gratuitously that the articles of faith in the Augsburg Confession stood in contradiction to modern scientific knowledge.[70]

Protestant churchmen in Saxony ultimately drew out their own mighty weapons in this fight over religious instruction. Pastors agreed to come to the schools to give religious instruction in place of the teachers. Announcements made by the church parish boards warned parents that children who did not take religious instruction in school would not be admitted to the church lessons in preparation for Confirmation. This admonition gained force when the church consistory issued an order on 28 December 1921 stating that parents had "to provide evidence" that their children had received religious instruction in school without interruption when they enrolled their children for Confirmation instruction.[71] Many communes began to make new teaching appointments dependent on whether applicants for the position were willing to give religious instruction. The Saxon Teachers' Association objected to this practice as a form of intimidation that threatened to curtail freedom of conscience, and appealed to Seyfert to put a stop to it.[72]

Why did the advocates of the secular school in the Saxon Teachers' Association adopt such an intransigent stand? These pedagogues persuaded themselves that the dissatisfaction of the parents was confined to small conservative circles and was instigated by the propaganda of church leaders and their political allies. They were confident that once they enlightened the public through the press and evening meetings with the parents, people would appreciate the value of instruction focusing on religious history and ethics in the schools and would accept the view that confessional education should be left up to the family and the church.[73] Moreover, the leaders of the teachers' association did not want a compromise settlement on the basis of the Zwickau theses. At two meetings on 6-7 November, the executive board discussed Seyfert's statement in the state parliament on 25 October and came to the decision that since the secular school alone guaranteed "the realization of a unified school system free of church influence," the association could "not retreat from its goal." The association would "not let itself be swayed in this decision by the minister's statement or similar attempts at persuasion made by many district school inspectors."[74]

The unyielding advocates of the secular school in the Saxon Teachers' Association did not believe that the majority of clergymen would accept religious education in the schools on the basis of the Zwickau theses and repeatedly pointed to statements made by clerical hard-liners in the press.[75] Behind this skepticism about the possibility of a moderate-liberal settlement was their own rejection of such a compromise. After the Revolution of 1918, they saw only "a certain lack of clarity, contradictions, and timidity" in the set of principles on religious instruction that the teachers' association had adopted in 1908.[76] They were intent on obtaining an unambiguous solution—the complete separation of school and church.

Erich Viehweg, the editor of the *Sächsische Schulzeitung*, thought that religious instruction in the schools would always be "a source of dissension," and could not see any possibility of retaining it without church supervision. "More distrustful" of the progressivist pedagogues in 1920, orthodox-Protestant churchmen would constantly try to find out how religion was being taught in the schools and would get involved in the elections of the parents' councils for this purpose. Viehweg contended that "a strong right wing" of clergymen and "a very strong orthodox laity" would demand to see the lesson plans and teaching materials and to have a voice in determining whether the instruction corresponded to church doctrines. Reminding the teachers of the clerical pamphlets written against the reform of religious instruction before 1914, he stated that they should "not harbor illusions" that the church would take a moderate position or that the orthodox circles in the Protestant parents' movement would acquiesce to the teaching of this subject according to the Zwickau theses.[77]

The leaders of the Saxon Teachers' Association also fostered intransigence by defining existentially the stakes in the conflict over religious instruction.

The secular school alone, Viehweg wrote, would "give us integrity and freedom and bring to an end all dishonesty and hypocrisy." In applications and appointments, teachers would no longer have to respond to direct or more subtle inquiries about their religious beliefs and method of giving religious instruction. Only in the secular school would teachers be "released from the oppression of their consciences" and from a relationship of subordination to the church.[78] Viehweg's articles cast much light on the tactics of the Saxon Teachers' Association in 1920. Although the Weimar Constitution prevented the secularization of the elementary school system, teachers had the right to refuse to give religious instruction. If teachers exercised this freedom, this change would come "in the course of historical development." "Any compromise [would] delay the coming of the secular school," he contended.[79]

The fight for secular schooling suffered a setback when the Reich Court on 4 November 1920 ruled that the article in Saxony's Transitional School Law and the decrees of the workers' and soldiers' councils in Bremen and Hamburg that excluded religious instruction from the public schools stood in conflict with the Constitution. Reich legislation superseded the laws of the federal states; thus, these regulations lost validity when the Constitution went into effect. The subject of religion now had to be taught in the schools in accordance with the beliefs of the religious communities.[80] Social Democratic reformers in the Saxon Teachers' Association conceded that the goal of a secular school system had "suffered a defeat." They found consolation in "the certainty of the course of historical development" toward a secular school system and in their "conviction of the inner necessity of [this] ideal."[81]

The conflict over religious education in the schools played a major role in the electoral campaign for the Saxon Landtag on 14 November 1920. In their fight to bring down the coalition government headed by the moderate Social Democrat Wilhelm Buck, the right-wing parties attacked the Transitional School Law and accused the progressivist pedagogues of striving to put a party ideology in place of the Christian religion in the schools. Helping the German National People's Party to exploit this issue for political advantage was a small band of disgruntled former school principals who organized the right-wing League of Saxon Educators in 1920. At German Nationalist rallies, these traditionalists delivered speeches defending religious instruction in the schools and lambasting the Saxon Teachers' Association for aligning with the party that was responsible for the November Revolution.[82] The outcome of the election deepened the political polarization of Saxony. The vote for the German Democratic Party slumped from 22.9 percent in February 1919 to 7.7 percent of the electorate; the Majority Social Democratic vote fell from 41.6 percent to 28.3 percent. On the political right, the German National People's and German People's Parties increased their share of the electoral vote and won 21 percent and 18.6 percent respectively. The Majority Social Democrats gave up their short-lived alliance with the German Democrats and formed a coalition government with the Independent Social Democrats.[83]

Before the opening of the new school year in the spring of 1921, a number of teachers who had declined to teach religion in the previous months notified the school boards and school inspectors of their intention to resume the instruction of religion. This change of mind was prompted by assorted feelings—a sense of isolation in their local communities in the face of the outrage of the pastors and Christian parents' associations, a deeper awareness of the strength and resolution of the opponents of secular schooling, and an uneasiness over the prospect that a large number of clergymen would come to the schools to substitute for the classroom teachers in the religion lesson.[84] In some localities these teachers encountered open distrust and resistance. The Christian parents' association in one section of Dresden objected to the instruction of religion by three pedagogues who had refused to teach the subject a year earlier. The parents contended that people could not change their ideology like a suit of clothes; they suspected that the three teachers had changed their mind simply because the local pastor had agreed to teach religion in the school.[85]

The Saxon Teachers' Association's attempt to obtain an unambiguous solution to the problematic relation of church and school left behind an abiding suspicion of the progressivist pedagogues in clerical circles. The intensity of this distrust bore little relationship to the modest results of the teachers' efforts to win over the parents to the cause of the secular school. When the Ministry of Education conducted a survey on the instruction of religion in the schools in August 1922, 5,505 out of 15,809 elementary schoolteachers in Saxony (34.8 percent) were still exercising their right to decline to give religious instruction. The number of children registered out of religious instruction, on the other hand, was no more than 13 percent or 94,945 pupils out of a total enrollment of 720,174.[86]

The Political Battle over the National School Law

By the time that the Reich government presented the draft of a national school law to the Reichstag in April 1921, Catholic and Protestant churchmen had mobilized large parents' movements, and the constellation of political forces in the Weimar Republic had changed. The swing to the political right in the elections for the Reichstag and state parliaments in 1920 enhanced the influence of the Center Party in the formation of coalition governments. Although State Secretary Heinrich Schulz in the Reich Interior Ministry was a Social Democrat with a long-standing commitment to the secular school, he took these political circumstances into account. In his address to the congress of the German Teachers' Association in May 1921, Schulz confessed that he had to write provisions of the school bill against which his inner feelings rebelled. The proposed law did "not emerge from the inner necessities of the German school," but represented "a compromise acceptable to parties with opposing views in the sphere of school politics."[87]

Drafting the school law became all the more difficult for Schulz and other councilors in the Reich Interior Ministry because Center politicians altered their interpretation of Article 146 of the Constitution. In the third reading of the draft constitution in the National Assembly and in the weeks immediately thereafter, Wilhelm Marx, Joseph Mausbach, and other Center deputies conceded that Article 146, paragraph 1, made the common school for children of all religious faiths the *Regelschule* for every commune and gave it precedence over the other school types. Paragraph 2 provided for the possibility of opening confessional and secular schools only under certain conditions as *Sonderschulen*.[88] The Center Party abandoned the Weimar school compromise when the Catholic bishops made the legal equality of the three types of schools the condition for accepting any new school legislation.[89]

In their petition to the Reich government and the Reichstag on 20 November 1920, the German bishops demanded that the confessional school be given full equality with the common school in the forthcoming law. The forceful language of the bishops' demands left no doubt that the Catholic Church would fight a school law that carried out the letter of Article 146. They closed the door to any compromise by declaring: "We would commit an offense against the faith of our people, the soul of our Catholic children, and our pastoral duty if we recognize the interconfessional school as being of equal worth with the confessional school and if we do not raise the sharpest protest against its introduction as the common school." If the state compelled Catholic parents to send their children to a school that was "indifferent or hostile" to their religion, that measure would be "a coercive encroachment on the inalienable natural rights" of the parents and "an intolerable oppression of their consciences." The clause pertaining to the "proper school organization" should not be interpreted so that it became an obstacle to the maintenance of confessional schools in areas where the Catholics were a minority. Confessional schools should be opened and maintained even if a small number of parents made this request.[90]

The bishops' haughty disregard for the letter of the Weimar Constitution alarmed the reformers in the teaching profession. In an open letter to the Reich chancellor on 9 February 1921, the executive committee of the German Teachers' Association argued that the bishops' demands for the preservation of the existing confessional schools contradicted the language and intent of Article 146. To underscore their view that the Constitution required the common school to be the rule for primary schooling in every commune, the reformers began to call it the community school (*Gemeinschaftsschule*) in the public debate on the school law. They contended that Article 146 left "no doubt" that the opening of confessional schools at the request of the parents "must satisfy specific conditions before [that request] can be taken into account." They emphasized the educational advantages of schools with classrooms for each grade and stated that the school administration and future legislation would be required "to bring to bear all of the pedagogical reasons" against the splintering of the school system within a district into small separate schools for each confession. A confessional school could be permitted only if the structure of classrooms for eight grades in the community school would not be adversely affected. The correctness of the teachers' interpretation of Article 146 was confirmed when Walter Landé, the legal councilor in the Prussian Ministry of Education, published his commentary on the Weimar Constitution later in the 1920s.[91]

When the draft of the national school law was unveiled, the German Teachers' Association criticized Heinrich Schulz and other officials in the Interior Ministry for applying the provisions of Article 146 in a manner that destroyed all prospects for a unified school system. Schulz's draft law made an ambiguous acknowledgment of the idea of the common school in the Weimar Constitution when it stated that "the *Gemeinschaftsschule* stands in principle open to all pupils." It did not require the establishment of this type of school in all communes and permitted the continuation of the existing confessional schools at the request of the parents. The progressivist pedagogues were disturbed by the introduction of a new principle in school legislation in Germany, namely, the right of the parents to determine the type of public school in each commune. They thought that the school bill did not give sufficient weight to the educational considerations that should restrict the opening of separate schools with a confessional or secular character (*konfessionelle Schulen* and *weltliche Schulen*). Instead, it left the definition and interpretation of the concept of a "proper school organization" up to the state parliaments, where the politicians of the Center and right-wing parties would argue for permitting confessional schools with one or two classrooms.[92]

Although the German Democrats and Social Democrats in the German Teachers' Association treasured individual freedom, they took issue with the expansive definition of parents' rights instigated by the partisans of confessional schooling. They thought that the provisions in the proposed law related to the choice of school by the parents would perpetuate conflicts over the schools and undermine the welfare of the republic and the development of a cohesive national community. From this perspective, they regretted that the school bill did not give expression to the moral ideal of tolerance. The progressivist pedagogues did not deny that parents had rights in respect to the education of their children, but the contentions of the defenders of parental choice made them uneasy. Because Catholic and Protestant clergymen routinely invoked the rights of parents in their opposition to the common school, educational reformers viewed this claim skeptically as "a cloak" for the interests and will of the politically organized church rather than as a fundamental right in a democratic and pluralist society. Johannes Tews contended that "the special privileges sought by the church" were presented to the public "in the guise of parents' rights."[93] In their response to this strategy, Tews and other reformers made a clear distinction between the right of a religious community to open private schools and the sovereignty of the state in the sphere of public education. They thought that the Reich as a *Kulturstaat* should uphold freedom and unity in the public school system against the claims of the church and use the public schools to promote national integration and a common civic identity. Georg Wolff saw the United States in this respect as a model for Germany. He admired the way in which the Americans used the public schools to acculturate people whose family origins were in diverse lands and who embodied diverse religious faiths, races, and ways of life.[94]

Pointing out that the *Begründung* or rationale appended to the draft of the school law stated that the entire instruction in the confessional school had to be "given in the spirit of the confession," the reformers in the teachers' association contended that this kind of public school would be closer to a parochial school than to an institution of the state. They saw in this vague phrase the disturbing prospect that teaching material for history and other subjects would be determined according to the wish of the churches and that the convictions and church activity of the teachers would be under constant scrutiny. Since school officials appointed by the state could not say whether the instruction was given completely and correctly "in the spirit of the confession," or whether the teachers fulfilled the requirements set by the churches, the draft law seemed to be opening the door for the churches to claim the right to supervise school instruction. The intent of this obscure phrase was evident to the progressivist pedagogues when they looked at the article in the school bill concerning the appropriate textbooks that had to be used in the confessional and secular schools. They feared that churchmen and political ideologues would interfere in the selection of schoolbooks and teaching materials, and envisioned clashes between the civic culture promoted by the republican state and the particularist ideologies of clerical and political parties.[95]

German Democrats and Social Democrats in the German Teachers' Association played a major role in the mobilization of public opposition to the school bill, and afterwards Heinrich Schulz bitterly held them responsible for the defeat of his draft of the school law. At the national congress of the German Teachers' Association in May 1921, Johannes Tews delivered a trenchant critique of the school bill, and the delegates voted to allocate funds to fight it.[96] Members of the executive committee voiced their objections in private meetings with deputies in the Reichstag and Prussian state parliament and with Heinrich Schulz in the Reich Interior Ministry. Tews gave speeches at numerous public meetings organized by the local chapters to drum up popular opposition. The rally in Frankfurt am Main drew a crowd estimated as large as two thousand. Teachers in Hamburg spoke at sixteen parents' meetings held within three days in July, each of which had an attendance of more than five hundred. On the platform at the massive meetings held in Dresden and Leipzig in June were city council members and deputies of the Saxon state parliament who belonged to the German Democratic and Social Democratic Parties.[97]

While the reformers worked to defeat the school bill, traditionalists in the Catholic and Protestant Churches mobilized popular support for it and made demands for amendments to protect confessional interests more securely. When the *Kirchentag*, the big conference of the German Protestant Church Federation, met in Stuttgart in September 1921, the representatives of the synods adopted a resolution supporting "the confessional school in which one integral worldview permeates the entire school life." The Protestant Church conference stated that the school law had to grant the confessional schools an unlimited right to remain open and to flourish. State-appointed officials could not decide whether religious instruction was taught "in accordance with the norms of the Christian faith and life as they are contained in the Gospels." The school law must include a provision for the formation of church organs that would "preserve the inner connection between church and school and guarantee to the church the influence that is indispensable for it."[98] To impress the deputies in the Reichstag with the strength of the popular support for confessional schooling, traditionalists in the Catholic and Protestant Churches launched a massive petition campaign. Declaring that the will of the people must be decisive in a democracy, the leaders of the Catholic School Organization boasted that the petitions circulated in the dioceses in Bavaria and Prussia bore the signatures of more than 76 and 80 percent of the Catholic people who were eligible to vote in those two states, respectively.[99]

Although the overwhelming majority of the reformers in the Prussian Teachers' Association took a moderate position on the issue of religious education, opposition to the school bill brought them frequently into polemical exchanges with churchmen. In the early months of 1922, the League for Protestant Education in the School and Home (Bund für evangelische Erziehung in Schule und Haus), led by Pastor Winkler in Frankfurt an der Oder, rallied clergymen in the eastern provinces of Prussia for the battle over the school law. Winkler traveled to many cities, delivering speeches at church meetings and recruiting members for his organization. He and other clerical propagandists described the *Gemeinschaftsschule* as a school in which "Christians as well as Jews, heathens, and blasphemers of God" could be appointed to teaching positions, and the children would no longer learn church hymns in the music lesson or begin the school day with prayer. After Winkler addressed a large gathering in the municipal auditorium in Königsberg on 15 January 1922, the leader of the local teachers' association seized the opportunity afforded by the discussion time to reproach clergymen in the province of East Prussia for starting the fight against the community school and striving to thwart the implementation of Article 146 of the Constitution. At another rally in Königsberg on 4 February, Hermann Bischoff, the chairman of the teachers' association in the province, delivered a speech emphasizing "the dangers" of the school bill. During the discussion time, a pastor provoked loud dissent when he contended that religious instruction would not be taught properly in the community school and that "only a shallow deism would prevail there."[100]

The political debate between schoolteachers and churchmen on the school bill became especially strident in the province of Saxony in the winter of 1921-22, when clergymen, stirred into action by Winkler, organized public meetings and delivered impassioned speeches against the community school and its champions in the German Teachers' Association. W. Horstmann and E. Becherer, two German Democrats in the teachers' association in the province of Saxony, attended these rallies in the company of other colleagues, and their attempts to refute the arguments of the clerical activists led to verbal clashes. After Winkler spoke at a public meeting in Delitzsch, Becherer chided him for flaunting the Constitution and failing to see the distinction between confessional doctrine and Christianity as a cultural heritage. When Becherer's request to respond to a pastor's harangue at a meeting in another town was denied, teachers who were present raised an outcry until they were ordered to leave. Another meeting ended in discord after Church Superintendent Leisegang closed off all discussion following his speech. When the chairman of the local teachers' association questioned the propriety of this action at a meeting open to the public, the high-strung church official lost his temper and angrily lashed out at him and Horstmann.[101]

Pedagogues in the eastern provinces of Prussia shared with their more left-wing colleagues in Saxony a profound distrust of the intentions of Catholic and Protestant churchmen. The demands of the Catholic bishops and the Protestant Church conference for "guarantees" in the school law that religious instruction would be taught in accordance with the confessional doctrines of the churches seemed to substantiate their suspicion that the clergy were striving to restore the church's supervision of the schools in another guise. These members of the Prussian Teachers' Association rejected any legal arrangement that would enable the church to determine the selection of the teaching material for the subject of religion. As a teacher in Magdeburg declared: "We do not want to open the way for the clergy to enter the school. If the church has a foot in the school again, we fear that it will soon recover its earlier power." He criticized churchmen in the German Nationalist ranks who wanted to return to the old times and restore the monarchy.[102]

Owing to a succession of governmental crises in 1921 accompanied by changes in the Reich cabinet, the first reading of the school bill in the Reichstag was delayed until January 1922. In the intervening months, the German

Teachers' Association's criticism of the draft law made a deep impression on the Social Democratic and German Democratic deputies. The speakers for the two parties in this Reichstag debate, Carl August Hellmann and Karl Weiss, were members of the teachers' association and referred repeatedly to its objections to the school bill when they stated their own opposition.[103] The debate in the Reichstag showed that the Weimar coalition parties were so deeply divided that there was little prospect of coming to any consensus. The school reformers were disappointed that the draft law was not voted down at once. Over the dissenting votes of the Independent Social Democrats, the other parties agreed to refer the school bill to the education committee for further deliberations and amendment.

The legislative work of the education committee was interrupted frequently because of governmental crises and the reshuffling of politicians sitting in the Reich cabinet. The Center politicians stuck to the demands of the episcopate, and the Social Democrats were even less willing to make accommodations to the Center Party after the Independent and Majority Social Democrats merged in the fall of 1922. Major decisions on the revision of the school bill were made by a slender majority of 15 to 13 votes.[104] The deputies of the Center and bourgeois conservative parties in the majority ignored altogether the views expressed by the German Teachers' Association in its petition to the Reichstag in February 1922. Johannes Tews and other educational reformers thought that the amendments made the proposed law all the more unconstitutional. Observing the interruptions in the committee's work, they were speculating hopefully in the summer of 1922 that this school bill would expire.[105] The committee's deliberations came to an end in December 1923 before an amended bill was brought to the full house for a vote.

As the result of the Reichstag's failure to enact a national school law, confessional schooling continued under the republic since Article 174 of the Constitution froze the existing school laws in the states of the German Reich until legislation implementing Article 146 was passed. In Saxony, the Transitional School Law of 1919 introduced the common school for children of all religious faiths before the Constitution went into effect. However, the Social Democrats who served in the Ministry of Education forestalled the outbreak of school strikes and other forms of protest by the Catholic minority by allowing 29 Catholic elementary schools to remain open, including 7 in Dresden and 4 in Leipzig. With few exceptions, Catholic children, who constituted 3 percent of the more than 717,400 pupils in the elementary schools in Saxony in 1922, were taught in schools of their own confession.[106]

For the more heterogeneous population in Prussia, confessional schooling continued to be the predominant form of elementary education in the Weimar years. Of the more than 5,461,000 pupils attending the elementary schools in 1921, Protestants constituted 62.8 percent of the enrollments, and the corresponding figures were 35.7 percent for the Catholics and 0.27 percent for the Jews. In spite of the fact that confessionally homogeneous school districts declined markedly after 1900 and more children lived in school districts with a mixed population, the percentage of Protestant and Catholic children who were taught in schools of their own confession was strikingly high: 95.9 percent for the Protestants and 92.3 percent for the Catholics. Moreover, Catholic clergymen continued to exercise a direct influence in the schools in Prussia. Whereas the Protestant Church relied on lay teachers to give religious instruction, this subject was frequently taught to Catholic children in the schools by priests as part-time religion teachers. In 1921, 80 percent of the 9,641 part-time Catholic religion teachers were priests, who gave religious instruction in 63 percent of the Catholic schools in Prussia. The other part-time clerical and lay religion teachers worked in non-Catholic schools to which the Catholic minority in the school district had to send their children.[107]

The disadvantageous effect of this system of confessional schooling for the Jewish minority in Prussia may have been offset by two trends in the 1920s. During the great inflation many Jewish public schools with a small enrollment in rural areas were closed so that the number of these schools declined from 153 in 1921 to 96 in 1931. On the other hand, new private Jewish elementary schools were opened in Berlin, Breslau, Cologne, and other cities. Within the Berlin synagogue congregation, Liberal Jews continued to oppose the separation of schoolchildren along religious lines and supported the city's interconfessional schools, but the Orthodox and Zionist factions, with the backing of Jewish immigrants from Eastern Europe, championed the opening of Jewish private schools. By 1931, 24 percent of the 8,873 elementary schoolchildren of the Jewish faith in Berlin were taught in Jewish private schools.[108] Furthermore, the enrollment of Jewish pupils continued to grow in the secondary schools. In the 1921–22 school year, almost 60 percent of Jewish youths of compulsory-school age, from six to fourteen years of age, were attending middle and secondary schools that did not have a confessional character. Of the Jewish boys and girls in this cohort, 16,949 attended public and private elementary schools, 5,970 were in middle schools, and 19,214 were in secondary schools. In comparison, a lower proportion of Christian children in this age group entered these upper-level schools: 11 percent for the Protestants and 7 percent for the Catholics.[109]

The Political Pragmatists in the School Reform Movement

The politics of culture in the early 1920s left the reformers in the German Teachers' Association with a somber view of the continuing power of the Catholic and Protestant Churches in the Weimar Republic. In the aftermath of the debate on the school bill, many teachers reassessed their professional organization's programmatic position and strategy. They thought that the political fight for an integrated school system could be waged more effectively if they described their goal as an interconfessional school based on a religious-moral foundation to distinguish it from the secular school. A favorite tactic of the clerical defenders of confessional schooling was to claim that the ultimate goal of the German Teachers' Association was the abolition of religious instruction in the schools and that the *Gemeinschaftsschule* would serve "only as the transition to the secular irreligious school."[110] Put on the defensive by this ploy, Tews and other reformers came to see that section 4 of their organization's school program was a hindrance. The national congress in 1919 met before the school articles of the Constitution had been drafted, and the delegates voted by a narrow margin in favor of leaving religious instruction as a subject up to the churches and synagogue congregations. Friedrich Nüchter in Bavaria now maintained that this vote had been a mistake as it gave the impression that religious education was not a matter of concern to the teachers. Section 4 of the school program gave the traditionalists "that weapon which they have been wielding ever since that congress," namely, the contention that the German Teachers' Association had "shut the school door on religious instruction."[111]

The problems created by the school program in the public debate on the school bill were aired at a meeting of the organization's central commission for school politics in Berlin on 11 December 1921. Becherer and Tews stated that the teachers had to wage their fight for school reforms in a manner that would not offend the religious sensibilities of people. When Kurt Wehner and Georg Winkler from Saxony contended that no political advantage would be gained by retreating from the school program, other members of the committee replied that the majority of German teachers did not endorse the exclusion of religious instruction from the schools.[112] Polls taken in the chapters in Breslau and Halle in 1922 indicate that even the progressivist pedagogues in the cities of eastern Prussia were more moderate than their colleagues in Saxony. In the Breslau and Halle chapters, only 5.1 percent and 1 percent of the teachers, respectively, supported the secular school. The majority favored the community school, in which religion would be taught as a subject without confessional doctrine and the catechism.[113]

When the national congress of the German Teachers' Association met in Hanover in June 1922 and took up the issue of revising section 4 of the school program, the political pragmatists in the ranks of the school reformers formed a cohesive group. The representatives of the chapters in Prussia and the southwestern states challenged the delegates from Saxony and Hamburg, who defended the 1919 school program. Oskar Gleissberg, the chairman of the Saxon Teachers' Association, contended that the secular school solved the old problem of the relation of church and school. As long as religion was a subject of instruction in the schools, he warned, the churches would demand the right to supervise it. Erich Viehweg appealed to the delegates to approach the issue of religious instruction not as school politicians but rather as a community of pedagogues. The school program should embody the goals and convictions of the membership, independent of current political circumstances or the extent of public support for these ideals in society at any given time. The revision of the school program out of tactical considerations, the Saxon delegates argued, could give the public the impression that the teachers' association was admitting a mistake and repenting or lacked the courage to uphold its principles.[114] Other delegates objected to this representation of the issue as a matter of principle versus tactical expediency. Oskar Hofheinz from Baden responded to Gleissberg and Viehweg by pointing to the school articles of the Constitution and noting that wide circles of society believed that children had a religious sensibility that should be nurtured in the school. Teachers were obliged "to respect such widely held views among the parents." If the teachers' association expended more energy in fighting for the secular school through a big propaganda crusade, it "shall not achieve this goal."[115] After ten hours of impassioned debate over two days, a majority of the delegates cast their votes for a compromise amendment.

The wording of the school program revised at the Hanover congress of 1922 captured the mixed emotions felt by the reformers in the German Teachers' Association during the Weimar era debates on religious education. The teachers' association considered, "now as before, the regulation of the relations between state, school, and church in the field of religious education described in its school demands of 1919 as the most advisable and the most just for all sides." After noting that the Constitution did not permit the exclusion of religious instruction from the school curriculum, the amended program endorsed a common school for all children in which religion was taught to them in separate groups according to confession.[116] Would this change in the official position of the German Teachers' Association make the reformers more effective in working for a national consensus in favor of a unified school system? The battle over the school bill of 1927 would show what effect their pragmatism and sensitivity to public sentiments would have in the cultural politics of the Weimar Republic.

Notes

1. *Sitzungsberichte der verfassunggebenden Preussischen Landesversammlung* (Berlin, 1921), 3 December 1919, pp. 7100-1; ibid., 5 December 1919, pp. 7392-93.
2. Quoted in *Sächsische Schulzeitung*, 15 October 1919: 428. See also Grünthal, *Reichsschulgesetz und Zentrumspartei*, pp. 80ff.
3. Quoted in *Sächsische Schulzeitung*, 3 December 1919: 545.
4. *Sächsische Schulzeitung*, 15 October 1919: 428.
5. *Zentralblatt für die gesamte Unterrichtsverwaltung in Preussen*, December 1919, no. 12: 663-64; *Gesetze und Verordnungen über das Volks- und Fortbildungs-Schulwesen im Freistaate Sachsen seit 1919* (Leipzig, 1927), p. 11; *Verordnungsblatt des Sächsischen Ministeriums für Volksbildung*, April 1920, no. 6: 57; ibid., March 1921, no. 4: 30.
6. *Lehrerzeitung für Ost- und Westpreussen*, 28 February 1920: 146-47; *Schlesische Schulzeitung*, 31 March 1920: 149.
7. *Sitzungsberichte der verfassunggebenden Preussischen Landesversammlung*, 18 February 1920, pp. 9479-81; Lohmann, *Das Schulprogramm*, pp. 35-36. See Gustav Menzel's article in *Lehrerzeitung für Ost- und Westpreussen*, 28 February 1920: 138; Erich Witte, *Die Elternräte* (Breslau, 1920), p. 12.
8. *Sächsische Schulzeitung*, 8 October 1919: 411; *Leipziger Lehrerzeitung*, 4 February 1920: 77-79.
9. Wilhelm Böhler, *Die Katholische Schulorganisation Deutschlands* (5th ed., Düsseldorf, 1926), pp. 3ff; Ulrich von Hehl, *Wilhelm Marx 1863-1946. Eine politische Biographie* (Mainz, 1987), pp. 62-66; Luise Wagner-Winterhager, *Schule und Eltern in der Weimarer Republik. Untersuchungen zur Wirksamkeit der Elternbeiräte in Preussen und der Elternräte in Hamburg 1918-1922* (Weinheim, 1972), pp. 236ff; Grünthal, *Reichsschulgesetz und Zentrumspartei*, pp. 70ff, 150.
10. Böhler, *Die katholische Schulorganisation*, pp. 7-14; Wilhelm Böhler, *Zum katholischen Schulideal* (Paderborn, 1922), pp. 12-15; Wagner-Winterhager, *Schule und Eltern*, pp. 232-33, 239-40. Among Catholic teachers there were mixed feelings toward the parents' councils and the Catholic School Organization—attitudes that can be traced to the issue of the clergy's supervision of school instruction. See *Westdeutsche Lehrerzeitung*, 31 January 1920: 53; ibid., 7 February 1920: 63; ibid., 15 January 1921: 37; ibid., 12 February 1921: 88.
11. Geheimes Staatsarchiv Preussischer Kulturbesitz [hereafter, GSA], Rep. 76 VII neu, Teil I, Sekt. 1B Gen., Nr. 2, Bd. 25, Blatt 83ff, Evangelischer Pressverband für Deutschland, *Elternbünde. Werden und Wachsen. Aufgaben und Einrichtung* (Berlin, n. d.), pp. 16ff; GSA, Rep. 76 VII neu, Teil I, Sekt. 1B Gen., Nr. 60, Bd. 1, Bl. 213, High Church Council to the minister of education, 20 May 1921.
12. *Deutsche Lehrerzeitung*, 20 September 1919: 416; ibid., 27 November 1920: 534; ibid., 27 December 1919: 581; ibid., 10 January 1920: 9.
13. Bezirksverband der christlichen Elternvereine, *Zehn Jahre christliche Elternbewegung in Leipzig* (Leipzig, 1930), pp. 9-11; *Sächsische Schulzeitung*, 20 April 1921: 231.
14. Quoted in Poste, *Schulreform in Sachsen*, p. 203.
15. *Lehrerzeitung für Ost- und Westpreussen*, 31 January 1920: 76; ibid., 7 February 1920: 97; ibid., 13 March 1920: 176-77; ibid., 27 March 1920: 203; *Schlesische Schulzeitung*, 18 February 1920: 94; ibid., 3 March 1920: 114-15; ibid., 9 June 1920; *Westfälische Schulzeitung*, 12 June 1920: 351-52; ibid., 10 July 1920: 419; *Schulblatt der Provinz Sachsen*, 12 May 1920: 188-89; GSA, Rep. 76 VII neu, Teil I, Sekt. 1B Gen., no. 2, vol. 24, two articles in *Reichsbote*, 3 May 1920, no. 185 and 8 August 1920, no. 361.
16. Ursula Bach, "Die Evangelische Stadtkirchengemeinde Neukölln und die Schulreform," in *Schulreform—Kontinuitäten und Brüche. Das Versuchsfeld Berlin-Neukölln*, ed. Gerd Radde et al. (Opladen, 1993), pp. 260-61; Stöhr, *Lehrer und Arbeiterbewegung*, pp. 228-29.

17. *Allgemeine Deutsche Lehrerzeitung*, Beiblatt, 18 August 1922: 205; Wagner-Winterhager, *Schule und Eltern in der Weimarer Republik*, p. 256.
18. *Sächsische Schulzeitung*, 20 April 1921: 230-31; ibid., 27 April 1921: 247-48. See also SHA, Nr. 13880/1, reports on the political-partisan contention in the elections of the parents' councils.
19. *Sächsische Schulzeitung*, 4 May 1921: 266; see also ibid., 28 January 1920: 53.
20. A complete statistical report of the results of the elections of the parents' councils in the elementary schools was not compiled during the Weimar years. The results of the elections in Berlin, Chemnitz, Dresden, and Leipzig can be found in Karl Foertsch, *Eltern an die Front! 10 Jahre Evangelischer Elternbund. Ein Beitrag zur Berliner Kultur- und Sozialgeschichte* (Berlin, 1930), pp. 39ff, 123; Walter Geissler, *Sechs Jahre Elternratswahlen an Sachsens Volksschulen* (Dresden, 1927), pp. 37-38. See also Poste, *Schulreform in Sachsen*, pp. 205-7.
21. *Sächsische Schulzeitung*, 29 June 1921: 390-91.
22. GSA, Rep. 76 VII neu, Teil I, Sekt. IB Gen., Nr. 60, Bd. 1, Bl. 312, Bl. 314, and Bl. 318, reports of the provincial district governments of Arnsberg, Cologne, and Düsseldorf, 7, 13 and 27 September 1921, respectively, to the Prussian Ministry of Education.
23. *Westfälische Schulzeitung*, 22 May 1920: 317; ibid., 5 June 1920: 342; ibid., 12 June 1920: 358; ibid., 26 June 1920: 382-85; ibid., 2 August 1920: 478-79; Böhler, *Zum katholischen Schulideal*, p. 25; Wagner-Winterhager, *Schule und Eltern*, pp. 219ff.
24. *Westfälische Schulzeitung*, 10 July 1920: 416-17.
25. GSA, Rep. 76 VII neu, Teil I, Sekt. IB Gen., Nr. 60, Bd. 1, Bl. 303ff., *Zentralblatt des Bundes der freien Schulgesellschaften Deutschlands*, October 1921, no. 10; Wagner-Winterhager, *Schule und Eltern*, pp. 206-8.
26. Günter Kehrer, "Soziale Klassen und Religion in der Weimarer Republik," in *Religions- und Geistesgeschichte der Weimarer Republik*, ed. Hubert Cancik (Düsseldorf, 1982), pp. 75ff.
27. Quoted in Wagner-Winterhager, *Schule und Eltern*, p. 204.
28. Wagner-Winterhager, *Schule und Eltern*, p. 209.
29. GSA, Rep. 76 VII neu, Teil I, Sekt. IB Gen., Nr. 2, Bd. 25, Bl. 50, Heinrich von Hähling, *Aufruf zum Kampfe für die freie konfessionelle Schule* (Paderborn, 1922), pp. 13, 36. See also Böhler, *Zum katholischen Schulideal*, p. 13.
30. GSA, Rep. 76 VII neu, Teil I, Sekt. IB Gen., Nr. 2, Bd. 24, Bl. 258, Minister of Education to the Independent Social Democratic club in Düsseldorf, 10 April 1920; *Zentralblatt für die gesamte Unterrichtsverwaltung in Preussen*, April 1920, no. 4: 278-79; ibid., June 1920, no. 6: 316.
31. GSA, Rep. 76 VII neu, Teil I, Sekt. IB Gen., Nr. 60, Bd. 1, Bl. 291, resolution adopted by the executive board of the League of Free School Societies on 25 June 1921, defending the use of school strikes; Bl. 312ff, reports on the school strikes submitted by the provincial district governments to the Ministry of Education in September 1921.
32. GSA, Rep. 76 VII neu, Teil I, Sekt.IB Gen., Nr. 60, Bd. 1, Bl. 346, minister of education to the Reich interior minister, 29 November 1921. See also Gustav Menzel's article in *Preussische Lehrerzeitung*, 7 January 1922: 1-2.
33. Poste, *Schulreform in Sachsen*, pp. 307-11. On the members of the German Communist Party who thought that the election campaigns for the parents' councils and the fight for secular schooling should be waged as a *Klassenkampf*, see Stöhr, *Lehrer und Arbeiterbewegung*, pp. 364-65.
34. *Allgemeine Deutsche Lehrerzeitung*, Beiblatt, 28 April 1922: 127-28; ibid., Beiblatt, 16 June 1922: 173; ibid., Beiblatt, 18 August 1922: 205.
35. Quoted in Stöhr, *Lehrer und Arbeiterbewegung*, p. 363.
36. GSA, Rep. 76 VII neu, Teil I, Sekt. IB Gen., Nr. 2, Bd. 25, Bl. 18ff and Bl. 28ff, two ministerial reports on the number of schoolchildren who did not receive religious instruction, and the teachers who declined to give it.

37. *Preussische Statistik*. Vol. 272: *Das Schulwesen in Preussen 1921 im Staate, in den Provinzen und Regierungsbezirken*, (Berlin, 1924), p. 8.
38. GSA, Rep. 76 VII neu, Teil I, Sekt. 1B Gen., Nr. 2, Bd. 25, Bl. 18ff, ministerial report on the schoolchildren and teachers who did not participate in religious instruction.
39. *Gesetze und Verordnungen über das Volks- und Fortbildungs-Schulwesen im Freistaate Sachsen seit 1919* (Leipzig, 1927), p. 4.
40. *Verhandlungen des Sächsischen Volkskammer*, 16 December 1919, pp. 2466-68.
41. *Verhandlungen des Sächsischen Volkskammer*, 16 December 1919, pp. 2473-75, 2494.
42. *Verhandlungen des Sächsischen Volkskammer*, 8 January 1920, pp. 2658-61.
43. Quoted in *Sächsische Schulzeitung*, 18 February 1920: 105.
44. SHA, Nr. 13365/5, Bl. 151.
45. *Verhandlungen des Sächsischen Volkskammer*, 8 January 1920, pp. 2653-56.
46. *Allgemeine Deutsche Lehrerzeitung*, 30 April 1920: 210-11.
47. *Leipziger Lehrerzeitung*, 24 March 1920: 208; *Verhandlungen des Sächsischen Volkskammer*, 8 January 1920, p. 2662.
48. *Sächsische Schulzeitung*, 18 February 1920: 111; *Allgemeine Deutsche Lehrerzeitung*, 16 July 1920: 339.
49. *Sächsische Schulzeitung*, 25 February 1920: 113.
50. SHA, Nr. 13365/5, district school inspectors' reports to the Ministry of Education.
51. SHA, Nr. 13365/5, Bl. 195, Superintendents Cordes and Zanker to the Ministry of Education, 1 May 1920; ibid., Bl. 201, Leipzig city magistrates to the Ministry of Education, 4 May 1920.
52. SHA, Nr. 13106/12, Bl. 56, magistrates of Pirna to the Ministry of Education, 1 March 1920; SHA, Nr. 13365/5, Bl. 216, Volkskirchlicher Laienbund to the Ministry of Education, 15 May 1920.
53. SHA, Nr. 13365/5, Bl. 219, Kircheninspektion for Oberlungwitz to the Ministry of Education, 17 May 1920; ibid., Bl. 221, the school inspector's decision, 5 May 1920; ibid., Bl. 222, the minister's decision, 10 June 1920.
54. SHA, Nr. 13365/5, Bl. 196, ministerial order of 15 May 1920.
55. *Leipziger Lehrerzeitung*, 18 August 1920: 472; *Sächsische Schulzeitung*, 1 September 1920: 426.
56. *Leipziger Lehrerzeitung*, 7 July 1920: 429-30.
57. SHA, Nr. 13365/6, Bl. 3, school principal to the district school inspector in Leipzig, 11 October 1920; ibid., Bl. 16, city magistracy of Klingenthal and district school inspector to the Ministry of Education, 19 October 1920; SHA, Nr. 13365/5, Bl. 304, mayor of Nossen to the Ministry of Education, 24 September 1920.
58. SHA, Nr. 13365/6, Bl. 1 and Bl. 2, Amtshauptmannschaft Pirna to the Ministry of Education, 15 October 1920, and the minister's reply of 27 October 1920; ibid., Bl. 13 and Bl. 15, Social Democratic club of Einsiedel to the Ministry of Education, 22 September 1920, and the minister's reply of 12 November 1920.
59. *Verhandlungen der Sächsischen Volkskammer*, 25 October 1920, pp. 4800-4801. For the minister's views on the continuation of religious instruction in the schools, see also Seyfert, *Das schulpolitische Programm*, pp. 31-33.
60. On this point, see SHA, Nr. 13365/6, Bl. 79, Ministry of Education to Reich interior minister, 15 January 1921.
61. SHA, Nr. 13365/6, Bl. 64, Leipzig district school inspector to the Ministry of Education, 29 November 1920; ibid., Bl. 68, Glauchau district school inspector to the Ministry of Education, 13 December 1920.
62. *Sächsische Schulzeitung*, 15 September 1920: 463.
63. SHA, Nr. 13365/5, Bl. 406b, proposal introduced in the Saxon Volkskammer on 14 October 1920.
64. SHA, Nr. 13365/6, Bl. 33 and Bl. 34, Pastor Wallenstein to the Ministry of Education, 2 November 1920, and the school inspector's report to the ministry, 12 November 1920.

The Politics of Education

65. Report on the synod in the *Leipziger Neueste Nachrichten*, cited in *Leipziger Lehrerzeitung*, 18 August 1920: 471.
66. SHA, Nr. 13365/5, Bl. 441, Superintendent Cordes to the Ministry of Education, 29 October 1920.
67. SHA, Nr. 13365/5, Bl. 452, city magistracy of Leipzig to the Ministry of Education, 12 January 1921.
68. Protest quoted in *Leipziger Lehrerzeitung*, 29 September 1920: 582.
69. SHA, Nr. 13365/5, Bl. 306, mayor of Eibenstock to the Ministry of Education, 23 September 1920; SHA, Nr. 13365/6, Bl. 50, League of Christian Parents' Associations of Leipzig to the Ministry of Education, 7 December 1920; ibid., Bl. 52 and Bl. 54, article from the *Pulsnitzer Wochenblatt*, 14 October 1920, and school inspector's report, November 1920.
70. SHA, Nr.13365/6, Bl. 158, church parish board in Gröba to the Ministry of Education, 15 October 1920; ibid., Bl. 160, leaflet entitled "Sittliche Lebenskunde oder konfessioneller Religionsunterricht?"
71. SHA, Nr. 13365/6, Bl. 165a, leaflet entitled "Über die Wahl von Elternräten"; ibid., Nr. 13365/7, Bl. 45, order of 28 December 1921 in the *Verordnungsblatt des Evangelisch-lutherischen Landeskonsistoriums*. See also *Sächsische Schulzeitung*, 10 November 1920: 581.
72. SHA, Nr. 13365/6, Bl. 135, the minister's order of 25 February 1921 on the religious freedom of teachers. See also *Sächsische Schulzeitung*, 10 November 1920: 580-81.
73. *Sächsische Schulzeitung*, 1 September 1920: 426; ibid., 15 September 1920: 463; ibid., 6 October 1920: 509-10.
74. *Sächsische Schulzeitung*, 17 November 1920: 605; see also ibid., 3 November 1920: 557.
75. SHA, Nr. 13365/6, article, "Zwickauer Thesen und Artikel 149 der Reichsverfassung," from *Evangelisch-lutherisches Volksblatt für Stadt und Land*, 1 November 1920, no. 45.
76. *Sächsische Schulzeitung*, 3 November 1920: 557-58.
77. *Sächsische Schulzeitung*, 1 September 1920: 426; ibid., 22 September 1920: 470.
78. *Sächsische Schulzeitung*, 22 September 1920: 469; ibid., 10 November 1920: 573.
79. *Sächsische Schulzeitung*, 22 September 1920: 470; ibid., 17 November 1920: 598.
80. SHA, Nr. 13365/5, Bl. 375ff, decision of the Reich Court of 4 November 1920.
81. *Sächsische Schulzeitung*, 8 December 1920: 667.
82. On the election campaign, see *Mitteilungen des Sächsischen Erzieherbundes*, November 1920, no. 2: 2-3; *Sächsische Schulzeitung*, 10 November 1920: 580; ibid., 24 November 1920: 614.
83. Benjamin Lapp, *Revolution from the Right: Politics, Class, and the Rise of Nazism in Saxony, 1919-1933* (Boston, 1997), pp. 44-46; Claus-Christian Szejnmann, *Nazism in Central Germany: The Brownshirts in 'Red' Saxony* (New York and Oxford, 1999), pp. 14-15.
84. See the discussion of this issue at the congress of the Saxon Teachers' Association in January 1921 in *Sächsische Schulzeitung*, 12 January 1921: 5.
85. SHA, Bezirksschulamt Dresden, Nr. 380, Bl. 20 and Bl. 23, Christian parents' association of Dresden-Stetzsch to the city magistracy and district school inspector, 31 May 1921; see also the same protest in the letter from members of the school board, 31 May 1921.
86. SHA, Nr. 13365/7, Bl. 169, survey on religious instruction conducted at the request of the state parliament.
87. Deutscher Lehrerverein, *Verhandlungen der 29. Vertreterversammlung vom 16.-18. Mai 1921 in Stuttgart* (Berlin, 1921), pp. 10-14; Schulz, *Der Leidensweg des Reichsschulgesetzes*, pp. 84-85.
88. Grünthal, *Reichsschulgesetz und Zentrumspartei*, pp. 83, 88-89. See also Hugo Stehkämper, ed., *Der Nachlass des Reichskanzlers Wilhelm Marx* (Cologne, 1968), vol. 2, pp. 409, 413.
89. For the influence of the Catholic episcopate on the change in the Center Party's understanding of the Weimar school compromise, see Grünthal, *Reichsschulgesetz und Zentrumspartei*, pp. 69, 86ff.
90. Wilhelm Offenstein, *Der Kampf um das Reichsschulgesetz* (Düsseldorf, 1925), pp. 21-26.

91. *Allgemeine Deutsche Lehrerzeitung*, 11 February 1921: 70; Walter Landé, *Die Schule in der Reichsverfassung* (Berlin, 1929), pp. 79ff.
92. *Allgemeine Deutsche Lehrerzeitung*, 27 May 1921: 229–30; *Lehrerzeitung für Ost- und Westpreussen*, 28 May 1921: 290; ibid., 18 June 1921: 328–31. For the text of the 1921 draft school law, see Schulz, *Der Leidensweg des Reichsschulgesetzes*, pp. 79ff.
93. *Sächsische Schulzeitung*, 8 June 1921: 329–30; *Lehrerzeitung für Ost- und Westpreussen*, 25 June 1921: 343–44; *Schulblatt der Provinz Sachsen*, 13 July 1921: 276–77; Tews, *Elternrecht und Staatsrecht*, pp. 5ff.
94. Georg Wolff, *Das Reich und die Schule* (Berlin, 1925), pp. 2–4.
95. *Allgemeine Deutsche Lehrerzeitung*, 3 June 1921: 245–46; ibid., 17 June 1921: 269–70.
96. Deutscher Lehrerverein, *Verhandlungen der 29. Vertreterversammlung*, pp. 20ff.
97. *Allgemeine Deutsche Lehrerzeitung*, 1 July 1921: 302; ibid., 29 July 1921: 350–51; ibid., 12 August 1921: 375; ibid., 16 September 1921: 429; *Sächsische Schulzeitung*, 15 June 1921: 357; ibid., 29 June 1921: 398; ibid., 6 July 1921: 419; Johannes Tews, *Der Reichsschulgesetzentwurf. Seine Gefahren für Volk, Staat und Schule* (Berlin 1921).
98. Quoted in *Allgemeine Deutsche Lehrerzeitung*, 30 September 1921: 449.
99. Offenstein, *Der Kampf um das Reichsschulgesetz*, pp. 98–104.
100. *Lehrerzeitung für Ost- und Westpreussen*, 21 January 1922: 51; ibid., 11 February 1922: 95–96; ibid., 4 March 1922: 139–40.
101. *Schulblatt der Provinz Sachsen*, 3 January 1922: 4–5; ibid., 1 March 1922: 109; ibid., 24 May 1922: 266; ibid., 31 May 1922: 276. For other confrontations between clergymen and teachers in the fight over the school law draft, see *Schlesische Schulzeitung*, 1 March 1922: 100; ibid., 26 April 1922: 193. On the oppositional tactics of right-wing Protestants, see August Grünweller, *Der Kampf um die Schule* (Neumünster, 1921), pp. 6–12.
102. *Schulblatt der Provinz Sachsen*, 20 September 1922: 427–28; ibid., 30 November 1921: 578. On the teachers' distrust of the church demands for "guarantees" in the school law, see also ibid., 24 May 1922: 265; *Lehrerzeitung für Ost- und Westpreussen*, 27 May 1922: 304; ibid., 9 September 1922: 467–68.
103. *Verhandlungen des Reichstages*, 23 January 1922, pp. 5481–86; ibid., 24 January 1922, pp. 5512–13.
104. Schulz, *Der Leidensweg des Reichsschulgesetzes*, pp. 112ff.
105. *Allgemeine Deutsche Lehrerzeitung*, 16 June 1922: 285; *Lehrerzeitung für Ost- und Westpreussen*, 22 July 1922: 391.
106. *Zeitschrift des Sächsischen Statistischen Landesamtes* 69 (1923): 96, 102.
107. *Preussische Statistik*. Vol. 272: *Das Schulwesen in Preussen 1921*, pp. 8–9, 12.
108. Rita Meyhöfer, *Gäste in Berlin? Jüdisches Schülerleben in der Weimarer Republik und im Nationalsozialismus* (Hamburg, 1996), pp. 62–72; Joseph Walk, *Jüdische Schule und Erziehung im Dritten Reich* (Frankfurt, 1991), pp. 22ff; Michael Brenner, *The Renaissance of Jewish Culture in Weimar Germany* (New Haven, 1996), pp. 59ff.
109. *Preussische Statistik*. Vol. 272: *Das Schulwesen in Preussen 1921*, pp. 11, 13–14.
110. See, for example, Becherer's statements on the common school for all children in *Schulblatt der Provinz Sachsen*, 5 April 1922: 173, and the discussion of the clergy's agitation against it at the congress of the East Prussian provincial teachers' association in February 1922 in *Lehrerzeitung für Ost- und Westpreussen*, 18 March 1922: 174.
111. *Allgemeine Deutsche Lehrerzeitung*, 26 May 1922: 260–61. See also *Preussische Lehrerzeitung*, 18 May 1922: 2.
112. *Jahrbuch des Deutschen Lehrervereins 1922* (Leipzig, 1922), pp. 133–34.
113. A poll of 529 Protestant, Catholic, and Jewish members in the Breslau chapter early in 1922 showed that 66.7 percent supported the community school, in comparison with 25.7 percent for the confessional school, 5.1 percent for the secular school, and 2.5 percent for the confessional school in cities and the community school in other localities where the school-age population was small. The reform of religious education in the public schools, that is, the elimination of confessional doctrines and the catechism, was

supported by 92 percent of these teachers in Breslau. *Allgemeine Deutsche Lehrerzeitung,* 14 April 1922: 182. In a poll of 339 members in the predominantly Protestant chapter of Halle, 72.5 percent supported the community school in comparison with 25.3 percent for the confessional school and less than 1 percent for the secular school. *Schulblatt der Provinz Sachsen,* 4 May 1922: 225.
114. Deutscher Lehrerverein, *Verhandlungen der 30. Vertreterversammlung am 5., 6. und 7. Juni 1922 in Hannover* (Berlin 1922), pp. 77–82.
115. *Verhandlungen der 30. Vertreterversammlung,* pp. 88–89.
116. *Verhandlungen der 30. Vertreterversammlung,* p. 127.

Chapter 4

EDUCATIONAL REFORMERS AND THE MODERN SCHOOL IN THE REPUBLICAN STATE

The progressivist pedagogues sustained their optimism and commitment to educational reforms throughout the political turmoil and economic distress of the early 1920s. The postwar years were stressful times for German elementary schoolteachers. A large number of them had served in the army in World War I and were now coping with wounds, shattered nerves, and the psychological effects of combat.[1] The hyperinflation of 1922–23 led to hardship and a decline in the standard of living in the households of teachers. With bewilderment and anger, they saw the real value of their salaries fall precipitously as prices skyrocketed from one month to another. Untenured young teachers worked under the threat of a layoff at the end of 1923 and in the early months of 1924, when the Reich and state governments adopted fiscal policies to stabilize the economy by cutting the personnel costs in the public administration. Empowered by the Enabling Act passed by the Reichstag, the government ordered on 27 October 1923 a sharp reduction in the size of the civil service in the Reich and federal states. The tremors of political violence in Germany during these years were also felt in the elementary schools. School life was disrupted in Upper Silesia during the intense conflicts between Germans and Polish nationalists in the plebiscite campaign and during the Polish uprisings in 1921. When the Reich government responded to working-class disturbances in Saxony by declaring a state of emergency in October 1923 and deposing the new coalition cabinet of Social Democrats and Communists led by Erich Zeigner, the troops who marched to Dresden and occupied public buildings manhandled and arrested several elementary schoolteachers.[2]

The physical and emotional stress in their own personal and professional lives did not keep teachers from being concerned about the welfare of the schoolchildren. Dependent on export markets for its industries, Saxony was hit hard by the economic recession after the war, and unemployment there was higher than the average rate for Germany. The deprivation of working-class families could be seen in the classrooms in industrial areas, where children suffered from malnutrition, anemia, and an outbreak of tuberculosis. The Leipzig teachers' association drew public attention to the poverty of working-class families in the city by conducting a survey, which disclosed the undernourishment of children who came to school without breakfast or had no warm midday meal. Poorly fed and underweight pupils grew weary quickly in the classroom, lacked mental alertness, and were unable to concentrate on schoolwork.[3] Teachers in Saxony appealed to the local and state authorities to establish rest homes for children with lung disease and to provide school meals and warm clothing for children in need. Teachers in Leipzig, Chemnitz, and other cities organized children's relief drives to raise money through appeals in the press, musical recitals, and dramatic performances. Teachers and parents worked together in relief actions. Volunteers mended old clothing, sewed new clothing, and repaired shoes. Mothers prepared and served school meals provided with funds from local donors and the Quakers in America. In some cities the teachers prevailed upon the municipal government to appoint school physicians for the medical examination of schoolchildren and to open dental clinics for them.[4]

The political instability of postwar Germany notwithstanding, the progressive education movement thrived and brought many changes to elementary school life in the cities. Wherever the Social Democratic and German Democratic Parties gained governmental power, schoolteachers found considerable support for the new pedagogy and other reforms. The education ministers in Prussia and Saxony in the early Weimar years were sympathetic to the aspirations of the progressivist pedagogues for more professional self-determination vis-à-vis the old traditions of bureaucratic regimentation and the reign of imperious school rectors. A system of collegial school governance (*collegiale Schulleitung*) was introduced in both states. The Transitional School Law of 1919 in Saxony abolished the office of the school rector (*Rektorat*), which had been customarily held for an unlimited term of appointment. The school principal, now bearing the less awesome title of *Schulleiter*, was elected by the local school board for a renewable term of three years. If a school had more than five teachers, the teachers' collegium was granted the right to nominate a person for this office by a majority vote and to submit this recommendation to the school board. The law widened the scope of pedagogical autonomy by permitting the teachers' collegium to discuss the lesson plans and other matters related to internal school affairs and to make decisions by a vote at meetings led by the school principal.[5]

In Prussia shortly thereafter, Haenisch demonstrated his own "courage to experiment" and his firm intention "to create a relationship of mutual trust between the big teachers' organizations and the government."[6] He dismantled the old hierarchy in the elementary schools by abolishing the requirement of a special examination for appointment to the office of school principal and by introducing collegial school governance. Although his decree of 20 September 1919 did not go as far as to make the office of school principal an elective position, as the reformers in the German Teachers' Association demanded, he supported their striving for more autonomy and responsibility in their professional work. "It corresponds to the spirit of our time to emancipate hitherto restrained energies in all areas of public life by the extension of self-governance," the minister declared in his decree. Under this regulation, the teachers' collegium was authorized to make decisions on internal school affairs. The office of school principal was divested of its supervisory power; the decree specified that the school principal acted as the chairman of the teachers' collegium when he visited classes "in order to become informed about school life." The school inspector was now the immediate supervisory authority over tenured teachers.[7]

The constellation of political power in the federal states and the entry of Social Democrats and German Democrats into the school administration do not alone explain the progress of educational reform in the Weimar years. With unflagging energy and optimistic idealism, the progressivist pedagogues worked for the democratization of the educational system and introduced the principles and methods of the active-learning school into practice. The opposition of the traditionalists in the Catholic and Protestant Churches and the Secondary Schoolteachers' Association (Deutscher Philologenverband) did not intimidate or dishearten them. The educational reforms in the early 1920s were to a large extent the achievement of elementary schoolteachers in the German Democratic and Social Democratic political camps.

"Open the Path to All Who Are Capable"

The German Teachers' Association revived the school reform movement in the closing years of the war with the publication of Johannes Tews's *Die deutsche Einheitsschule* in 1916. Commissioned by the association's executive board to write this book, Tews defended the demand for a unified school system adopted at the teachers' congress in June 1914, and proposed an agenda of school reforms for the postwar years in the name of social justice and equality of opportunity. The subtitle of his pamphlet—"open the path to all who are capable"—became the motto for school reformers who demanded a more democratic and equitable educational system in Germany in the aftermath of a long war that was claiming a heavy toll on human life. In 1917 Social Democratic and left-wing liberal deputies in the Reichstag called on the Reich chancellor to summon a school conference after the war to discuss the reorganization of the educational system and to advise the government on the preparation of a new school law.

Although the National School Conference (*Reichsschulkonferenz*) did not convene until June 1920, the reformers' demands were widely publicized from 1916 onward. Johannes Tews, Richard Seyfert, and other reformers proposed the abolition of the *Vorschulen*, the preparatory schools and elementary-level classes connected to the secondary schools, and the instruction of children of all class and religious backgrounds in the common school for a period of six years. The separation of pupils on diverse educational paths would begin at the earliest at the age of twelve rather than the age of nine, when German children generally entered secondary school at that time. Tews called the first six grades of the elementary school, which would be obligatory for all children, the *Grundschule* or basic school because it provided the foundation of learning leading up to all types of secondary schools. The elementary and secondary schools would no longer function in isolation from each other as two separate worlds, different in their purpose, ethos, and methods and in the social origins of their clientele. The reformers assumed that the nine-year duration of the secondary schools would be shortened by one year. Tews proposed the creation of a new kind of secondary school (*Aufbauschule*), which would admit pupils after the completion of seven years of elementary schooling. This secondary school, with a six-year course of study, would give gifted pupils who went through the upper grades of the elementary school the chance to take the examination for the *Abitur* and to have access to a university education.[8]

To defuse the criticism of the conservatives, the reformers stated that they were not striving for a mechanistic uniformity and the elimination of the diverse types of schools in secondary education (*Gymnasium, Realgymnasium,* and *Oberrealschule*). They wanted to connect "organically" the elementary school and the institutions of secondary education and to widen the passageway to secondary and higher education so that all children would receive an education commensurate with their abilities, regardless of their social origins. The *Aufbauschule* would have equality with the older types of secondary schools in respect to the eligibility of its students to attend the universities. In contrast to the emphasis on Latin and Greek in the *Gymnasium*, the curriculum of the new high school would focus on the culture of Germany and modern languages. Tews's wartime pamphlet did not digress into a debate over which secondary school curriculum provided the best education for most young people and the free professions. His position was clearly evident, however, when he stated that the "overestimation of the benefits" of learning the two ancient languages in the secondary schools had a detrimental effect on German society and culture.[9]

Aware that structural changes alone would not eliminate the socially inequitable nature of the traditional educational system, Tews wanted to remove the economic impediments that prevented intelligent youths from families with little means from attending the institutions of higher education.

He proposed the abolition of tuition fees for the secondary schools and universities and the provision of stipends from public funds to cover the living expenses of lower-class students. Anticipating the financial objections that would be raised, Tews pointed out that the state's present expenditures for the secondary schools and universities made instruction there almost free since the fees paid by the students represented only a very small portion of the costs of their education. To prevent the secondary schools from being overcrowded by pupils who performed poorly or eventually dropped out, he proposed more stringent conditions for admissions and higher standards in the entrance examinations. Tews did not think that the secondary school system could be based on the one pillar of intellectual merit and ignore the will of middle- and upper-class parents who had the social ambition and financial means to educate their children for professional and business life. To limit the number of less worthy applicants, he recommended that students of average ability and achievements be required to pay the full costs of their education.[10]

Although the reformers in the German Teachers' Association were proposing the obligatory attendance of all children in the common school, they did not want their ideas to be confused with state coercion and an educational monopoly of the state. Tews was especially sensitive to this issue. He considered education in the public schools to be desirable for all children, but he also believed that the state should grant "full freedom" to parents who wanted to educate their sons and daughters in another way. Private activity had to be allowed in the sphere of education "for reasons of self-determination and civic freedom," he wrote. "The free public school has nothing to fear from the competition of the private school" if the state improved its schools through the necessary public expenditures. Since private schools required substantial costs that only the wealthy could afford, he thought, they were not likely to spread in Germany, with its strong tradition of public education, as long as the public schools retained the confidence of the people. He held the anticlerical school policy of the Radicals in the Third Republic responsible for the development of the extensive system of private Catholic schools in France.[11]

After the November Revolution, the progressivist pedagogues emphasized the nature and requirements of the new democratic state when they framed their arguments for school reforms. Georg Winkler declared that Germany's stratified educational system, built according to the principles and purposes of the old "class state," had lost its raison d'être in the republic. He wrote: "All people have the same right to acquire an education for which they are destined by their mental faculties and innate talents. This principle must be the criterion for the organization of the school system in the democratic state." A genuine democracy, Fritz Gansberg stated, would not separate children on the basis of social class in the early years of schooling and nurture arrogance and social elitism in a privileged group of children. The tracking of pupils by ability could be done with greater justice and certainty in the later years of elementary schooling.[12]

When elementary school pedagogues argued for the establishment of a new kind of secondary school in 1919-20, they criticized the curriculum of the *Gymnasium* more sharply than Tews had done. Gansberg observed how grammar and vocabulary drills in classical language instruction kept philologists in the secondary schools from adopting modern pedagogical practices. He contended that experiential learning in the elementary school developed a ten- or eleven-year-old child's curiosity, imagination, and ability to discover and think for him- or herself more effectively than the traditional methods of instruction in the lower level of the *Gymnasium*.[13] The reformers in the German Teachers' Association were not bent on demolishing the classical secondary school. They were challenging the sacrosanct view of the traditionalists that the study of ancient and foreign languages should be "the only and exclusive way to higher education." They believed that "the dominance" of the *Gymnasium* "must be broken" and that a new secondary school of "equal standing," built upon the curriculum of the elementary school, should be established.[14]

In 1920 the Reich interior minister introduced in the National Assembly the first bill for the reform of elementary education. The proposed law designated the first four grades of the elementary school as the *Grundschule*, the foundation upon which the secondary schools rested. A clause allowed the states to extend the basic school beyond four years and opened up the possibility of lengthening its duration to six years, as the reformers advocated. The draft law mandated the dissolution of public and private preparatory schools—beginning with the first grade in the school year of 1920-21 or 1921-22 at the latest and reaching completion in 1924-25—and promised compensation from public funds to the owners of the private schools. The closing of private preparatory schools could be postponed up to the school year of 1929-30 if an earlier shutdown would cause material hardship for the teachers, but the total number of their pupils during this time could not exceed the previous enrollment.[15]

The Basic School Law of 28 April 1920 was passed in the National Assembly without difficulty because the Center Party saw no threat to confessional interests in this reform measure. The new legislation did not touch the confessional character of the elementary schools and deferred to a subsequent school law the settlement of this hotly contested issue. Moreover, the defenders of the preparatory schools were an isolated rear-guard faction of German Nationalists. The Basic School Law had a greater impact on the heavily Protestant areas of Prussia and Hamburg, where the preparatory schools were concentrated, than in other parts of Germany. In Saxony, the Transitional School Law of 1919 had already dismantled the differentiated system of elementary schooling built on the class structure of society by requiring all children, irrespective of the income of their parents, to attend the common school in their local district. The Social Democrats and German Democrats supported this bill as the first step in the reorganization of the school system. They expected that a more comprehensive school law would soon extend the duration of the basic school to six years, and looked ahead to the coming National School Conference to provide the momentum for reforms on a grander scale.[16] Elementary schoolteachers in Prussia, who had opposed the preparatory schools for many years, greeted the first enactment of Reich legislation for the schools all the more enthusiastically because it constituted "the first breach in the old system of schools based on social class."[17]

Unhappy over the passage of the Basic School Law, traditionalists in the secondary schools fretted that the National Assembly had ignored their objection that the *Volksschule*, devoted to the task of providing the populace with the rudimentary skills of reading, writing, and arithmetic, could not also prepare a selected group of pupils for the rigor of instruction in the *Gymnasium*. They had rejected the proposal for a unified school system before the war and had intensified their opposition to it since the publication of Tews's book in 1916. After the November Revolution, most members of the Secondary Schoolteachers' Association supported the bourgeois conservative German People's and German National People's Parties and responded to the new parliamentary democracy with an ambivalent accommodation or with disdain and hysterical pessimism.[18] The secondary schoolteachers saw Tews's blueprint for school reforms as a threat to the structural arrangements that were designed to preserve traditional culture in Germany and the hegemony of the bourgeoisie over the establishments of secondary and higher education. They assumed a leading role in the fight against a unified school system. Kurt Kesseler, a secondary schoolteacher in Berlin, accused the progressivist pedagogues of striving to "dethrone philology and the philologists." He contended that the leveling and egalitarian tendencies of the reformers' proposals threatened the tradition of cultivation and academic learning in Germany.[19] Secondary schoolteachers organized a protest demonstration in Leipzig in February 1920 to oppose a plan for the reorganization of the educational system that the Saxon Ministry of Education was drawing up. In a leaflet warning parents and former students that the secondary school was "in danger," they stated that lengthening the *Grundschule* to six years would amputate the lower grades from the secondary school and lead ultimately to a culturally shallow educated class. In such a "mutilated" secondary school, the future leaders of Germany's economic and cultural life would no longer receive a thorough education.[20]

In the fight against educational reform, conservative secondary schoolteachers found many allies in the university faculties. The traditionalists feared that the connection of elementary and secondary schools into a single system would not only shorten the course of study in the existing nine-year secondary schools but also produce a massive influx of lower-class pupils into the schools of higher learning. They defended separate and distinct educational paths for children of different social classes in the earliest years of schooling. The cultivation of the habits of intellectual discipline indispensable for academic study would be weaker, they argued, if the instruction of the classical languages was put off to the age of twelve rather than beginning at the age of nine in the *Gymnasium*. A nine-year-long course of study in the secondary schools was necessary to prepare the pupils sufficiently for study in the universities. They predicted that if the reforms were implemented, the academic performance of students in the universities would decline because young people entering from a six-year secondary school would lack the mass of factual knowledge, intellectual discipline, and aesthetic cultivation required for higher education. Ferdinand Jakob Schmidt, a professor in Berlin, lamented that the secondary schools and universities would be "degraded to one-sided training institutes for the acquisition of useful knowledge" and would no longer educate the bearers of high culture or provide a genuine ethos of academic learning.[21] These apprehensions led the representatives of the university faculties attending a meeting of the Corporation of German Universities (Verband der deutschen Hochschulen) in Halle in February 1920 to issue a strong public statement in opposition to the creation of a six-year secondary school, the incorporation of teacher education into the universities, and other trends of democratic "leveling" and "mediocrity" in the reform movement. A professor from Berlin, Eduard Spranger, insisted that the character of the philosophical faculty of the university, as a body devoted to "pure scholarship," must be preserved and that the professional education for elementary school teaching should take place in institutes located outside of and without any affiliation to the universities.[22]

The conservatives in the educated elite had every right to speak out on the questions of the duration of secondary schooling and the standards of admission to the university. However, as Fritz Ringer pointed out, the mandarins "failed to disentangle the problem of academic standards from the whole complex of social prejudices that had grown up around the ideal of classical 'cultivation.'"[23] They refused to admit that there were any imperfections or injustices in the old educational system. Instead, they parried Tews's criticism of the inequality of opportunity for secondary education by claiming that the reformers were advocating a process of admission on the basis of a "controlled selection of the capable" and a "one-sided" standard of intelligence without any consideration for the wish of the parents, family heritage and traditions, and personal character and values.[24]

The traditionalists' class bias and defense of social privilege were unveiled when they argued for a rigid distinction between the elementary and secondary schools, each functioning as a self-contained unit. Wilhelm Hartnacke, a school official in Dresden during the republic, and Friedrich Wilhelm Foerster, a university professor in Munich, defended the "healthy and necessary" stratification of the existing school system by stressing the different cultural and social upbringing, intellectual abilities, and educational needs of children in the propertied and working classes. They thought that each type of school had the educational goals and curriculum appropriate to the socioeconomic and cultural backgrounds of its pupils. Stressing the relationship of the home environment and the learning ability of children, Hartnacke contended that children in middle-class families received more cultural nurturing in the preschool years than the children of poor parents, and on the average had higher intellectual aptitudes and made quicker progress in school. He berated the partisans of the active-learning school for viewing the differences in the ability and achievements of children "as the result of the social guilt of the ruling classes rather than as the impediments of heredity and fate to the fulfillment of the dream of human equality."[25]

The traditionalists believed that the changes proposed under the name of the unified school system would unsettle the old social hierarchy and foster restlessness and aspirations for social mobility within the lower classes. Foerster deplored the "extreme and artificial pushing of talented individuals of the populace upward into the highest levels of education." To seat children of proletarian and bourgeois families on the same school bench would merely stir up envy and resentment on one side and breed a sense of superiority on the other side. The reformers' expectations of the reconciliation of the "two nations" and other social benefits from the basic school were based on assumptions that stood "in stark contradiction to the certain fundamental truths of human knowledge." In no way did these "illusory sociopolitical effects" justify "venturing on such a big experiment," as Tews was proposing.[26] The conservative academics were convinced that the reasons driving the reformers to abolish the preparatory schools were "not pedagogical but socialist in nature." Schmidt declared that it was "dangerous utopianism" to try "to achieve the social leveling of ranks and classes by the compulsory means of the egalitarian school."[27]

Before the National School Conference convened, the lines between the traditionalists and progressivists in the teaching profession were sharply drawn. Reformers in the German Teachers' Association discerned behind the rhetoric of the philologists an elitist struggle against the democratization of German society and paranoid fears of losing social prestige. A progressivist pedagogue in Leipzig observed: "What separates the secondary schoolteachers from us and what leads them to stand in the way of our struggle for the improvement of popular education are not differences in pedagogical views but reasons related to class and politics." The traditionalists rejected any organizational and curricular ties between the secondary and elementary schools because they feared that these changes would tear down the walls separating the educated elite from other classes in society and would "shatter their old privileges." Tews did not deny the relationship between home environment and school achievement but took a less deterministic view of the education and development of working-class children. He detected in Hartnacke's objections to the unified educational system "a crass claim to privilege for those who are socially and economically better placed."[28]

The opening of the National School Conference in the Reichstag building on 11 June 1920 was not the most favorable moment for the reformers. The swing to the political right in the recent Reichstag election in May affected the atmosphere of this assembly. While the Social Democratic and German Democratic Parties had lost ground at the polls, the German Nationalists had increased their share of the popular vote, and the Center Party had maintained its bedrock of electoral support. The 36 representatives of the German Teachers' Association at the National School Conference sensed that the timing was not to their advantage, but they did not succumb to fatalism. They were determined to work in the committees set up for the deliberation of specific school questions with confidence in the weight of their ideas, the power of their arguments, and their experience as professional educators. The conference gave them a national platform whereby the people and government officials would hear their voices.[29]

Envisioned at first as an assembly of some 50 school reformers, the National School Conference turned out to be a massive gathering of more than 600 educators and representatives of political parties and interest groups. The list of invited participants grew when organizations involved in cultural politics lobbied State Secretary Schulz in the Reich Interior Ministry for a greater representation. When the leaders of the German Teachers' Association finally saw the published list of participants, they noticed unhappily the sizable contingents of Catholics and secondary school teachers.[30] Political divisions affected the school conference's deliberations from the start. Representatives of the universities, secondary schools, and Catholic and Protestant parents' organizations sat on the right side of the chamber. Members of the German Teachers' Association took their seats to the left side of the center, and further to the left were the representatives of Socialist organizations. The results of the recent Reichstag election had given the opponents of school reform greater assertiveness and confidence. Objecting to Schulz's plan to record the views of the majority by holding a series of votes on the final day of the conference, Wilhelm Marx, a Center Party leader and the chairman of the Catholic School Organization, contended that the opinions of pedagogues who were invited by an office in the Reich Interior Ministry could not be taken as a reflection of the views of the nation. Reinhard Mumm, a Protestant churchman and German Nationalist politician, stated gloatingly that the vote of participants at the school conference had importance only in relation to the strength of the ideological group that they represented.[31]

In the deliberations of the National School Conference, traditionalists in the secondary schools and universities put up a strong fight against the "threats" that the establishment of a six-year basic school and a new six-year secondary school would pose to the university as a place of *Bildung* and *Kultur*. Rudolf Erzgräber, the director of a secondary school in Pomerania, protested that the Basic School Law had been enacted too hastily. He defended the tracking of children early in their schooling and complained that the parties in the National Assembly had ignored the secondary schoolteachers' view that the preparatory school provided "a better selection" of pupils for the secondary schools than did the *Volksschule*. He demanded a revision of the Basic School Law so that able children could be taught in separate classes and could enter secondary school after the third year. When Johannes Tews rose to deliver an address, Paul Mellmann, the chairman of the German Secondary Schoolteachers' Association, interrupted the proceedings to protest the decision to invite Tews to speak on the organization of a unified school system. Parading his elitism and snobbishness, another philologist berated the elementary schoolteachers for having the audacity to propose radical changes for the secondary schools without having been educated there. Professors from Heidelberg, Jena, and Marburg joined the debate in defense of the nine-year secondary school and argued that the proposed reforms would lead to the admission of poorly prepared students to the universities.[32]

Intent on preserving the hierarchy of social prestige within their profession, secondary schoolteachers and university professors at the National School Conference fought to keep *Lehrerbildung*, the professional training for elementary school teaching, out of the universities. The attack opened before the school conference began its discussion of the reformers' proposal to eliminate the nonacademic institutions for teacher education (*Präparandenanstalten* and *Lehrerseminare*) and to upgrade it to a university-level course of study. In March a group of professors at the University of Berlin signed a declaration in opposition to this reform. For tactical reasons they waited until the eve of the school conference to distribute it to the political press and the conference participants. They claimed that the appointment of faculty members for teacher education would bring "inferior personnel" into the universities, and "the inevitable results" would include "a noticeable decline in the general level of German universities."[33] Eduard Spranger, the professors' spokesman at the school conference, contended that the university had always given primacy to the education of scholars and could be "a professional school only for secondary schoolteachers." He warned the reformers that the professors would "fight for the preservation of the academic atmosphere [of the universities] as lions." Ernst Troeltsch, another professor from Berlin, criticized the "artificial egalitarianism and schematism" of the idea of educating prospective elementary and secondary schoolteachers as members of one profession in the same institutions.[34]

The reformers rejected the social distinctions and exclusiveness that the traditionalists sought to preserve through a differentiated system of professional training—the universities for educators in the *Gymnasium* and the nonacademic teachers' training seminaries for pedagogues in the *Volksschule*. Speaking for the German Teachers' Association, Carl Louis Pretzel refuted the charge that the reformers were striving for "a superficial mechanistic uniformity" in teacher education, and defended the education of prospective elementary schoolteachers in the universities for the sake of their own development as cultivated human beings. He criticized the present course of study for secondary schoolteachers in the universities for its neglect of the disciplines of psychology and pedagogy. To Spranger and other professors, who insisted that the universities must pursue only scholarly research and could not incorporate institutes for teacher education, Pretzel replied that learning was not an end in itself but "must serve life." The universities could not maintain their claim to be places for the expansion of knowledge if they continued to neglect research on child and adolescent psychology and on the education and socialization of the youth.[35]

The conclusion of the National School Conference diminished whatever influence its deliberations could have had on the making of school legislation. In the committees set up to discuss specific questions, the representatives of the German Teachers' Association worked with earnestness and won the support of other forward-looking participants. The *Leitsätze* or guiding principles for the reorganization of the school system submitted by these committees for a formal vote in the plenum came close to the reformers' own proposals. They were elated and thought that once these principles were adopted, it would be impossible for any Reich government to file away and ignore the results of the school conference's deliberations. In the final days of the school conference, however, secondary schoolteachers and university professors formed a coalition with Catholic and Protestant defenders of the confessional elementary school to block a vote on the *Leitsätze* in the full assembly. A motion that no vote should take place in the final meeting on 18 June was hastily introduced and passed.[36]

The opposition of the right-wing secondary schoolteachers to a unified school system made the reformers all the more vigilant when reports circulated in the winter of 1920-21 that the implementation of the Basic School Law had come to a standstill in Prussia. The law did not specify how the owners of the private preparatory schools would be compensated from public funds after the closing of these schools. When the negotiations between the Reich and Prussian governments on the question of sharing the costs led to no settlement, Minister President Braun informed the Reich chancellor in February 1921 that it would not be possible for Prussia to execute this provision of the law as long as the Reich did not appropriate funds for this purpose.[37] The opponents of the four-year *Grundschule* were exultant. In Prussia, close to half of the children entering the secondary schools had been instructed in the three-year preparatory schools or privately tutored. Since the Basic School Law did not shorten the nine-year curriculum of the secondary schools, the obligatory attendance of the basic school meant the addition of one more year to the length of schooling. In a backhanded attempt to defeat the purpose of the law, conservatives in the Secondary Schoolteachers' Association demanded the opening of accelerated learning classes (*Förderklassen*) for a selection of able children in the basic schools so that the pupils on this fast track could be admitted to secondary school after only three years of instruction. In the meantime, parents with financial means were enrolling their children in private preparatory schools in complete disregard for the letter and spirit of the law.[38]

Elementary schoolteachers in Prussia suspected that the Reich government's financial situation would be used by the opponents of the Basic School Law as a pretext for delaying its execution. They feared that public confidence in the possibility of achieving school reforms in the future would be undermined if the republic's first important national school legislation was not implemented scrupulously.[39] The representatives of the chapters of the Prussian Teachers' Association held a special meeting in Berlin on 17 February 1921 in response to disturbing reports that public preparatory schools in some cities were accepting pupils for the first grade and that the enrollments in the private preparatory schools were expanding.[40] Three members of its executive board met with officials in the Reich Interior Ministry in the following month to contest the legality of an order, issued by the Prussian Ministry of Education on 2 March, that permitted the continuation of the preparatory schools up to 1924-25.[41] Thereafter, the Reich Interior Ministry drafted guidelines for the proper execution of the Basic School Law so that the Prussian school administration had to cancel its regulation. A new order on 13 April required the closing of the first-year classes in all public preparatory schools in 1921 and the elimination of the other classes year by year without interruption.[42]

The Secondary Schoolteachers' Association was not reconciled to the compulsory four-year basic school. The fear that it jeopardized the nine-year curriculum of the secondary schools was reinforced when Hamburg shortened the length of secondary school attendance to eight years. At their convention in Jena in 1921, the philologists vowed to fight any change in the duration of the *Gymnasium* and demanded the creation of a separate track of classes in the basic schools for a select group of children.[43] At a meeting of the Berlin municipal council, the delegation of the German People's Party introduced a motion on 6 April 1922, urging the magistracy to set up accelerated learning classes in the first three years of elementary schooling for the more intelligent pupils so that they could enter secondary school a year earlier. On 3 July, German Democrats and Social Democrats in the city council voted down this proposal.[44]

The reformers in the German Teachers' Association fought the movement to create separate accelerated learning classes within the basic schools in Berlin, Chemnitz, Magdeburg, and other cities. They thought that tracking would institutionalize a division of social classes in elementary education and undermine the social purposes of the common school. Georg Wolff stated: "Assembled in the special classes would probably be the children of the wealthier families, who can receive immense family help and support in their school work and make themselves noticeable by their articulateness." Two elementary schoolteachers in the Prussian Landtag, German Democratic deputy Ferdinand Hoff and Social Democratic deputy Waldemar Holtz, contended that this proposal was a reactionary ploy to "sabotage" the Basic School Law.[45] In the press, the progressivist pedagogues criticized the traditionalists in the secondary schools for defining the function of primary education too narrowly and for demanding that the basic school provide "artificially premature" intellectual training as quickly as possible. They stated that ability grouping should be institutionalized in the later years of schooling, not in the first three or four years. Striving to develop all of the faculties of the child in the active-learning school, they could see no benefit in a system that sorted out children in the earliest years of schooling and questioned whether a mental aptitude test at that young age could provide a basis of selection that would prove satisfactory for everyone. They believed that the different talents and levels of ability of the pupils in a classroom should be handled through pedagogical methods rather than through the creation of a separate track for a selected group of children.[46]

Right-wing secondary schoolteachers suffered a defeat in their fight against the basic school. The guidelines for the execution of the Basic School Law issued by the Reich Interior Ministry on 18 July 1921 forbade the creation of separate classes for the purpose of preparing a select group of children for admission to secondary school in three years. Otto Boelitz, a secondary schoolteacher by profession and a member of the German People's Party, had no other choice but to comply with this interpretation of the law when he became minister of education in Prussia. In March 1923 he issued a directive prohibiting municipalities from creating special classes in the basic schools for the purpose of accelerating admission to the secondary schools.[47] Swallowing their disappointment with Boelitz's policy, right-wing secondary school educators shifted to another tactic in their fight against the school reforms. Speaking in the Prussian Landtag in May 1923, Wilhelm Steffens of the German People's Party lamented that Germany was sinking into a "cultural crisis." "Wherever we look, in our school, in all educational institutions in the country, we have the painful impression that our cultural level has already fallen," he said.[48]

The reformers attained another goal in their plan for a unified school system in the spring of 1922, when the first six-year secondary schools (*Aufbauschulen*) were opened in Prussia, in 47 buildings that once housed the preparatory schools and seminaries for training elementary schoolteachers. In its directive on the new secondary school issued on 18 February 1922, the Ministry of Education gave official endorsement to the idea of linking the elementary schools more closely to the system of secondary education. Officials in the ministry expected the *Aufbauschule* to serve as a bridge over the chasm that had separated working-class people and the educated class in Germany for centuries. Its curriculum, which emphasized German cultural studies, made the new secondary school more a "natural continuation of the elementary school" than the *Gymnasium* could be. Pupils were admitted to it after the completion of seven years of instruction in the elementary schools. The value of this educational foundation was enhanced when the ministry granted the graduates of the six-year *Aufbauschule* a degree equal to that of the nine-year *Gymnasium* and entitled them to take the examination for the *Abitur* and to enter the university.[49] The Social Democrats had high expectations of the social impact of this reform and wanted to open *Aufbauschulen* in the big cities. Their model was the high school in Berlin-Neukölln under the direction of Fritz Karsen, whose enrollment consisted of many youths from working-class families. By the end of the decade, most of the 112 *Aufbauschulen* in Prussia were located in small towns and had a predominantly lower-middle-class enrollment.[50]

The introduction of the obligatory four-year *Grundschule* can be called one of the achievements of the reformers during the Weimar years. By 1923–24, the closing of the public preparatory schools had been completed. The number of children who were taught outside the basic schools declined in the following years, despite the fact that the amendment of the Basic School Law in February 1927 opened up the possibility of a further postponement of the closing of private preparatory schools. Under the amended law, the complete closing of private preparatory schools could not take place before financial compensation for the owners and teachers was regulated by national legislation and paid. In most of the federal states, the introduction of the four-year basic school was carried out without difficulties. The private preparatory schools were predominantly concentrated in Hamburg, Prussia, and Württemberg, and were attended overwhelmingly by girls. In Prussia in 1921–22, 19,092 boys and 33,475 girls were taught in private preparatory schools; five years later, the corresponding figures were 788 boys and 12,507 girls. By 1930–31, the number of children instructed in private preparatory schools in Germany had fallen to 10,894, a very small figure in comparison with the total enrollment of 7.6 million children in the elementary schools.[51]

The Active-Learning School and Civic Education

The founding of the republic gave the active-learning school movement a new sense of purpose. The values of ethical socialism and political democracy informed the philosophy of education and practices of the progressivist pedagogues, many of whom either joined or stood close to the Social

Democratic and German Democratic Parties. In addition to the goal of child development, they now related the principles and methods of the new pedagogy to the requirements of civic education in the republican state. They were convinced that the active-learning school contributed more to the civic and moral education of the youth than the traditional school could do because it gave the pupils the opportunity to put cooperativeness, tolerance, and other civic virtues into practice. To nurture in the pupils a sense of obligation to work for the good of the whole, the teachers turned each class in the active-learning school into a "working community" in which mutual help and support in word and action, a shared responsibility for the quality of the work that was done, and a common obligation to bring the work to completion were regarded as the collective duty of the pupils. Group work and interactive learning altered the physical appearance of the classrooms. School desks nailed to the floor were replaced by movable tables and chairs, and the children worked and discussed their work in groups. The progressivist pedagogues took pleasure in seeing this atmosphere of joyful vitality and movement in the classrooms and, unlike the traditionalists, did not confuse it with clamor and chaos.[52]

Otto Erler and Martin Weise, who taught in active-learning schools in Leipzig and Dresden respectively, observed how the teaching methods and process of learning released the potential for leadership residing within young people and prepared them for a life of civic responsibility and self-government. The teachers recognized the rights as well as the duties of the pupils and made the participation of the pupils in the governance of the school an educational principle. Pupils in the upper grades were entrusted with specific responsibilities in school festivals and during field trips, and in the school library, garden, or equipment room. Weise wrote: "If self-initiative, independence of thought, courage, endurance, the ability to organize and the art of handling people are required for leadership, is it not the nature and purpose of the active-learning school to enhance and strengthen these abilities?"[53]

Teachers in the active-learning schools dispensed with the use of severe punishments and maintained a comradely relationship with the pupils. They rejected the image of the teacher as an infallible authority enthroned in the classroom and cast themselves in the roles of "wise friend," to whom the pupils could trustingly turn for help in school matters as well as in their personal sorrow and cares. A school built on the principle of external authority, they thought, would never be able to draw out and cultivate the talents of the children. As Weise observed, notwithstanding the freedom allowed to the pupils, discipline and order prevailed in the classrooms because the teachers led on the basis of the inner consent of the pupils rather than through external authority. Abandoning the use of corporal punishment, they thought that unruly pupils could be corrected more effectively by excluding them from school activities for a time.[54]

The reformers in the elementary schools also fostered civic education and affirmation of the republican state through the instruction of history. During the Weimar years, German Democrats and Social Democrats in the German Teachers' Association worked to change the traditional methods of teaching history in the schools. Committees in the local chapters drafted guidelines for the revision of the instruction of history and prepared new curriculums for this subject. These proposals were discussed and put to a vote at the meetings of the full membership. The progressivist pedagogues criticized the overemphasis on the ruling dynasty and warfare in the lesson plans for the subject of history used in the past. They thought that history instruction should become a chronicle of the people—their customs and ways of life, religious and cultural life, and economic development—and recommended the addition of material on the "heroes" who labored and contributed to civilization. A teacher in Breslau said: "Even the lower classes, up to now always the big nobody in history, should speak to us through representative individuals."[55]

The progressivist pedagogues argued for an unvarnished and truthful treatment of Germany's military tradition and the mistakes and weaknesses of the monarchy in the instruction of history. Franz Strauss, a teacher in the province of East Prussia, stated that war should not be idealized and glorified and that the history lessons should teach young people the tragic effects of war. He acknowledged the difficulties of being emotionally objective in handling World War I in the instruction of history, but he insisted that the youth had a right to learn how the war came about, how it ended in defeat, and what its political effects were.[56] At a meeting of the Berlin teachers' association, Wilhelm Rödiger maintained that the instruction of history should be informed by the ideals of democracy and the League of Nations. He thought that teachers should draw a line between school instruction and nationalistic politics in handling the subject of Germany's territorial losses. The yearning for reunification with fellow Germans living outside the postwar boundaries was a natural instinct, but the way to recover these lands could "never be a war, which would totally destroy the Western world."[57]

The transformation of the political consciousness and behavior of the German people following the collapse of the old authoritarian state, as the progressivist pedagogues knew very well, could not be realized simply by the adoption of a democratic constitution. They thought that an appreciation of and a respect for the institutions of the republic should be imparted to elementary school pupils in the instruction of history; they advocated an increase in the instruction time allocated to this subject in the upper grades from two to three hours weekly.[58] Most of these teachers did not support the idea of adding civics (*Staatsbürgerkunde*) as a separate subject to the elementary school curriculum. When the Ministry of Education asked the Saxon Teachers' Association to submit proposals for a civics curriculum,

Oskar Gleissberg replied in February 1921 that its members thought that the instruction of civics as a discrete subject was more suited for students in secondary schools. After a discussion of this issue at a recent congress, the teachers had taken the position that lessons providing elementary schoolchildren with an understanding of the civic requirements and institutional forms of the state community should be done within the entire instruction in a way that was meaningful at their young age. The elementary school served the needs of civic education most effectively by becoming "a working and living community according to the model of the active-learning school."[59] The national congress of the German Teachers' Association reached the same conclusion a year later, when the representatives of the chapters discussed how schoolchildren could be educated to have a consciousness of belonging to the state community and loyalty to the republican state as an expression of the national integration and will of the people. They agreed that the reform of education in the direction of the active-learning school offered a more effective pedagogical means of socializing schoolchildren into a democratic society than teaching civics as a subject.[60]

The link between the active-learning school and civic education in the Weimar Republic was already forged when the Reichstag passed the Law for the Protection of the Republic of 18 July 1922, in the aftermath of the assassination of Foreign Minister Walther Rathenau by right-wing terrorists. This legislation empowered the states to prohibit organizations and assemblies that endangered the republic. Also acting in response to the political violence that threatened the stability of the republic, Reich Interior Minister Koch, a German Democrat, summoned the education ministers to a conference in Berlin on 19 July to discuss the responsibilities of the schools in the work of building up allegiance to the republic. The leadership of the German Teachers' Association not only supported these actions but praised Minister of Education Fleissner in Saxony for issuing a stern administrative order on 6 July 1922 on the relationship of schoolteachers to the republican state.[61] Fleissner stated that all teachers had "the unconditional obligation to perform their professional work in the spirit and interests of the new republican state institutions." Teachers were told to refrain from any disparagement of persons "in the anti-Semitic manner" and to follow the precepts of objectivity, tolerance, and reconciliation in their instruction. The minister threatened to remove teachers from the schools and to open formal disciplinary procedures for their dismissal if they acted contrary to these obligations of their office or belonged to organizations that worked to destroy the republican form of the state.[62]

German Democrats and Social Democrats in the elementary school teaching profession took issue with the critics of these modest measures within the Secondary Schoolteachers' Association. Georg Wolff, who served as the editor of the *Allgemeine Deutsche Lehrerzeitung* until his election as the chairman of the German Teachers' Association in 1925, contended that the requirement that schoolteachers support the Weimar Constitution wholeheartedly was "not gagging free thought and imposing constraints on one's conscience" but a natural duty for them as state employees. He criticized the nostalgic views of the monarchy held by philologists in the German Nationalist ranks. He thought that they acted irresponsibly when they brought into the *Gymnasium* the ideological conflicts between the monarchists and republicans over the form of the state, the colors of the German national flag, and the celebration of Constitution Day, the republic's national holiday, on 11 August.[63] The progressivist pedagogues were no less critical of those colleagues with equivocal and lukewarm attitudes toward the republic. Paul Ruchatz, who taught in the province of East Prussia, said that teachers could be successful in civic education only if they were "firmly convinced and fully aware of their duties toward the existing state constitution." It was "not sufficient," he added, for them "to stand merely on the basis of facts, go along outwardly, and bow to the unavoidable; a correct manner of teaching out of consideration for the present circumstances is not sufficient either."[64]

Concerns about the political socialization of the young generation in the republic were in the foreground of the discussions at a conference on school politics and pedagogy organized by the Prussian Teachers' Association in Magdeburg from 28 August to 2 September 1922. The choice of Wilhelm Tittel, the chairman of the teachers' association in Westphalia, to deliver the keynote address was clearly intended to turn this meeting into a strong demonstration of allegiance to the republican state. A member of the Social Democratic Party and a newly appointed municipal school official in Dortmund, Tittel was known to be a fervent and resolute champion of the new democratic order. He extolled the democratic liberties and genuine parliamentary government under the republic compared to the authoritarian controls and the treatment of citizens as subjects during the empire. He deplored the number of citizens whose emotions were still tied to the old monarchical state and who made disdainful remarks about the republican state and parliamentary democracy. He stated that the Law for the Protection of the Republic must be applied to the schools. The republican state could tolerate such behavior so long as it was confined to private life and did not disturb its institutions. However, the schools should "not sabotage the republic" with teaching corrupted by reactionary ideologies and nostalgia. Without scorning the past, "school instruction must do justice to the new [state] and understand its inevitability and historical necessity." Tittel believed that the government was fully justified in demanding that the schools educate the youth to be loyal to the democratic state and in dismissing those teachers who misused their positions to instill contempt for the republic in the hearts of the young generation. He stated: "A person cannot be compelled to embrace the republic, but he cannot demand that the republican state allow him to propagate his hostility to it in the schools."[65]

A photograph of Johannes Tews taken in 1930, after three decades of public advocacy for school reform. (Ullstein Bilderdienst)

With their teacher's encouragement, these first-grade children in Berlin did their first writing exercise on the sand in the schoolyard, 1928. (Ullstein Bilderdienst)

The teaching of children in the experimental elementary school in Dresden-Hellerau with the active-learning methods of the new pedagogy, 1924. (Ullstein Bilderdienst)

Developing the imaginative, creative, and constructive faculties of the children through manual arts instruction in the experimental elementary school in Dresden-Hellerau, 1924. (Ullstein Bilderdienst)

Group work and interactive learning changed the physical appearance of this classroom in a modern school in Unterteutschenthal, located near Halle, 1929. (Ullstein Bilderdienst)

In an anatomy lesson in this modern school, boys and girls together learned about the breathing organ of human beings by observing a plaster model of the body and a living specimen, 1924. (Ullstein Bilderdienst)

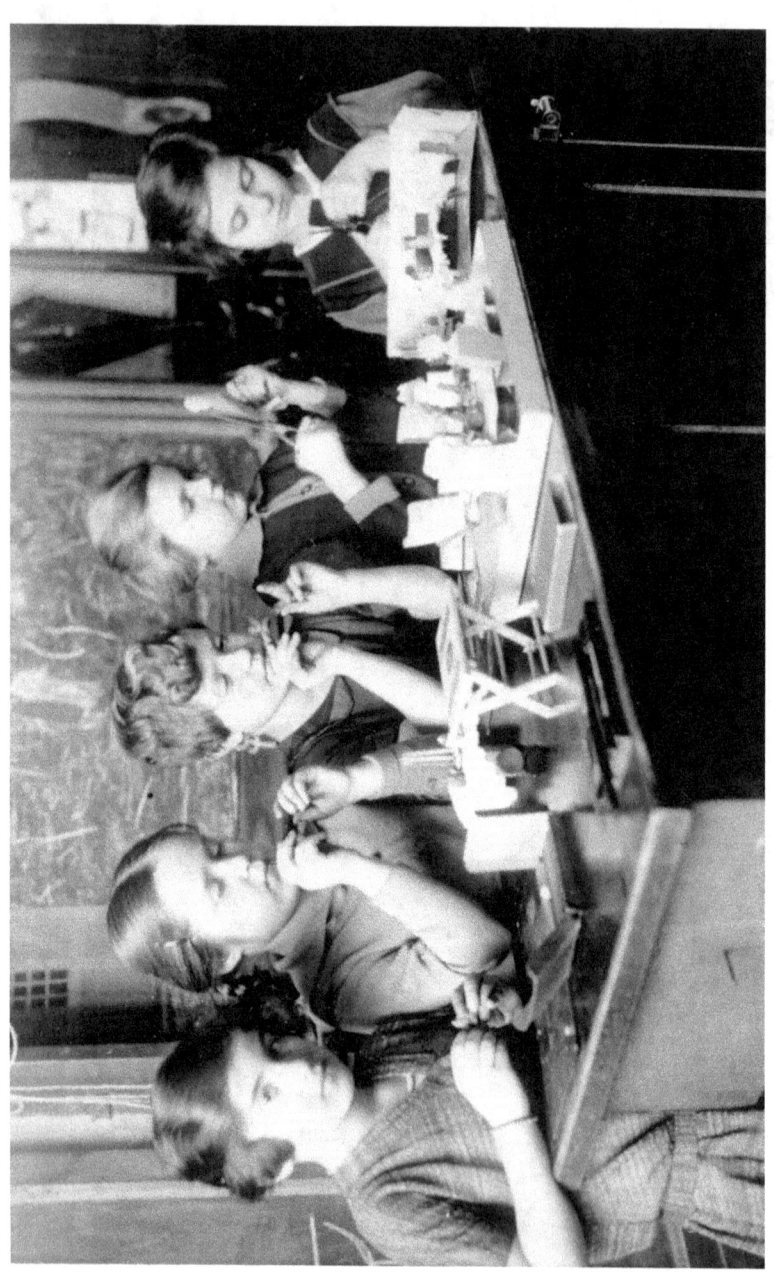

A group project during art and handicraft instruction turned this classroom of girls into a "working community" in a modern school in Berlin, 1927. (Ullstein Bilderdienst)

Progressive Education in the German Schools in the 1920s

In the 1920s school officials who were affiliated with or stood close to the German Democratic and Social Democratic Parties gave a big boost to the transformation of the traditional school into an active-learning school. Supporters of the *neue Pädagogik* occupied key positions in the education ministries in many German states. In Prussia, Minister of Education Konrad Haenisch and his successor Carl Becker as well as Paul Kaestner, the ministry's director throughout the 1920s, promoted the active-learning school, and this policy shaped the "Guidelines for the Curriculum of the Basic School" issued on 16 March 1921. The councilor in the ministry who drafted the curriculum guidelines was Carl Louis Pretzel, who had served on the executive board of the German Teachers' Association since 1898. His work on behalf of educational reform began in 1912, when he was chosen to head the office set up by the association to advance the cause of the modern pedagogy.[66]

Before the curriculum guidelines were officially announced, the Prussian Ministry of Education sent a draft to the leaders of the teachers' organizations and invited them to express their views at a meeting on 8 January 1921. In this discussion, Pretzel stated that the ministry's intention was to remove the hindrances to change and to open the way for the implementation of the principles of the active-learning school.[67] At the same time, he took into account that many teachers were still wedded to the traditional methods, and decided "not to impose the new pedagogy on anyone against his conviction." A left-liberal reformer with a nondogmatic and conciliatory temperament, Pretzel said in an address to the Berlin teachers' association: "If the new pedagogy does not fight its way through and conquer the hearts of teachers, then it makes no sense to introduce it by force." A coercive implementation of the reform pedagogy would only generate ill will and rejection. Pedagogical innovations could only "prove themselves in the fullest sense" if they were "accepted and done out of free conviction."[68]

The curriculum guidelines for the basic school endorsed the concept of the active-learning school and encouraged teachers to practice the modern pedagogy. The entire instruction in the basic school should follow the principle that "almost everything children learn is experienced by them inwardly and acquired through self-activity." Teachers should take care to connect their instruction to the child's native regional surroundings. For the first four years of schooling, the ministry did not require a strict division of the lesson plans by subjects and permitted *Gesamtunterricht*, a method of interactive teaching in which the pedagogue moved spontaneously from one subject matter to another in a dialogue with the pupils.[69] In the selection of the instruction material, the criteria should be, first, the children's cognitive abilities and developmental needs and, secondly, the importance of this particular subject matter for their future practical life. Teachers were urged to avoid instruction material that was "premature" and "overburdening," beyond the comprehension of pupils at that age. The contents of instruction in the first two grades should be drawn from the child's immediate surroundings and experience. From the third grade on, *Heimatkunde* was to be taught to prepare the pupils for the instruction of geography, history, and natural science. The curriculum guidelines did not prescribe a single course for the instruction of reading and writing and granted teachers enough autonomy to pursue new ways of teaching these subjects so long as the goals of learning achievement in reading, writing, and grammar set for the pupils at the completion of the fourth year of the basic school were fulfilled.[70]

In the final stage of this curricular reform, the Ministry of Education had to make concessions to the demands of the Catholic bishops in respect to the guidelines on Catholic religious instruction. Afterwards, conservatives in the Protestant Church regretted that they had not shown as much political muscle and tenacity.[71] In the discussion in the ministry on 8 January, State Secretary Wildermann, who had close ties to the Center Party, insisted that the demands of the Catholic episcopate should be heard before the curriculum guidelines became official policy. Subsequently, Pretzel held discussions with Catholic and Protestant church officials separately. As a result of the resistance of Catholic churchmen to any changes in the contents and the hours of religious instruction in the schools, Pretzel revised the draft document so that different regulations for Catholic and Protestant religious education were set. Whereas the instruction for Catholic children would continue to adhere to the traditional practices, the guidelines for the Protestant instruction reflected the thinking of the pedagogues. Catholic children received religion lessons each week for three hours in the first grade and four hours in the other three years of the basic school. The religion lessons for Protestant children were shortened to one and one-half hours per week in the first grade, two hours in the second grade, and three hours in the third and fourth years. For the Protestant religion, the guidelines simply stated that the teaching material should consist of "Bible stories from the Old and New Testaments suitable for comprehension at the age level [of the children]." The more comprehensive instruction for Catholic children covered the Bible, the catechism, and preparation for the rites of Holy Communion and Confirmation.

The publication of the curriculum guidelines lifted the hopes of the progressivist pedagogues. One teacher in Silesia called them "a significant sign that the idea of a sound school reform, particularly that of the active-learning school, is taking off." Another teacher in the province of Saxony stated: "The guidelines, born out of a progressive spirit, demonstrate to us clearly that the Prussian Ministry of Education has the firm will to develop school life on a modern foundation."[72] The curriculum guidelines were a major reform initiative of the Prussian Ministry of Education under Konrad

Haenisch. His successor, Carl Becker, took a strong interest in the training of teachers in the active-learning school methods and provided funds for them to participate in workshops on the modern pedagogy that were sponsored by the Central Institute for Education and Instruction, an office within the Reich Interior Ministry.[73]

In the early years of the republic, the active-learning school movement extended beyond the circles of Protestant pedagogues in the big cities. Committees of teachers in many inspection districts prepared new curriculums in the spirit of the reform pedagogy and with a particular regional character. County chapters of the Prussian Teachers' Association devoted meetings to the discussion of the methods and goals of the active-learning school and to proposals for applying them in schools with two or three classrooms.[74] The defensiveness and resentment that many village teachers expressed toward the modern school and big-city pedagogues suggest that pedagogical reform theories affected rural schoolhouses to a lesser extent than schools in the cities. The standards set by the progressivist pedagogues did, however, prompt rural school reformers such as Walter Popp to advocate the creation of school union districts in the countryside, following the American model of rural schooling.[75]

Catholic teachers who had remained distant from the active-learning school movement in earlier years were now eager to keep pace with their Protestant colleagues in the cities. In 1921, in an article in the *Westdeutsche Lehrerzeitung*, an organ of the Catholic Teachers' Association, Friedrich Schneider, a teacher in Münster, criticized "a certain conservatism" that characterized the theory and practice of Catholic educators. He observed that Catholic teachers were "mostly cool, wary, critical, and often skeptical" toward pedagogical innovations. While they claimed that this caution toward new ideas gave their school work tranquility and steadiness, Schneider believed that there were "disadvantages and dangers" in this outlook. "There is a tranquility that signifies the absence of vitality and a steadiness that is unthinking routine," he remarked. As Schneider recognized, the fight over religious instruction in the schools had also affected Catholic attitudes toward the new pedagogy. He did not share the belief that the exclusion of religious instruction from the school curriculum inevitably followed from the principles of experiential learning and learning as an activity of the self. He pointed out that the concept of the active-learning school in the writings of Hugo Gaudig and Franz Weigl, a less well-known Catholic philosopher of education, was not antithetical to the instruction of religion and could be embraced by Catholic teachers.[76]

The active-learning school was discussed in the meetings and in the press of the Catholic Teachers' Association with greater sympathy in the 1920s. The convention of its biggest branch in the province of Westphalia in December 1921 adopted a resolution supporting the principles of the new pedagogy. Catholic teachers there agreed that all local chapters should form working groups (*Arbeitsgemeinschaften*) for the study of the psychology of education and that the membership should be encouraged to carry out "the reasonable demands of the active-learning school movement" by a program of lectures and courses and by visits to schools where the modern pedagogy was already in practice.[77] In June 1922, Franz Weigl was invited to speak on the active-learning school at the national congress of the Catholic Teachers' Association. In the discussion that followed, the comments made by teachers from the Rhine Province, Westphalia, and Silesia showed that they were already participating in groups organized for the study of the new pedagogy. These teachers were conscious of the fact that their own professional society had trailed far behind the German Teachers' Association in promoting the cause of pedagogical reform and that Hugo Gaudig, Johannes Kühnel, and other Protestant reformers in Saxony had achieved a national reputation that no Catholic educational theorist could as yet claim. They were eager to prove that Catholic pedagogues were no less forward-looking and innovative.[78]

Worries about the economic inflation did not prevent elementary schoolteachers from devoting time and their own resources to acquire the training that would enable them to practice the new pedagogy in their classrooms. Teachers from all parts of the country made pilgrimages to Leipzig to visit the teachers' training seminary under the direction of Gaudig and the reopened experimental schools. After a school principal in Silesia completed a three-week visit to Leipzig in the spring of 1921, he commented that the work of the reformers in the schools and in the Institute for Experimental Pedagogy and Psychology of the Leipzig teachers' association provided a comprehensive view of progressive education that other German cities could scarcely match.[79]

The chapters of the German Teachers' Associations organized training workshops running from three to five days. Hugo Gaudig, Otto Scheibner, and other reformers in Leipzig traveled to many cities in the provinces of Saxony and Silesia to give lectures and classroom demonstrations of the teaching methods of the active-learning school in the summer and fall of 1921. In the city of Bunzlau, Johannes Kühnel, an instructor in the teachers' seminary in Leipzig, taught in the course sponsored by the local chapter from 27 June to 1 July 1921. Nearly three hundred teachers attended his lectures. During his visit, Kühnel also observed the classes in one of the city's schools, where the modern pedagogy was already in practice. Impressed by the number of his colleagues who attended this course, which had no direct bearing on their material interests, one teacher commented that "the idealism of the nation's educators is now as before unbroken despite the immense economic distress."[80]

Gaudig and Scheibner led other pedagogical workshops that were organized and funded by the Central Institute for Education and Instruction. Large numbers of teachers registered for these workshops held in Breslau,

Erfurt, Halle, and other cities in 1921–22. Representatives of the school administration were often present and praised the dedication of the teachers who took the training courses on their own initiative. These workshops won over many teachers to the active-learning school movement and particularly to the pedagogical methods expounded by Gaudig.[81] Even Erich Pabel, a pedagogue in Magdeburg who thought that Gaudig's concept of the active-learning school was too intellectually oriented and did not give as much attention to the manual arts as did the reformers in Hamburg, had to admit by 1923 that these workshops had made Gaudig's school the model for most teachers in Prussia who were receptive to the ideas of progressive education. Shortly after Gaudig died in 1923, a school principal in Halle wrote: "In the pedagogical world in recent years, no other name has been mentioned more than Gaudig's."[82]

Why was Gaudig so effective in attracting teachers in Prussia to the active-learning school movement? Gaudig's charisma and intuitiveness made a strong impression on the teachers who heard his lectures and observed his demonstrations of the new pedagogy in the local schools. A pedagogue of extraordinary gifts, he was able to enliven and capture the attention and trust of children whom he had never met before.[83] Teachers appreciated Gaudig's understanding of the proper relationship between freedom and compulsion in education. He applied the principle of learning as an activity of the self without going to extremes. He was known to be critical of some of the radical exponents of "pedagogy from the perspective of the child" in Bremen and Hamburg, who were inclined to overstate the child's ability to develop into a whole person through his or her inner resources, and who believed that the "interference" of the teacher could even be harmful in the child's natural development. As Otto Scheibner noted in 1921, Gaudig's broad perspective and practical schoolwork had preserved him from the "high-flown and utopian" ideas of the radicals in the active-learning school movement.[84] Moreover, Gaudig's theory of education in the service of the whole person lent a socioethical purpose to education that had immense resonance for teachers who believed that the needs of the new republican state placed special demands on the schools. He distinguished between the individual with his or her innate, natural instincts and the whole person with acquired abilities and ethical norms. The whole person as an ideal was the individual who led a good life in full self-determination and at the same time was cognizant of an obligation to be active in the service of the community. In Gaudig's model of the active-learning school, the pupil was not viewed as a solitary individual but as a human being with all of the social relationships of life in a community.[85]

Since Gaudig had never advocated the exclusion of religious instruction from the schools, his model of the active-learning school could appeal to reform-minded teachers in Prussia who took a moderate position on this controversial issue. Gaudig was the son of a Protestant pastor and grew up in a village parish in Saxony. Throughout his life he maintained a deep personal faith and an appreciation for the place of religion and the church in society.[86] In 1920 he disavowed the efforts of the reformers in the Saxon Teachers' Association to eliminate religious instruction from the schools against the wish of large numbers of parents. Questioning the political wisdom of their confrontational relationship with the church and their claims about the autonomy of pedagogy, Gaudig stated that teachers were "not masters of the school" and did not have the right to exclude the parents and legitimate representatives of the churches in the formulation of the purposes of education. He doubted that Catholic and Protestant church leaders would ever agree to an instruction of religion in the schools that set aside the beliefs and observances of the confessional community and simply imparted the moral teachings of Jesus. "Even a modest degree of political realism suffices to see that the state has a strong interest in cooperation with the churches in the school sphere," he said.[87]

The Opening of Experimental Schools amid Public Controversy

The school boards in many cities in Weimar Germany opened experimental public schools with the approval of the state governments. Hamburg led the way with the establishment of three experimental schools in the spring of 1919 and another one in 1920. The Saxon Ministry of Education authorized the opening of experimental schools in Chemnitz, Dresden, and Leipzig in the early 1920s. Prussia caught up with these two innovative states when experimental schools were created in Breslau in 1921, Magdeburg in 1922, and Berlin in 1923. These schools had large enrollments and were far from being an exotic phenomenon. The school in the Georgplatz in Dresden had 16 classes with 590 pupils, and the school in the Tieloh-Süd section of Hamburg had 20 classes with 770 pupils. Despite the controversies over the new pedagogy, experimental schools continued to spread in the following years so that by the early 1930s there were about 200 in Germany. The registration of children for the experimental schools, left up to the free choice of the parents, continued to grow despite the decline in the birth rate. Between 1927 and 1932, the enrollment in the experimental schools increased from 17,820 to 40,149 pupils. Because of the shortage of space, several experimental schools could not admit all of the children whose parents wished to enroll them.[88]

Considerable controversy surrounded the decision to open experimental schools in some cities, and the progressivist pedagogues who worked in these schools had to contend with people who had unfavorable preconceptions and made disparaging remarks. Bourgeois parents with a conservative outlook doubted that the modern schools would provide the foundation of knowledge and intellectual discipline necessary for the traditional educational system in the *Gymnasium*. Opposition was strongest wherever the experimental school was started as a "district school," with obligatory attendance for the children living in that area. The Protestant Parents' League in Magdeburg took up the cause of those parents who wanted to transfer their children out of the experimental school, and demanded that this school be classified as a "voluntary school."[89]

The Humboldt School for girls in Chemnitz, which opened in the spring of 1921, went through a few years of instability when progressive education in general—and this school in particular—came under attack in the right-wing press. After the pedagogues in the Humboldt School declined to teach religious instruction, Protestant churchmen in the city refused to admit the pupils who attended this school to the Confirmation lessons. Thereafter, parents withdrew hundreds of children from the Humboldt School. It became coeducational in 1923, and the gaps in the enrollment were filled by the registration of boys. Some of the teachers faltered under the psychological strain of this public opposition and requested to be transferred; vacancies in the teaching staff had to be filled every year. By the mid 1920s, the teaching staff had become more stable and had the satisfaction of seeing the number of children whose parents wanted to register them in the school exceed what the classroom space would permit.[90]

The political uproar over the appointment of Wilhelm Paulsen, an educational reformer from Hamburg, to the office of superintendent of the school system of Greater Berlin in 1921 delayed the opening of the experimental schools there until 1923. Paulsen had been the editor of the *Pädagogische Reform* in Hamburg for several years and had spoken out for the elimination of confessional instruction from the schools. After the November Revolution, he joined the Social Democratic Party and broke off his affiliation with the Protestant Church. The left-wing majority in the Berlin city council selected Paulsen for the school post over the protests of the Center and bourgeois conservative parties. Resistance to his appointment and to the opening of experimental schools based on his ideas of ethical socialism and progressive education, which were called "living community schools" (*Lebensgemeinschaftsschulen*), proved to be stronger than his Social Democratic supporters had expected. A Catholic priest in Berlin made inquiries in Hamburg about Paulsen's work as the principal of a school there and published a highly critical report of Hamburg's modern schools in *Germania*, a newspaper tied to the Center Party. Catholic politicians attacked Paulsen as an "atheistic 'school expert.'" The *Tägliche Rundschau*, which served as the political mouthpiece of the Protestant Church leadership, declared that Berlin's large school system could "not possibly be delivered over to the experiments of a teacher" who wanted "a revolution in the school." Paulsen's philosophy of education would bring to the Berlin schools "egalitarianism and the disintegration of all discipline."[91]

Although the left liberals in the Berlin teachers' association would have preferred the appointment of Johannes Tews, Paulsen was at least familiar to them as an active member of the German Teachers' Association, and he soon gained their confidence. At a massive assembly in December 1921, the Berlin teachers' association adopted a resolution urging the school administration to establish a few "living community schools" on an experimental basis. Shortly thereafter, Paulsen requested official permission to open experimental schools in the spring. He admitted that the appeal of his educational ideas was likely to be confined to Social Democratic parents at first and that the "living community schools" would be attended mainly by working-class children. He hoped that over the course of time the non-Socialist and wealthier sections of the population would become more receptive to his thinking and send their children to these schools. A faction in the provincial school board that was not sympathetic to Paulsen's plan tried to block it. It was not until March 1923 that the Ministry of Education issued a directive permitting the opening of nine experimental elementary schools in Greater Berlin. The district of Neukölln housed three of these schools and became a hub of educational innovation in the 1920s; its school superintendent, Kurt Löwenstein, was one of the Social Democratic Party's "resolute" educational reformers.[92]

School administrators granted the teachers in the experimental public schools considerable autonomy and did not bind them to a prescribed lesson plan. Under the system of collegial school governance, the teachers in each school discussed their work and made decisions on school life in weekly conferences. The vote of the majority at these meetings was binding. With a few exceptions, collegial school governance worked well in the experimental schools because the teachers formed a community based on shared democratic and socioethical values.[93] The mature pedagogues, such as Ottomar Fröhlich, Martin Weise, and Paul Vogel in Saxony; Johannes Gläser and Wilhelm Lamszus in Hamburg; and Adolf Jensen and Wilhelm Wittbrodt in Berlin, had been active in the educational reform movement before 1914. The experimental schools in Hamburg and other cities in northern Germany also attracted teachers of a younger generation who had been socialized in the Youth Movement of the prewar years. Filled with disdain toward the traditional school, they were fired with a glowing desire to bring about change and make school life better.[94] The professional demands and psychological and physical stress of teaching in the experimental schools were immense. Active-learning school instruction, the teachers' warm and caring relationship with the pupils, and the frequency of teacher-parent meetings required a greater sacrifice in time than work in the traditional school. In addition, teachers in the experimental schools made themselves available to other members of the profession, who visited their schools and sought training in the modern pedagogy. A visiting teacher from Altona, who was a skeptical observer of some aspects of the experimental schools in Hamburg, could not deny the idealism and commitment of the teachers there. "They are undoubtedly among the best of our profession," he reported.[95]

Without neglecting the development of the mental faculties of the child, the pedagogues in the experimental schools strove to cultivate an ethical social consciousness in the pupils by transforming each class and the entire school from a place of mechanical individual activity into a vibrant working community. The teachers formed a relation with their pupils based on the bonds of trust and fostered by group work and dialogue in classroom instruction. The comradeship between teachers and pupils was strengthened through school festivals, field trips, and wilderness hikes. The experimental schools relaxed the rigid discipline maintained in the traditional school and allowed the pupils greater freedom of movement. The teachers abandoned the system of numerical grades and instead wrote descriptive assessments of the pupils' performance. While they recognized that successful schoolwork required discipline, they relinquished the use of corporal punishment. They sought to transcend the system of classroom order imposed by the threat of caning and to achieve obedience and order through the pupils' own understanding, consent, and self-restraint.[96] Student councils and school assemblies were introduced for the classes of the intermediate and upper grades. Georg Schwenzer, who taught in the experimental school in Dresden, stated that the pupils must have an active share in the direction of school life. The value of their help in maintaining school discipline, leading field trips and games, running the school library, tending the school garden, and taking care of the equipment in the workrooms lay "above all in the moral dimension of such leadership and self-government."[97]

The idea of community also informed the lively participation of the parents in school life. Most of the children in the experimental schools came from working-class families. The teachers established a close rapport with the parents in order to gain their confidence and to give them a correct understanding of the new pedagogy. Teacher-parent meetings held in the evenings became a forum in which the teachers propagated the cause of educational reform. At the experimental schools in Chemnitz and Dresden, the parents came to a consensus on the issue of religious instruction and registered their children out of it. Facing the opposition of clergymen and other conservatives organized in the League of Christian Parents' Associations in Leipzig, teachers in the city's experimental schools worked to unite the parents "on the neutral ground of a purely scientific practice of pedagogy."[98] Pedagogues in the experimental schools in Saxony observed that the parents of their pupils donated money and time for school needs more willingly than the parents of children attending other elementary schools. Parents with craft skills volunteered to help the teachers in courses for woodworking and needlework. Mothers assisted the school physician and supervised the bathing of girls in the school shower. School associations formed by the parents collected funds for the acquisition of summer camps for the children. With contributions from the parents, the experimental school in Chemnitz was equipped with a piano, slide projector, and duplicating machine.[99]

The experimental schools in Bremen and Hamburg had a more troubled existence, and the progressivist pedagogues in Saxony were very conscious of the differences between the modern schools in their cities and in northern Germany. Teachers in the experimental schools in Saxony successfully resisted the attempts of radical Marxist parents to influence the instruction. In Hamburg, some of the radical reformers regarded the experimental schools as a "revolution in education" and boldly associated the new schools with "the ideology of the proletariat."[100] Other pedagogues there struggled to keep the politics of the working-class parties out of school life. A few teachers and a small group of parents belonging to the German Communist Party in Hamburg sought to use the schools as a place for partisan agitation. Disputes broke out among the teachers in the Breitenfelder-Strasse-Schule and Berlinertor-Schule. Most of the teachers were Social Democrats and objected to Marxist ideas about the function of the school in the politics of class conflict. Both schools entered a calmer phase later in the 1920s, when the Communists on the teaching staff realized their isolation and departed.[101]

Philosophical and didactic divisiveness also afflicted the experimental school in Bremen. In the spring of 1920 the collegium of teachers chose Heinrich Scharrelmann to be the school leader. His educational theories captivated those members of the Bremen teachers' association who came out of the Youth Movement and for whom the experimental school meant "a rebellion against the obsolete methods of the schoolmaster." Christian Paulmann, one of the disenchanted pedagogues who taught at this school, related that the teachers gave extensive freedom to the pupils and assumed that the common sense and understanding of the pupils would lead them to see the necessity of order for people living together. The teachers took seriously and applied consistently Scharrelmann's theory that a new order in the classroom coming from the children themselves could only emerge out of the destruction of the old forms of discipline. It was not long before the problems of teaching children who caused disturbances began to dominate the weekly discussions of the collegium. Most of the teachers thought that they had an obligation to assess their classroom experiences critically. They argued that compulsion and requirements were justified in educational work for the benefit of the schoolchildren. Scharrelmann and his disciples thought that these colleagues were spoiling the experiment and would continually make concessions to the traditional school. The teachers' association sided with the critics of Scharrelmann in this dispute. The two factions parted company when the school administration opened a second experimental school.[102]

Educational reformers in Saxony were critical of the extreme manner in which the "pedagogy from the perspective of the child" was carried out in the experimental schools in Bremen and Hamburg. For them, the active-learning school did not mean the end of planned instruction or free rein for arbitrariness. They thought that exercises in reading, writing, and arithmetic should not be neglected and that these "learned skills" should be taught as discrete subjects. "Pedagogical dilettantism should find no place in the experimental school," remarked Paul Vogel. Martin Brethfeld contended that "an unrestrained freedom in teaching" could lead to "subjectivism of all types and degrees up to pedagogical anarchy." Later in the 1920s, Ottomar Fröhlich observed that "the sentimental pedagogy 'from the perspective of the child' causes much less mischief in the schoolrooms than it could have seemed from the pedagogical literature in the years immediately after the revolution." It seemed "superfluous" to him "to refute it again and again and to 'beat it to death.'"[103]

The Spread of Progressive Education in the Elementary Schools

The experimental schools were not an exotic phenomenon in the world of public education in Weimar Germany. Pedagogues in the experimental schools wanted to provide a model for the regular schools and to facilitate the extension of progressive education throughout the elementary school system. The experimental schools in Chemnitz, Dresden, and Leipzig welcomed hundreds of visiting educators and school administrators from all parts of Germany. An official in the Prussian Ministry of Education visited the experimental schools in Dresden and Leipzig in February 1923 to observe the instruction and to learn how these schools were organized and equipped. Ottomar Fröhlich and other teachers in the experimental schools worked with the chapters of the Saxon Teachers' Association in drafting curriculum guidelines in order to establish the reform pedagogy firmly in the regular schools.[104]

In November 1922, the executive board of the Saxon Teachers' Association proposed to the Ministry of Education that courses for training teachers in the methods of the active-learning school be offered in the experimental schools. Oskar Gleissberg enclosed in his letter to the minister a plan for the training courses that had been prepared by the reformers in the Leipzig teachers' association. He recommended that the participants be selected from among "those teachers who had been interested in the concept of the active-learning school for a long time but had not yet had the opportunity to realize it to any great extent." After the completion of the course, they must be willing "to work together with other teachers in their schools to ensure that the principles of active-learning instruction gain a foothold in their localities." In an impressive demonstration of support for the new pedagogy, officials in the ministry accepted this proposal within a week and announced that the courses would be offered in 1923 and that a subsidy from state funds would cover the travel expenses of the participants.[105]

More than sixty Saxon teachers between the ages of thirty and thirty-nine attended the training courses held in February 1923. The school inspectors selected teachers who were already familiar with the theories and practices of the active-learning school, and who had indicated a willingness to introduce these concepts to their colleagues at the meetings of the school staff and the local teachers' association. The participants in the training courses observed classroom instruction in the experimental schools and were given the opportunity to practice the new methods themselves. They heard lectures given by teachers in the experimental schools and participated in discussions with these seasoned pedagogues. They attended teacher-parent meetings at the experimental schools to observe how the teachers gained the confidence and goodwill of the parents.[106] Interest in the practical application of the modern pedagogy among Saxon teachers was so strong that the Ministry of Education made arrangements for training courses at the experimental schools in the three cities again in the fall of 1923 and in the following two years. School inspectors who promoted the active-learning school encouraged teachers in rural areas to attend the courses. Otto Erler wrote to the ministry that his inspection district in the Vogtland was very remote from the social world of educational reform and needed a boosting. Many of the teachers selected for the courses offered in the fall of 1925 came from schools located in small towns and villages.[107]

Over the course of the 1920s, the principles of progressive education influenced the practice of teaching in many of the regular elementary schools in Saxony. Many teachers in Dresden and Leipzig were already in the forefront of the educational reform movement before 1914, and during the republic the new pedagogy was widely practiced in the schools there. Kurt Wehner, the school inspector in Leipzig, reported in 1923 that the experimental schools already had "a strong impact on the entire school system of Leipzig." He saw classes in many regular schools in which the instruction was hardly different from that in the experimental schools.[108] A progressivist pedagogue in Dresden observed in June 1923: "More and more old schools are being transformed into active-learning schools. It is gratifying to see how the new pedagogical wave takes hold of more and more schools and teachers and draws them into the general movement."[109]

Progressive education extended beyond the big cities and changed the practices of teaching in schools in the medium-sized cities and the towns in Saxony. The implementation of the modern pedagogy was affected by generational lines within the teaching profession and by the disposition of the district's school inspector. The school inspectors' reports indicate that teachers in the early and middle phases of their professional life were more receptive to the innovations. Older teachers were less willing to alter their traditional methods. They said that the active-learning school was "a vogue that would pass away in time." They fretted that the modern school did not instill discipline and obedience in the children and would diminish the authority of and respect for the teacher. It neglected memorized learning and exercises in reading, writing, and arithmetic. On the other hand, wherever teachers practiced the new pedagogy, the school inspectors observed that the children were more lively, gained self-confidence, came to school happily, and worked with greater eagerness than before. Teaching in the active-learning school was mentally and physically demanding but brought deep personal and professional gratification. When Martin Weise conducted a survey of twenty-eight teachers who had attended the training course in Dresden and were practicing the modern pedagogy in their schools, they responded that the active-learning school strengthened their sense of obligation to the child and their educational work and spurred them to find the right balance between the learning of subject matter and the development of the child and between compulsion and freedom.[110]

The new pedagogy was practiced more extensively in areas of Saxony in which the school inspectors were favorably disposed to the reform than in other districts, where they did not disguise their hostility. Some of these officials maintained that the active-learning school neglected exercises and did not reinforce the learning of subject matter. One inspector complained about the relaxation of school discipline and associated it with "the excessive freedom of the newer methods [of teaching]." "If the teacher evaluates the new methods objectively and is conscientious," stated another inspector, "he will refrain from unfruitful experimentation."[111] What is striking in Saxony, however, was the number of school inspectors, such as Otto Erler, Otto Hertel, August Schneider, William Stenzel, Erich Viehweg, and Kurt Wehner, who encouraged the teachers under their supervision to practice the new pedagogy, and who took a lively interest in the training of teachers for the active-learning school. For this purpose, Stenzel founded a voluntary association in his inspection district, which held workshops in the city of Glauchau quarterly and later monthly. He praised the dedication of the teachers who came from distant towns and villages to these meetings without claiming compensation for their travel fare.[112]

Although the school inspectors in Saxony did not assess quantitatively the extensiveness of the changes in schoolteaching, their reports indicate that the practice of the modern pedagogy in the regular schools was widespread, if somewhat uneven among the generations within the teaching profession. Many school inspectors observed that teachers were well informed about active-learning instructional methods through the voluminous writings on educational reform put out by the press in Germany after 1918, participation in workshops and other organized discussions, and visits to the experimental schools. The number of teachers who were influenced by the active-learning school movement made a strong impression on them. Hertel wrote that only a "very small" number of teachers "remained completely untouched by the new currents of thought." In his district, the educational methods of the active-learning school were applied most widely in the classes for children in the lower grades. The majority of teachers in his district, Viehweg reported, were "caught up by the pedagogical movement and the change to an active-learning school, but of course to a varying extent." The new methods of teaching were introduced in the classrooms "at a various pace and in degrees of different shades." The school inspectors were not surprised to find out that the younger generations in the profession were the most receptive to the reforms. They had the good sense not to demand that older teachers, who had grown up in another intellectual world, cross over to the camp of the reformers with waving banners.[113]

The school inspectors' reports indicate that the progressivist pedagogues in Saxony eschewed extreme theories and practices. School Inspector Wahl wrote: "It is a good sign of their levelheadedness that nowhere has one thrown out the baby with the bath." He praised the teachers in his district for appreciating the place of exercises in the instruction of reading, spelling and grammar, and arithmetic, besides their use of other teaching methods oriented toward experiential learning and self-expression. Viehweg described the reform in his district as "a moderate adaptation of traditional instruction to the ways of teaching of the active-learning school." An overview of the entire school system would show, he contended, "how wrong it is to speak of an impetuous shattering of the elementary school caused by radical breaks with the customary system of teaching." The majority of teachers continued to follow a schedule setting the time for each subject and to work with lesson plans in the traditional manner, but the school inspector was "pleased" to see that they made an effort "to foster the self-activity of the children [in the learning process] more than they did before, and to carry over to their work the ideas of the active-learning school, whose correctness must be clear to everyone."[114]

The progress of educational reform was more gradual in Prussia than in Saxony. In 1923 a progressivist pedagogue in the province of Saxony stated that Prussian teachers who were receptive to the new pedagogy and willing to change the traditional methods of teaching were "still a minority." He was not disheartened and realized that the old *Lernschule* could not be abolished and the active-learning school could not be brought into existence overnight by administrative decree. Teachers of the younger generations were more willing to follow the principles of the active-learning school and to teach the four grades of the basic school than were older teachers. Erich Pabel, who taught in an experimental school in Magdeburg, observed that many school principals were still attached to the traditional school and that principals who were enthusiastic supporters of the modern pedagogy were "in the minority." A Catholic teacher in Westphalia reported in 1927 that the theories of the active-learning school had affected rural schools less than schools in the cities of the Ruhr because pedagogues in the countryside could not easily apply these ideas in a one-classroom schoolhouse.[115]

And yet the advocates of the active-learning school in Prussia found reasons to be hopeful. Moritz Bartsch in Breslau reported in 1922 that "many of the most capable members of the teaching profession are devoting themselves to pedagogical reforms with diligence and energy." The number of teachers who wanted to promote active learning in their classrooms was "growing more and more."[116] Fritz Karsen told pedagogues in Germany that it would be a mistake to conclude from the controversy surrounding the opening of the experimental schools in Berlin that the modern pedagogy had found little support in that city. He cited two reasons for being optimistic about the extension of the new methods of teaching to the other schools in Berlin. Beyond the realm of these experimental schools, there were "already many teachers who are working in the modern spirit in their classes." Recalling how the Prussian state authorities in the past were bent on exercising controls, Karsen saw two major milestones in the progress of educational reform: the school administration's approval of the opening of experimental schools that were not bound to any prescribed lesson plan, and the ministry's new curriculum guidelines for the basic school that were "influenced most strongly by the ideas of the active-learning school."[117]

Notes

1. In Prussia, for example, 60 percent or 56,559 of the 94,303 men in elementary school teaching positions were conscripted for military service in World War I. More than 9,400 teachers died in combat. By the end of the war, 4,952 teachers serving in the military suffered from war wounds or the loss of a limb. See Carl Louis Pretzel's report on the effects of the war on the elementary schools in *Zentralblatt für die gesamte Unterrichtsverwaltung in Preussen*, March 1920, no. 3: 258–63.
2. *Leipziger Lehrerzeitung*, 28 November 1923: 573–74; ibid., 5 December 1923: 585–86; *Sächsische Schulzeitung*, 5 December 1923: 573–75. On conditions in postwar Saxony, see Walter Fabian, *Klassenkampf um Sachsen* (1930; reprint, Berlin, 1972); Lapp, *Revolution from the Right*, pp. 21ff.
3. SHA, Nr. 13586, Bl. 364ff, report of School Inspector Wehner in the Leipzig district. See also *Leipziger Lehrerzeitung*, 7 November 1923: 533–34; Poste, *Schulreform in Sachsen*, pp. 87ff.
4. SHA, Nr. 13586, reports of the school inspectors of the Chemnitz, Dresden, and Leipzig districts; *Leipziger Lehrerzeitung*, 20 June 1923: 297–98.
5. *Gesetze und Verordnungen über das Volks- und Fortbildungs-Schulwesen im Freistaate Sachsen*, pp. 9–10.
6. See Haenisch's addresses to large gatherings of schoolteachers on visits to the cities of Königsberg and Halle in *Lehrerzeitung für Ost- und Westpreussen*, 29 January 1921: 51–54; *Schulblatt der Provinz Sachsen*, 23 February 1921: 71–73.
7. *Zentralblatt für die gesamte Unterrrichtsverwaltung in Preussen*, no. 10, October 1919: 615ff.
8. Tews, *Die deutsche Einheitsschule*, pp. 44ff; Richard Seyfert, "Für die allgemeine Volksschule," in Seyfert and Foerster, *Für und wider die allgemeine Volksschule*, pp. 13–14, 18–19.
9. Tews, *Die deutsche Einheitsschule*, pp. 30–31, 43–44.

10. Ibid., pp. 50–57.
11. Ibid., pp. 58–59.
12. Georg Winkler, *Aufbau des Schulwesens* (Langensalza, 1919), pp. 4–5; Fritz Gansberg, *Grundlinien der Schulorganisation im neuen Volksstaate* (Berlin, 1920), p. 7.
13. Gansberg, *Grundlinien der Schulorganisation*, pp. 8–9.
14. Winkler, *Aufbau des Schulwesens*, pp. 14–16; *Schlesische Schulzeitung*, 18 February 1920: 92–93; ibid., 6 April 1921: 144; *Allgemeine Deutsche Lehrerzeitung*, 8 January 1920: 15.
15. For the text of the Basic School Law of 28 April 1920, see Führ, *Zur Schulpolitik*, pp. 161–62.
16. *Verhandlungen der Deutschen Nationalversammlung*, 8 March 1920, pp. 4763–66; ibid., 16 April 1920, p. 5195.
17. *Schulblatt der Provinz Sachsen*, 28 April 1920: 170–71; *Lehrerzeitung für Ost- und Westpreussen*, 24 April 1920: 257; *Allgemeine Deutsche Lehrerzeitung*, 7 May 1920: 217.
18. On the political orientation of secondary schoolteachers, see Jarausch, *The Unfree Professions*, pp. 68–71; Ekkehard Meier, "Geschlossene Gesellschaft – Zur Mentalität deutschnationaler Gymnasiallehrer," in *Schulreform – Kontinuitäten und Brüche*, ed. Radde, pp. 102–15. A survey of 500 politically active secondary schoolteachers in 1926 showed that only 3.8 percent and 11 percent of these educators were involved in the Social Democratic and German Democratic Parties respectively, whereas 30.4 percent belonged to the German People's Party and 27.8 percent to the German National People's Party, and 18.3 percent gravitated to the right wing of the Center Party.
19. On the secondary schoolteachers' agitation against the school reforms, see Kurt Kesseler, *Die Erhaltung des wissenschaftlich gebildeten Lehrerstandes eine Notwendigkeit* (Leipzig, 1920) and the reports in *Allgemeine Deutsche Lehrerzeitung*, 19 February 1920: 100; ibid., 14 May 1920: 239; ibid., 13 August 1920: 355. See also Franz Hamburger, "Lehrer zwischen Kaiser und Führer. Der Deutsche Philologenverband in der Weimarer Republik" (Ph.D. diss., University of Heidelberg, 1974), pp. 177–88.
20. Quoted in *Sächsische Schulzeitung*, 10 March 1920: 155.
21. Ferdinand Jakob Schmidt, *Volksvertretung und Schulpolitik* (Berlin 1919), pp. 27–32; idem, *Das Problem der nationalen Einheitsschule* (Jena, 1916), pp. 3–4, 13–15.
22. *Allgemeine Deutsche Lehrerzeitung*, 4 March 1920: 128–29; ibid., 9 April 1920: 167–68.
23. Fritz Ringer, *The Decline of the German Mandarins: The German Academic Community 1890–1933* (Cambridge, 1969), pp. 78–80.
24. Wilhelm Hartnacke, *Das Problem der Auslese der Tüchtigen. Einige Gedanken und Vorschläge zur Organisation des Schulwesens nach dem Kriege* (Leipzig, 1916), pp. 45–49.
25. Wilhelm Hartnacke, *Naturgrenzen geistiger Bildung* (Leipzig, 1930), pp. 5–8; idem, *Das Problem der Auslese*, pp. 16–17.
26. F. W. Foerster, "Bedenken gegen die Einheitsschule," in Seyfert and Foerster, *Für und wider die allgemeine Volksschule*, pp. 41–44, 47–49. See also Paul Cauer, *Aufbau oder Zerstörung? Eine Kritik der 'Einheitsschule'* (Münster, 1919), pp. 27ff; August Grünweller, *Schulreform, Volksschule und Volkswohl. Zugleich ein Protest gegen die heillose Auspowerung der Volksschule* (Berlin, 1918), pp. 6–10.
27. Schmidt, *Volksvertretung und Schulpolitik*, p. 15. See the views of Otto Braun, a Privatdozent at the University of Münster, quoted in Emil Saupe, *Die Einheitsschule* (Langensalza, 1919), p. 53.
28. *Leipziger Lehrerzeitung*, 3 March 1920: 162–63; see also *Sächsische Schulzeitung*, 19 May 1920: 277–78; *Lehrerzeitung für Ost- und Westpreussen*, 10 April 1920: 230–31; Tews, *Die deutsche Einheitsschule*, p. 66.
29. *Allgemeine Deutsche Lehrerzeitung*, 11 June 1920: 281.
30. See the report written by Fritz Rupprecht of Breslau in *Schlesische Schulzeitung*, 16 June 1920: 241.
31. *Die Reichsschulkonferenz 1920. Ihre Vorgeschichte und Vorbereitung und ihre Verhandlungen* (1921; reprint, Glashütten, 1972), pp. 451–52.

32. *Reichsschulkonferenz 1920*, pp. 479, 483–85, 698–99. On this controversy, see Remigius Stölze, *Universität und Lehrerbildung* (Langensalza, 1920); Johannes Kühnel, *Gedanken über Lehrerbildung* (Leipzig, 1920); Richard Seyfert, *Der Streit des Herrn Dr. Ernst Boehm gegen die akademische Lehrerbildung. Eine Abwehrschrift* (Leipzig, 1926).
33. *Allgemeine Deutsche Lehrerzeitung*, 18 June 1920: 299–300.
34. *Reichsschulkonferenz 1920*, pp. 635–37.
35. Ibid., pp. 630–32.
36. Ibid., pp. 882–83; *Allgemeine Deutsche Lehrerzeitung*, 25 June 1920: 309–11; *Westdeutsche Lehrerzeitung*, 17 July 1920: 197–98.
37. Führ, *Zur Schulpolitik*, pp. 89–91.
38. Georg Wolff, *Grundschulfragen und Grundschulgegner* (Osterwieck, 1923), pp. 27–31.
39. *Lehrerzeitung für Ost- und Westpreussen*, 1 January 1921: 2; ibid., 19 February 1921: 90, 96; ibid., 26 February 1921: 104; *Schulblatt der Provinz Sachsen*, 23 February 1921: 73; *Schlesische Schulzeitung*, 23 February 1921: 81.
40. *Allgemeine Deutsche Lehrerzeitung*, 25 February 1921: 85–87.
41. *Zentralblatt für die gesamte Unterrichtsverwaltung in Preussen*, no. 6, June 1921: 133–36; *Allgemeine Deutsche Lehrerzeitung*, 25 March 1921: 143.
42. *Zentralblatt für die gesamte Unterrichtsverwaltung in Preussen*, no. 9, 5 May 1921: 199–201.
43. Hamburger, "Lehrer zwischen Kaiser und Führer," pp. 209, 213ff.
44. *Allgemeine Deutsche Lehrerzeitung*, Beilage, 22 September 1922: 242.
45. *Sitzungsberichte des Preussischen Landtages*, 8 May 1923, p. 17063; ibid., 9 May 1923, p. 17140.
46. Wolff, *Grundschulfragen*, pp. 48–50; see also the articles of Martin Weise in *Sächsische Schulzeitung*, 21 January 1920: 34; ibid., 8 September 1920: 438–40; ibid., 15 September 1920: 458–60; *Schulblatt der Provinz Sachsen*, 11 April 1923: 138–39; ibid., 16 May 1923: 193–94.
47. *Zentralblatt für die gesamte Unterrichtsverwaltung in Preussen*, no. 9, 5 May 1923: 187–88.
48. *Sitzungsberichte des Preussischen Landtages*, 7 May 1923, pp. 17011, 17024–26.
49. For the ministry's directives on the *Deutsche Oberschule* and the *Aufbauschule*, see *Zentralblatt für die gesamte Unterrichtsverwaltung in Preussen*, Beilage, no. 6, 20 March 1922: 1–6.
50. Gerhardt Petrat, "Die gezielte Öffnung der Hochschulreife für alle Volksschichten in der Weimarer Republik," in *Sozialisation und Bildungswesen in der Weimarer Republik*, ed. Manfred Heinemann (Stuttgart, 1976), pp. 79–80; Wittwer, *Die sozialdemokratische Schulpolitik*, pp. 270–71.
51. *Vierteljahrshefte zur Statistik des Deutschen Reichs. Das Schulwesen im Deutschen Reich. Schuljahr 1926–27*, vol. 39, no. 5, pp. 3, 5; *Statistik des Deutschen Reichs*. Vol. 438: *Das Schulwesen im Deutschen Reich. Schuljahr 1931–32* (Berlin, 1933), pp. 4, 14.
52. *Allgemeine Deutsche Lehrerzeitung*, 12 February 1920: 82–83; ibid., 22 April 1921: 181–82. See also Ottomar Fröhlich's views on the school class as a "working community" in ibid., 1 December 1920: 627–29; Johannes Boeger, *Staatsbürgerkunde als Lehrfach der Schulen* (Berlin, 1921), pp. 34ff; Fritz Karsen, *Die Schule der werdenden Gesellschaft* (Stuttgart, 1921), pp. 22ff; Artur Buchenau, *Wesen und Aufgaben der Schule* (Langensalza, 1919), pp. 7ff.
53. *Sächsische Schulzeitung*, 15 September 1920: 459; Otto Erler, *Die Volksschule im Lichte des demokratischen Staates und des Sozialismus* (Leipzig, 1919), pp. 3, 9–11.
54. *Sächsische Schulzeitung*, 15 September 1920: 459; *Allgemeine Deutsche Lehrerzeitung*, 22 April 1921: 182–83.
55. *Allgemeine Deutsche Lehrerzeitung*, 19 February 1920: 106; *Schlesische Schulzeitung*, 18 February 1920: 89; *Leipziger Lehrerzeitung*, 28 April 1920: 262–63; Horst Schallenberger, *Untersuchungen zum Geschichtsbild der Wilhelminischen Ära und der Weimarer Zeit. Eine vergleichende Schulbuchanalyse deutscher Schulgeschichtsbücher aus der Zeit von 1888 bis 1933* (Ratingen, 1964), pp. 215ff.
56. *Schlesische Schulzeitung*, 24 November 1920: 426–27; *Lehrerzeitung für Ost- und Westpreussen*, 25 September 1920: 555–57; ibid., 2 October 1920: 567–68; *Sächsische Schulzeitung*, 18 April 1923: 148–49.

57. *Allgemeine Deutsche Lehrerzeitung*, 19 February 1920: 106.
58. *Schlesische Schulzeitung*, 18 February 1920: 89; *Lehrerzeitung für Ost- und Westpreussen*, 17 July 1920: 418-19; ibid., 25 September 1920: 555-57.
59. SHA, Nr. 14563, Bl. 15, order of the Saxon Ministry of Education on civics in the schools, 23 December 1920; ibid., Bl. 17, the reply of Oskar Gleissberg in his capacity as the chairman of the Saxon Teachers' Association, 9 February 1921; see also ibid., Bl. 123, the report sent to the ministry by Fritz Barth, a progressivist pedagogue in Leipzig, who participated in a workshop on civic education sponsored by the Zentralinstitut für Erziehung und Unterricht in Berlin on 4-9 June 1923.
60. For the deliberations on civic education at the congress and the text of August Möller's address, see *Allgemeine Deutsche Lehrerzeitung*, 16 June 1922: 285ff; ibid., 14 July 1922: 325-27; ibid., 28 July 1922: 338-39.
61. *Zentralblatt für die gesamte Unterrichtsverwaltung in Preussen*, no. 16, 20 August 1922: 363-64; *Allgemeine Deutsche Lehrerzeitung*, 28 July 1922: 337-38; ibid., 25 August 1922: 384-86; *Schulblatt der Provinz Sachsen*, 16 August 1922: 367-68.
62. *Gesetze und Verordnungen über das Volks- und Fortbildungs-Schulwesen im Freistaate Sachsen*, pp. 148-49.
63. *Allgemeine Deutsche Lehrerzeitung*, 28 July 1922: 337-38; ibid., 11 August 1922: 353-54. For other statements on the responsibilities of teachers in the political socialization of the youth, see *Schulblatt der Provinz Sachsen*, 16 August 1922: 367-68; *Katholische Schulzeitung für Norddeutschland*, 10 August 1922: 435-36. On the secondary schoolteachers' unfavorable views of these administrative measures to protect the republic, see Jarausch, *The Unfree Professions*, pp. 68-69.
64. *Lehrerzeitung für Ost- und Westpreussen*, 17 July 1920: 419.
65. *Preussische Lehrerzeitung*, 7 September 1922: 1-2; ibid., 26 September 1922: 2-3.
66. See Pretzel's comments on civic education and the active-learning school in the report of the meeting of the German Teachers' Association's Erziehungswissenschaftliche Hauptstelle held in the chamber of the Ministry of Education on 8 and 9 March 1924 in *Allgemeine Lehrerzeitung*, 28 March 1924: 189. On Pretzel's career, see Leonhardt, *50 Jahre Berliner Lehrerverein*, pp. 194-95.
67. GSA, Rep. 76 VII neu, Teil I, Sekt. 1B Gen., Nr. 61, Bd. 2, Bl. 34, Prussian minister of education to the chairmen of the teachers' associations, 13 December 1920; ibid., Bl. 46ff, minutes of the discussion held on 8 January 1921.
68. *Allgemeine Deutsche Lehrerzeitung*, 7 October 1921: 461-63.
69. Berthold Otto, an exponent of this method of instruction, maintained that the division of teaching material by discrete subjects was alien to the way a child of six or seven years of age looked at the world. Gertrud Ferber, *Berthold Ottos Pädagogisches Wollen und Wirken* (Langensalza, 1925), pp. 22ff.
70. *Zentralblatt für die gesamte Unterrichtsverwaltung in Preussen*, no. 9, 5 May 1921: 185-88.
71. GSA, Rep. 76 VII neu, Teil I, Sekt. 1B Gen., Nr. 61, Bd. 1, Bl. 454 and Bl. 471, minutes of the discussions of the representatives of the Protestant Church with officials in the Ministry of Education on 21 October 1921 and 4 May 1922.
72. *Schlesische Schulzeitung*, 17 August 1921: 353-54; *Schulblatt der Provinz Sachsen*, 7 March 1923: 91-92. See also *Lehrerzeitung für Ost- und Westpreussen*, 3 September 1921: 483.
73. GSA, Rep. 77, Tit. 1124, Nr. 76, Bd. 1, Bl. 15, Reich interior minister to the Prussian education minister, 18 January 1922 [copy]; ibid., Bl. 21, minister of education to the Prussian finance minister, 30 May 1922 [copy].
74. *Lehrerzeitung für Ost- und Westpreussen*, 15 January 1921: 35; ibid., 22 January 1921: 47; ibid., 29 January 1921: 58; ibid., 19 February 1921: 97; ibid., 26 November 1921: 659; *Schlesische Schulzeitung*, 16 March 1921: 105-7, 113; *Schulblatt der Provinz Sachsen*, 23 March 1921: 112; ibid., 7 March 1923: 91-93; ibid., 14 March 1923: 109.
75. Paul Bode, "Grenzen und Aufgaben moderner Landschularbeit," in *Stimmen zur Landschulreform*, ed. Franz Kade (Frankfurt am Main, 1932), pp. 1-3; Max Wolf, "Zur Landschulreform,"

in ibid., pp. 124-29; Anton Strobel, "Landliche Zentralschule," in ibid., pp. 101-13. See also Walter Popp, *Neuorientierung der Volksschule* (Langensalza, 1917), pp. 16-18.
76. *Westdeutsche Lehrerzeitung*, 28 May 1921: 329-30.
77. *Westdeutsche Lehrerzeitung*, 2 April 1921: 191-93; ibid., 4 June 1921: 351; ibid., 3 December 1921: 757. See also *Pädagogische Post*, 17 January 1922: 83; ibid., 18 February 1922: 206; and the defense of the modern pedagogy by Catholic teachers in the Ruhr region in ibid., 26 February 1931: 135-37.
78. *Pädagogische Post*, 21 June 1922: 669-71.
79. *Schlesische Schulzeitung*, 17 August 1921: 353-54; see also ibid., 2 March 1921: 90; *Hugo Gaudig zum Gedächtnis. Worte seiner Mitarbeiter* (Leipzig, 1924), p. 29.
80. *Schlesische Schulzeitung*, 31 August 1921: 380; ibid., 10 August 1921: 348; ibid., 17 August 1921; 360-61; ibid., 9 November 1921: 489; ibid., 23 November 1921: 513; ibid., 29 December 1921: 556.
81. *Schulblatt der Provinz Sachsen*, 3 January 1922: 7-8; ibid., 15 February 1922: 87; ibid., 30 March 1922: 159; ibid., 10 May 1922: 238. For an assessment of Gaudig's influence among the elementary schoolteachers, see ibid., 29 August 1923: 345.
82. *Schulblatt der Provinz Sachsen*, 7 February 1923: 57; ibid., 31 October 1923: 418-21.
83. *Schlesische Schulzeitung*, 26 April 1922: 192-93.
84. Otto Scheibner, *Zwanzig Jahre Arbeitsschule in Idee und Gestaltung* (Leipzig, 1930), pp. 10, 153.
85. Gaudig, *Die Schule im Dienste der werdenden Persönlichkeit*, vol. 1, pp. 29ff; *Schulblatt der Provinz Sachsen*, 31 October 1923: 418-21.
86. Scheibner, *Zwanzig Jahre Arbeitsschule*, p. 161.
87. Gaudig, *Die Schule im Dienste der werdenden Persönlichkeit*, vol. 1, pp. 31-33; ibid., vol. 2, pp. 146-59; idem, *Elternhaus und Schule als Erziehungsgemeinschaft* (Leipzig, 1920), pp. 3-6.
88. Hanno Schmitt, "Topographie der Reformschulen in der Weimarer Republik. Perspektiven ihrer Erforschung," in *'Die Alte Schule Überwinden'. Reformpädagogische Versuchsschulen zwischen Kaiserrreich und Nationalsozialismus*, ed. Ullrich Amlung et al. (Frankfurt am Main, 1993), p. 21.
89. Margarete Behrens, "Die Magdeburger Versuchsschule," in *Die neuen Schulen*, ed. Karsen, p. 106. See also Reinhard Bergner, "Magdeburger Schulversuche mit Berthold Ottos Schulkonzept zur Zeit der Weimarer Republik," in *Die Alte Schule*, ed. Amlung, pp. 158-84.
90. *Die Chemnitzer Versuchsschule. Ein kurzer Bericht über ihre Entwicklung und ihren derzeitigen Stand* (Dresden, 1928), pp. 7-8. See also Pehnke, *Sächsische Reformpädagogik*, pp. 107ff.
91. On the opposition to Paulsen's appointment, see *Allgemeine Deutsche Lehrerzeitung*, Beiblatt des Lehrerverbandes Berlin, 28 January 1921: 27-28; ibid., 29 April 1921: 132-33.
92. Fritz Karsen, "Die Entstehung der Berliner Gemeinschaftsschulen," in *Die neuen Schulen*, ed. Karsen, pp. 161-81; Gerd Radde, "Schulreform in Berlin am Beispiel der Lebensgemeinschaftsschulen," in *Die Alte Schule*, ed. Amlung, pp. 89-106.
93. *Allgemeine Deutsche Lehrerzeitung*, 3 February 1922: 55-57.
94. *Versuchsschule Telemannstrasse 10, 1919-1929. Ein Bericht über ihre Entwicklung und ihren gegenwärtigen Stand* (Hamburg, 1929), p. 7. For other contemporary reports on the experimental schools, see Wilhelm Lamszus, "Der Weg der Hamburger Gemeinschaftsschule," in *Die neuen Schulen*, ed. Karsen, pp. 24-84; *Allgemeine Deutsche Lehrerzeitung*, 3 February 1922: 55-57; *Pädagogische Arbeitsgemeinschaft. Beilage zu der Sächsischen Schulzeitung*, 21 March 1923, no. 2, 11-14. See also Reiner Lehberger, "'Schule als Lebensstätte der Jugend'. Die Hamburger Versuchs- und Gemeinschaftsschulen in der Weimarer Republik," in *Die Alte Schule*, ed. Amlung, pp. 32-64.
95. *Preussische Lehrerzeitung*, 26 August 1922: 1-2.
96. *Die Chemnitzer Versuchsschule*, pp. 22-23; *Preussische Lehrerzeitung*, 26 August 1922: 1-2.
97. Georg Schwenzer, "Die Dresdener Versuchsschule," in *Die neuen Schulen*, ed. Karsen, p. 118.
98. Ibid., p. 123; SHA, Nr. 13588, Bl. 45ff, memorandum on the experimental school in Leipzig-Connewitz written by Paul Schnabel, a member of the teaching staff.

99. *Die Chemnitzer Versuchsschule*, pp. 70-71; *Pädagogische Arbeitsgemeinschaft. Beilage zu der Sächsischen Schulzeitung*, 21 March 1923: 148.
100. Lamszus, "Der Weg der Hamburger Gemeinschaftsschule," pp. 27-31; 73-76.
101. Lehberger, "'Schule als Lebensstätte der Jugend,'" pp. 38, 49-50; Ewald Fabry, "Die Schulpolitik der Linken in der ersten Phase der Weimarer Republik," in *'Der Traum von der freien Schule'. Schule und Schulpolitik in der Weimarer Republik*, ed. Hans-Peter de Lorent and Volker Ullrich (Hamburg, 1988), pp. 66-67.
102. Christian Paulmann, "Zwei Jahre Arbeit. Grundlage und Fortgang der Versuchsschule Schleswigerstrasse/Theodorstrasse zu Bremen," in *Die neuen Schulen*, ed. Karsen, pp. 125-30; Fritz Aevermann, "Anarchie oder soziale Bindung," in ibid., pp. 130-33; *Allgemeine Deutsche Lehrerzeitung*, 3 March 1922: 102-4.
103. *Leipziger Lehrerzeitung*, 1 September 1920: 501-3; ibid., 28 November 1923: 571-72; *Sächsische Schulzeitung*, 18 February 1920: 101-2; *Die Chemnitzer Versuchsschule*, p. 9.
104. SHA, Nr. 13838, Ministerialrat Karstädt of the Prussian Ministry of Education to the Saxon minister of education, 30 January 1923, requesting permission to visit the experimental schools; *Pädagogische Arbeitsgemeinschaft. Beilage zu der Sächsischen Schulzeitung*, no. 4, 20 June 1923: 31-32. See also Poste, *Schulreform in Sachsen*, pp. 305-7, 374-77.
105. SHA, Nr. 13915, Bl. 1, Saxon Teachers' Association to the minister of education, 24 November 1922; ibid., Bl. 6, the ministry's order to the district school inspectors, 30 November 1922.
106. SHA, Nr. 13915, Bl. 12ff, district school inspectors' reports on the selection of the teachers for the training courses; ibid., Bl. 88-90, list of the participants and the amount of the subsidy given to each one; ibid., Bl. 145ff, report of the course held in the Dresden school written by Martin Weise and sent to the ministry, 15 April 1923.
107. SHA, Nr. 13915, Bl. 234, School Inspector Erler in Ölsnitz to the ministry, 4 October 1923; ibid., Nr. 13915/1, Bl. 2 and Bl. 185, ministry's announcements of the training courses; ibid., Bl. 196-97 and Bl. 322-27, lists of the participants.
108. Quoted in Poste, *Schulreform in Sachsen*, pp. 342-43.
109. *Pädagogische Arbeitsgemeinschaft. Beilage zu der Sächsischen Schulzeitung*, no. 4, 20 June 1923: 31.
110. SHA, Nr. 13915, Bl. 145ff, report on the training course held at the Dresden experimental school and the summary of the responses of twenty-eight participants on the extent to which the reform pedagogy had been put into practice in the schools of their localities.
111. SHA, 13586, Bl. 331ff, report of School Inspector Fritzsch of the Grimma district; ibid., Bl. 549ff, report of School Inspector Zesch of the Bad Schandau district.
112. SHA, Nr. 13586, Bl. 202ff, report of School Inspector Stenzel in the Chemnitz II district.
113. SHA, Nr. 13586, Bl. 316ff, report of School Inspector Hertel in the Glauchau district; ibid., Bl. 429ff, report of School Inspector Viehweg in the Löbau district; ibid., Bl. 202ff, report of School Inspector Stenzel in the Chemnitz II district.
114. SHA, Nr. 13586, Bl. 31ff, report of School Inspector Wahl in the Bautzen district; ibid., Bl. 429ff, Viehweg's report cited above.
115. *Schulblatt der Provinz Sachsen*, 14 February 1923: 66-68; ibid., 16 May 1923: 193-94; *Pädagogische Post*, 19 November 1927: 925-27.
116. *Schlesische Schulzeitung*, 20 April 1922: 178-79.
117. Karsen, "Die Entstehung der Berliner Gemeinschaftsschulen," p. 178.

Chapter 5

THE CULTURE WARS OVER THE SCHOOLS IN THE WEIMAR ERA

The shift of governmental power to the political right in 1924 gave heart to ideological groups who opposed the school reforms and harbored feelings of ambivalence or outright hostility to the republican state. The Social Democratic Party in Saxony was left divided and weakened after the Reich government's intervention to depose the Socialist cabinet of Erich Zeigner in October 1923. The great coalition government formed by the Social Democratic Landtag deputies with the German Democratic and German People's Parties in January 1924 diminished Social Democratic influence in Saxon politics. The consequences of this coalition for school politics became evident immediately after Fritz Kaiser, the new minister of education from the German People's Party, entered office. Kaiser gave the traditionalists a clear signal of the ministry's break with the policies of the Social Democrats by repealing Fleissner's decree of 24 August 1922, which did not permit religious observances, prayers, and the singing of church hymns in the schools outside of the time designated for religious instruction. Fleissner had issued this directive as an act of tolerance toward people of diverse faiths and convictions and out of consideration for the pupils who were registered out of religious instruction. Politically conservative churchmen and parents, however, had viewed this order as a concerted attempt by the Social Democrats to "de-Christianize the school" and "repress the freedom of Christian religious belief and practice."[1] With Kaiser now at the head of the school administration, the traditionalists in the church and teaching profession launched a polemical battle against the active-learning school in 1924. In no other large state in Germany were the culture wars over the modern pedagogy waged with as much vehemence as in Saxony from 1924 to the early 1930s.

The implementation of the school articles in the Weimar Constitution was also affected by the outcome of the Reichstag election in May 1924. The losses suffered by the German Democratic and Social Democratic Parties and the gains made by the German Nationalists and splinter parties on the right gave the Center Party greater political leverage. With a secure block of seats in the Reichstag and the Prussian Landtag, Center politicians used their position in governing coalitions with the Social Democrats in Prussia to limit the reform of teacher education. They joined a Reich coalition cabinet with the German Nationalists in 1927 with the intention of enacting a national school law that would fulfill the demands of the Catholic episcopate. In anticipation of this battle over the school law, church leaders in Prussia, confident of the support of the massive Catholic and Protestant parents' organizations, conducted a test of strength with the state and challenged the policies of school officials who sought to carry out the provisions of the Weimar Constitution. Why were the culture wars over the *Volksschule* fought with such intensity in the Weimar Republic? With what objectives did the traditionalists and progressivist pedagogues enter these battles for the school?

The Attack on the Modern School and the New Pedagogy

Although Fritz Kaiser knew that it was not yet politically feasible to revise the school legislation of the early Weimar years, he expressed his opposition to the policies of his Social Democratic predecessors in the early months of 1924 by removing Alwin Wünsche from his post in the ministry and shelving his plan for the reorganization of the school system and by orchestrating a campaign against the active-learning school. His political motivation was apparent when he chose a major conference of the German People's Party as the platform for inaugurating the assault on the new pedagogy. Kaiser stated that the Ministry of Education had received many complaints from parents who were dissatisfied with the instruction in the elementary schools and that the booming enrollments in the secondary schools were the result of "this flight from the elementary schools."[2] He repeated these charges in the Saxon parliament on 20 March, when he announced that the ministry was conducting an inquiry to find out whether "the learning achievement of the basic school is so poor that it affects the first year of secondary schooling." He contended that parents wanted more school supervision and that "some of the teachers have not always made the proper use of the freedom that the Transitional School Law granted to them." The rise in secondary school enrollments was "a sad sign that our elementary school no longer has the confidence of our parents."[3]

In response to the minister's order of 25 March 1924, thirty-four district school inspectors and the directors of 105 secondary schools in Saxony submitted reports. The inspectors who based their reports on visits to the schools in 1923, a time of economic hardship for working-class families, cautioned against generalizations and mentioned the difficulties of making an assessment of the new teaching methods in so short a time. The Saxon Teachers' Association demanded that the complaints be submitted to an objective review by professional educators and that the teachers be given the right to examine the material collected by the ministry. Brushing aside this request, the ministry hastily prepared a report on the faults of the Saxon elementary schools, and Kaiser issued it to the public at a press conference on 9 December 1924.[4] The ministry distributed nearly 3,000 copies of this report to journalists, members of the teaching profession, and school administrators, as well as to government officials and parliamentary deputies in Saxony and in other German states. Articles quoting sections of the report appeared in the daily press.[5] This sensational publicity put the modern pedagogy and the active-learning school in the national spotlight.

The negative evaluation of the elementary schools in Kaiser's report rested heavily on the comments of secondary schoolteachers, who carped about the deficiencies in the performance of the pupils on the entrance examinations and in the first grade (the *Sexta*) of the secondary schools. They claimed that the results of the tests showed a decline in the children's abilities in reading, writing, and arithmetic. The pupils in the *Sexta* lacked the necessary mental discipline and training in grammar for Latin instruction and had difficulty in memorizing the material by heart. The gains in the intellectual curiosity, liveliness, and self-expression of the pupils were offset by the "superficiality of their learning," their inability to concentrate and be attentive, and their unwillingness to exert their energies in doing difficult assignments. The traditionalists in the secondary schools also observed a decline in the moral conduct of these pupils. In explaining this condition, the report presented their criticism of "the *Zeitgeist* with its restlessness, nervousness, and superficiality, with its flabby concept of duty, with its emancipation from moral and religious obligations."[6]

Kaiser's report gave little attention to the favorable observations of those school inspectors who wrote that the basic schools were achieving the educational goals set by the school administration and that the pupils had more curiosity, initiative, and self-motivation. Instead, the report quoted other inspectors, without mentioning their names and districts, who thought that "experimentation" in the schools had gone too far. They claimed that many teachers had no set lesson plan and that the instruction proceeded "according to the wishes and opinions of the liveliest children." The theory of the child-centered school, sound in itself, led "frequently to aimless chattering, play, and dillydallying." Instruction in spelling and grammar was often "neglected by the most zealous advocates of the new education consciously or unconsciously as an unnecessary waste of energy and time."[7]

Ignoring the explanation for the increase in school enrollments given by most of the school inspectors, the minister concocted a myth that blamed the overcrowding of the secondary schools on an exodus from the elementary schools. The report offered anecdotal evidence and listed the complaints that parents conveyed to secondary school educators at the time of registration. The parents said that the pedagogues in the modern schools underestimated the importance of positive knowledge, neglected exercises and learning by memory, and "no longer developed in the children the moral will for earnest work, discipline, and order." After the school principal's office was divested of its supervisory authority, and collegial school governance was introduced, the teachers were left with too much freedom to follow their own arbitrary wishes.[8]

The "flight from the elementary school" became a shibboleth in the campaign against the new pedagogy, despite the efforts of the reformers in the teaching profession to bring reason and objectivity into the public debate on the surging enrollments in the secondary schools. Although the school-age population declined in the postwar years, secondary school enrollments expanded from 3.2 percent of the youth between eleven and nineteen years of age in 1911 to 7.1 percent in 1926, and 8.8 percent in 1931. At the same time, less than half of the students who entered secondary school succeeded in attaining the *Abitur* certificates.[9] The Saxon Teachers' Association held the secondary schoolteachers responsible for the problem of "overcrowding" and for the admission of pupils of average abilities. A scrutiny of the grades of children who entered the secondary schools revealed that the representatives of the secondary schools on the admissions committees did not follow a highly selective process. In a debate on this issue in the Chemnitz city council in March 1924, a municipal school official refuted the criticism published in a local right-wing newspaper by pointing out that the admissions committee had accepted applicants whose ability for academic work was "doubtful" on the basis of their development up to the age of ten. He reminded the city council of the conditions under which schoolchildren had grown up during the war and postwar years, and implored it not to act too hastily and reject the school reforms.[10]

Five school inspectors reported to the ministry that the secondary schools gave an easy entrance examination and admitted many pupils who had received low grades and were not recommended by their elementary schoolteachers. The Saxon Teachers' Association challenged the philologists to look at their own standards when it published a long rebuttal to Kaiser's report in 1925.[11] The policy in practice was to admit a relatively large number of applicants, to become more selective as the pupils ascended to the higher grades, and to weed out the pupils who did not perform well. By the time that the Ministry of Education in Prussia under the Social Democrat Adolf Grimme recognized this practice as one of the causes of overcrowding in the secondary schools and ordered a tightening of the selection process in 1931,[12] the myth of the decline of learning achievement in the elementary schools had gained wide currency.

Kaiser's criticism of the elementary schools launched an organized polemical campaign against the new pedagogy in the right-wing press in 1924–25. Karl Rothe, the German Nationalist mayor of Leipzig, started another round in this fight with his criticism of the elementary schools in his New Year's address to the city council in 1927.[13] Articles in the *Leipziger Neueste Zeitung* and other right-wing newspapers in the spring of 1924 painted a picture of noise, disorder, and indiscipline in the modern school, and attributed the expansion of the secondary school enrollments to the dissatisfaction of the parents and the "flight from the elementary school."[14] The education minister's report gave these newspapers more ammunition for continuing their attack on the pedagogues.

The polemic written by Alfred Spitzner, a *völkisch*-nationalist teacher, for a newspaper in the city of Plauen, a foothold of Nazi agitation, shows how the culture wars over the new pedagogy took a politically antidemocratic direction in the mid-1920s. Spitzner portrayed this debate as part of a larger clash between opposing ideological orientations: the traditionalists' affirmation of ethical norms and the *Volksgemeinschaft* on the one side, and the moral relativism and egoistic individualism of the liberals and leftists on the other side. Calling for the recovery of "authoritative norms" in school instruction, Spitzner maintained that the schools must emphasize the formation of character and nurture religious devoutness, consciousness of duty, a sense of discipline and order, and a respect for the authorities, so that a barricade could also be "created in the schools against the *Zeitgeist* that is driving inevitably toward chaotic conditions." He lambasted "the advocates of the 'development of the individual' who claim domination over the schools today" for being indifferent to the *Volk* and the fatherland and for seeing schooling as "a matter of letting the youth grow up in unlimited freedom and educating them through freedom for individual liberty." After assailing the active-learning school as a product of the November Revolution, he proceeded to denounce Germany's parliamentary democracy for possessing no moral and spiritual claim to authority and respect.[15]

The fight against the new pedagogy was waged by a coalition of conservative educators and clergymen. Secondary schoolteachers and the clerical leaders of the Protestant Parents' League in Saxony fed scurrilous material to the press for articles on the elementary schools. The attack on the modern school had begun even before the minister of education opened his inquiry in 1924. At public meetings of the Dresden secondary schoolteachers' association in October and December 1923, Wilhelm Hartnacke, a diehard opponent of the unified school system, spoke about the decline in the learning achievement of the pupils and charged that the elementary schools were "heading toward cultural Bolshevism." A German Nationalist school official in Dresden, Hartnacke repeated these assertions at a school board meeting in November and gave evasive replies when he was challenged to give evidence for his claims. Afterwards, he summoned a meeting of secondary schoolteachers in Dresden to inquire about the complaints of the parents that they might have heard and to collect their judgments of elementary school work. Early in 1924 he supplied this tendentious material to the political press.[16] Like Hartnacke, many of the polemicists in the culture wars were political right-wingers in the teaching profession who fought school reforms on political and ideological grounds and for reasons of social status and self-interest.

For elementary school educators who were adamantly opposed to collegial school governance and the position taken by the Saxon Teachers' Association on the issue of religious instruction, the controversy over the new pedagogy became a useful vehicle for agitating for the restoration of the *Schulrektorat*. Before 1919, school principals had enjoyed tenured appointment and had exercised more authority than the school principals (*Schulleiter*) under the new system of self-governance currently possessed. School principals were now nominated by the collegium of teachers and elected by the school boards for a limited and renewable term. From 1919 to 1921, disgruntled former school principals in Saxony fought a long and losing battle in the law courts to recover their old offices. They argued that the paragraph of the Transitional School Law of 1919 abolishing the *Schulrektorat* violated their appointment contracts and rights as tenured civil servants. They suffered another defeat when the Social Democratic majority in the Saxon parliament refused to amend the law.[17] Many school rectors experienced the loss of their professional authority as a painful humiliation. Remaining in the schools as classroom teachers, they were vehemently hostile to the Social Democratic Party and disaffected from the republic. "We no longer live in a state under the rule of law," protested Walter Kühn, a German Nationalist school rector. He viewed political life in the Weimar state as "a culture war," a struggle between a Marxist ideology bent on destroying bourgeois culture and an ideology of national renewal.[18]

The conservatives who bolted from the Saxon Teachers' Association founded a competitive organization in May 1924 with the financial support of the German People's Party. From the beginning, the raison d'être of the New Saxon Teachers' Association was to fight the school reformers and to stir up divisiveness and rebellion within its older and larger rival. Its leaders, Edmund Leupolt and Paul Sättler, were bitterly opposed to the school politics of the Social Democrats in the teaching profession and in the postwar government of Saxony. Benefiting from the patronage of Minister of Education Kaiser and his party, the New Saxon Teachers' Association absorbed another splinter group that had been formed by Kühn and other German Nationalists in 1920. The secessionists accused the postwar leadership of the Saxon Teachers' Association of betraying the profession by supporting the parties on the political left.[19] The Saxon Teachers' Association did not crumble under the assault of its right-wing foes. It lost only 248 members in 1924, and its membership rose to more than 18,900 by the end of the decade. The membership of the new teachers' organization remained so embarrassingly low that its officers did not disclose the figures.[20]

The conservatives in the New Saxon Teachers' Association sought to persuade the public that the introduction of collegial school governance was linked to the alleged decline in the learning achievement of the pupils. A former school principal stated in a daily newspaper: "It is an open secret that, under self-governance, a steep decline in teaching energies, work without lesson plans and goals, and experimentation of a dangerous kind are to be observed. The 'flight from the elementary school' is not a shabby slogan but has become a means by which conscientious parents can ensure the education of their children." A firmer supervision of the teachers by the school principals would "eliminate the distrust toward the schools that wide circles of parents still feel, and would be a way to cleanse the atmosphere in school politics."[21]

Attacks on the active-learning school remained a staple of the propaganda of the New Saxon Teachers' Association. Its opposition to the new pedagogy seldom went beyond mockery, vague ideological catchwords, and unsubstantiated generalizations. The author of one polemical article admitted that he had "painted in crass colors" and that there were "earnest people practicing the principles of the active-learning school in a moderate manner." And yet he proceeded to attack "faddish pedagogy" without mentioning names and places. The traditionalists deplored the influence of the discipline of psychology on schoolteaching and correlated the theories of child development and experiential learning with the *Zeitgeist* of materialism and individualism.[22] The progressivist pedagogues were ridiculed as "pale imitators of the Frenchman Rousseau." In the modern school, Leupolt jeered, the teacher stood "reverentially before the child, the new idol," and became "the slave of the child."[23]

The leaders of the New Saxon Teachers' Association frequently contrasted the conservatives' ideal of the "German Christian school" to the active-learning school in their efforts to appeal to teachers of the older generation who clung to traditional methods of instruction and to nationalist values with a religious hue. Leupolt lamented that elementary schoolteachers had become a very restless profession. Changes in the schools had produced "confusion, ferment, and fever, mental states of exhilaration and deepest despair" in the profession. He criticized the modern pedagogy for not developing "the virtues of German competence, German industriousness, strong determination and purposefulness, and steadfast subordination and adaptation." Leupolt described the educational ideal of the traditionalists as "the German school," which led the pupils "across the path of compulsion and behavioral training to freedom," nurtured patriotism, and did "not preach class conflict as many exponents of the new education" did. Reinforcing his insinuation that the active-learning school did not foster patriotic values, he contended that "the new education neglects the cultivation of the characteristics of the 'social' person that are of the highest value for a *Volksgemeinschaft*."[24] Ernst Laube, another former school principal and a member of the executive board of the New Saxon Teachers' Association, accused the progressivist pedagogues of advocating "the ideas of a cowardly pacifism and a zealous glorification of the reconciliation of nations at the expense of Germany." He maintained that wide circles of society viewed elementary schoolteachers with distrust and no longer respected them because so many members of the Saxon Teachers' Association preferred "to serve internationalism and pacifism."[25]

For conservative secondary schoolteachers, the public debate over the new pedagogy became a convenient handle for discrediting the school reform movement. They viewed the enactment of the Basic School Law and the opening of new types of secondary schools, the *Deutsche Oberschule* and the six-year *Aufbauschule*, in the 1920s as a threat to the social exclusiveness and cultural elitism of the traditional *Gymnasium*. The fast growing enrollments in the secondary schools and universities aroused a deeply felt fear of academic overproduction and proletarianization and a sense of crisis among the traditionalists. Their perceptions of change and their reaction to the perceived threat of democratic "leveling" were out of proportion to the actual effects of the school reforms. The potential access to the *Abitur* was increased with the creation of the basic school and the new types of secondary schools, but the practical effects were quite modest. The two new types of secondary schools had an enrollment of about 33,000 out of a total of 823,000 secondary school students (that is, 4 percent) in Germany in the 1926–27 academic year. The *Aufbauschulen* proved to afford less upward mobility for working-class youths than the reformers had expected; the largest number of pupils in these schools were the offspring of lower-middle-class parents. By 1931, only 7 percent of the students in all grades in the secondary schools came from working-class homes.[26]

The traditionalists in the secondary schools associated the active-learning school with a negative attitude toward the cultivation of the mind and an indifference to the spiritual and moral purposes of education. They claimed that a vague kind of experience was put in place of intellectual work and learning and that instruction in the lower grades was "reduced to playing and dillydallying."[27] A common tactic employed by these opponents of school reform was to link the German Teachers' Association to the parties of the political left. One secondary schoolteacher charged that the political behavior of a "not inconsiderable" number of elementary schoolteachers, who professed their support for the Social Democratic Party after the November Revolution, aroused alienation throughout Germany and damaged the public reputation of their profession. It was not appropriate for pedagogues who had to teach the children of all parents "to be politically active in a very one-sided manner with conspicuous zeal."[28]

Hermann Rolle, a secondary schoolteacher in Bautzen, chastised the progressivist pedagogues for being indifferent to spiritual values and for placing the new pedagogy on the foundation of child psychology. "Educational psychologism falls into the dangerous error of seeing the child in the perverse light of an untrue idealization of his nature," he wrote. It conceived of the child's nature as innately good and promoted "a naturalistic pedagogy of freedom that determines the methods of education exclusively 'from the perspective of the child.'" Under the influence of these theories, the lesson plans in the modern school were no longer determined by the mature understanding of the teacher and curriculum regulations but by the inclinations of the pupils. Lamenting that "no requirements, obligations, and restraints" were placed on the schoolchildren, he declared that the reform pedagogy led to "a complete reversal of the relationship between teacher and child" and to "total anarchism in education." Rolle also condemned the "subjectivism" and the "cult of the individual self" in the new education and contended that the modern school failed to transmit the "objective values" and cultural heritage of the German people and to integrate the youth into the communities of social life. He bewailed: "We need such an extremely individualistic pedagogy least of all today, when we must knit together a society atomized by brutal egoism into a community through the renewal of social virtues."[29]

The polemical campaign against the modern pedagogy gained a wide hearing in Germany through the agitation of the League of Christian Parents' Associations. The league's officers submitted to the Saxon Ministry of Education the complaints that parents had sent to their headquarters in Dresden. Many of these letters contained accusations of promoting "nudism" (*Nacktkultur*) in the schools and raised questions about the moral character of the teachers. The parents objected to the attire worn by schoolgirls in sports, and complained that teachers weighed and measured schoolgirls dressed in their underclothes when the school physicians conducted medical examinations. In the election campaigns for the parents' councils, the league spiced its propaganda with anecdotal evidence about nudism in the modern school.[30]

Scurrilous propaganda about sexual instruction in the upper grades of the modern school was manufactured also from hearsay evidence about instruction on the human body and reproduction. At the experimental school in Chemnitz, a male teacher and his class of girls went to a public exhibition on the human species. Afterwards, with the aid of pictures in a biology book he answered their questions about childbirth. A drawing made by one of the pupils fell into the hands of a pastor. Without the knowledge of the parents, the pastor took the drawing to Robert Giertz, a German Nationalist in the city council and the chairman of the parents' league in Chemnitz. In the election campaign for the parents' councils in May 1923, an exaggerated tale of this school lesson was disseminated in a propaganda leaflet against the new education and secular schools. An article by Giertz in a Chemnitz daily related that thirteen- and fourteen-year-old girls at the experimental school were given sexual instruction and had to make drawings of the sexual organs of the body. This story became more distorted when it was retold in right-wing newspapers elsewhere in Germany.[31]

In several localities the Christian parents' associations lodged complaints about the modern pedagogy at school board meetings and sent petitions to the school authorities demanding the transfer of the teachers. A Protestant pastor in the town of Callenberg instigated a school strike in the spring of 1923 as a protest action against two teachers who were following the methods of the active-learning school. He was able to persuade only a small number of parents to keep their children home on the first day of the new school year. The teachers reacted quickly by inviting the parents and other local citizens to a meeting at which the district school inspector spoke in support of their work. The Ministry of Education, at that time under the Social Democrat Fleissner, acted firmly to discourage such protest tactics. The school authorities imposed fines on the pastor for calling the strike and on nine fathers who kept their children out of school.[32]

Schoolteachers who were the target of protest actions were known to be Social Democrats and had incurred the ill will of conservative townspeople because of their political views. The school inspector who investigated the complaint against two teachers in one rural locality wrote in his report to the minister of education that the strong objections to them within the middle-class population were to be attributed to "the offense taken [by these parents] at seeing their children instructed by Socialist-oriented teachers."[33] Teachers who broke their church affiliation also ran into opposition in small towns and rural villages. In 1923 some of the parents in Breunsdorf demanded the removal of Rudolf Leonhardt from the local school because he had given instruction about "sexual matters," with reference to the biological reproduction of animals. When the school inspector recommended Leonhardt's transfer to another school, he protested that he was being punished because he was a Social Democrat and had left the Protestant Church. When a Social Democratic official in the ministry examined how this case had been handled, he criticized the school inspector's decision. "Anger among the parents," Alwin Wünsche wrote, could not be grounds for transferring Leonhardt because "otherwise numerous teachers who decline to give religious instruction, leave the church, or join the Social Democratic and Communist Parties would have to be transferred continually from one locality to another."[34]

Conservative townspeople chafed at the school inspectors who withstood their efforts to drive the progressivist pedagogues out of the local schools. School Inspector Erich Viehweg called the accusations groundless after concluding his investigation of several complaints filed against these teachers in his district. In one of these cases, the inhabitants of a rural school district sent petitions to the minister of education in March 1924, demanding the removal of Johannes Schumann. Since Schumann had begun to practice the methods of the active-learning school, his critics claimed, the children had wasted hours of school time in playing and were behind in the subjects of reading, writing, and arithmetic. Members of the school board who visited his class found "the greatest conceivable disorder and indiscipline." The petitioners gave vent to their anger at Viehweg because he had not acceded to their earlier request to transfer Schumann and had treated it as a political vendetta.[35]

After Viehweg observed Schumann's work in the school and made inquiries in the local community, in his report to the minister he praised the teacher's knowledge of the discipline of pedagogy and his competence in the classroom. Schumann, Viehweg wrote, followed "the new methods with enthusiasm but also with moderation." His colleagues and other people in the local community spoke of his dedication and concern for the welfare of his pupils and noted that he voluntarily tutored three children of Polish workers at his home in after-school hours. Most of the people who had signed the petitions did not have school-age children or firsthand knowledge of his teaching. Viehweg discerned the political subtext in the opposition to Schumann when his critics on the school board made references to his political activities as a Social Democrat. A year earlier, a delegation representing local conservative opinion had come to Viehweg with the demand for Schumann's transfer and complained that he had spoken at a meeting of the Social Democratic Party. The pressure to remove him was intensified in 1924, after he was elected to the town council as a Social Democrat.[36]

The reformers in the elementary school teaching profession in Saxony and elsewhere in Germany condemned these attacks on the active-learning school as a politically motivated smear campaign. The role of politicians in the right-wing parties in this agitation in Saxony and Kaiser's choice of party conventions as the platform for two of his speeches against the new pedagogy in 1924 had not gone unnoticed. The reformers of the Saxon Teachers' Association contended that right-wing educators in the secondary schools who made "unproven allegations" about the decline in the learning achievement of the schoolchildren were bent on discrediting the basic school and were making an argument for a socially stratified educational system. They deplored the philologists' "distant and critical stance" toward modern views of education, and stated that these traditionalists would "be seen as an anachronism in the cultural life of the nation" if this resistance continued.[37]

The propaganda war against the modern pedagogy under the guise of news reporting provoked indignation within the Saxon Teachers' Association. Several articles signed by "a schoolman" presented a distorted picture of disorderly classrooms and frivolous instruction in the elementary schools. The reformers saw in this journalism a deliberate strategy of undermining public confidence in the active-learning school and its teachers. Slanderous insinuations about the immoral character of the progressivist pedagogues offended them. As the district school inspector of Leipzig pointed out, these tales were not based on facts and had "not passed the test of investigation" conducted by school officials.[38] The congress of the

Saxon Teachers' Association in 1924 denounced the unscrupulous tactics of the League of Christian Parents' Associations and its allies in the teaching profession. A teacher in Leipzig declared: "It is a fight with means against which we are almost powerless." Other teachers who felt vulnerable and unprotected remarked that by the time the investigations of the school administration revealed the untruthfulness of the allegations, the scandalous stories had spread, and the correction seldom reached those people who carried the stories further.[39]

The executive board of the Saxon Teachers' Association published a pamphlet in response to Kaiser's report on the elementary schools in an attempt to bring factual evidence and reason into the public discussion. The teachers reminded German citizens of the circumstances under which children lived and were taught during the war and postwar years. School life became unstable after 1914. In the city of Leipzig alone, 597 elementary schoolteachers were called into the army at the beginning of the war. To cover the vacancies in the teaching staff, substitutes with little professional experience were hired, and classes in the schools had to be merged. The schools did not return to normal conditions after 1918. In the wake of the inflation came shortages in the supply of paper, pens, and other school needs. Wherever municipalities did not have the funds to purchase coal to heat the classrooms, schools were closed down for weeks or the hours of instruction were cut during the winter months. The teachers gathered statistical data on the unemployment or short-time working hours of the fathers to document the poverty of schoolchildren in the industrial centers of Saxony, which experienced a severe economic recession in the postwar years. The physical conditions of the schoolchildren were described with a wealth of statistical material on their nourishment, health, and clothing. The teachers did not deny the presence of deficiencies in the work performed by these pupils, but they attributed them to malnutrition and poor health and to school conditions during these times of immense economic distress.[40]

The Churches and the Politics of Culture in the Republican State

Apart from the propaganda war against the modern pedagogy, educational reformers in Germany had other reasons to be troubled by the electoral shift to the political right. The constellation of power in the Reichstag after the election in May 1924 produced a majority for a national school law that moved further away from the school articles of the Weimar Constitution and closer to the demands made by the Center and German Nationalist Parties. The demagogic propaganda and volatility of the voters in this election campaign left many German Democrats in the German Teachers' Association with a disturbing sense of the intensified ideological polarization of the German people. After the election, Otto Schulz, a member of the executive board, wrote that the teachers would have to show the nation the way to unity and agreement on "the important nonpartisan principles in school politics."[41]

Otto Schulz and other reformers in the German Teachers' Association deplored the lack of a consciousness of the republican state as an integrating political community among many deputies in the newly elected Reichstag and in German society at large. In their view, Germany was experiencing "a new strong wave of particularism in domestic politics." Religious and ideological groups were placing subcommunities and subcultures above the idea of the state and the nation. Clergymen were misusing the concepts of democracy and parents' rights to serve the particularistic purposes of their churches and to weaken the sovereignty of the state in the cultural sphere. In reaction to these trends, German Democrats in the teachers' association placed greater emphasis on the idea of the *Kulturstaat*, the state as a cultural power, from 1924 on. Otto Schulz thought that the republic should be viewed not only as a state that regulated the relations of its citizens according to norms of justice and fairness, but also as a civic body that subsumed the cultural goals of the diverse groups within society in its own purposes.[42] When the Reichstag was dissolved after months of rowdy partisan debating and deadlock, the teachers' association urged its members in December 1924 to work for the election of a new Reichstag that would fulfill its public responsibilities, to make the campaign a fight over policies and principles rather than demagogic slogans, and to speak out for the *Kulturstaat*, "a state that strives to unite our people together inwardly through cultural-political work and to overcome the debilitating and damaging particularism by intellectual weapons."[43]

Developments in *Kulturpolitik* deepened the school reformers' impression of the weakness of the Weimar state in relation to the power of the Christian churches. When the government of Bavaria negotiated an accord with the Vatican in 1924, German Democrats and Social Democrats in the teaching profession denounced this act as a blow inflicted on the German Reich as a national state. Members of the Bavarian Teachers' Association viewed many provisions in this treaty apprehensively. Fresh in their memories were the school strikes incited by parish priests and the Catholic School Organization in 1922 to drive out of the schools teachers who spoke out in favor of the community school or joined the Social Democratic Party.[44] The concordat stipulated that the education of Catholic schoolchildren in Bavaria must "be entrusted only to such teachers who are suited and prepared to instruct Catholic religious doctrine in a reliable manner and to educate [them] in the spirit of the Catholic faith." It granted the bishops the right to commission priests to inspect public elementary schools and to lodge complaints about "any offenses to the religious faith and sensibilities [of the Catholics] in the instruction." The school authorities were obliged under the terms of this agreement to redress these grievances. The church obtained guarantees in respect to the maintenance of confessional public schools for Catholics in Bavaria that were similar to the maximalist demands for a national school law laid down by the German bishops in 1920. The state's obligation to provide institutions that would train teachers for Catholic schools "corresponding to the above principles" virtually gave the bishops the power to veto any reform of teacher education in Bavaria.[45]

Notwithstanding the electoral strength of the Catholic Bavarian People's Party in the state parliament, the Bavarian Teachers' Association organized an opposition movement to the concordat in November and December 1924 to arouse the public's awareness of the consequences of this agreement and to influence the position of the other parties. Its members staged protest rallies in Munich, Nuremberg, and Kaiserslautern.[46] In Berlin, the executive board of the national organization appealed to the Reich cabinet and Reichstag to block the ratification of the concordat. Eschewing anticlerical rhetoric, they hammered away at the treaty's violations of the school articles in the Weimar Constitution and the grave threat to the freedom of the teachers. They contended that the terms of the concordat would "lead inexorably to the observation and supervision of the teacher from a church perspective even in his life outside of the school—in his church attendance, choice of a wife, and membership in professional and political organizations."[47]

After the ratification of the concordat by the Bavarian parliament in January 1925, German Democrats and Social Democrats in the German Teachers' Association criticized the Reich cabinet for raising no objections to Bavaria's unilateral negotiation of a treaty with the Vatican. Ottomar Fröhlich was dismayed to see how the Reich government allowed the church "to interfere very extensively in the sphere of state authority, especially in the area of the schools." He thought that the concordat was "the worst self-abasement of a German state before the church at the expense of the schools above all." Georg Wolff pointed out in a cutting remark that throughout the controversy State Secretary Heinrich Schulz in the Reich Interior Ministry had not uttered a word to uphold a national school policy that would place common national values and interests above particular confessional, ideological, and regional concerns. Anxious to avoid a conflict with the Center Party, the Social Democrats in the Reichstag likewise disappointed the teachers with the sluggishness of their opposition to the concordat.[48]

Schoolteachers witnessed the powerful influence of political Catholicism again during the long debate over the enactment of a national law on teacher education. Under Article 143 of the Constitution, the professional training of elementary schoolteachers was to be regulated uniformly in the German Reich according to the principles used for secondary schoolteachers. The reformers in the German Teachers' Association and the German Democratic and Social Democratic Parties believed that this article required the republican state to shut down the *Lehrerseminare* and to make teacher education an academic course pursued in the universities.[49] When the deputies of these two parties in the Reichstag pressed the Reich government to introduce a draft law on teacher education in November 1920, Heinrich Schulz gave the evasive reply that the Ministry of the Interior had to examine first the financial consequences of the legislation. In 1921 and 1922, the teachers' association implored the Reich cabinet and Reichstag to enact a national law on teacher education, and in March 1922 teachers in Berlin staged a massive demonstration to protest the government's inaction. After several years of stalling, the Reich cabinet announced in February 1924 that it would not propose any national law for the integration of teacher education within the universities.

Political considerations rather than the financial costs led the Reich government to relinquish its constitutional power to regulate teacher education uniformly throughout Germany. The Center Party's hope for preserving the confessional character of the institutions for teacher education could be realized only by leaving legislation in this matter up to the states. In Saxony, Thuringia, Hesse, and Hamburg, all of which had a predominantly Protestant population, left-wing majorities in the state parliaments passed laws that fulfilled the intent of Article 143 of the Constitution. On the other hand, Bavaria kept intact the old system of confessional *Lehrerseminare*. In Prussia, the Social Democrats in the governing coalition were willing to accommodate the Center Party on this issue, and the Prussian State Ministry made the decision as early as February 1922 that the education of prospective elementary schoolteachers would not be consigned to the universities.[50]

The Center Party and its Protestant allies in the German National People's Party in Prussia fought attempts to bring the professional training of elementary schoolteachers within the universities. When the debate on the question of teacher education reached a decisive phase in 1925, the bishops of the Catholic dioceses in Prussia issued a warning that "only teachers who have received sufficient training in Catholic academies can be considered as qualified for working in Catholic schools in the future." In their petition sent to Minister of Education Carl Becker in September, the bishops laid down the condition that teachers for Catholic elementary schools must be trained in institutions staffed exclusively by instructors of the Catholic faith and that Catholic theology must be included in the material for the subject of religion. Other teachers would not be granted the *missio canonica*, the church's authorization to give Catholic religious instruction.[51] The Catholic School Organization used the same stern language in a statement issued to the press in November. The establishment of nonsectarian institutions for teacher education over the will of the Catholics, as the Social Democrats and German Democrats in the Prussian Landtag were striving to do, "would mean an open *Kulturkampf*."[52]

The plan for the reorganization of teacher education in Prussia announced by Becker in June 1925 fell far short of the reformers' demands.

The state government intended to establish twenty-six pedagogical academies (*Pädagogische Akademien*), which would not be affiliated with the universities. Candidates for elementary school teaching would receive their general education in secondary schools up to the attainment of the *Abitur* and then complete a two-year professional course in either a Catholic or Protestant pedagogical academy. Most elementary schoolteachers wanted to eliminate the isolation of their training in institutions that did not have the professional standing or social prestige of the university. They opposed Becker's proposal to no avail. In 1926 two Protestant academies in Elbing and Kiel and one Catholic academy in Bonn were opened.

For reasons of coalition politics, the Prussian State Ministry yielded to the demands of the Catholic episcopate and Center Party for a confessionally divided institutional structure for teacher education. In the Landtag on 3 November 1925, Becker defended the necessity of making this concession by citing the bishops' warning. A left liberal who grew up in Frankfurt am Main, Becker was personally sympathetic to the system of interconfessional schooling in that city. He understood the aspirations of the reformers who wanted the institutions of teacher education to be places where pedagogy was pursued as an academic discipline. He was prepared to support the opening of one interconfessional pedagogical academy, but he rejected the reformers' entreaty to place teacher education entirely in institutions with a mixed faculty and student body.[53] By a close vote of 182 to 173, the deputies defeated a motion to establish all pedagogical academies as interconfessional institutions. A more modest German Democratic proposal for the establishment of an interconfessional pedagogical academy in Frankfurt am Main won a majority vote on 15 December.

The reformers in the German Teachers' Association resented bitterly the influence exercised by the Center Party in school politics by virtue of its leverage in the formation of governing coalitions in Prussia and the Reich.[54] The circumstances regarding the Prussian law on teacher education impressed upon them the weakness of the Weimar state, with its unstable governmental leadership and incoherent and fluctuating parliamentary majorities, in relation to the resolute will of the episcopate and the unified voice of the Catholic subculture in Germany. In 1926, Otto Schulz noted that the parents' associations that uttered threats of political militancy and were determined to attain their objectives "without any concern for political compromise" made it difficult to regulate reasonably the place of the state and the church in the sphere of public elementary education. He deplored how school politics had become "a culture war," and he could foresee no end to this strife in the near future.[55]

The Catholic bishops and Center politicians turned the opening of the pedagogical academy in Frankfurt into a test of strength with the Weimar state. After the Prussian Landtag voted to establish this institute with an interconfessional faculty and student body in December 1925, they filed protests with the Reich interior minister and argued that this decision violated Article 174 of the Constitution. This opposition led him to appeal to the State Court for a ruling and forced the Prussian Ministry of Education to postpone the opening of the academy in Frankfurt. When the State Court did not sustain the contention of the Catholic opposition, the Catholic School Organization waved aside this judicial decision and argued that "legal formalism in questions of cultural and school politics is intolerable and destructive." In a joint pastoral letter in December 1926, the bishops of the dioceses of Limburg and Fulda declared that the Catholic Church would not allow schoolteachers trained in the pedagogical academy in Frankfurt to give Catholic religious instruction. Nor would the church grant the *missio canonica* to any instructor at that academy to teach the Catholic religion.[56]

The Catholics boycotted the pedagogical academy in Frankfurt when it finally opened in May 1927. The bishops' unyielding opposition to the establishment of institutions for teacher education with an interconfessional faculty and student body had significant consequences for the making of a national school law. This skirmish led many Germans in public life to ponder the obstacles to the attainment of a confessionally integrated elementary school system. One of these skeptics was Carl Becker. The Prussian minister of education now questioned the wisdom of "imposing the interconfessional school by a parliamentary majority" and "applying dogmatically the interconfessional principle," which was "appropriate for the purely intellectual goals of the university," to the nature and tasks of the elementary school.[57] Becker's comments on the segmentation of German society lent a somber tone to his speech at the opening ceremony of the pedagogical academy in Frankfurt. He observed how difficult it was for the German people to overcome partisan strife and confessional divisiveness because it was "quintessentially German" to put diverse opinions in contention against each other by the creation of ideological organizations that were powerful forces in society. When he pleaded for the enactment of a national school law, he made a distinction between the "practical facts" of politics and the interconfessional school as "the theoretical regular school" in the Weimar Constitution. Given the realities of coalition politics, he saw no other alternative than to forsake the goal of a confessionally integrated elementary school system for the present time.[58]

Protestant Pastors and the School Strike in Westphalia

Protestant churchmen exercised their own political muscle in a test of strength with the Weimar state when they organized a school strike in Westphalia in 1926 to protest the appointment of a school inspector. In 1924 Minister of Education Boelitz named Martin Nischalke to a school inspection office in the province of East Prussia, although he knew at that time that Nischalke was a Social Democrat and had ended his affiliation with the Protestant Church. The Protestant High Church Council raised objections, and pastors in the area tried to discredit Nischalke by circulating innuendoes about the effect of his political convictions on his work. Schoolteachers in his inspection district praised his professional competence and conscientiousness. However, his clerical opponents argued that a school inspector who disowned the church had neither the competence nor the legitimacy to judge whether religious instruction in the schools was given in accordance with the teachings of the church. To conciliate church officials, Carl Becker transferred Nischalke in 1926 to the Dortmund *Landkreis*, where a quarter of the schoolchildren attended secular schools. Since this county already had one Protestant and two Catholic school inspectors, the minister of education thought that none of the ideological groups in school politics had grounds for complaining.

The church synod, Protestant Parents' League, and conservative parties in the county and city of Dortmund formed a united front and threatened to stage a school strike if the minister of education did not revoke Nischalke's appointment. The executive board of the teachers' association in Westphalia came to his defense and pointed out that under Article 136 of the Constitution the eligibility of a citizen for public office may not be dependent on any religious confession. The school boycott that began in Nischalke's inspection district on 15 November 1926 was instigated by clergymen who urged the parents to keep their children out of the school. When Becker refused to remove Nischalke, the school strike was extended to neighboring towns and the city of Dortmund. The executive board of the Protestant Parents' League in Westphalia, chaired by Pastor Winckler, decided on 27 November to extend the school strike throughout the province, and instructed the local chapters to start the boycott on 8 December and continue it up to the Christmas recess. The underlying intention of the clerical activists was revealed when Winckler stated in the instructions: "It is necessary now to take resolute action that demonstrates to the government and the public that the will of Protestant parents is a reality and power that must be considered."[59]

Strike meetings organized and led by the pastors were held in the churches. Propaganda leaflets with a defiant tone were distributed house to house, telling the parents that they should not be intimidated by the admonitions of the teachers and that the state authorities would not dare to carry out the threat of imposing fines on the parents who kept their children out of school. To induce the parents to join the movement and to reinforce their defiance, the pastors handed out to the right-wing press inflated reports on the numbers of pupils on strike. The teachers later criticized government officials in Westphalia for not issuing the real figures immediately. More than 50 percent of the schoolchildren were on strike in the Dortmund *Landkreis* in mid December. The participation rate was much lower elsewhere:

8.6 percent of the schoolchildren in the city of Dortmund, 11 percent in Hörde, and 31 percent in Bochum on 17 December.[60]

The leaders of the Protestant Parents' League pursued political objectives that went beyond the removal of a school inspector who was a dissenter and Social Democrat. They wanted to use the school strike as a demonstration of the political strength of the parents' league and to show how far parents' rights should be applied in respect to the choice of a school type in the enactment of a national school law in the near future. One leaflet justified the use of politically militant tactics by declaring that parents had to get public attention and be heard. State officials and the political parties must "never forget again that Protestant parents will allow none of their parental rights and freedom of conscience to be curtailed."[61] Winckler and other conservative Protestant churchmen frequently mentioned the Center Party's political power in Prussia and the rights and concessions that had been granted to the Catholics through school strikes and the Bavarian concordat. They sought to emulate the firmness with which the Catholic bishops held to their maximalist demands.

The chapters of the German Teachers' Association in Westphalia fought the school strike vigorously, and in the propaganda of the parents' league these teachers were described as "indifferent or even hostile to the Gospel and the church" and as "the enemy in the school." Leaflets circulated just before Christmas asserted that if the teachers had their way, the story of the birth of Jesus would no longer be taught in the schools nor would Christmas carols be sung.[62] Activists in the teachers' association went to the meetings held in church buildings to refute the arguments of the strike ringleaders. In some localities, they were shouted down and prevented from speaking further or the pastors posted the church sextons at the doors to keep them out. In house visits and at parents' meetings the teachers pointed out the harmful effects of the school boycott on the children and exposed the political objectives pursued by the clerical organizers of this movement. These defensive actions were a significant factor in dooming the strike to failure in the heavily populated city of Dortmund.[63]

When the fate of the school strike was sealed, the ringleaders directed their wrath at Minister of Education Becker and the republican state. Becker refused to bow to the pressure of right-wing deputies in the Prussian Landtag who demanded the removal of Martin Nischalke. He declined to negotiate with the representatives of the Protestant Parents' League and reproached the pastors in Westphalia who had incited the parents from the pulpit. Rather than levying fines and penalties on the strike leaders and parents, the minister preferred to wait for the protest to peter out.[64] In an open letter to the minister, Winckler reproached Becker for allying himself with the enemies of religion and lashed out that since Nischalke's appointment Westphalians had "sensed all kinds of Bolshevik tendencies, whose spread by the state government in Prussia" confounded them. At a parents' meeting in Dortmund, another churchman declared: "Certainly, the state in itself exists. But we will create the right state only when the November Socialists and office-hunters have finally disappeared."[65]

The agitation of the Protestant Parents' League eventually alienated Protestant pastors in Westphalia who supported the Weimar state. A group of clergymen led by Pastor Tribukeit of Dortmund disassociated themselves from the right-wing activists in the strike movement. "As the strike extends," they declared in a public statement, "there exists the danger that other motives, which we do not approve, could slip in." They implicitly objected to the way in which the fight over the confessional school was assuming the political nature of a movement against the republican state. Tribukeit was more blunt in his own letter to the editor of the newspaper published by the Westphalian Teachers' Association. Any perceptive person could see in the conduct of the strike leaders, he wrote, "the motive of an instinctive hostility toward the republican state and the democratic minister behind the banner of the fight for the Gospel" and, in the background as a second motive born out of distrust, the ambition of clergymen to supervise the teachers in respect to their instruction materials and methods as well as their personal religious faith.[66]

The members of the Westphalian Teachers' Association could take pride in the courage with which they resisted the strike agitators, but they saw little cause for rejoicing when the protest ended before the Christmas recess. They thought that officials in the provincial district of Arnsberg responded too mildly to this challenge to the state's authority. The government did not fine the parents who joined the strike. Nor did it officially reprimand the pastors who exhorted the children during Confirmation instruction not to go to school. Pedagogues in other areas of Germany observed the school strike in Westphalia with dismay. They criticized the churchmen there for undermining the authority and dignity of the republican state, and regretted that the Weimar state seemed unable to defend itself against reactionary groups who scorned and defied the law.[67]

The Battle over the School Law in 1927

In January 1927 the leaders of the Center Party joined a Reich cabinet with the German Nationalists and German People's Party with the blessings of the Catholic bishops, who assumed that this governing coalition would command a majority in the Reichstag to ratify a concordat with the Vatican and to pass a school law that fulfilled their conditions.[68] When Chancellor Wilhelm Marx announced the government's program in the Reichstag on 3 February, he stated that a school bill would grant an equal standing to the confessional, interconfessional, and secular elementary schools and would ensure the right of the parents to choose the school type for their children.

The Social Democrats and German Democrats chided the Center politicians for turning their backs on the school compromise of 1919 and for forming a coalition government with the antirepublican German Nationalists. They saw the reactionary school politics of this parliamentary bloc as a new danger threatening the republic at a time when it was gaining stability. *Vorwärts*, the Social Democratic daily in Berlin, warned Catholic politicians that their alignment with the German Nationalists would "provoke a culture war of such an intensity of passion as Germany has not yet experienced." A school law that was "passed against the will of a large mass of people with force or with parliamentary tricks will produce continual resentment and never bring peace."[69]

Looking ahead to the introduction of a school bill, Catholic and Protestant church leaders asserted their terms and conditions in statements issued to the public in the spring of 1927. The Protestant Church Senate in Prussia drafted guidelines on the execution of Article 149 of the Constitution that underscored the church's right to supervise religious instruction in the schools. While these churchmen realized that the old office of local school inspector occupied by the parish pastors could not be restored, they were too distrustful of the teachers who were left to give religious instruction under the supervision of the state alone. They stated that the school law must contain "certain external guarantees" through which the clergy could be certain that religion was taught in the schools in accordance with church doctrines, specifically, the rights of the church to approve the lesson plans and school books, to have a voice in the appointment of instructors for religion in the pedagogical academies, to interrogate the candidates in the examination for the teachers' license, and to observe religious instruction in the elementary schools.[70]

Reaffirming their maximalist position in the pastoral letter published after their conference in Fulda, the Catholic bishops declared that the school question was a matter on which the Catholics could "never compromise" and that the opposing side should understand "the tenacity" with which the Catholics held fast to their demands.[71] Although the bishops justified this hard line by invoking the rights of the parents, their understanding of this principle was related far more to their defense of the confessional school than to any concept of free parental choice. In a letter to Wilhelm Marx, Bishop Matthias Ehrenfried of Würzburg wrote that the Bavarian episcopate would reject any school law that granted the secular school a legal status equal to that of the other school types. The party's leaders would become morally culpable if they gave legal recognition to the secular school. The bishop pointed to the possibility that several secular schools would be opened in the working-class suburbs of Würzburg, where many members of the Social Democratic and Communist Parties lived. He then stated: "There is no parents' right to disbelief and atheism and therefore no parents' right to have their children receive an education without religion."[72]

In July 1927 Reich Interior Minister Walther von Keudell, a German Nationalist, submitted to the Reichstag the draft of a school law that gave the church extensive influence in school affairs. The drafting of this legislation showed clearly the hand of Ludwig Pellengahr, a member of the Center Party, who was placed at the head of the ministry's Cultural Affairs Department after Heinrich Schulz was ousted. In a flagrant violation of the Constitution, which gave precedence to the common school as the *Regelschule*, Keudell's school bill granted the "free possibility of development" to all three school types. Under article 4, the lesson plans, teaching materials, and schoolbooks in the confessional school would have to fit its religious character. Only teachers who belonged to the corresponding confession could be appointed to full-time positions in this school. In school life, the religious exercises and customs of the church were to be practiced, and the religious holidays and commemoration days were to be observed. Article 13 was worded to create, in effect, confessional qualifications for the appointment of school inspectors. Representatives of the church whose religion was taught in the schools were granted a seat and a vote on the local school boards. Article 16 gave church officials the capacity to find out whether religious instruction was given properly by requiring the state to appoint persons selected by the church to supervise it.[73]

Throughout the summer and fall of 1927, German Democrats and Social Democrats in the German Teachers' Association stood in the forefront of the battle against Keudell's school bill. The impact of their opposition should not be underestimated. Their critical analysis of its provisions defined the issues and shaped the public debate. As early as 14 July, Johannes Tews's opposition was aired on the front page of the *Berliner Tageblatt*. In another article in this left-wing liberal newspaper, Georg Wolff, the chairman of the organization's executive board, called public attention to the harmful effects that the proposed school law would have in practice. Ferdinand Hoff, an elementary school educator and German Democratic deputy in the Prussian Landtag, pointed out how it was breaking historic tradition and changing the state institution of the *Volksschule* into a "church school."[74]

The executive board of the German Teachers' Association summoned a meeting of the larger policymaking committee on 28 July to discuss plans for the fight against the school bill. In the following months, teachers in the regional branches organized public meetings and wrote articles for the daily press to mobilize opposition within the middle and left-wing parties. At a mass rally in Leipzig in August, speeches calling for the rejection of the school bill were delivered by Fritz Barth, the editor of the *Leipziger Lehrerzeitung*, and German Democratic Reichstag Deputy Heinrich Rönneburg. Georg Wolff opened another attack on the school bill at the large German Democratic demonstration that took place in Berlin just after the Reichstag began its deliberations in October. Several branches of the German Teachers' Association polled their members, asking whether they would decline to teach religion if the school bill with article 16 on the church's supervision of this instruction was passed. In the polls conducted in the provinces of Prussia, 74 percent of the respondents in Westphalia as well as in Hanover, 88 percent in Pomerania, and 92 percent in Schleswig-Holstein said that they would then choose to give up the instruction of religion. The results of these polls were used by the organization's leadership to influence the deliberations of the Reichstag deputies.[75] The German Teachers' Association fought the Keudell bill without any help from the Secondary Schoolteachers' Association, whose executive board announced a policy of neutrality in respect to elementary school legislation of "an ideological nature" and advised educators in the secondary schools to stay out of the fray.[76]

German Democrats and Social Democrats in the German Teachers' Association objected that the proposed law did not establish a national, confessionally integrated educational system for the German people but would splinter the public school system. The community school was not recognized as the *Regelschule* that the state was required to establish in every school district; it was relegated to the status of one of three school types that could be opened at the request of the parents. The school bill disregarded the clause in the Constitution on "a proper school organization" with classrooms for each grade, and required the state to open and maintain a confessional or secular school in a commune for a small number of children at the request of the parents. The opponents of the school bill contended that the intent of the Constitution was to prevent the community school from being torn apart by the unrestricted opening of public confessional and secular schools (*Sonderschulen*). To support this argument on the unconstitutionality of Keudell's draft law, they noted that Friedrich Giese and other legal scholars confirmed their interpretation of Article 146.[77]

The members of the teachers' association in the opposition also argued that the paragraphs of the school bill on the opening of any one of the three types of schools in a district at the request of the parents would provoke constant political strife and diminish the influence of the state in public education. If the draft law was enacted, they said, the state would be a passive observer of the conflicts that would break out once every three years, when the fate of the school in every commune could be decided by a ballot vote. They rebuffed the Center Party's contention that the opposition wanted to give the state unlimited coercive power in the school system. They thought that the politicians who defended the parents' right to choose a confessional public school were overlooking the social role performed by the common school. Upholding the state's sovereignty in the school sphere and the ideal of a common school for all children, the teachers declared that the *Volksschule* was an important means at the disposal of the state for the cultural integration of a diverse population into a civic community. They emphasized at the same time the state's responsibility to protect minorities. While Catholic and Protestant advocates of the confessional school invoked the freedom of religious conscience, for Jews and other minorities in a commune the provisions of the school bill could mean the oppression of their consciences.[78]

In the polemical crossfire over the school bill, the argument for parents' rights was rhetorically powerful in Germany's young republican state. The defenders of confessional schooling claimed that Keudell's draft law was "genuinely democratic" because it gave parents the right to determine which type of public school their children would attend. The German Teachers' Association refused to retreat when Center and German Nationalist politicians referred to "the democratic instrument of the will of the parents." From the school strikes staged by the parents' associations, the teachers knew that democratic control over the schools in the form of parental sovereignty could produce undemocratic outcomes. Otto Schulz argued that the concept of parents' rights formulated in the debate over the schools was not democratic in nature but "merely an illusory right." Catholic churchmen championed the rights of the family in the school system "not for the sake of the freedom of the parents but for the sake of their duties toward the church." On several occasions since 1918, as several teachers pointed out, church officials did not hesitate to deny the right of parents to register their children out of religious instruction. In 1925 a Catholic prelate declared: "Even if the state would compel freethinking parents to send their children to Christian religious instruction, that would not mean the suppression of conscience for the children" in a free country.[79] The teachers contended that no provision of the Constitution of 1919 stipulated that the rights of individual parents should be "the unconditional and ultimate criterion" in public education. The state should be sovereign over the school system because it constituted the whole civic community of the nation.[80]

While the Secondary Schoolteachers' Association remained aloof from the fight over the school bill, more than 1,500 university professors decided to voice their opposition and signed a declaration addressed to the German people and the Reichstag in October 1927. They warned that Keudell's draft law not only violated the Constitution but also threatened the peace and sense of community in the nation. It went too far in surrendering the state's sovereign rights and subordinated the entire life of the school to confessional and ideological influences. The academic protesters wasted few words in communicating their fears for the future: "It endangers the freedom of the teaching profession, drags the political conflict over the school into every village and family, and makes the school the football of confessional, ideological, and partisan groups."[81]

The Social Democratic and German Democratic Parties formed a united front in opposition to the school bill in the Reichstag's deliberations. The German Democrats took a decisive stand quickly. Gertrud Bäumer, a German Democratic Reichstag deputy, and other party leaders were resolved to wage a stout fight to defeat it.[82] The Social Democratic leadership's first reactions were ambiguous and less decisive. When they joined the opposition alongside the German Democrats, they conducted the fight with an eye to the political situation and the political future—their government coalition with the Center Party in Prussia and the prospect of working together with Center politicians in the Reich cabinet after the 1928 elections.[83]

Before the introduction of the school bill in the Reichstag, Heinrich Schulz, representing the party's executive committee, met with other Social Democrats in the spring of 1927 to discuss the party's position and strategy in this debate and to write a resolution that would be presented to the Social Democratic congress in Kiel. The resolution adopted at the congress called for the opening of secular schools at the request of the parents and expressed the expectation that Social Democratic supporters by a voluntary consensus and party members generally would prevail on the school administration to establish secular schools. The Social Democrats in effect gave priority to the distant goal of a secular school system over the principle of unity in the educational system based on the model of the common school in the Constitution. Schulz told the congress that the secular school was "the school of the working class and socialism" and fulfilled the party's demands in every respect. He identified the interconfessional *Gemeinschaftsschule* with the ideology of the left liberals and insisted that the Social Democrats could never support this type of school.[84]

This strategy was clearly evident in Heinrich Schulz's first public remarks on the school bill. Ignoring the letter and spirit of the school articles in the Constitution, he spoke of the "unity of the school system on the basis of secularization." With the sharpening of ideological conflicts in recent years, the interconfessional school had become more and more "a utopia [and] a cause for dreamers and politicians with illusions." "We must reckon with the division of our school system as an unavoidable fact," he contended. In the deliberations on the proposed law, the Social Democrats would give "their special attention to the treatment of the secular school" and would fight to obtain for the secular school "at least the same rights, freedom, opportunities, and privileges that a school law [drafted by] the Center and German Nationalists provides for the confessional school." In an apparent attempt to justify this strategy, he stated that the opening of secular *Sonderschulen* meant "no increase in the splintering of the school system; instead, in the course of time [this school] shall exercise such a power of attraction that it will gradually become more and more a school of integration."[85]

Opponents of Keudell's draft law in the German Teachers' Association and in the left-wing liberal press criticized Schulz's position. They thought that the Social Democrats had to concede that in the cultural life of the German people presently there was no prospect for the expansion of secular schooling. Not even in the ranks of the working class were the Social Democrats able to win many adherents to the secular school. The secular school could never become a serious competitor to the confessional school. If the Social Democrats wanted to prevent the passage of a reactionary law, the *Frankfurter Zeitung* stated, they had to work with those parties that defended the constitutional rights of the community school.[86]

Social Democrats who wanted to wage a strong fight against the school bill also took issue with Schulz's views and thought that their party had to see clearly the real intent of the draft law—the "connection of the German elementary school to the church." Rudolf Breitscheid urged the Social Democrats to oppose the concessions to the churches in the school bill and to support a law that would carry out Article 146 of the Constitution correctly. Wilhelm Paulsen reminded his party that there was no mass public support for the secularization of the school system. He urged the Social Democrats to reassess their negative position on the interconfessional school and to align with the German Democrats in the fight for a school law that gave a high priority to the preservation of unity and the defense of freedom and independence in the school system. The Social Democrats would make "a grave tactical mistake" if they concentrated on the draft law's provisions for the secular schools and ignored the danger that it posed to the existing "free" and confessionally integrated school systems in Baden, Hamburg, Hesse, and Thuringia. "We would sell out the entire school system to the ultraconservatives for a dish of lentils," Paulsen declared. The place of religion as an optional subject in the curriculum of the community school, he thought, should not prevent the Social Democrats from collaborating with the German Democrats in school politics. For many years the Social Democrats in Baden and Hesse supported the preservation of interconfessional schools against Catholic efforts to introduce a confessionally divided school system. In these schools the instruction of the profane subjects was "secular."[87]

When the Social Democratic leaders came to see that they had to put up a stiff fight against the school bill, they sought to avoid the appearance of attacking the Center Party and directed their ammunition instead at Reichstag Deputy Mumm and other antirepublican, "orthodox-Protestant demagogues" in the German Nationalist camp. The tactical guidelines for Social Democratic propaganda in this battle, issued by the party's executive committee in September, described Keudell's draft law as "a challenge to the young republic and one of its strongest and most faithfully committed parties, the Social Democrats" and as "a hard blow to ideological tolerance, which the young republic needs." The Social Democratic leaders appealed to the left side of the Center Party to return to the Weimar coalition that had agreed to the school compromise in 1919, motivated by the will to strengthen the democratic state. They reminded the Center politicians of their deceased leaders, Adolf Gröber and Franz Hitze, who had once agreed with the Social Democrats that "a school law in Germany should never be made against the wide masses of workers, because such a law would be a constant source of strife and unrest." The party leaders provided the motto for the Social Democratic opposition when they declared that the school bill "breathes the spirit of Potsdam, the spirit of the old Prussia—intolerant, authoritarian, and hostile to the workers and to freedom." In the Social Democratic fight against it, the issue was not religion, but the protection and stability of the republic.[88]

This Social Democratic strategy reflected the views of the party's pragmatic politicians, who sat in the Reichstag and participated in the coalition governments with the Center Party in Prussia and in other states. They did not want the issue of school legislation to divide the two big pro-republican parties. Since the differences between the two parties on the school question could not be reconciled, they practiced a policy of mutual tolerance and avoided conflicts in cultural politics that could jeopardize their collaboration. In 1925, when it seemed that a school bill drafted in the Interior Ministry under the German Nationalist Martin Schiele would set off a culture war, Social Democratic Party leaders had urged the Center politicians to return to the school compromise of 1919 and had warned that the passage of a school law that violated the Constitution would be detrimental to the republic. The discussion of this issue at the party congress in 1925 showed that Hermann Müller, Otto Wels, and other Social Democratic leaders were loath to invest too much political capital in any propaganda campaign for secular schooling or to be pushed into a confrontation with the Center Party. School politics for them did not possess the same central importance as it did for the Center Party, but remained subordinate to general political considerations that were decisive for the development of parliamentary democracy in Germany.[89]

The Propaganda Campaign for the School Bill of 1927

Protestant churchmen in Prussia and Saxony were among the strongest supporters of the school bill of 1927 and provided the German National People's Party with a cadre of active propagandists. They entered the battle with fervor and a sense of urgency. The introduction of this draft of the school law in the Reichstag was for them the long-awaited start of the counterrevolution in cultural politics. They were convinced that the present time, with a German Nationalist as the Reich interior minister, offered the best and possibly the last chance to obtain a national school law that would preserve the confessional schools and provide guarantees for a Protestant education in these schools. In the discussions of the provincial synods of the Protestant Church in Prussia, clergymen frequently referred to events in Saxony and contended that the Marxist parties would attempt again and again to pursue their ideological goals in a unified school system.[90]

Church officials mobilized the parish pastors for the political campaign in support of the school law and issued instructions to guide them in matters of propaganda and tactics. In the province of Brandenburg, a special course was set up to train sixty to seventy pastors to work as political activists. During the public debate on the school bill, clergymen appeared as speakers at mass meetings held under the sponsorship of the Protestant Parents' League and other organizations. At rallies organized by the opposition, they gave rebuttals to the arguments made by schoolteachers. As the guidelines issued by the consistory in Westphalia indicate, parish pastors were under heavy pressure to organize public meetings at which defenders of the school bill delivered speeches. Pastors who refused to participate in this campaign were to be reported to the church authorities. The consistory masked the political nature of these meetings by advising the pastors to add choral music and hymns to the program.[91]

Right-wing churchmen sought to deflect public attention from the question of the constitutionality of Keudell's draft law by dismissing the opposition of the German Teachers' Association as mere "slogans" and by assailing the *Gemeinschaftsschule* as "a disguised secular school." A pastor in the German Nationalist Reichstag delegation called the notion of a uniform education for the politically and culturally divided German nation "a big lie, a cloak, under which unscrupulous elements agitated against everything that is sacred to the Christian section of the population." He stated: "Helpless Christian parents are frequently at the mercy of the terror of un-Christian school inspectors and teachers. The Reich school law shall put an end to such terror by giving Christian parents the right to decide on the beliefs in which their children should be educated." German Nationalist agitators described the community school as "a step toward the secular school" and the teachers' fight for it as "a skirmish for the outposts" to the secular school in which "an education imparting a fanatical hostility to religion is the duty of every appointed teacher."[92]

Protestant churchmen in Baden, Hesse, and Thuringia, who had reconciled themselves to the interconfessional schools there, criticized the right-wing clergymen who fought for Keudell's school bill. Pastors who had liberal or social-democratic political sympathies saw grave harm to the nation and the Protestant Church in the stubborn fight for confessional schooling. In the columns of the *Frankfurter Zeitung*, Pastor Diehl criticized church officials in Berlin for not acting to prevent the school question from dividing the Protestant community. In many Protestant working-class homes, he wrote, the wives attended church and belonged to Protestant women's clubs even though their husbands were members of Social Democratic trade unions and clubs. Pastor Karl König in Thuringia contended that it was better for children from working-class families to be taught along with middle-class children in interconfessional schools than to force the Social Democrats into a situation in which they had to demand the opening of secular schools. The tendency of many churchmen to lump all socialists together as atheists, he stated, ignored important developments within the Social Democractic

Party, particularly "the turn away from the philosophical materialism of the earlier Marxist period toward idealism as well as religion."[93]

With the backing of the bishops, the Catholic School Organization made a massive effort to mobilize support for the school bill within the Catholic community. Besides Wilhelm Böhler, its general secretary, eight priests and teachers on the staff at its headquarters in Düsseldorf performed propaganda work, writing tracts and leaflets and delivering speeches at public rallies.[94] The annual Congress of German Catholics provided Center politicians with a public forum in September 1927 for drumming up popular support for the school bill. On the last day of the congress in Dortmund, the Catholic School Organization staged a rally to demonstrate the unity of Catholic popular opinion in defense of the confessional school. Addressing a crowd of more than 10,000 people, Reich Chancellor Marx defended the school bill as a work of tolerance and concluded by urging the parents to voice their dissatisfaction if the deputies did not perform their duty in the upcoming Reichstag deliberations.[95]

The Catholic School Organization's campaign for the school bill was especially intensive in regions where interconfessional schools had been established for a long time—Baden and Hesse and in the Prussian province of Hesse-Nassau. Catholics attending a rally in Frankfurt am Main in September adopted a resolution that followed the organization's hard line. They were gratified that the proposed law permitted the conversion of interconfessional schools at the request of the parents, but the interim of five years that would be required before the change could occur was too long for them. They warned the parties in the Reichstag that Catholics would never accept a school law with a special paragraph that preserved the interconfessional schools in these areas, and threatened to stage a massive school strike if such an amendment was added to it.[96]

Center politicians in the Reichstag were put on the defensive by the German Democratic argument that the proposed school law would produce constant ideological strife in the republican state and did not create a unified school system that would foster a shared sense of national culture. Their discomfort increased when Joseph Wirth and Adam Röder, two Center deputies in the Reichstag from Baden, voiced their opposition to Keudell's draft law in the *Berliner Tageblatt* and *Frankfurter Zeitung*. Wirth disapproved of his party's decision to join a coalition government with the German Nationalists and was concerned about the impact of the school conflicts on the political stability of the republic. He thought that the Center's school politics should be less controlled by the episcopate and that questions of state politics and the needs of the democratic state should be brought into the public discourse on the national school law.[97] Wirth's political comrades were reluctant to rebuke him in the press. Their irritation over the publicity surrounding his open dissent was expressed when Wilhelm Offenstein and other propagandists for the Catholic School Organization reproached him for breaking with the party's position on the school question, a matter that had been considered "something inviolable for the Center since its founding."[98]

In their response to the critics of the school bill, publicists for the Catholic School Organization and Center politicians questioned whether a unified national culture actually existed in Germany and whether the task of nurturing a consciousness of a common German culture could be imposed on the elementary schools. Anton Rheinländer, the chairman of the Catholic Teachers' Association of Germany and a Reichstag deputy, stated that the advocates of the community school were ignoring the hard reality of confessional and ideological divisions within German society and had a mentally constructed school model that could never eliminate this legacy of Germany's historical past. "A community school for all future German citizens that imparts all educational material in absolute religious and political neutrality is a theory without any relation to human life and reality," stated *Germania*. A school that sought to find commonalities among the diverse ideological groups and to impart shared civic and cultural values would become a "coercive school of irreligiosity." The defenders of confessional schooling attributed the school politics of the German Democrats to naiveté and a fanatical urge to impose uniformity. They argued that peace would come to the realm of cultural politics when the choice of a school type was left to the will of each parent. "Tolerance" and "to each his own" became the watchwords of the Catholic School Organization in the fight over the Keudell bill.[99]

The leaders of the Catholic School Organization began to fear that "non-Catholic ideological influences" were sowing "confusion" within their religious community when other Catholics in public life joined Wirth in speaking out against Keudell's draft law. They were annoyed at Leo Weismantel, a Catholic deputy in the Bavarian parliament, for expressing views that were no different from those of a German Democrat. In a widely publicized article he wrote that the school bill, based wholly on "party and ecclesiastical politics," was oblivious to modern developments in pedagogy and was drafted without any consideration given to the interests of education and the state. He criticized the expansion of parental rights and the confessional character of the schools.[100]

Another Catholic critic of the Center's school politics, Ernst Michel, declared that the confessional schools in Germany had hindered the process of forming a culturally unified nation. Suggesting a comparison that he considered to be relevant to Germany, Michel pointed out that American Catholic intellectuals were critical of the parochial schools for leading to a "Catholic ghetto" and "social isolation." He supported an interconfessional school system in the interests of fostering a greater integration of the German people and creating a *Volksgemeinschaft*. Conscious of the emotional power of this argument, publicists working for the Catholic School Organization justified the church's unyielding position by stating that the demand for confessional schools came "from the very nature of the Catholic faith." Joseph Schröteler, a Jesuit priest, wrote that the entire school life should pulsate with the spirit of Catholicism and be anchored in the Catholic faith. Catholics could not separate religion and life; the spirit of confession should penetrate the thought, will, and action of a human being. "Intermixing is not a feasible course" for Catholics because that would mean giving up Catholic principles for living and an education rooted in the core of the Catholic religion.[101]

Dissatisfaction with the school bill of 1927 within the Catholic Teachers' Association of Germany was not publicized at first because its politically ambitious leaders tried to dampen the discontent. In contrast to Anton Rheinländer and Adolf Gottwald, who hewed to the Center Party's line as deputies in the Reichstag and Prussian Landtag, Catholic elementary schoolteachers remained for the most part strikingly aloof from the political battle. Catholic teachers in the organization's branch in Westphalia were unhappy with the proposals for the church's supervision of religious instruction in the public schools, adopted at the bishops' conference in Fulda in August 1927. They were convinced that the bishops intended to restore the old system of clerical inspectors. By means of quiet diplomacy, representatives of the teachers in Westphalia tried without success to prevail upon the church leaders to modify their demands. At a meeting of the chapter in Dortmund on 15 October, the chairman declared that if the bishops' proposals became the law, Catholic teachers would exercise their constitutional right to decline to give religious instruction. A week later, the congress of the Catholic teachers' association in the province voted to reject the bishops' proposals.[102]

In the *Vereinsboten*, the newspaper published by the separate Catholic Teachers' Association of Württemberg, Aegidius Schweizer revealed the tensions between Catholic pedagogues and the church hierarchy when he lamented that "the principle of authority is stretched excessively and the freedom of conscience of individuals is limited too much." Catholic teachers were told explicitly or implicitly that it was their duty "to say yes and amen to all that is considered politically right by the Center Party, that is, the church side." Schweizer thought that behind the façade of the parents' associations the Center Party was striving to create a "church school" and to enhance the power of the church in respect to the appointment of teachers. Catholic teachers could not develop a relationship of trust with the Center Party because its influential clerical wing had "a very low opinion of the elementary school and its teachers" and considered "their own opinions, above and beyond the framework of the doctrines of faith, as infallible."[103]

The Defeat of the School Bill—a Victory without Euphoria

When the Reichstag began its deliberations on the draft of the school law in October 1927, the teachers and parties in the opposition pinned their hopes on the German People's Party. Uncertainty hovered over the fate of the school bill as soon as the two representatives of the German People's Party in the cabinet, Gustav Stresemann and Julius Curtius, informed the other ministers that their party's delegation in the Reichstag would assume no obligation to support it. In the Reichstag debate on 18-20 October, the spokesmen for the German People's Party defended the interconfessional school. The German Teachers' Association sought to influence the position of the party's two representatives on the education committee of the Reichstag, Elsa Matz and Heinrich Runkel. Teachers who lived in the constituencies of Matz and Runkel in Pomerania and Schleswig-Holstein reminded them of the liberal tradition of the German People's Party in cultural politics and sought to prevail upon them to oppose the school bill. The chasm between the coalition partners was widened irrevocably in November, when the deputies of the German People's Party announced their conditions for supporting any school law: (1) the long-established interconfessional schools in the states of Baden and Hesse had to be preserved; (2) a preferential position had to be given to the community school, as the Weimar Constitution stipulated; (3) freedom of teaching in the confessional schools must be safeguarded against any attempt to place confessional constraints on the entire instruction; (4) the state's sovereignty in the school system must also extend to the instruction of religion.[104]

In the winter of 1927-28 the Reich's governing coalition faced a crisis over the future of the school bill. The leaders of the Center Party and the Catholic School Organization were coming to the conclusion that a school bill amended as the German People's Party proposed would be unacceptable. When the deputies of the German People's Party in the education committee broke with the other government parties in voting for amendments in January, the governing coalition drew the consequences of this action and accepted the failure of the Keudell bill. The resistance among the teachers and the strength of the opposition within the German People's Party and in southwestern Germany made a deep impression on Wilhelm Marx. He thought that a period of calm was needed and that the Center Party should not push for the introduction of another school bill in 1928. He advised Wilhelm Böhler in June 1928 to let the matter rest.[105]

Since the "embargo clause" in Article 174 of the Constitution, in effect, protected the existing confessional schools until the enactment of a national school law, Catholic traditionalists considered the status quo to be more favorable to them than to the reformers. Elementary education in Saxony, Thuringia, Hesse, Baden, Hamburg, and Bremen was provided in integrated school systems, but the schools in these heavily Protestant regions accounted for only 16.2 percent of the more than 52,800 elementary schools in Germany (excluding the Saargebiet) in 1926-27. Confessional schools predominated in elementary education in the large states of Prussia, Bavaria, and Württemberg and in the smaller states of Braunschweig, Oldenburg, and Mecklenburg. The vast majority of Catholic and Protestant pupils in the German states (excluding Hamburg, for which no figures on the confessional affiliation of the pupils were submitted for these official statistical reports) were still taught in schools of their own confession: 84.9 percent for the Catholics and 74.6 percent for the Protestants in the school year 1931-32. The school arrangements in Prussia made the status quo look even more advantageous to church interests. In 1926-27, 92.9 percent of the Catholics and 94 percent of the Protestants attending elementary schools in Prussia were taught in schools of their own confession. The enrollments in the interconfessional and secular schools accounted for only 5 percent of the pupils.[106]

The defeat of Keudell's school bill did not produce a triumphant mood within the German Teachers' Association. In the aftermath of the fight, Georg Wolff called for "a pause for reflection," a stretch of time that would lead the German people to a solution of the school question based on the nature and interests of education. Wolff and other German Democrats in the teachers' association thought that it was debilitating for the republican state to move from one culture war to another. They stressed the necessity of depoliticizing the organization of the school system and winning the parents and wider public over to "the pedagogue's perspective on the school question." They reproached the Center Party and German Nationalists for treating this issue as a matter of the ideological will and political power of the parties.[107]

The introduction of Keudell's draft law in the Reichstag impressed upon the school reformers once again the influential role that the Center Party had attained in cultural politics in the Weimar Republic. In all of the vicissitudes of politics since 1919, the Center Party had succeeded in preserving its pivotal position in the formation of governing coalitions. Intent on stabilizing and protecting the young democratic state, the Social Democrats and German Democrats wanted to maintain a political partnership with the Catholic party and were often ready to make accommodations to it in school politics. On the issue of the school law, however, the episcopate and Catholic School Organization had set maximalist demands with little regard for the school articles of the Constitution. Conforming to the bishops' hard line, Center politicians disavowed the school compromise of 1919 and later entered a coalition government with the German Nationalists, closely tied to the clerical conservatives in the Protestant Church. The Center's deputies in the Reichstag did not discuss with clarity and candor the fatal discrepancy between the bishops' demands on the one hand and the constitutional law and political reality on the other hand. Thereby, they abetted an illusion held by sections of the Catholic population that the Center Party could achieve a school law fulfilling these conditions. Some Catholic defenders of the school bill of 1927 showed a contempt for the Constitution by pitting the "theoretical" principles of Article 146 against the "actual facts" of parental choice. Refusing to be deterred by the Constitution, Böhler had earlier contemplated the possibility of a referendum on a national school law.[108]

By the end of the 1920s, some observers noted "a certain weariness and disappointment" within the German Teachers' Association. While memories of the conditions for the teaching profession under the authoritarian monarchy were no longer fresh, many teachers had come to "realize how difficult the public direction of school affairs could be in a democratic state, from which they had expected at first more rapid and consistent progress in the school system." The reformers had bitter feelings toward conservative churchmen who had misrepresented their views and goals. Otto Schulz remarked that "only ill will or a blinding quest for power could draw out of [the teachers' association's school program of 1919] a hostility to religion and the church."[109] In many parishes teachers who spoke out against the school bill incurred the ill will of the pastors and experienced petty acts of retaliation. With strong indignation, a teacher in Magdeburg reported that Protestant pastors threatened to exclude teachers from employment as church organists and choirmasters if they took part in the opposition.[110]

The mobilization of Catholic and Protestant parents by right-wing churchmen in the fight against school reforms was for many teachers a disquieting dimension of public life in the Weimar Republic. Reflecting on the last ten years in school politics in 1929, Friedrich Nüchter, a leader of the Bavarian Teachers' Association, wrote that the parents' movements had not been a benefit for public education. The parents were organized not to lobby the government to provide more funds for school improvements but to weaken the influence of the state and to fragment the school system to suit the wishes of confessional groups. He added: "Through extreme demands and propaganda in school politics on one side and skillful political tactics on the other side, this genuinely democratic means for the improvement of the school system became a veritable double-edged gift for the young German democracy."[111]

The "Irreligious Republic" and the Culture Wars

The culture wars over the schools in the Weimar Republic were ignited to a large extent by traditionalists in the Christian churches and teaching profession who saw the school reforms advocated by German Democrats and Social Democrats as a threat to their values and interests. The school compromise that formed the basis for Articles 146 and 149 of the Constitution offered the possibility of settling the issue of religion in the public schools in a manner that would satisfy the wish of a large majority of parents for some form of religious education for their children and yet respect freedom of conscience in a diverse society and fulfill the desire of the progressivist pedagogues for the separation of church and school. The Center Party disavowed the school compromise in 1920 and rebuffed the entreaties of the Social Democratic leaders to return to it. Although the Constitution provided for the instruction of religion as a school subject, traditionalists in the Catholic and Protestant Churches could not reconcile themselves to the model of the community school for all children. For more than a century clergymen had exercised considerable influence and supervisory authority in the elementary schools and viewed religious instruction not only as the preeminent subject informing the entire education but also as a vital part of the church's preparation of young people for Confirmation. After 1918, they could not accede to the pedagogues' emancipatory aspirations or demand that the initiation of children into the doctrines and observances of their confession be left up to the family and the churches. They were profoundly distrustful of the reformers in the teaching profession. The political activity of a minority of teachers who joined the Social Democratic Party during the Weimar Republic was a disturbing phenomenon to them.

Conservative clergymen and other traditionalists believed that under the "irreligious republic" Socialists, with their ideology of Marxist materialism, had gained immense influence in Germany. From their perspective, the agitation of leftists in the League of Proletarian Freethinkers (Zentralverband der proletarischen Freidenker Deutschlands) to promote disaffiliation from the church and the secularization of the elementary schools threatened to "de-Christianize" German society and the schools and to break the links between German culture and Christianity. These apprehensions were especially pronounced among clergymen in the Protestant Church, which suffered a greater loss of membership in the massive waves of disaffiliation in 1919–21 and 1930–32 than the Catholic Church had experienced. In the Weimar years, more than two and one-half million Germans gave up church membership. Workers in the cities of Berlin and Hamburg and the industrial areas of the Ruhr, Lower Rhineland, Saxony, and Thuringia, who were supporters of the Independent Social Democratic and Communist Parties, formed the bulk of this exodus out of the churches.[112]

Heightening the clergy's anxiety about the influence of Marxism in the republic were the reports of the agitation of Socialist groupings for the secularization of the schools. In the mid-1920s a faction of freethinkers, who stood on a radical Marxist platform within the League of Free School Societies, gave a militant, partisan tone to the propaganda for secular schooling. At its national convention in 1925, the league made no pretense of political neutrality and adopted a resolution that harnessed its fight for the secular school to the "struggle for the emancipation of the proletariat." Its position in support of the secular school as a "school for the proletarian class conflict" was reconfirmed in 1929, when the convention voted for a resolution that called "the demands of Socialism in cultural politics binding for the league." "The league sees its main task," declared the resolution, "in the consolidation and extension of the secular schools, which are a base for the development of a proletarian class ideology and will become thereby a cultural center of the workers' movement."[113]

To the leaders of the Catholic School Organization and Protestant Parents' League, the agitation for secular schools seemed to be a serious threat because they were convinced that the education ministers after 1918 had appointed many Social Democrats and German Democrats to offices in the school administration on the basis of party politics and as a concession to the demands of the "left-wing" teachers' associations. After Konrad Haenisch left office, Protestant conservatives in Prussia continued to air the allegation that the ministry's personnel policy was influenced by party affiliation. "We are quickly falling into the danger that our school administration will become a spoils system following the American example," asserted a German Nationalist in the Prussian Landtag in 1925. The German Nationalists complained that Protestant religious and church interests were not well represented in the school administration.[114]

In their perceptions of school politics under the republic, right-wing churchmen overestimated the influence of the partisans of secular schooling within the Majority Social Democratic Party and showed an inability to distinguish between pragmatic and radical Social Democrats and between progressivist pedagogues and doctrinaire left-wing ideologues. They lumped all Social Democrats together as hostile to religion and did not see the different perspectives on the school question within the party.[115] In the 1920s the responsible leaders of the Majority Social Democratic Party realized the impossibility of achieving a secular school system by democratic means in the foreseeable future. They doubted that an aggressive propaganda campaign for secular schooling would be successful. They showed greater moderation and sensitivity in matters of religion. At the party's congress in 1925, Hermann Müller rejected Kurt Löwenstein's demand for the formation of a "proletarian front" to fight for secular schooling. Löwenstein and Adolf Hoffmann, two former Independent Social Democrats, complained that the party treated the school question as a marginal matter and argued that it was time for the Social Democrats to give up the politics of accommodation and concession to the Center Party. Hermann Müller, Gustav Radbruch, and other Social Democratic politicians feared that a political battle for secular schooling would alienate Catholic workers and women voters, drive the Center Party into the arms of the antirepublican German Nationalists, and compound the political difficulties besetting the democratic state. They thought that the interconfessional school designated as the rule in the Constitution was the "school of democratic tolerance" and that the school compromise of 1919 opened "the way to a conciliatory *Kulturpolitik* that moderated differences."[116] The Social Democratic leaders also distanced themselves from the agitation of leftist freethinkers. Despite the tireless efforts of these radicals, the movement of disaffiliation from the church had "limited success" owing in no small measure to the abstention of the Majority Social Democratic Party from this crusade.[117]

Contrary to a widely held opinion in right-wing circles, the personnel policy of the Prussian Ministry of Education did not give preference to Social Democrats. During his years in office, Konrad Haenisch showed a deep respect for professional competence and followed a cautious policy of changing gradually the personnel in the school administration held over from the years of the monarchy. Carl Becker, a left liberal, had a sufficient sense of fairness to admit that the discrimination against the Social Democratic Party in the appointment of school officials in the past had to be redressed. Replying to German Nationalists' charges in the Prussian Landtag in 1925, he stated that the entry of Social Democrats into the school administration had been magnified for purposes of partisan agitation. The minister's report on the political affiliation of school officials showed that Social Democrats were underrepresented and that the claim that Protestant Church interests were not represented sufficiently was groundless.[118]

Right-wing churchmen also overestimated the threat of the secular school movement and the effect of the verbal radicalism of the ideologues in the League of Free School Societies. The secular school movement was stagnant by the late 1920s. The special secular schools (*Sammelschulen*) opened after 1918 did not develop into a significant part of the elementary educational system. These schools, 289 in number by 1931, were a small fraction of the more than 33,400 elementary schools in Prussia, and the pupils taught in them constituted only 2 percent of all schoolchildren.[119]

Most working-class parents proved to be traditional in their views on religious education and did not withdraw their children from religious instruction in the registration for schooling as much as the Social Democratic activists in school politics expected or the clergy feared. Propaganda work to persuade parents to register their children out of confessional instruction had modest results in Hamburg and Saxony. The percentage of pupils who did not take religious instruction was lower than the share of the vote won by the parties of the political left in parliamentary elections. Twelve percent of the children attending the elementary schools throughout Saxony in 1931 were registered out of religious instruction. In the three big cities, the percentage of entering schoolchildren whose parents made a formal request for no religious instruction at the time of their enrollment indicates that this practice remained the choice of a small minority: in Chemnitz, 7 percent in 1925 and 11 percent in 1930; in Dresden, 16 percent in 1925 and 14 percent in 1930; and in Leipzig, 25 percent in 1925 and 27 percent in 1930. In Prussia the proportion of schoolchildren who did not participate in religious instruction was much lower: 2.9 percent of the more than 4.6 million schoolchildren in 1931.[120]

The available evidence suggests that the pedagogues in the *Sammelschulen* and experimental schools did not subscribe to the political line followed by the League of Free School Societies from 1925 on. At the league's conventions in 1928 and 1929, political leftists argued that teachers in the secular schools should have the same political ideology as the working-class parents of the pupils. The pedagogues repudiated this interference. In Berlin they resisted the attempt of a faction of Communist parents to turn the secular schools into antireligious, "class-conflict schools."[121] An experimental school principal in Madgeburg drew a clear distinction between partisan indoctrination and the civic education of future citizens authorized by the Constitution. He contended: "We do not want to promote the development of the secular school into a party school with its intolerance and fanaticism. The secular school should nurture religious tolerance in the pupils; we want to teach respect for every religious faith and, through a nonconfessional study of religion, impart an understanding of the nature and historical importance of religion in human civilization. We do not agree with the demand that teachers in the secular school should belong to no church."[122] In 1929 a group of teachers in the experimental schools in Bremen, Hamburg, Dresden, Berlin, Madgeburg, and Halle issued a collective declaration announcing that the advocates of the new education and the League of Free School Societies must go separate ways.[123]

Right-wing clergymen overreacted in their perceptions of hostility to religion and the church within the elementary school teaching profession. Only 2,087 of the 192,227 full-time male and female teachers (barely more than 1 percent) gave up church membership during the Weimar period, not counting the teachers in Hamburg, where the school administration did not make figures on the church affiliation of schoolchildren or teachers a matter of public record. In the early 1920s, several branches of the German Teachers' Association conducted polls on the issue of religious instruction; an overwhelming majority of the members who responded were in favor of retaining religious instruction in the schools.[124] Teachers who supported a secular school system were clearly a minority. By 1927 many of them were becoming more realistic about the political situation. Like the Social Democratic reformer Wilhelm Paulsen in the debate on the school bill, they thought that it would be better to give priority to the unity of the school system over the principle of secularization.[125]

Within the Saxon Teachers' Association, some members became impatient with the advocates of a secular school system who clung to this distant goal. Their sense that the secular school was a lost cause was expressed at the 1926 congress of the Saxon Teachers' Association. In an address on the relations between state, church, and school, Ottomar Fröhlich admitted that there was little hope for the realization of a secular school system for all children, given the school articles of the Constitution and the influence of the Center Party in national politics. Loyal to his school ideal, he cried out: "We shall remain at our posts and know what we are fighting for." Other delegates from Chemnitz and Dresden took issue with his stubbornness and argued that the secular school for all children could not be a battle cry in the coming fight over the school law. A teacher from the outskirts of Dresden contended that large numbers of parents who were receptive to the educational reforms in the active-learning school wanted religious instruction for their children and would not send them to a secular school. In the next fight over the school law, members of the teachers' association must "stand with both feet on the ground of reality" and choose one of two political options in the Constitution: the community school for all children with a separation by confession only for the subject of religion or a segmented educational system with confessional and secular *Sonderschulen*. Another teacher from Waldheim saw in Fröhlich's remarks about the secularization of cultural life in modern times "a false understanding of conditions." It was important to remember, he told the delegates, that "the religious dimension in the cultural heritage of Germany is a part of reality. It is a mistake to close our eyes to reality."[126]

The unhappy relationship of the modern pedagogues to the churches during the Weimar years arose not from any hostility to religion but from the teachers' resentment of the Center Party's power in school politics and their disapproval of clerical activists on the far right. The politics of pastors in the German Nationalist ranks provoked severe condemnation among many Protestant teachers who continued to adhere to their religious faith.[127] They reproached these clergymen for forgetting too quickly the faults of the government under the old monarchy and for attacking the republic as a "godless" state. Hans Schlemmer, a devout Protestant educator in Silesia, deplored how "the church has placed itself almost entirely on the side of the parties hostile to the Revolution of 1918." The ill will of these clergymen toward the new parliamentary democracy and the Social Democrats seemed to him so unwarranted because the Weimar Constitution stated explicitly that religious instruction must be offered as a subject in the public schools. The republican state continued to support the churches with funds and to maintain the theological faculties at the universities. Schlemmer criticized Reinhard Mumm, Friedrich Winckler, and other churchmen who were active in the German National People's Party, and pastors in the eastern provinces of Prussia who joined the right-wing Stahlhelm veterans' organization.[128] Respect for churchmen within the teaching profession was also diminished because of their leading role in the school strikes and in the parents' movements organized in opposition to school reforms. Many teachers thought that the formation of the parents' associations and the use of parental rights had more to do with the fears and ambitions of the clergy than with the interests of the schools.[129]

The most important cause of the culture wars over the schools and the strained relations between pastors and pedagogues in Weimar Germany was the issue of religious education. The controversies over the instruction of religion among the progressive pedagogues after the founding of the republic produced within the Protestant and Catholic Churches an abiding distrust of these reformers. Far from receding over the years, suspicion of the schoolteachers was rekindled time and again. Progressivist pedagogues were never fully reconciled to the clergy's demands that the confessional doctrines in the catechism should be covered in the instruction of religion in the schools. They wanted to teach the subject with a freer hand and a modern viewpoint. As the Dresden teachers' association stated in a leaflet distributed to the parents in 1929, "orthodoxy in a narrow church sense" should not be decisive in determining the curriculum for religious instruction, but "the pedagogical question of whether it is possible to make the doctrines [in the Augsburg Confession] comprehensible to a child."[130] In July 1929, Bernhard Claus, an elementary school educator and a German Democratic deputy in the Saxon Landtag, introduced a motion calling for the elimination of religious instruction in the first two years of schooling. The motion was passed by a close vote of 44 to 40, with the support of the German Democratic, Social Democratic, and Communist Parties.

Such incidents led churchmen in Saxony and elsewhere in Germany to raise the question of whether Christian parents could have confidence in the reliability of the teachers who were giving religious instruction in the schools. Right-wing newspapers discussed the dilemma of parents who were obliged to entrust their children to teachers who gave "expression to their contempt for religion before the full public."[131] Distrustful of the pedagogues, conservative clergymen were determined to recover the church's right to supervise school instruction. By the end of the 1920s, the foes of educational reform had created within conservative sections of society a "crisis of confidence" in the modern schools. In the early 1930s, in an atmosphere of political crisis and cultural pessimism, neoconservative and *völkisch*-nationalist ideologues tapped the resentments of the traditionalists, generated in the culture wars, and a vague public sensibility that "experimentation" in the schools had come too quickly and gone too far.

Notes

1. For the ministerial order of 24 August 1922, see *Gesetze und Verordnung über das Volks- und Fortbildungs-Schulwesen im Freistaate Sachsen*, p. 149. On the opposition to Fleissner's decree, see *Verhandlungen des Sächsischen Landtages*, 11 January 1923, pp. 164ff.
2. *Leipziger Lehrerzeitung*, 6 February 1924: 76–77.
3. *Verhandlungen des Sächsischen Landtages*, 20 March 1924, pp. 2660–62.
4. *Leipziger Lehrerzeitung*, 17 December 1924: 714–17.
5. SHA, Nr. 13925, Bl. 17ff, ministry's records of the number of copies of the report that were printed and the groups to whom the report was sent.
6. SHA, Nr. 13925, Bl. 16ff, the ministry's report on the Saxon elementary schools (pp. 32–41).
7. The report cited above (pp. 48, 60).
8. The report cited above (pp. 24–26, 67).

9. Fritz Ringer, *Education and Society in Modern Europe* (Bloomington, 1979), pp. 54-55.
10. *Leipziger Lehrerzeitung*, 26 March 1924: 205-6. See also the statement made by a teacher from Chemnitz in *Bericht über die 49. ordentliche Vertreterversammlung des Sächsischen Lehrervereins vom 14. bis 16. April 1924 in Bautzen* (Leipzig, 1924), p. 29.
11. SHA, Nr. 13925, Bl. 16ff, the school inspectors' findings were mentioned casually in the ministry's report (p. 68) without any comment; ibid., Bl. 98ff, Sächsischer Lehrerverein, *Zum Kampf um die Volksschule* (Leipzig, 1925), p. 92.
12. Milberg, *Schulpolitik in der pluralistischen Gesellschaft*, pp. 208-9; Wittwer, *Die sozialdemokratische Schulpolitik*, p. 265.
13. *Leipziger Lehrerzeitung*, 12 January 1927: 7-9; ibid., 19 January 1927: 34-36. See the newspaper articles in SHA, Nr. 13925, Bl. 146, Bl. 148, Bl. 149, Bl. 152.
14. SHA, Nr. 13925, Bl. 2, Bl. 3, Bl. 10, and Bl. 11, articles from the *Dresdner Arena* and *Leipziger Neueste Nachrichten*.
15. SHA, Nr. 13925, Bl. 86, Spitzner's article in the *Vogtländischer Anzeiger und Tageblatt*, 22 February 1925.
16. *Leipziger Lehrerzeitung*, 19 March 1924: 181-82. On Hartnacke's role in the polemical campaign against the modern school in 1923-24, see SHA, Nr. 13925, Bl. 71ff, Dresdner Lehrerverein, *Die masslos heruntergewirtschaftete Volksschule* (Dresden, 1924), pp. 6-8. This pamphlet with an ironical title was published as a rebuttal to the attacks in the right-wing press.
17. SHA, Nr. 13854, protests and petitions of the Saxon School Principals' Association sent to the Ministry of Education and the state parliament; the correspondence and court decisions concerning the lawsuit of Ernst Pätzold, Otto Augustin, and Ernst Laube of Dresden.
18. *Mitteilungen des Sächsischen Erzieherbundes*, no. 2, November 1920: 2-3. The title of this newspaper was changed to *Der Schulwart* in 1921.
19. *Mitteilungen des Sächsischen Erzieherbundes*, no. 2, February 1921: 9; ibid., no. 2, November 1920: 3-5.
20. On the founding of the New Saxon Teachers' Association, see *Neue Sächsische Schulzeitung*, 22 October 1924: 1-2, 5; *Leipziger Lehrerzeitung*, 2 July 1924: 403; ibid., 9 July 1924: 424-25; ibid., 3 September 1924: 476.
21. Quoted from the *Sachsenstimme* in *Neue Sächsische Schulzeitung*, 26 November 1924: 1-2. See a similar argument in *Der Schulwart*, October 1921, no. 10: 154-55.
22. *Der Schulwart*, 15 May 1922: 201-3.
23. *Neue Sächsische Schulzeitung*, 29 October 1924: 1-2.
24. *Neue Sächsische Schulzeitung*, 22 October 1924: 1; ibid., 7 January 1925: 2-3; ibid., 29 October 1924: 1-2.
25. *Neue Sächsische Schulzeitung*, 4 March 1925: 2-4; ibid., 1 April 1925: 3-5.
26. Ringer, *Education and Society*, pp. 60, 78-79, 272-74.
27. Posselt [Dr. Eccartus], *Die Volksschule, ein Sorgenkind. Eine Kritik des deutschen Volksschulwesens* (3rd ed., Leipzig, 1923), pp. 19, 30; Willy Moog, *Grundfragen der Pädagogik der Gegenwart* (Osterwieck and Leipzig, 1923), pp. 203-4.
28. Posselt, *Die Volksschule, ein Sorgenkind*, pp. 63-66, 77.
29. Hermann Rolle, *Bildungskrisis. Gesammelte pädagogische Aufsätze* (Habelschwerdt, 1926), pp. 141-44, 219-23.
30. SHA, Nr. 13106/14, Bl. 150ff, protests of parents and officers of the League of Christian Parents' Associations in Saxony to the Ministry of Education in 1924.
31. *Leipziger Lehrerzeitung*, 20 June 1923: 303. See the remarks on this affair in *Bericht über die Vertreterversammlung des Sächsischen Lehrervereins* (1924), pp. 14-15.
32. *Leipziger Lehrerzeitung*, 6 June 1923: 272.
33. SHA, Nr. 13906, Bl. 276 and Bl. 277, article in the *Meissner Tageblatt*, 10 May 1924, criticizing the two teachers in the village of Wiesa, and the district school inspector's report to the minister, 19 June 1924.

34. SHA, Nr. 13906, Bl. 129, memo written by Wünsche, 9 July 1923; ibid., Bl. 132, Rudolf Leonhardt to Minister of Education Fleissner, 4 August 1923.
35. SHA, Nr. 13906, Bl. 180 and Bl. 183, two petitions from the inhabitants of Euldorf and Grosshennersdorf to the Ministry of Education, 22 March and 23 March 1924.
36. SHA, Nr. 13906, Bl. 185, district school inspector's report to the minister, 5 April 1924. See also SHA, Nr. 13907, Bl. 8, for Viehweg's report of 23 May 1924 to the minister after the investigation of the complaint lodged against another teacher, Albert Tränkler, who practiced the modern pedagogy.
37. *Leipziger Lehrerzeitung*, 6 February 1924: 76–77; ibid., 26 March 1924: 197–98; *Sächsische Schulzeitung*, 26 September 1924: 677–78; Dresdner Lehrerverein, *Die masslos heruntergewirtschaftete Volksschule*, pp. 7–9, 14.
38. *Leipziger Lehrerzeitung*, 19 March 1924: 181–82; ibid., 28 May 1924: 332; ibid., 9 July 1924: 418–19.
39. *Bericht über die Vertreterversammlung des Sächsischen Lehrervereins* (1924), pp. 16, 38–42.
40. SHA, Nr. 13925, Bl. 98ff, Sächsischer Lehrerverein, *Zum Kampf um die Volksschule* (Leipzig, 1925), pp. 3ff.
41. *Allgemeine Deutsche Lehrerzeitung*, 16 May 1924: 311–12, 315. See also the discussion of the situation in school politics in the aftermath of the election at the congress of the German Teachers' Association in ibid., 20 June 1924: 391ff.
42. *Allgemeine Deutsche Lehrerzeitung*, 2 May 1924: 271; ibid., 4 July 1924: 435–37.
43. *Allgemeine Deutsche Lehrerzeitung*, 31 October 1924: 789–90.
44. See the reports of such cases in the *Allgemeine Deutsche Lehrerzeitung*, 11 August 1922: 358; ibid., 24 November 1922: 541.
45. For the school articles of the Bavarian concordat, see Johannes Tews, *Zum deutschen Schulkampf. Die deutschen Reichsschulgesetzentwürfe in ihrem Verhältnis zu Staat, Kirche und Erziehung* (Frankfurt am Main, 1926), pp. 14–15.
46. *Allgemeine Deutsche Lehrerzeitung*, 12 December 1924: 935–38. See also Johannes Guthmann, *Der Bayerische Lehrer- und Lehrerinnenverein. Ein Jahrhundert Standes- und Vereinsgeschichte* (Munich, 1961), vol. 2, pp. 277–79.
47. *Allgemeine Deutsche Lehrerzeitung*, 5 December 1924: 901–2; ibid., 12 December 1924: 925. On the debate over the Bavarian concordat in national politics, see Grünthal, *Reichsschulgesetz und Zentrumspartei*, pp. 170ff.
48. Georg Wolff, *Das Reich und die Schule*, pp. 10–11. See Fröhlich's speech on the relations of state, church, and school in *Bericht über die 51. Vertreterversammlung des Sächsischen Lehrervereins vom 29. bis 31. März 1926 in Plauen* (Leipzig, 1926), pp. 20–21.
49. Carl Louis Albert Pretzel, *Die Neuordnung der Lehrerbildung* (Berlin, 1920), pp. 18ff, 42–44; Preussischer Lehrerverein, *Die Zukunft der Pädagogischen Akademien* (Magdeburg, 1930), pp. 5–7.
50. Rita Weber, *Die Neuordnung der preussischen Volksschullehrerbildung in der Weimarer Republik* (Cologne, 1984), pp. 113ff, 284ff; Bölling, *Volksschullehrer und Politik*, pp. 169ff.
51. For the petition of the Fulda Bishops' Conference, see Wilhelm Gerhard Schuwerack, *Der Kampf um die simultane pädagogische Akademie in Frankfurt am Main* (Düsseldorf, 1929), pp. 20–22.
52. Quoted in Schuwerack, *Der Kampf*, pp. 49–50.
53. *Sitzungsberichte des Preussischen Landtages*, 3 November 1925, pp. 5714–17.
54. *Allgemeine Deutsche Lehrerzeitung*, 14 January 1926: 28; ibid., 27 May 1926: 389–90.
55. *Allgemeine Deutsche Lehrerzeitung*, 4 March 1926: 157–61; ibid., 10 June 1926: 433–34.
56. Schuwerack, *Der Kampf*, pp. 87–95.
57. See Becker's *Denkschrift* on the pedagogical academies in *Die Pädagogischen Hochschulen. Dokumente ihrer Entwicklung 1920–1932*, ed. Helmut Kittel (Weinheim, 1965), pp. 136–37.
58. The report of Becker's speech in the *Frankfurter Zeitung*, 11 May 1927, quoted in Schuwerack, *Der Kampf*, pp. 109–12.

59. *Der Westfälische Schulkampf. Materialsammlung zusammengestellt vom Geschäftsführenden Ausschuss des Westfälischen Lehrervereins* (Iserlohn, 1927), pp. 7-11.
60. *Der Westfälische Schulkampf*, pp. 18-26; *Westfälische Schulzeitung*, 1 January 1927: 1-4; ibid., 8 January 1927: 21.
61. *Der Westfälische Schulkampf*, pp. 18, 28
62. Ibid., pp. 27-28, 31.
63. Ibid., pp. 32-38.
64. Ibid., pp. 50-57.
65. Ibid., p. 29.
66. Ibid., pp. 30, 33.
67. Ibid., pp. 50-57.
68. Grünthal, *Reichsschulgesetz und Zentrumspartei*, pp. 142-43, 208ff. See also Ellen Lovell Evans, *The German Center Party 1870-1933* (Carbondale, 1981), chap. 16.
69. *Vorwärts*, no. 200, 29 April 1927.
70. Wilhelm Offenstein, *Der Kampf um das Reichsschulgesetz. Die Entwürfe der Jahre 1925 und 1927* (Düsseldorf, 1928), pp. 123-24.
71. *Germania*, no. 194, 27 April 1927.
72. *Der Nachlass des Reichskanzlers Wilhelm Marx*, ed. Stehkämper, pp. 438-39.
73. For the text of the draft law, see Offenstein, *Der Kampf um das Reichsschulgesetz*, pp. 32ff.
74. *Berliner Tageblatt*, no. 328, 14 July 1927; ibid., no. 359, 1 August 1927; ibid., no. 363, 3 August 1927.
75. *Allgemeine Deutsche Lehrerzeitung*, 4 August 1927: 609, 631; ibid., 11 August 1927: 654; ibid., 29 September 1927: 829; *Vorwärts*, no. 400, 25 August 1927; *Berliner Tageblatt*, no. 504, 25 October 1927. See also Bölling, *Volksschullehrer und Politik*, pp. 164, 270.
76. *Allgemeine Deutsche Lehrerzeitung*, 1 December 1927: 1049-51; Offenstein, *Der Kampf um das Reichsschulgesetz*, p. 143.
77. *Allgemeine Deutsche Lehrerzeitung*, 28 July 1927: 585-86; *Leipziger Lehrerzeitung*, 28 September 1927: 725-29. See also the commentary on the school articles, written by the legal counselor of the Prussian Ministry of Education, in Landé, *Die Schule in der Reichsverfassung*.
78. Sächsischer Lehrerverein, *Das Keudellsche Reichsschulgesetzentwurf* (Dresden, 1927), pp. 18ff; *Allgemeine Deutsche Lehrerzeitung*, 28 July 1927: 585-86.
79. Quoted in *Das Keudellsche Reichsschulgesetzentwurf*, pp. 72-73.
80. *Allgemeine Deutsche Lehrerzeitung*, 8 September 1927: 742-43; ibid., 16 June 1927: 460-61.
81. *Berliner Tageblatt*, no. 495, 19 October 1927; Offenstein, *Der Kampf um das Reichsschulgesetz*, p. 145.
82. *Berliner Tageblatt*, no. 340, 21 July 1927; ibid., no. 363, 3 August 1927; Konstanze Wegner, ed., *Linksliberalismus in der Weimarer Republik. Die Führungsgremien der Deutschen Demokratischen Partei und der Deutschen Staatspartei 1918-1933* (Bonn, 1980), pp. 419, 434ff.
83. *Allgemeine Deutsche Lehrerzeitung*, 22 December 1927: 1121-22.
84. *Protokoll des Sozialdemokratischen Parteitages 1927 in Kiel* (reprint, Bonn, 1974), pp. 149-50.
85. *Vorwärts*, no. 330, 15 July 1927. See Schulz's criticism of the left-liberal reformers in the German Teachers' Association in Schulz, *Der Leidensweg des Reichsschulgesetzes*, pp. 72, 88.
86. Quoted in *Allgemeine Deutsche Lehrerzeitung*, 21 July 1927: 573; see also ibid., 9 June 1927: 446-47; ibid., 16 June 1927: 460-61.
87. *Vorwärts*, no. 333, 16 July 1927; ibid., no. 341, 21 July 1927; ibid., no. 365, 4 August 1927.
88. *Vorwärts*, no. 430, 11 September 1927; see also Schulz's article in ibid., no. 349, 26 July 1927; Heinrich Schulz, *Kirchenschule oder Volksschule? Ein Kampf gegen den Reichsschulgesetzentwurf der Rechtskoalition* (Berlin, 1927), pp. 40-41.
89. *Protokoll des Sozialdemokratischen Parteitages 1925 in Heidelberg* (reprint; Bonn, 1974), pp. 213-15; 218-19; Wittwer, *Die sozialdemokratische Schulpolitik*, pp. 130-34. For a different interpretation of the Social Democrats' position on the church and religious life during the Weimar Republic, see Frank Gordon, "Protestantism and Socialism in the Weimar

Republic," *German Studies Review* 11 (1988): 423-46. Gordon disputes the view that the Social Democratic Party moderated its stance, and contends that on the state and local levels "its anticlericalism and anti-Christianity took on a new virulence" and that "Socialist assaults on the churches ranged from gratuitous insults to major threats to the churches' existence and work" (p. 430). For his evidence, Gordon uses polemical articles in the church press and statements made by German Nationalist politicians, without questioning the reliability of these sources.

90. Offenstein, *Der Kampf um das Reichsschulgesetz*, pp. 120ff; *Allgemeine Deutsche Lehrerzeitung*, 18 August 1927: 660.
91. Hans Schlemmer, *Die Schulpolitik der evangelischen Kirche Preussens* (Görlitz, 1928), pp. 29-30.
92. Quoted from the right-wing press in *Leipziger Lehrerzeitung*, 31 August 1927: 642; *Allgemeine Deutsche Lehrerzeitung*, 21 July 1927: 571-72; Schlemmer, *Die Schulpolitik der evangelischen Kirche*, p. 27; Offenstein, *Der Kampf um das Reichsschulgesetz*, pp. 130-31.
93. Quoted in Schlemmer, *Die Schulpolitik der evangelischen Kirche*, p. 38; Diehl's article in the *Frankfurter Zeitung*, 26 November 1927, quoted in Offenstein, *Der Kampf um das Reichsschulgesetz*, pp. 127-28.
94. *Germania*, no. 412, 5 September 1927.
95. *Germania*, no. 417, 8 September 1927.
96. Offenstein, *Der Kampf um das Reichsschulgesetz*, pp. 103-8.
97. See Wirth's article in *Berliner Tageblatt*, no. 380, 13 August 1927 and Röder's article [*Frankfurter Zeitung*, no. 580, 7 August 1927] reprinted in ibid., no. 371, 8 August 1927; Grünthal, *Reichsschulgesetz und Zentrumspartei*, pp. 220-21.
98. *Germania*, no. 387, 21 August 1927; see also ibid., no. 379, 17 August 1927; ibid., no. 386, 20 August 1927. See also Offenstein, *Der Kampf um das Reichsschulgesetz*, pp. 81-85.
99. *Pädagogische Post*, 15 October 1927: 809-10; *Germania*, no. 327, 17 July 1927; ibid., no. 355, 3 August 1927; Ernst Föhr, *Bekenntnis- oder Simultanschule* (Karlsruhe, 1927), pp. 70-72, 82-83.
100. Weismantel's article was reprinted in *Berliner Tageblatt*, no. 388, 18 August 1927.
101. Joseph Schröteler, *Um die Grundfrage des Schulkampfes* (Freiburg, 1928), pp. 9-19, 31-32. This pamphlet was an expansion of Schröteler's article in *Germania*, no. 389, 23 August 1927.
102. *Berliner Tageblatt*, no. 506, 26 October 1927; *Westfälische Schulzeitung*, 22 October 1927: 676-77; ibid., 3 December 1927: 787-89; *Pädagogische Post*, 12 November 1927: 905-6; ibid., 25 January 1928: 66; ibid., 4 February 1928: 104-5; ibid., 15 February 1928: 140. See also Ernst Cloer, "Aspekte der Schulpolitik der katholischen Lehrerverbände in der Weimarer Republik," in *Der Lehrer und seine Organisation*, ed. Manfred Heinemann (Stuttgart, 1977), pp. 151-66.
103. Quoted in *Pädagogische Post*, 25 June 1927: 541-42.
104. Bölling, *Volksschullehrer und Politik*, pp. 159-64.
105. *Der Nachlass des Reichskanzlers Wilhelm Marx*, ed. Stehkämper, pp. 440-44. See also Grünthal, *Reichsschulgesetz und Zentrumspartei*, pp. 237-44.
106. *Vierteljahrshefte zur Statistik des Deutschen Reichs. Das Schulwesen im Deutschen Reich. Schuljahr 1926-27*, vol. 39, no. 5, pp. 6, 33; *Statistik des Deutschen Reichs. Das Schulwesen im Deutschen Reich. Schuljahr 1931-32*, vol. 438, p. 12.
107. *Allgemeine Deutsche Lehrerzeitung*, 7 June 1928: 491ff; ibid., 1 November 1928: 911; ibid., 23 February 1928: 173-75.
108. *Germania*, no. 327, 17 July 1927; Grünthal, *Reichsschulgesetz und Zentrumspartei*, pp. 150-52, 250-53.
109. *Allgemeine Deutsche Lehrerzeitung*, 16 May 1929: 393-94; ibid., 22 November 1928: 969-72.
110. *Schulblatt der Provinz Sachsen*, 14 November 1929: 440.
111. Friedrich Nüchter, *Über schulpolitische Grundfragen der Gegenwart* (Munich, 1929), pp. 12-13.

112. Kehrer, "Soziale Klassen und Religion in der Weimarer Republik," pp. 75, 79–81; Jochen-Christoph Kaiser, *Arbeiterbewegung und organisierte Religionskritik. Proletarische Freidenkenverbände in Kaiserreich und Weimarer Republik* (Stuttgart, 1981), pp. 40ff.
113. Quoted in *Schulblatt der Provinz Sachsen*, 5 September 1929: 332.
114. *Sitzungsberichte des Preussischen Landtages*, 2 November 1925, pp. 5654–56. See also ibid., 14 December 1921, p. 5921; ibid., 15 April 1929, p. 5757; ibid., 16 April 1929, pp. 5820–21.
115. See Wilhelm Offenstein's propaganda pamphlet written for the Catholic School Organization, *Die Schulpolitik der Sozialdemokratie* (Düsseldorf, 1926), pp. 37ff.
116. See this debate in *Protokoll des Sozialdemokratischen Parteitages 1925*, pp. 151–52, 204–5, 211–13, 218–19, 304–5; Wittwer, *Die sozialdemokratische Schulpolitik*, pp. 59–73, 130–34
117. Kaiser, *Arbeiterbewegung und organisierte Religionskritik*, pp. 39–40, 46.
118. *Sitzungsberichte des Preussischen Landtages*, 3 November 1925: 5724–27.
119. GSA, Rep. 76 VII neu, Teil. I, Sekt. 1B Gen., Nr. 60, Bd. 3, Bl. 137ff, ministry's statistical data on the enrollments and teachers in the secular schools in Prussia in 1931 and 1932.
120. *Statistik des Deutschen Reichs*, vol. 438, pp. 52–53; *Sächsische Schulzeitung*, 3 February 1932: 93.
121. *Allgemeine Deutsche Lehrerzeitung*, 7 February 1929: 105–7; *Westfälische Schulzeitung*, 5 March 1927: 156–58.
122. *Schulblatt der Provinz Sachsen*, 5 September 1929: 334. According to the ministry's record cited in note 119, by 1931, 30 percent of the 2,580 male and female teachers in the secular schools in Prussia had broken their church affiliation.
123. *Schulblatt der Provinz Sachsen*, 24 October 1929: 410–12; ibid., 24 November 1929: 439–40.
124. Bölling, *Volksschullehrer und Politik*, pp. 86ff.
125. See also this argument made by Otto Leist, a teacher in a secular school in Berlin and a Social Democrat, in *Allgemeine Deutsche Lehrerzeitung*, 7 February 1929: 105–7.
126. *Bericht über die Vertreterversammlung des Sächsischen Lehrervereins vom 29. bis 31. März 1926 in Plauen* (Leipzig, 1926), pp. 33–39.
127. Meyer-Dinkgräfe, *Der Lehrerstand*, p. 193. In this poll conducted in 1926, teachers in Prussia were asked about their relations to the church and religion.
128. Schlemmer, *Die Schulpolitik der evangelischen Kirche*, pp. 9–12.
129. Tews, *Elternrecht und Staatsrecht*, pp. 17, 24–25; *Allgemeine Deutsche Lehrerzeitung*, 22 April 1926: 295.
130. SHA, Nr. 13365/10, Bl. 117, leaflet of the Dresden teachers' association. See also *Sächsische Schulzeitung*, 17 April 1929: 302–3.
131. SHA, Nr. 13365/10, Bl. 125 and Bl. 128, two articles from the *Sächsische Volkszeitung*, 10 April 1929 and 21 April 1929; ibid., Bl. 118a and Bl. 127, two articles from the *Dresdner Anzeiger*, 4 April 1929 and 20 April 1929. See also the protests related to Claus's motion in the state parliament, made by the League of Christian Parents' Associations, 29 October 1929, and the church consistory of Saxony to the Ministry of Education, 10 February 1930, in ibid., Bl. 63 and Bl. 110.

Chapter 6

SCHOOLTEACHERS AND THE NAZI MOVEMENT DURING THE CRISIS OF THE REPUBLIC

The disintegration of parliamentary democracy in Germany began after Chancellor Heinrich Brüning dissolved the Reichstag on 18 July 1930 and resorted to the expedient of carrying out his fiscal reform policies by presidential emergency decrees. In the Reichstag election on 14 September the Nazi Party swept into the mainstream of German politics by skillfully exploiting public discontent and capturing 18 percent of the vote. The relationship of schoolteachers to the Nazi movement from 1930 to Hitler's takeover of political power in 1933 appeared to some contemporaries and to historians many years later as an enthusiastic embrace. In 1930–31, Theodor Geiger and Ernst Riggert, two observers of the volatile political behavior of the middle-class electorate and the decline of the "middle parties," commented on the susceptibility of elementary schoolteachers to National Socialism. A left-wing Social Democrat, Riggert blamed the "illusionistic liberalism" of the German Teachers' Association for their "flight into the mysticism of Nazi ideology." Their participation in the Nazi movement was not incomprehensible, he asserted, if one remembered their class background and the army-like regimentation and drilling in the teachers' seminaries.[1] Similar assumptions about the "ideological affinities" of elementary schoolteachers to fascism have informed historical research on this profession during the late Weimar period. Historians have discussed "the specific predispositions that made it easy for them to identify with National Socialism" and have contended that the German Teachers' Association "proved to be more a precursor than an opponent of fascism."[2]

Recruiters for the National Socialist Teachers' League (Nationalsozialistischer Lehrerbund) in 1932 and 1933, on the other hand, often complained about "hard and difficult soil" and "impenetrable" regions.[3] On his propaganda tour in Westphalia in July 1932, Ernst Krieck encountered considerable opposition from elementary schoolteachers who adhered to democratic liberalism even after the German Democrats failed to make a political recovery in 1930 with a slightly altered program and image as the German State Party.[4] He disdainfully described the left-wing liberals and Social Democrats in the German Teachers' Association, especially the generation of teachers who were "older than forty years of age," as "frozen solidly in an obsolete past." He could not fathom why they continued to "believe that the ideas of 1848, ideas rooted politically and pedagogically in the eighteenth century, can master the problems of the newly emerging times."[5] Krieck's remarks suggest that schoolteachers were a more politically differentiated profession than is often portrayed in the historical literature and that the German Teachers' Association was seen by the Nazi recruiters as a block in their path.

How did elementary schoolteachers respond to National Socialism's threat to the democratic state? Did the pedagogues who supported the republic since its founding abandon it during these fateful years? Which specific groups within the teaching profession were most receptive to National Socialism and what attracted them to this movement? Did their anger over Heinrich Brüning's fiscal policy of reducing public spending through deep cuts in the salaries of civil servants alienate them completely from the republican state? School principals and teachers protested the emergency decrees of the Reich and state governments in 1930–32 and were certainly embittered by the reductions in their salaries. However, an examination of the actual penetration of National Socialism in the teaching profession shows that its appeal for sections of this profession was more than a matter of material interests. Its success in winning the support of elementary school principals and teachers lay to a large extent in the field of cultural politics. The leaders of the National Socialist Teachers' League were quick to grasp the possibilities that opposition to educational reforms offered them in their propaganda against the republic. In 1931–32 Nazi agitators tapped the resentments and hostilities generated in the culture wars over the schools to win over traditionalists in the teaching profession from the camp of the bourgeois conservative parties.

The Emergency Decrees and the Political Disaffection of Teachers

The relationship of teachers to the Weimar Republic was shaken during the economic crisis of 1930–32, when Reich Chancellor Brüning pursued a policy of fiscal reform and retrenchment. A member of the Center Party's conservative wing, Brüning was determined to push through cuts in public expenditures for social welfare and reductions in the salaries, pensions, and other benefits of civil servants. After the opposition to the socially regressive proposal for a poll tax led to the defeat of the government's budget bill, he dissolved the Reichstag on 18 July 1930 and invoked the emergency powers vested in the Reich president under Article 148 in order to introduce by decree an "emergency levy" on the salaries of civil servants. The Reichstag election in September increased the seats held by the Communist and Nazi Parties and made it more difficult for Brüning to base his cabinet on a parliamentary majority. When the Reichstag convened in October, the German Nationalists, Nazis, and Communists brought a motion of no confidence against the government. Only the flexibility of the Social Democrats enabled Brüning's cabinet to survive. In the face of fierce polemics from the opposition parties on the extreme left and right, he adjourned the Reichstag until 3 December and, after a brief session, once again until February 1931. The chancellor had no intention of working with a "nonfunctional Reichstag" and pursued a deliberate strategy of introducing emergency legislation when the Reichstag was not in session. The Social Democrats and the parties of the moderate center went along with the legislature's intermittent exclusion from a meaningful role in political life; they adopted a policy of tolerating Brüning's government rather than helping the antirepublican opposition to bring it down.[6]

The emergency decrees issued by the Reich and state governments cut the salaries and pensions of civil servants. Further reductions were made in the salaries of the teaching profession by slashing the supplements for administrative responsibilities paid to school principals and head teachers and the supplements given to married teachers with dependent children. All of the salary reductions alone added up to 19.5 to 28.8 percent of the salaries of school principals and tenured and untenured teachers. Younger teachers were especially hurt by the emergency decrees that imposed a one- or two-year freeze on promotion to a higher grade in the salary scale. By mid-1932, over 6,600 teaching positions in the elementary school system in Prussia were eliminated. To save as many positions as possible for young teachers, the state government encroached on the "duly earned rights" of the civil service, and the decree of 23 December 1931 lowered the age of compulsory retirement for elementary schoolteachers alone to sixty-two years.[7]

Elementary schoolteachers recognized the necessity of closing deficits in the Reich and state budgets and accepted the emergency levy in July and, more unhappily, the salary reduction in December 1930. In 1931 the reports of upcoming emergency decrees that leaked to the press kept them in a state of despondency and anxiety, not knowing when the next cut in their salaries would be imposed, and not trusting the government's denial of these rumors.[8] Their angry indignation exploded in massive public rallies when the emergency decrees were issued by the state governments in 1931. In public demonstrations and meetings of the local chapters and in the press, members of the German Teachers' Association protested that the emergency decrees did not distribute the burden of sacrifices fairly to all parts of society, according to their capacity to pay. They saw no social justice in the retrenchment policy and contended that the Reich and state governments imposed greater exactions on civil servants than on persons in private employment and on big business.[9]

Left-wing liberals and Social Democrats in the German Teachers' Association criticized Brüning's use of Article 48 of the Constitution to issue decrees that encroached on the rights of civil servants. They argued that the Constitution permitted the use of the presidential emergency powers only when disturbances gravely threatened public security and order. They deplored the irresponsible behavior of the deputies on the extreme left and right in the Reichstag and thought that the Reichstag's abdication of its political responsibilities had struck a damaging blow to German parliamentarianism.[10] To their dismay, the "inequitable" and "unjust" emergency decree of 12 September 1931 in Prussia had been issued by a cabinet in which the minister president and finance minister, Otto Braun and Hermann Höpker-Aschoff, belonged to the Social Democratic and German State Parties respectively. Heinrich Diekmann, the chairman of the Prussian Teachers' Association, met with state officials prior to the publication of this emergency decree and warned them that the teachers' confidence in the justice and lawfulness of the state was faltering.[11] In a speech at the national congress of the German Teachers' Association in 1932, a member of the executive committee argued that the Reich government had committed a grave error in pursuing relentlessly a retrenchment policy full of pinpricking provocations. It did not produce the revenues for the state treasuries that were promised, but it drove "some of those colleagues who once supported the government parties into the army of the discontented."[12] One of the most fateful effects of the emergency decrees was the political radicalization of the civil service. In the election campaigns the Nazi Party's propaganda leadership identified civil servants as a prime target and courted them assiduously.[13]

Teachers on the political right lost confidence in the value of their professional associations, whose strenuous efforts to protect their material interests had been of no avail, and whose leaders continued to support Weimar's parliamentary democracy. They ceased to pay dues and let their membership lapse. The membership of the German Teachers' Association declined from its peak of 154,126 in 1928 to 147,844 by the end of 1932. The association suffered its biggest loss, 3,122 members, in Prussia between 1930 and the end of 1932. Since 1929, nationalistic right-wingers there had been sulking over the executive board's "pacifistic" views in international relations and opposition to the German Nationalists' referendum campaign to block the implementation of the Young Plan on the payment of war reparations.[14] The smaller Catholic Teachers' Association, which was tied to the cohesive Catholic subculture, also reported a loss of members in Prussia.[15]

The National Socialist Teachers' League

Up to the Great Depression, elementary schoolteachers who belonged to the Nazi movement were a minute segment of the profession. After the National Socialist Teachers' League was founded in 1929[16] by Hans Schemm, a teacher in Bayreuth who knew Adolf Hitler, many of its members came from small local groupings of *völkisch*-nationalist teachers. The league organized teachers in the elementary, secondary, and vocational schools and took pride in overcoming the social snobbery that kept university-educated teachers in the *Gymnasium* apart from pedagogues in the *Volksschule*. In its early years, the league's membership, about 900 by the end of 1929 and 2,000 by the end of 1931, came predominantly from the Bavarian region of Franconia, the Vogtland and Erzgebirge areas in Saxony, and Thuringia. The rapid expansion of its membership took off in the summer of 1932; from April 1932 to January 1933, the membership in Germany rose from 5,000 to 11,000.[17]

From an analysis of the statistical data on Nazi Party membership, Konrad Jarausch and Gerhard Arminger concluded that 2.9 percent of the educators of all school types joined the party before 1933 and that teachers who became National Socialists were more likely to be Protestant, to belong to the younger generation, and to live in small towns and medium-sized cities. Some of these "Old Fighters" who joined the Nazi Party and teachers' league before 1933 belonged also to the German Teachers' Association.[18] The meaning of dual affiliations can be seen in the cases of Arthur Göpfert and J. Döring, who were members in the Saxon Teachers' Association before their public appearances as Nazi agitators. Although they rarely attended the meetings of the association's chapters in Glauchau and Limbach, they wanted the security of belonging to its sickness insurance fund (*Krankenkasse*). Göpfert dropped out of the teachers' association in 1931, and Döring in 1932, when they heard that formal proceedings to expel them would be opened.[19]

A Nazi Reichstag deputy since 1928, Hans Schemm envisioned the National Socialist Teachers' League as a "combat battalion for Adolf Hitler" rather than as a conventional professional society. The subordination of profession to political party was clearly expressed when the *Nationalsozialistische Lehrerzeitung*, the league's organ, described "the National Socialist teacher" in a 1930 article: a fanatical political radical, the member of the league had little or no interest in questions related to pedagogy and the profession. "Removing himself from the profession," its associational life and ethos, the Nazi teacher was "not first and foremost an educator." He did "not consider everything from the narrow standpoint of the teacher."[20]

Men of the "Front generation," the leaders of the National Socialist Teachers' League were strongly marked by their postwar experiences and never acquired the professional identity of the generations that entered schoolteaching before 1914. Hans Schemm became involved in *völkisch* party politics in Bavaria after serving in the Free Corps in 1919. Party politics became his exclusive commitment when he joined the Nazi Party formally in 1926 and, from 1929 on, served as the national leader of the league and the party's *Gauleiter* in Upper Franconia.[21] Otto Raatz, the secondary schoolteacher who led the *Ortsgruppe* in Königsberg, was born in the province of West Prussia in a county close to the "Polish Corridor." Psychologically shattered by Germany's military defeat and loss of territory to Poland under the terms of the Versailles treaty, he joined a *völkisch*-nationalist splinter party in 1921.[22] Rudolf Knoop, who headed the district organization in southern Westphalia, completed his professional training as a war veteran and then suffered the humiliation of being an unemployed teacher. Failing to obtain a school appointment in the 1920s, Knoop had to earn a living as a coal miner and later as a worker in a machine factory. After a brief stint of schoolteaching in 1923, he was laid off when the Reich and state governments carried out a massive downsizing of the civil service in 1924 as a consequence of the policy for economic stabilization. He joined the Nazi Party and became a propagandist for the league in Westphalia when he returned to teaching.[23]

The National Socialists and *Kulturpolitik*

After the Reichstag election of 1930 the Nazi Party's political platform became a matter of great concern to the teaching profession. Its vague and ambiguous position in school politics aroused a suspicion of deceptiveness among many elementary schoolteachers. The party program adopted in 1920 skirted school issues and stated that the National Socialists stood for "positive Christianity." With the intention of cutting through the party's vaporous propaganda and promoting a meaningful discussion of its *Kulturpolitik*, Leo Raeppel, the editor of the *Allgemeine Deutsche Lehrerzeitung*, wrote to Josef Goebbels in the fall of 1930, inquiring about the Nazi Party's position on the idea of a unified school system as well as on the civil rights and status of teachers as tenured civil servants. In another inquiry sent to Hitler on 14 October, the Catholic editor of a newspaper in Bavaria wanted to know whether the Nazi Party supported confessional schooling and was ready to work hand in hand with the Center and Bavarian People's Parties in the fight for the schools.[24] Neither Goebbels nor Hitler responded with a programmatic statement. They knew that school politics would be slippery ice for the National Socialists and thought that the best strategy would be an imprecise and noncommittal school program. The replies to these inquiries were left to Nazi deputies in the Reichstag and state parliaments, whose remarks could always be labeled as unofficial.

One group within the Nazi movement made no attempt to disguise its antipathy toward confessional particularism in Germany's cultural life and the influence of political Catholicism in the republic. Martin Löppelmann, a secondary schoolteacher in Berlin and Reichstag deputy, replied to Raeppel in November that his party rejected the negotiation of state concordats with the Papacy and would not support confessional schools. The "state schools" should rest on "a general Christian foundation." The meaning of this statement became elusive when Löppelmann added that religious instruction should be left up to the churches.[25] Reichstag Deputy Georg Usadel, another secondary schoolteacher, also spoke openly of his opposition to confessional schooling. Joseph Grohé, the editor of a Nazi newspaper in the Rhineland and a member of the city council of Cologne, said in December 1930 that "[the demands of] the bishops are not decisive for us in school questions because we want a German school."[26]

Johannes Stark, a university professor in Würzburg, gave so clear an argument against confessional schooling in his pamphlet *Nationale Erziehung* that covert Nazis propagating the party's ideology in the chapters of the German Teachers' Association later used it to demonstrate cunningly the similarities of the school goals of National Socialism and the teachers' own professional society. Stark deplored the failure of Weimar's parliamentary democracy to create a national educational system. When he described the separation of the rights and duties of the state and church in a future Nazi Germany, he claimed for the state exclusive power in school affairs. Turning over the instruction of religion to the churches, he argued, would promote peaceful relations between church and state in the school sphere. As long as religion was taught in the schools, the churches would insist on the right to supervise "public servants of the state." He assailed the advocates of confessional schooling, calling their philosophy of education "the outcome of either narrow-mindedness or confessional fanaticism." Their demands for confessional schooling were "an offense to the principles of a national education and the *Volksgemeinschaft* itself." He wrote: "The argument that within the confessional school the consciousness of belonging to a national community is fully developed flies in the face of logic and truth." Because "the political misuse of religion and the church" had brought so much confessional strife to Germany, it was "necessary to counteract the harm that it threatens to inflict on national feeling" by providing children of all confessions a common secular instruction and national education.[27]

Another group in the Nazi Party saw greater political advantage in ambiguous rhetoric and a noncommittal school program and thought that the culture wars over the schools provided a fertile ground for agitation against the republican state and for the recruitment of supporters among the traditionalists. Hans Schemm was a leading proponent of this strategy. After the Reichstag election of 1930, he began to soft-pedal those aspects of the propaganda of the National Socialist Teachers' League that were likely to alienate Protestant churchmen and conservatives. In the Nazi press, Schemm attacked the Center and Social Democratic Parties and employed the vague and elastic concept of the "Christian school" to define the school ideal of National Socialism. He contended that the political parties had "reduced the schools to objects of haggling over political power." The confessional schools were "purely objects of the [Center] Party's power politics," and the interconfessional schools in many areas of Germany were "already in the claws of unpatriotic and atheistic Marxism."[28] Schemm's strident assault on the German Teachers' Association served to distance the Nazis' cultural politics from the reforms advocated by left-wing liberals and Social Democrats in the teaching profession.[29] The National Socialists withdrew Stark's *Nationale Erziehung* from the bookstores because it was offensive to the Protestant Parents' League and was damaging the Nazi Party's appeal to these voters.[30]

Rudolf Buttmann, the head of the Nazi delegation in the Bavarian Landtag, defended his party in response to the criticism of the Catholic bishops. One of his speeches acquired a semiofficial character after it was published in the party's newspaper, the *Völkischer Beobachter*. Buttmann denied the charge that his party opposed confessional schooling, and in a counteroffensive thrust he made a caustic reference to the Center Party's participation in governing coalitions with the Social Democrats in the Reich and in Prussia: "We accuse the governmental parties in the Reich of postponing the enactment of the national school law again and again because of political horse-trading with the atheistic Marxists."[31] The Nazi Party's ideological program, he contended, could never contain any heresy because it did not interfere in the internal affairs and doctrines of the Catholic and Protestant Churches. He declared: "For us as a party—the Führer has stated this often enough and this is the criterion for our actions—there is no further search for a new worldview, a new religion. Rather, positive Christianity is the foundation for us as a party."[32]

Schemm cultivated close ties with Protestant pastors who were open and receptive to the Nazi ideology. When the National Socialist Teachers' League produced its first official program in 1930, the definition of its goals included the fight against the "liberal and Marxist teachers' associations" and opposition to "cultural bolshevism in all areas of life." Schemm added his own idea of organizing "all German-minded clergymen of both confessions into a working group within the league under the great motto: the education of our nation on a Christian religious foundation."[33] Protestant clergymen who were attracted to the *völkisch* nationalism and anti-Bolshevism of the Nazi Party were more numerous than the 200 hardcore followers (out of around 15,700 pastors in Germany) who belonged to the Working Group of National Socialist Pastors.[34] Schemm was invited to address several large assemblies of Protestant churchmen who wanted to engage in a "dialogue" with National Socialism. At the national convention of the Inner Mission in April 1931, he sought to dispel their doubts about his party's position on church and school issues and stressed the possibilities of collaboration between National Socialism and the church. Capitalizing on their fear of the left-wing parties, Schemm contended that only the National Socialists could protect Christianity from its Marxist enemies and the *Volksschule* from the freethinking secular school movement.[35]

The Reactions to National Socialism in the Teaching Profession

The National Socialist Teachers' League had great difficulties in recruiting members even after the Reichstag election of September 1930. The Prussian State Ministry's decree of 25 June 1930 prohibited civil servants from belonging to and working for the Nazi Party. This ban was by no means the only obstacle. In 1930-31, the newspapers of the German Teachers' Association and Catholic Teachers' Association repeatedly exposed the tactical opportunism of the Nazi politicians by drawing attention to their ambiguous and contradictory statements on the school question. Antifascists in the *Lehrerpresse* impressed upon the teaching profession the need to look at the hollow promises of Nazi propaganda with a critical eye. Raeppel wrote that Löppelmann drew the only logical conclusion of his party membership when he broke his affiliation with the Protestant Church, "since 'German Christianity,' which is promoted by the racist ideology of National Socialism, is completely irreconcilable with a confessionally true Christianity." Other Nazi leaders had not done so "because the tactical plan of the party is to draw the real political consequences for religion from its *völkisch* ideology only when it achieves political power."[36]

The *Sächsische Schulzeitung* frequently contrasted the clarity with which Catholic Church leaders drew a line of separation against National Socialism to the ambivalence and division of opinion among Protestant theologians. Pointing out that the concept of "positive Christianity" in Nazi propaganda was imprecise, pedagogues in Saxony stated that the Protestant parents' associations were mistaken in concluding that this motto signified support for the confessional school. Singled out for sharp reproach were those pastors who propagated National Socialism enthusiastically in the newspapers published by the Protestant Church in Saxony. Writing in the *Sächsisches Kirchenblatt* in 1931, one of these preachers made excuses for the Nazi Party's reluctance to take a programmatic position on the school question. He swept aside the misgivings of other Christian believers about the party's racial theories and rowdy political activism by pointing to "a healthy, vital core" and "the striving for ideal goals" in the movement.[37]

Catholic educators were concerned that sections of the Catholic population were being deceived by Nazi propagandists who tried to win votes in election campaigns by emphasizing the party's fight against Social Democratic educational reformers and "irreligious schools." Johannes Brockmann, who was a leader of the Catholic Teachers' Association in Westphalia and a Center Party deputy in the Landtag, thought that the Nazi movement posed a threat that required the greatest vigilance and clearest thinking. Early in 1931 he called upon church leaders "to make a clear and unambiguous statement on National Socialism's position in cultural and school politics." Joseph Güsgens urged the Catholic School Organization to express publicly its opposition to National Socialism. He criticized the racism and intolerance of the National Socialists and stated that out of hostility to the Jews or opposition to Marxism would come no positive Christianity.[38] The German bishops' pronouncements on the incompatibility of National Socialism with the teachings of the Catholic Church, issued in the spring of 1931, made a strong impression on Catholic educators. One Rhinelander declared that any Catholic teacher who would "seek salvation in a flight from the teachers' association or its party [Center Party] out of justified anger" at the government's emergency decrees would "act politically unwise and in a manner unworthy of a Catholic teacher." He added for emphasis: "Our bishops whose authority we respect have given their judgment."[39]

The newspapers published by the German Teachers' Association erected another barrier to the penetration of National Socialism in the elementary school teaching profession. Leo Raeppel did not interpret the association's policy of nonpartisanship in a way that disallowed critical reporting on the Nazi Party in the columns of the *Allgemeine Deutsche Lehrerzeitung*.[40] He published so much unflattering news about the National Socialists that the party's press, ignoring the fact that his parents were Catholic, criticized the association for selecting a Jew to be the editor of its national newspaper.[41]

Raeppel seized upon the brutally frank statements on the exercise of power in a Nazi-controlled state, which were made by Landtag Deputy Manfred von Killinger of Saxony and other party politicians, to warn civil servants about the "ultimate consequences" of the Nazi ideology. In a state governed by a dictatorship, he warned in 1931, there could be no independent judiciary, no freedom of the press, speech, and assembly, no freedom of teaching, and no civil servants' rights. Anyone could understand how an unemployed person in the depths of despair could place his hopes in Nazi promises of rescue and salvation, but it was "unimaginable how a civil servant [could] be ready to exchange the legal guarantees of a constitutional state for the blank check of an arbitrary dictatorship."[42] During the Reichstag election campaign in 1932, the *Allgemeine Deutsche Lehrerzeitung* stressed the gravity of the Nazi Party's threat to the republic and the responsibility that citizens bore in casting their votes. "It could be the final fight for the republic, to decide whether new structures and laws should emerge that will deprive the state of its democratic character," wrote a Berlin teacher who was a Social Democrat. On the eve of the election, Raeppel described the situation of the schoolteachers in Italy under the Fascist dictatorship. The same fate could befall the German people, he warned, if under the spell of irrational ideologies they ceased to value individual liberties and abdicated democratic rights and responsibilities.[43]

From 1930 up to the winter of 1932–33, Raeppel and other editors of the *Lehrerpresse* published numerous news reports on the abuses of power by the National Socialists who became education ministers in coalition governments: Wilhelm Frick and Fritz Wächtler in Thuringia, Anton Franzen in Braunschweig, and Heinz Spangemacher in Oldenburg. Members of the German Teachers' Association in these states resisted courageously the infringements of their civil liberties and the clumsy ideological interference of Nazi politicians in school instruction. While the effect of this unfavorable publicity cannot be measured, the conduct of the Nazi education ministers seems to have prevented their party from making deeper inroads in the teaching profession than it did.[44]

After Wilhelm Frick took office in Thuringia in January 1930, he announced a "relentless fight for the spiritual renewal of the minds and will of the German people against the Jewish-Marxist, internationalist-pacifist contamination." He ordered that the palace art gallery in the city of Weimar be "cleansed of cultural-Bolshevik, so-called works of art," and, thereafter, the paintings and graphic prints of Kandinsky, Kokoschka, and other modernists were removed from its exhibition rooms. The ministry blacklisted Erich Maria Remarque's *All Quiet on the Western Front* and prohibited the use of this book in school instruction. On 16 April 1930 Frick issued a regulation on prayers that had to be recited in the elementary schools. The prayers imploring God to free the German fatherland from "deception and betrayal" contained Nazi ideological allusions to the Jews, the Social Democrats, the revolution of November 1918, and the Versailles peace treaty. Left-wing liberals and Social Democrats in the Thuringian Teachers' Association objected to the propagandistic text of these school prayers and supported the decision of Reich Interior Minister Wirth to challenge the constitutionality of Frick's decree before the Reich Court. The judicial ruling on 11 July sustained their contention that the school prayers violated Article 148 of the Constitution, which prohibited teachers from manifesting intolerance in school instruction. Frick left office after a second Social Democratic motion of no confidence in him finally secured a majority vote in the Thuringian Landtag in April 1931.[45]

The teachers' association in Thuringia resisted another Nazi education minister when the Nazi Party won a major victory in the state election in July 1932 and formed a government. Although Fritz Wächtler had taught in an elementary school, teachers in Thuringia knew him as a Nazi Party politician and strident speaker in the Landtag and did not respect him. In a decree on the instruction of history issued on 10 October 1932, Wächtler assigned to the schools the task of instilling in the youth "the will to fight" the injustices done to the German people by the Treaty of Versailles. He ordered that the instruction of history taught in the upper grades of the elementary schools must cover the provisions of the treaty and "lead the youth to the understanding that the ultimate cause of our present distress lies in the *Diktat* of Versailles." The pupils were required to learn by heart the language of Article 231 on Germany's "war guilt." From the seventh year of schooling on, in the last hour of instruction each week one pupil in each class had to recite the offending paragraph, and the other pupils had to respond collectively with the refrain: "The German shame should burn in our souls until the day of honor and freedom." The newspapers published by the German Teachers' Association widely publicized and repudiated this intrusion of Nazi Party agitation in the schools of Thuringia. Two officers of the teachers' association, O. Becker in Weimar and E. Linde in Gotha, demanded the repeal of this order in a petition addressed to the minister. They objected to "the intention that is evident in the decree, and especially in the refrain, to kindle in the hearts of children a consuming fire of hostility toward other nations and the demand for vengeance." They indicated to the minister that there would be passive resistance if the order was not revoked: "We German teachers, who derive our educational goals from ethics, cannot give our help to this. To plant feelings of hatred and vengeance in the souls of children goes against our consciences as educators." Wächtler unleashed a vituperative campaign against Becker and Linde, and in the winter of 1932–33 his lackeys within the Thuringian Teachers' Association began to agitate for the resignation of the executive board and the election of new officers.[46]

The politically motivated purges and the curtailment of the civil liberties of teachers were other aspects of the policies of the Nazi education ministers that were widely reported and condemned in the *Lehrerpresse*. Expecting to win the applause of clergymen and other traditionalists, the National Socialists in Braunschweig set themselves to the task of rooting out "Marxist influences" in the school system after they entered a coalition government with the bourgeois conservative parties in October 1930. Minister of Education Anton Franzen dismissed seven school inspectors and transferred out of the ministry a German Democratic school councilor who had been the chairman of the Braunschweig Teachers' Association for many years. In their place he appointed Dietrich Klagges and other party hacks. The number of classes in the secular schools was reduced, and notices of dismissal were sent to twenty-six teachers who were no longer affiliated with the Protestant Church. Franzen issued a decree prohibiting teachers from expressing their views on the school question in parents' meetings as well as in other public forums and the press.[47] In the fall of 1932, the state government suspended a school principal named Freienberg in the city of Braunschweig and trumped up charges to prosecute him. His colleagues suspected that Dietrich Klagges, now holding the office of education minister, was acting out of political motives. At a meeting of the teachers' association in 1931, Freienberg had criticized both the appointment of professionally unqualified "party men" to the school administration and the minister's regulation on the teaching of the subject of racial hygiene and heredity in the schools.[48]

Teachers of the Younger Generation and National Socialism

When the leaders of the National Socialist Teachers' League intensified their propaganda and recruitment work in 1931–32, in the reservoir of potential prey they were quick to target the large number of young teachers who were estranged from the associational life of their profession and alienated from the republican state. In the Weimar era, *Junglehrer* became a distinctive label for the generation of untenured teachers who returned from the battlefields of World War I only to confront grim job prospects at home. Many young teachers had an unstable and unhappy life throughout the 1920s. A sudden oversupply of teachers seeking school offices in Prussia emerged when German teachers took flight from the areas of Poznan and West Prussia ceded to Poland in 1919. In the spring of 1920, young teachers in the provinces of Silesia and East Prussia were laid off so that the Ministry of Education could relocate tenured refugee teachers in new schools.[49] By October 1921, there were more than 15,200 unemployed young teachers, who were dependent upon temporary jobs as clerical and commercial employees and blue-collar workers for their livelihood. In 1928, 14,653 candidates for teaching appointments (*Schulamtsbewerber*) were still unemployed; 8,827 young teachers held untenured offices at the bottom of the salary scale; and another 3,000 earned a meager pay as assistant teachers. Without financial security, many of these young teachers could hardly contemplate the responsibilities of bringing up children and postponed marriage.[50]

Already in 1927, members of the interconfessional and Catholic teachers' organizations observed and were profoundly troubled by the estrangement of the young generation from the profession and by the signs of political radicalization in its circles. In the constant struggle for a job, young teachers had become intensely self-absorbed and were not developing "the pedagogue's social-ethical consciousness."[51] Relations between the generations in the profession were often strained because some young teachers suffered from an "inferiority complex" and were oversensitive and defiant in their behavior toward older colleagues. Unemployed young teachers were alienated from their profession and yet were "not part of the working class." They were "wanderers between two worlds," wrote Arthur Hennig in 1927. Their "negativism" led "frequently to an impulsive rejection of all earlier ideals" held by generations of German elementary schoolteachers since the 1840s, and they succumbed to a "dark pessimism" and "hatred of the existing social order."⁵² Young teachers were "putting their energies at the disposal of movements hostile to the state," warned Paul Kluke in 1927. "For its own sake and the sake of schoolchildren, the state should strive to preserve the civic loyalty of young teachers. How could the young generation of teachers instill affection for the republican state in their pupils after that state had given them stones rather than bread?" he asked.⁵³

Young teachers staged protest demonstrations soon after the Prussian Finance Ministry's plan to eliminate 10,000 teaching positions was leaked to the press in 1930. To close increasing deficits in the state budgets, the governments of Prussia and other German states ordered reductions in the number of school positions in the fall of 1931. At the time of the Great Depression, in the army of radicalized *Junglehrer* who lived under the "the sword of Damocles" that threatened joblessness were two age cohorts: untenured teachers in their early thirties, many of whom had fought in the world war and had completed their professional training in the teachers' seminaries in the early Weimar years, and men and women in their twenties who had graduated from the new pedagogical academies.⁵⁴ Enthusiasm for National Socialism among students training for the profession in the early 1930s ran very high. The Nazi slate won 39.4 percent of the votes cast in the student government elections at the Pädagogisches Institut in Leipzig in 1931 and picked up more votes in 1932 in spite of the lighter turnout.⁵⁵

The National Socialist Teachers' League reaped rich political dividends when its recruitment propaganda targeted young teachers. About two-thirds of the teachers of all school types who joined the league before 1933 came from the two cohorts of young teachers.⁵⁶ Nazi propagandists had an acute understanding of their psychological needs and yearnings. Capitalizing on the ideological cleavage between the generations, they charged that "liberal-democratic ideas and to some extent even Marxist false doctrines have found too much credence within the older generation of German teachers." They used polemical attacks on the "internationalism" and "pacifism" of the German Teachers' Association as a foil to promote the league's own school program in favor of an "education for love of the fatherland, for the capacity to fight, and for heroic courage." National Socialism's most compelling appeal was the promise of a transformation that would lift *Junglehrer* out of resignation, demoralization, and a negative self-image to a new and more positive perception of themselves as forward-looking activists serving paramount national goals.⁵⁷

Traditionalists in the Culture Wars and National Socialism

When the National Socialists intensified their drive to penetrate the professional associations of German elementary school principals and teachers, they made inroads with little or no resistance in those organizations whose members had fought the reformers in the German Teachers' Association with an unrelenting ideological zeal throughout the 1920s. Standing on a Christian-conservative platform in defense of confessional schooling, the League of German Protestant Teachers' Associations reached a membership of close to 3,600 by the end of the 1920s, failing in its efforts to become a serious competitor to the much larger German Teachers' Association. The Prussian School Principals' Association (Preussischer Rektorenverein) attracted some 4,000 conservatives in the profession,[58] who were adamantly opposed to the reformers' demands for the abolition of the office of school rector and the introduction of collegial school governance. In the highly polarized political landscape of Saxony, the traditionalists who formed the New Saxon Teachers' Association were consumed by a burning hostility to their older and bigger rival and to the parties on the political left.

Early in 1931 Nazi Landtag Deputy Emil Fischer, who was also a school principal in Plauen, intensified the recruitment drive of the National Socialist Teachers' League in Saxony by assigning to specific lieutenants the task of infiltrating and creating cells in the various organizations of the teaching profession in the state. When Schemm spoke at the league's big rally in Dresden on 7 November 1931, his harangue against the Saxon Teachers' Association for advocating the secular school and aligning with the "Marxist parties" excited and energized conservative school principals and teachers in the audience.[59] Schemm and other Nazi agitators contended that the modern pedagogy was "an education for godlessness" and that the experimental schools opened in Dresden, Leipzig, and other German cities were "sprouting cells of Bolshevism." They criticized the progressivist pedagogues' comradely relations with the pupils and cultivation of self-initiative and self-responsibility in the active-learning school. "Our hard future needs people in whom conformity to order, inner discipline, and obedience have been instilled," stated a young Saxon teacher, who described himself as an "advocate of a pedagogy rooted in the soil." The Nazis' polemics against the active-learning school fostered a distorted perception of flux, discord, and confusion in the world of pedagogy and trumpeted slogans claiming that the elementary school was suffering from "the fever of reform" and "the crisis of education."[60]

The National Socialists' infiltration of the organizations of conservative Protestant school principals and teachers took the form of a dialogue with National Socialism on the basis of Ernst Krieck's writings. Krieck taught at the pedagogical academy in Frankfurt am Main until his Nazi sympathies, thinly veiled in a speech delivered at a student rally in 1931, came to the attention of Social Democrats in the Prussian Landtag, who pressed Minister of Education Grimme to take disciplinary action against him.[61] *Nationalpolitische Erziehung*, which was published after Krieck was transferred to Dortmund for disciplinary reasons and had joined the Nazi teachers' league in January 1932, was a potpourri of *völkisch* educational theory and polemical denunciations of progressive education, liberalism, and parliamentary democracy.[62] Nazi infiltrators used Krieck's book as a façade for their propaganda work in the meetings of right-wing teachers' organizations, whose members were especially susceptible to the message of National Socialism because they had imbibed the discourse of antiliberalism and cultural crisis in the writings of Spengler and other ideologues associated with *Die Tat*, a neoconservative magazine.[63] Conservative school principals and teachers applauded National Socialism's call for the return of authority and discipline to the classrooms and the cultivation of "national moral values" in school instruction. They thought that the cultural politics of the Nazi and German Nationalist Parties ran parallel in respect to the elimination of "educational experiments" in the schools. A school principal in Frankfurt am Main made an unwitting confession of self-delusion when he stated at a meeting of the executive committee of the Rektorenverein on 25 June 1932: "National Socialism has not made a decision on the form of the state. One can imagine the possibility of a healthy republican form."[64]

Although the electoral vote for the Nazi Party cast by school principals and teachers as an occupational group within the civil service cannot be quantified precisely,[65] the available evidence indicates that by 1932 many members of the right-wing professional organizations were openly supporting National Socialism. Otto Arnhold, the editor of the newspaper published by the New Saxon Teachers' Association, defended the actions of Nazi Minister of Education Franzen in Braunschweig, the censorship of school books "with a Marxist-materialist orientation," and the dismissal of school officials who had been appointed by his Social Democratic predecessor. Richard Otto Kabisch, the head of the Leipzig *Ortsgruppe* of the Nazi teachers' league, was invited to the convention of the New Saxon Teachers' Association in March 1932 and gave a "welcoming address" to the delegates.[66]

Members of the League of German Protestant Teachers' Associations took care not to mention the Nazi Party by name in the public discourse at their convention in Barmen in May 1932, but the references to the "big national current" hardly concealed their sympathy for National Socialism. The debate brought out the hopes that the Nazi Party awakened in these educators as well as the trepidation that they felt about its position on Christianity and its lack of a clear school program. School principals and teachers who were attracted to National Socialism thought that it was "an advantage" for the party to postpone the drafting of a school program because all of its energy could instead be devoted to "the first task of breaking the power of the Marxists." As for the future, they clung to the illusion that devout Protestants would gain influence in the party and would be able to integrate Christianity into the *völkisch* ideology and prevent the predominance of the neopagan stream.[67]

Why were some conservative Protestant school principals and teachers willing to set aside their doubts and discount the warnings of their colleagues? In the election campaigns of 1932, the dynamic energy and mass constituency of the Nazi Party made a deep impression on them, especially in light of the erosion of electoral support for the bourgeois conservative parties.[68] The capacity "to mobilize a phalanx of men who can enter the battle against the exponents of the modern pedagogy with the prospects of success" enhanced the value of the Nazi Party in their eyes.[69] August Grünweller, a retired school principal in Rheydt and the editor of one of the newspapers of the League of German Protestant Teachers' Associations, became a fervent admirer of Adolf Hitler and was hoping for a "Hindenburg-Hitler political synthesis," in which the traditional conservatism of the German Nationalists would be reinvigorated through the new forms of popular politics of the radical right.[70] The Nazi Party, with its mass following and its image of being decisive, dynamic, and able to accomplish a job, won over these traditionalists who were hoping for a thoroughgoing reaction in school politics.

Progressivist Pedagogues and the Challenge of National Socialism

The active members of the German Teachers' Association resisted the penetration of National Socialism in their profession. When the National Socialist Teachers' League organized propaganda and recruitment meetings in the cities of Germany in 1931–32, Schemm, Krieck, and the other speakers were challenged by opponents of National Socialism who belonged to the German Teachers' Association. The league brought in Nazi storm troopers in uniform to ensure a large and enthusiastic crowd, but observers from the teachers' association were not deceived. At the rally in Königsberg on 10 September 1932, they noticed that "a considerable percentage of the people" in the audience of "about 400" were not teachers and that Otto Raatz was "led to the speaker's podium by eight SS men."[71] In the discussion following Schemm's diatribe in Dresden, Karl Trinks, the chairman of the Saxon Teachers' Association, courageously stood up and refuted Schemm's inflammatory accusations.[72] After Krieck delivered his speech in Dortmund on 11 July 1932, Albrecht Brinkmann, Ernst Müller, and Wilhelm Tittel from the Westphalian Teachers' Association spoke out against National Socialism in the discussion. They refuted Nazi propaganda again in a lively exchange with two of the league's agitators at a heavily attended meeting of the Dortmund chapter on 16 July.[73] Opposition to National Socialism in the German Teachers' Association was greater than historians have indicated in their studies of the elementary school teaching profession during these years.[74] This struggle can be documented by a close examination of its membership's response to National Socialism's threat to the democratic state and by the case studies of penetration and resistance in the teachers' associations in the provinces of Brandenburg and Silesia.

After the Nazi Party's victory in the Reichstag election of 1930, Georg Wolff, the 48-year-old chairman of the executive board of the German Teachers' Association, began to worry about the effects of the polarized political landscape on his profession. He brought to his strategical calculations the mindset of a functionary rather than the courage and deep conviction that this critical time required. Apprehensions of divisiveness and internal fighting within the association weighed heavily on him. He did not know precisely how many of its members were already followers of National Socialism. However, the activism of the National Socialists in the universities and the growing support for their slates in the student self-government elections made a deep impression on him. He realized that a sizable number of the younger generation of teachers was drawn to the ideology of *völkisch* nationalism and that the association's leadership could not close their eyes to this phenomenon. In the course of 1931, his perspective focused increasingly on the sole problem of preserving the association's unity.[75]

The strategy mapped out by Georg Wolff at a meeting of the larger executive committee on 5 December 1931 was muddled and politically naive. He proposed that the German Teachers' Association should enter a "dialogue" with National Socialism. Straying from the association's humanistic and liberal heritage, he urged the older members to reexamine the values held by generations of German pedagogues "in the light of new ideological currents and the outlook of the new generation of teachers." The association could not expect the younger generation "to put on the uniform of a teachers' union and agree to a traditional dogmatic program." He mentioned "the possibility of a synthesis" between *völkisch* nationalism and liberal humanism, and declared: "We can explain and defend the fundamental ideas of our association also from a completely different mindset." Wolff proposed, in addition, that the association should adhere to a policy of neutrality in party politics. The association could preserve its unity and "protect itself from open and disguised [National Socialist] recruitments" by emphasizing its character as a professional community.[76]

Wolff's strategic proposals provoked a big controversy within the German Teachers' Association in the early months of 1932. Objections were raised not only in Hamburg and Saxony, known as the "left wing" of the association, but also in the eastern and western provinces of Prussia. In the newspapers published by the state branches of the German Teachers' Association, Wolff was more sharply rebuked than any other chairman had been in its long history. Liberal and Social Democratic opponents of National Socialism in the association deplored Wolff's "lack of courage" and chided him for "standing aside passively" during "the fateful hour of the democratic republic."[77] They were not persuaded by his argument on the separation of the *Berufsverein* (professional association) and *Politik* and stated that he did "not assess correctly" the authoritarian nature and goals of the Nazi Party or grasp the consequences of a dictatorship concerning the right of free association and other democratic liberties presently exercised by teachers and other civil servants in the republic. Helmut Braun, a teacher in Pomerania, repudiated Wolff's strategy of preserving the unity of the association through political neutrality and appealed to German teachers to form a *"Kampffront"* in defense of the Weimar Republic. Neutrality would be a fatal mistake "in our situation, when not only the state but also the existence of our organization are critically endangered," he argued.[78]

The opponents of National Socialism also contested Wolff's proposal for a "dialogue" with National Socialism. They pointed out that the National Socialists rejected the ideals and values that the German Teachers' Association had represented for decades—democracy, the right to participate in decision-making, the need to assume responsibility, and the promotion of tolerance and international understanding. Quoting statements from *Mein Kampf*, they criticized Hitler's racial theories and moral precepts drawn from Social Darwinism.[79] In contrast to Wolff, they emphasized the "choices" that the teachers' association had to make. Wilhelm Tittel told the convention of the Westphalian Teachers' Association on 1 April 1932: "Never have two political worlds in Germany confronted each other so starkly as dictatorship and democracy do today." To loud applause, he added: "As public educators, we have an obligation to deliberate clearly and then to decide firmly which course we want to take— toward democracy or dictatorship. A profession that aspires to educate people to be free, autonomous, and morally responsible human beings requires clear, unequivocal decisions, namely, the decision in support of democracy and the great ideas of humanism."[80]

Other members of the German Teachers' Association, however, spoke out in favor of political neutrality for diverse and complex reasons. Regional leaders such as Erhardt Wolff in Breslau thought that the policy of neutrality would act as a shield and prevent the formation of Nazi cells in the local chapters.[81] Wilhelm Voigt in Madgeburg hoped that it would induce teachers who were sympathetic to National Socialism to keep their party activity and professional association apart as two separate worlds.[82] Two other defenders of nonpartisanship, Karl Schmidt and Carl Pretzel, were demoralized and disillusioned German Democrats. They thought that the fragmentation of party politics based on the representation of special interests had obstructed the development of an integrated national community and an effective parliamentary system in the Weimar Republic. They were disheartened by the magnitude of the defeat suffered by the German Democrats, now reorganized as the German State Party, in the Reichstag election of 1930, and saw the forces of liberalism in disarray.[83]

Many teachers living in small towns and the countryside felt vulnerable in regions where the electoral vote for the Nazi Party was heavy. Though personally loyal to the republic, they, too, argued that political neutrality was the right position for the German Teachers' Association. Hermann Trebbin, a teacher who lived in the area of Beeskow, a stronghold of National Socialism in the province of Brandenburg, confided in 1931 that it was no longer advisable for teachers to participate actively in political life. He had served as the leader of the local German Democratic club and experienced personally the ire of right-wing groups toward politically progressive schoolteachers. In the current feverish atmosphere, he stated, teachers could not work effectively if they were perceived by the public as political activists for a democratic party. Even if they performed their professional work scrupulously, they were "suspected, insulted, and disdained." This problem was "especially acute for teachers in small towns" because "in these smaller communities party divisions loom very large."[84]

By the time the national delegates' congress met in Rostock on 17–18 May 1932, the question of how the German Teachers' Association should respond to National Socialism's challenge to the republic became even more urgent in view of the fact that the Nazi Party had scored big victories in the state parliamentary elections held in April. A handful of Nazi insurgents at the congress assailed Leo Raeppel for violating the policy of nonpartisanship. Representing a small group of politically conservative teachers in Hamburg,[85] Günther contended that articles in the *Allgemeine Deutsche Lehrerzeitung* followed the "Social Democratic line of the *Vorwärts*" and were hostile to the National Socialists. Fritz Thiele, a delegate from Stettin, came to Raeppel's defense and proposed a resolution expressing confidence in his editorship of the newspaper. In spite of the intimidating remark of another insurgent who referred to the Nazi Party's electoral strength, the assembly of about 500 delegates adopted Thiele's resolution against "seven or eight" dissenting votes.[86]

For the national congress, Wolff had prepared an address charting the course that the German Teachers' Association should follow in these troubled times. Before the resolution drafted by Wolff was put to a vote, delegates from Bremen, Hamburg, Saxony, and Westphalia objected that its language was too vague in affirming support for the *Volksstaat*, a word that had different meanings for democrats loyal to the Weimar Constitution and for the National Socialists. Convinced that the association should "not pursue a head-in-the-sand policy" and that the delegates "would have looked like fools if they closed their eyes to this powerful movement and acted as if things were the same as in the past," the opponents of National Socialism demanded a more clearly worded resolution. A subcommittee amended the resolution to read that the German Teachers' Association unequivocally endorsed the democratic state of the Weimar Constitution.[87] Gustav Küchler, the chairman of Hamburg's largest teachers' association (the Gesellschaft der Freunde des vaterländischen Schul- und Erziehungswesens founded in 1805), with a membership of over 3,800, drafted an alternative resolution that made the expression of loyalty to the republic firmer by adding a passage on the will to "fight against all efforts to replace democracy with dictatorship."[88]

Ignoring the criticism of his strategy, Wolff continued to promote his shortsighted policy. His address essentially outlined a policy for shielding the teachers' association from the conflicts of the political world by placing the concept of profession in the foreground of associational life and separating the program of the *Berufsverein* from the ideals and values of liberalism.[89] The delegates supporting a decisive position in defense of the republican state were dismayed at Wolff's speech. They complained about the "indecisiveness" of his leadership and deplored the lack of clarity of his thinking and his tendency to lapse into pathos and hollow rhetoric in dealing with important issues. His speech did "not promote an understanding for the necessity of making clear decisions."[90]

Although delegates from Hamburg, Saxony, and Frankfurt am Main defended Küchler's proposed resolution in the debate that followed Wolff's speech, the majority gave their votes to the resolution amended by the subcommittee. Did this vote at the national congress of May 1932 mean that the German Teachers' Association had turned its back on the Weimar Republic? The delegates departed from Rostock with varied impressions of the decision. Kurt Wunsch left the congress with a feeling of "alienation and estrangement." A school principal and an apostle of the neoconservative *Tat* Circle in the region of the Riesengebirge in Silesia, Wunsch moved closer to National Socialism in 1931–32. He concluded that he could no longer belong to the executive committees of the German Teachers' Association and its branch in his province, and he resigned both offices in August.[91] Some delegates from Braunschweig took satisfaction from their understanding that solidarity based on the *Berufsidee* would keep the teachers' association united whatever political convictions individual members may have "on the outside." Other delegates from Baden noted that in contrast to Wolff's "anxious [and] cautious" behavior "stood the clear spirit of the assembly, which by its spontaneous applause manifested open support for the fundamental idea of the democratic republic."[92] The tenor of the debates and the stunning defeat suffered by a handful of Nazi insurgents who sought to censor the association's national newspaper left many regional leaders convinced that the outcome of the congress was an affirmation of loyalty to the republic.[93] *Parteipolitische Neutralität* did not mean political passivity to most delegates. They did not think that the teachers' association should form paramilitary defense units and enter the political power struggle against the Nazi Party, but they were far from being indifferent to the fate of the democratic republic and the penetration of National Socialism into their professional association.[94]

The Nazi Teachers' League and Its Opponents in Brandenburg

The struggle that took place when the National Socialists sought to infiltrate the chapters of the German Teachers' Association can be examined closely on the provincial level in Brandenburg. A covert Nazi group calling itself the "league of national teachers" was formed in Potsdam in the winter of 1930-31. The leadership of the Brandenburg Teachers' Association, with a membership of 8,005 (not counting the 6,885 members in the Greater Berlin organization),[95] quickly put up a guard against the formation of Nazi cells in their chapters.[96] Up to the summer of 1932, the growth of the membership in the National Socialist Teachers' League in the province was slow. Most of the teachers who were recruited did not belong to the German Teachers' Association, and if they were members, they had no record of active service in their local chapters.

Soon after Reich Chancellor Papen's coup d'état against the Prussian state government in July 1932 and the lifting of the ban forbidding Prussian civil servants to join the Nazi Party, Ewald Sablotny, a secondary schoolteacher who led the National Socialist Teachers' League in the province, announced a campaign to double the membership by the end of August 1932.[97] To give the recruitment drive momentum, Hans Schemm came to Brandenburg to speak at the league's rallies. By the end of 1932, the league had a network of *Ortsgruppen* located in small towns.[98]

While the recruitment campaign of the National Socialist Teachers' League profited from the profession's low morale and anger at the government's cuts in the salaries of civil servants, the main themes of the league's propaganda were issues of cultural politics and national pride rather than material interests. As Sablotny knew very well, the discrepancies in the salaries paid to rural and urban teachers and to teachers in elementary and secondary schools under the legislation of the 1920s had divided the profession into conflicting interest groups. Nazi propagandists made a point of stating that the league was not devoted to the pursuit of narrow occupational interests as were other professional organizations. Politics for the National Socialist teacher was not a matter of economic advantage but "the fight for the freedom and independence of the fatherland." The politics of liberation must be prepared by "an education that instills in the youth the will to fight, religious feeling, and an understanding of the fundamental principles of racial hygiene for our people." The league's agitators then launched into an attack on the modern pedagogy and the active-learning school. Identifying progressive education with Social Democratic pedagogues, they contended that since 1918 the *Volksschule* had become "a Marxist experimental school."[99] Their polemics against the modern school appealed to the defensiveness and resentments of rural and small-town teachers, whose work in small schoolhouses without a separate classroom for each grade had been changed very little by the theories of the active-learning school

- 217 -

movement. In comparison with the reform of elementary education in the cities, rural schools were frequently perceived as "backward." Many country schoolteachers were profoundly unhappy with their professional situation and viewed big-city pedagogues with resentment.[100]

Nazi propagandists courted Protestant rural and small-town teachers in Brandenburg also by communicating a sympathetic understanding for their longing for a new, more harmonious relationship with the clergy. Besides their opposition to the church's claims to a right to supervise religious instruction in the schools, a sizable number of teachers in rural and small-town parishes in the eastern provinces of Prussia were unhappily placed in school offices that were tied to the obligatory performance of church duties (*vereinigte Kirchen- und Schulämter*). Throughout the 1920s, Protestant teachers in these appointments, striving to be liberated from a deferential relationship with the parish pastors, fought for the separation of the school and church offices. Still traditional in their Christian religious beliefs, they wanted to work as church organists and choirmasters on the basis of free contractual arrangements that would give them more dignified conditions of work. Since these schools were built by donations to the parish churches, however, the protection of these property rights by the provincial consistories of the Protestant Church limited the state's ability to fulfill the teachers' demands. The negotiations for the separation of these dual offices were further impeded by the hostility of conservative churchmen to any innovation that could "de-Christianize" the schools.[101]

Sablotny made vague promises about the "liberation of teachers from various patronages" and used Protestant clergymen in the Nazi camp as speakers in the league's campaign to recruit teachers. In the coming Nazi state, one of these pastors claimed, the long-standing conflicts between church and school would be resolved because clergymen would trust teachers who were rooted in the German national culture and Christian faith. He made a point of stressing that the National Socialist Teachers' League did not endorse the church's demands to oversee religious instruction in the schools. If teachers and pastors were filled with "a National Socialist spirit," he declared, the supervision of school instruction by the church authorities would "not be necessary because they would then be striving for the same goals."[102]

Refugee teachers from the areas of Poznan and West Prussia ceded to Poland after the war were also fervent propagandists for National Socialism in Brandenburg and elsewhere in eastern Prussia. During the *Kaiserreich*, German teachers had become the executors of the government's Germanization policy in the schools in the Polish-speaking regions.[103] Although state officials in Berlin in 1919 discouraged the flight of teachers from the annexed areas in order to ensure the preservation of German culture in localities with a sizable German population, teachers feared Polish harassment and reprisals and were among the first wave of German nationals who emigrated.[104] In the 1920s, the Polish government pursued a policy of phasing out the public schools for the German minority, and teachers who stayed in Poland hoping to serve as stalwarts of German national culture were dismissed. School officials fired German teachers who refused to sing the Polish national anthem and to take a loyalty oath to Poland. In some counties the German teachers were expelled immediately, and pianos, sewing machines, and other items of furniture in their households were confiscated.[105]

Extreme nationalism, an intense enmity toward Poland, and a negative view of the Weimar Republic marked the political perspective of many refugee teachers who were resettled in new school positions in Prussia. From 1930 on, refugee teachers intensified their propaganda activity on behalf of the grievances of the German minority in Poland relating to provisions for German-language schools.[106] The "bleeding frontiers" was the theme of the speeches delivered by these nationalists at Nazi propaganda meetings for teachers. They denounced the Social Democrats in the government in the early Weimar years for allowing German lands to be torn away from the national body and millions of Germans to be "placed under the yoke of the inferior *völkisch* Polish state."[107]

Under the plan devised by Sablotny, National Socialist teachers who belonged to the Brandenburg Teachers' Association were instructed to retain their membership and to fight for the goals of the Nazi movement within it. Their first objective was to remove left-wing liberals and Social Democrats who were opponents of National Socialism from the executive committee. The league was determined to oust Max Karstedt, the editor of the *Brandenburgische Schulzeitung*, because he had published critical news reports on the schools in Fascist Italy; the policies of the Nazi education ministers in Braunschweig, Oldenburg, and Thuringia; and the raucous disturbances caused by Nazi students at the University of Leipzig.[108] During the fall of 1932, Nazi cells were formed in the chapters in the rural county of Frankfurt an der Oder and in several small towns. Moving rapidly and aggressively, the National Socialists made a bid for power in the election of the executive committee that was to take place at the upcoming delegates' convention on 3–4 October 1932. This attempt to gain a commanding position on the executive committee reveals that the Nazi adherents in the Brandenburg Teachers' Association at this time were still a small faction. In August, the nominating committee prepared a slate of candidates with Artur Schilde, a school principal in Eberswalde and the present chairman, at the head of the list. The nominating committee decided not to permit another slate proposed by Nazi teachers to be put on the ballot because ten of the candidates were not members of the teachers' association.[109]

Nazi insurgents at the convention introduced a motion nullifying the election of the nominating committee and calling for a new election.

Aware of the far-reaching significance of this dispute, many teachers had come to the convention as spectators, in addition to the more than 150 voting delegates. In the debate on this motion, three rural teachers argued that the Nazi slate had been improperly disqualified. They characterized the challenge of the Nazi teachers as a conflict between the generations and contended that the present leadership no longer possessed the confidence of the members. In a counterattack, Romberg, a school principal in Finow, pointed to the Nazi Party's dictatorial ambitions. He charged that the Nazi slate was merely a front for the National Socialist Teachers' League, whose ultimate goal was the absorption of the other professional associations. Another delegate criticized Minister of Education Heinz Spangemacher in the Nazi government in Oldenburg for purging the school administration and putting party hacks in public offices. The convention voted for the reelection of the executive committee by an overwhelming majority. With four dissenting votes on their side, the National Socialists were far from dominating the Brandenburg Teachers' Association.[110]

Later in the fall of 1932, the committee on school politics of the Brandenburg Teachers' Association held a conference in the city of Neustadt, devoted to the issue of National Socialism, and provided Romberg and other republican stalwarts with another forum for criticizing the authoritarianism of the Nazi movement and rallying teachers to defend their civic rights and the freedom of their profession. Close to 200 teachers came to this meeting. A report on this conference in the *Brandenburgische Schulzeitung* stated that although the National Socialists were "a numerically small group within the membership," it was necessary to confront this assertive movement. The National Socialists had committed "the tactical blunder of placing party leaders who were not members of the teachers' association in the fighting line." Teachers at the delegates' convention and the Neustadt conference had rejected National Socialism because of the "impossibility of reconciling two worldviews that are very different in their essential nature and principles." They knew what was "at stake" when they repudiated the authoritarian principles of the Nazi Party: "Collegial school governance, elected representative teachers' councils, modern school instruction 'from the perspective of the child,' and many other achievements would automatically be abolished with the destruction of democracy. No teacher can want autocratic rule. One of the most important intrinsic aspects of our profession is the capacity to govern ourselves, make our own decisions, and act on our own responsibility in freedom, according to our best knowledge and consciences." They saw "no possibility for compromise, only the necessity of drawing the line and making the distinction clear."[111]

National Socialism and Teachers in the Frontier Province of Silesia

Resistance to the infiltration of National Socialism in the Silesian Teachers' Association was courageous but less extensive because the political conservatism and nationalistic frontier perspective of a large section of its membership made the organization more porous. Before the summer of 1932, the National Socialist Teachers' League recruited a small number of dedicated followers in Silesia. Karl Dittberner, a Protestant teacher and church organist, founded a branch of the National Socialist Teachers' League and led it until he suffered a heart attack and died in 1931. Its first members came from a small club of *völkisch*-nationalist teachers in the central and northern sections of the province, who had been meeting monthly in Breslau since 1926. Dittberner propagated National Socialism within the circle of conservative rural and small-town schoolteachers in the province who belonged to the Vereinigung der Organisten und Kantoren, a subgroup of organists and choirmasters within the Prussian Teachers' Association that represented the particular interests of those members whose school positions required them to perform church duties.

The National Socialist Teachers' League made very slow progress in expanding its membership rolls in the province. When the members of the league in Silesia held their first convention in October 1931, "around 30 male teachers and a few female teachers" assembled in the town of Braunau and heard the speeches delivered by Hans Schemm and Helmut Brückner, the leader of the Nazi Party in the Silesian *Gau*. About 100 teachers came to another meeting organized by Nazi teachers in Breslau on 17 November 1931. Here Schemm vented his frustration over the slow growth of the league's membership and assailed the "stubborn heads" in the German Teachers' Association. The Landtag and Reichstag election campaigns in 1932 were also a time of intensified Nazi efforts to make inroads in the teaching profession. With "a feeling of defiance" toward the political system, which prohibited civil servants from belonging to the Nazi Party, members of the league worked tirelessly to propagate their ideology and win followers.[112] By the beginning of July 1932, the league had recruited only 211 members in the heavily Protestant provincial district of Liegnitz, an area in which the Nazi Party had won 48 percent of the vote in the Reichstag election in that same month and 42 percent in the November 1932 election.[113]

Although the percentage of elementary schoolteachers who cast their ballots for the Nazi Party in 1932 cannot be assessed, there can be no doubt that sympathy for National Socialism in the ranks of the elementary school teaching profession in Silesia extended far beyond the membership of the Nazi teachers' league there. The observation of one teacher that most rural teachers in his area of the Liegnitz district voted for the Nazi Party does not seem off the mark.[114] In this electoral district in the predominantly

Protestant Lower Silesia, the vote for the two bourgeois middle parties together fell from 12.9 percent in the 1928 Reichstag election to less than 2 percent in the election in July 1932. Rural and small-town schoolteachers constituted 71 percent of the membership of the Silesian Teachers' Association in 1932, and a sizable section of these teachers were more conservative than the elected officers in Breslau. Although the association's membership included Catholics and Jews, Protestant teachers were far and away the majority.[115] Moreover, the political outlook of teachers in this border province was deeply affected by the violent political struggle between the Germans and Poles before and immediately after the plebiscite of 20 March 1921 in Upper Silesia. In matters of foreign politics, teachers in the East often contrasted their "German frontier perspective" with the "internationalism" and "pacifism" of the German Democrats and Social Democrats in the other branches of the German Teachers' Association, who supported the aspirations of the League of Nations and a policy of reconciliation between Germany and the victorious Allies.[116]

In the plebiscite campaign of 1920–21, German elementary schoolteachers in Silesia were ardent patriots and high-profile activists. As volunteer workers in the Defense League for Germans on the Frontier and Abroad (Deutscher Schutzbund für die Grenz- und Auslandsdeutschen), they registered Germans who were eligible to vote in the referendum, and provided assistance to those persons living outside the plebiscite zone to encourage them to return to their place of birth and vote for Germany. As local agents of the League of Patriotic Upper Silesians (Verband heimattreuer Oberschlesier) in many towns, they delivered speeches promoting loyalty to Germany as the homeland of the Upper Silesians and wrote propaganda for the press.[117] This volunteer service became more intensive when the minister of education ordered the governor of the Liegnitz provincial district on 10 January 1921 to release a number of teachers from schoolwork so that they could work longer hours in the last phase of the plebiscite campaign.[118]

As Upper Silesia descended into disorder and lawlessness, Polish nationalists stoked the fires of popular antipathy to German teachers. Derogatory articles about schoolmasters who allegedly insulted and whipped Polish pupils appeared in the Polish-language press. In localities where the Poles organized school strikes, gangs broke into the schoolhouses, destroying books and vandalizing the classrooms. Teachers whose lives were threatened had to flee. Polish hostility toward teachers who were active in the German loyalist campaign escalated to terrorism when the Polish nationalists staged a revolt in August 1920. Insurgents broke into the teachers' homes, beat them with clubs, and robbed them of their valuables. Some of these teachers were arrested and brought to internment camps. In another wave of political terrorism in the winter of 1920–21, several attempts to assassinate teachers by gunfire and hand grenades took place. Even when the teachers had the good fortune to escape unhurt, they found their homes heavily damaged.[119]

The division of Upper Silesia, after Germany had won a majority vote in the referendum, left teachers in the province with an enduring hostility toward France and Poland. They attributed Poland's acquisition of the eastern part of Upper Silesia to the "vengefulness" of the French. In the preceding months they had frequently complained that the French on the Interallied Commission sided with the Polish nationalists and did not keep their promise of impartiality and fairness, and that the French occupation troops were too tolerant of the violence of the Polish nationalists. They saw the negotiations of the final settlement of Upper Silesia at the League of Nations as "a mask of hypocrisy" for the purpose of giving a proper appearance to "an injustice."[120]

Schoolteachers in Silesia did not reconcile themselves to Germany's new boundaries in the East. In the following years they frequently deplored the divisive party politics and instability of the "gravely sick German state" and thought that the German people had to concentrate their energy on foreign politics and the revision of the Versailles settlement. Writing on the occasion of Constitution Day in 1923, one teacher lamented that the German people lacked a unified national will and were not ready for the freest constitution in the world. Another teacher decried the "pacifists" and praised the Germans who were resisting the French occupation of the Ruhr. Contending that the Versailles treaty was the fundamental cause of Germany's wretched situation, he stated that it was high time that the German people understood the priority of foreign policy before all other questions because only thereby could a united front in domestic politics be formed to overturn the Versailles settlement.[121]

In the early 1930s many conservative rural and small-town schoolteachers, whose lukewarm affirmation of the republican state had been shaken by the emergency decrees, were drawn to the neoconservative movement and its denunciation of parliamentary democracy, the cultural decadence of the big city, and the modern pedagogy. Hermann Schaller, a head teacher and church organist in Erdmannsdorf, and Kurt Wunsch, a principal in Hermsdorf, became fervent disciples of the neoconservative prophets of the *Tat* Circle and began to disseminate their ideas in the Silesian Teachers' Association. A reading circle in Schaller's chapter in Erdmannsdorf had been meeting regularly since 1928 to discuss articles in *Die Tat*. In 1930–32, Schaller and Wunsch frequently traveled to other chapters in the predominantly Protestant regions of the Riesengebirge and Eulengebirge to give speeches on the "crises of education," the "crisis of liberalism," and related themes at their monthly meetings.[122] Wunsch became a convert to National Socialism, and in these same chapters he and other Nazi sympathizers were soon using lectures on Krieck's *Nationalpolitische Erziehung* as a screen to propagate their new political faith.[123]

In 1932 many Protestant rural and small-town teachers became fellow travelers in the Nazi movement. Schaller and the other teachers in his chapter, for example, did not join the Nazi Party and storm troopers, but they were attracted to the charisma and *völkisch* nationalism of Hitler. Their monthly meetings were devoted to lectures and discussions on the grievances of the German minority in Poland, the Treaty of Versailles and reparations, and the crisis of the state, under such titles as "Germany in Chains" and "When Will the Rescuer Come for Our Times?" The chapter sponsored a series of lectures based on Hans Freyer's *Revolution von Rechts*, Moeller van den Bruch's *Das dritte Reich*, and the writings of other neoconservative pundits.[124]

In numerous articles in the association's press, Schaller and other tragically foolish epigones of the *Tat* Circle presented National Socialism as the hope for the renewal of all institutions in German society and for "the assertion of a strong national will to freedom" from the conditions imposed by the Treaty of Versailles. Referring to a vague concept of a Nazi revolution as the only way of rescuing Germany from the "total crisis," they advocated "a turn to the total state with a corporate foundation below and a forceful leadership at the top."[125] They criticized Hugo Gaudig's "individualistic" philosophy of education. Rejecting the idea of the autonomy of pedagogy and the educational goals of the active-learning school, which had been "inspired by the liberal ideology," they called for a new school that would stand in the service of the integral nation and would drill social discipline and a *völkisch*-nationalist consciousness into the pupils.[126] As an activist in the Nazi teachers' league in Breslau confirmed in April 1933, the propagandists of the *Tat* Circle in the Silesian Teachers' Association had helped to disseminate the ideology of National Socialism in the teaching profession. Many of the teachers who found their way to National Socialism came through the neoconservative movement.[127]

In 1931 and 1932, National Socialists infiltrated and formed cells in the chapters of the Silesian branch of the German Teachers' Association. A survey of the agendas and reports of the chapter meetings suggests that the National Socialists were more active in this organization than in the branch of the Catholic Teachers' Association in the province. Only in October 1932 did the chapter of the Catholic Teachers' Association in Ratibor, located near the boundary separating the German and Polish sections of Upper Silesia, announce that a member would speak on Ernst Krieck's book.[128] Nazi sympathizers formed cells in the chapters of the Silesian Teachers' Association in the cities of Gleiwitz, Oppeln, Liegnitz, Bunzlau, and Münsterberg and in the rural regions of the Riesengebirge and Eulengebirge. National Socialism appealed to conservative rural and small-town teachers and to other right-wing teachers who bewailed the fate of their German "brothers" living across the border under Polish rule.

As early as 1930, a small core of National Socialists who were assertive and tenacious in fighting for their cause began to agitate for the "depoliticization and complete political neutrality of the German Teachers' Association and its press organs." They tried to impose a right-wing political agenda on the provincial branch in October 1931, when the rural chapter in Zackenthal submitted a seemingly innocent proposal to the executive committee, demanding that the association take up the "new tasks" placed before the teaching profession by the "crisis of the German people." The executive committee chaired by Ernst Knappe, a school principal in Breslau, withstood this maneuver.[129] After this setback, the supporters of the Nazi Party began to attack the leadership of the German Teachers' Association on the provincial and national levels. Otto Fröhlich, a rural schoolteacher in the Münsterberg chapter who became the spokesman for the Nazi faction, assailed the "petit-bourgeois" conduct of the leadership in an article published in the Schlesische Schulzeitung. He urged the teachers to examine the reasons for the "failure" of their professional organization and to change its political direction. It should become an opposition movement against the government "system" and big business. "Fight against reparations, lies about war guilt, the men of high finance, bank scandals connected with the Jew Jacob Goldschmidt," he exclaimed.[130]

At a meeting of teachers on the radical right in the city of Hirschberg on 23 January 1932, Kurt Wunsch unleashed another assault on the leadership of the German Teachers' Association. The tenor of his speech was disclosed to his colleagues through a report on this meeting in a Nazi newspaper, the Hirschberger Beobachter, which denounced the leadership of the teachers' association for "selling themselves out to the liberal-Marxist system." The article called for the demolition of the organization to the ground so that the younger generation could rebuild it anew and bring "new ideas and young blood into the leadership." It ended with an intimidating threat: "The Nazi storm shall sweep the board here also. Young teachers and the up-and-coming generation are at work. Their next task is the conquest of the teachers' associations, the overthrow of their bosses, the change of their programs and conduct."[131] Ernst Knappe, Traugott Kapuste, and other members of the executive committee criticized Wunsch's speech in Hirschberg at their meeting on 30 March 1932. Wunsch absented himself from this meeting, most likely to dodge a face-to-face confrontation. The opponents of National Socialism on the executive committee confronted him personally at a meeting on 26 June. Thereafter, he resigned from the association's executive committees on the provincial and national levels.[132]

The supporters of the republican state in the leadership of the Silesian Teachers' Association publicly stated their opposition to the agitation of Wunsch and other teachers on the far right in the Schlesische Schulzeitung. Traugott Kapuste, who wrote this article, was a German Democrat and a highly respected elder statesman in the association, having served as its chairman in the 1920s. He criticized the contempt for democracy expressed by ideologues on the extreme right, and added emphatically that the German

Teachers' Association did not endorse dictatorship and would not do so in the future. Addressing teachers who were angry at the government because of the emergency decrees, Kapuste gave a strong defense of the teaching profession's ties to the republic. He stated that anyone who was deeply committed to the well-being of the elementary schools and wanted to devote his or her life's work to the progressive development of the nation had to agree that a democratic state based on the intellectual and moral maturity of citizens had an inherent need to improve the education of the youth to a far greater extent than did an authoritarian state that viewed people as subjects. Even if one held the opinion that the German people were not yet prepared for the responsibilities of parliamentary government, this view did not require the nation's educators to reject the democratic form of the state but to eliminate these shortcomings as soon as possible.[133]

With growing confidence and assertiveness, Nazi teachers made a bid to take control of their professional society after the popular vote for the Nazi Party soared in the Breslau and Liegnitz electoral districts in the Reichstag election of July 1932. The chapter in Gröditzberg that had been taken over by Nazi agitators sent to the executive board in Breslau a resolution that laid down the guidelines according to which the teachers' association should work. The Nazi faction called for changes in the educational goals and curriculum of the schools in line with *völkisch*-nationalist ideology. Opposing collegial school governance, they proposed that school principals be appointed by the government for the remaining duration of their careers and that political ideology be a decisive criterion in these appointments. The officers of the Silesian Teachers' Association were resolved to fight this attempt by a political party to dictate principles and policies to them. They circulated the Gröditzberg proposal to the chapters so that the membership could take a position, and summoned the local chairmen to a meeting on 30 October. Representatives of the executive boards of the national and state organizations in Berlin came to Breslau for this showdown. The remarks made by a National Socialist who led the Gröditzberg chapter provoked considerable dissent. In the heated exchange, Knappe told him that if the demand for a reexamination of the ideological position of the leadership was intended "to bring the teachers' association into an accommodating relationship with the Nazi Party, then we reject this demand decisively."[134]

Knappe's remarks at this meeting, subsequently published in the *Schlesische Schulzeitung*, were an unequivocal repudiation of the Nazi movement. He criticized its hostility to the Weimar Republic, its demands for a strong state leadership that would be independent of parties and parliamentary institutions, and the attempts of the Nazi education ministers in the state governments of Braunschweig and Mecklenburg to indoctrinate the schoolchildren and to repress dissent. Contending that teachers had to take a position on recent political developments, he criticized the Reich cabinet's coup of 20 July 1932 against the state government in Prussia, the use of presidential emergency powers, and the exclusion of the Reichstag from the government. He reminded civil servants of the constitutional rights and benefits that they had received from the republic. They had a vital interest in seeing that democratically elected representative institutions were preserved in the government of the state. An authoritarian state would not provide civil servants with securer rights or give their interest groups more influence.[135]

Within the Silesian Teachers' Association the centers of opposition to National Socialism were the urban chapters, especially in the cities where the Social Democratic Party had a strong following. In a lecture at a meeting of the big chapter in Breslau in 1931, Walter Kowalski condemned the unrestrained anti-Semitism of the Nazi movement and Hitler's extreme statements in *Mein Kampf* about the removal of Jews from the national community.[136] A teacher in Schweidnitz voiced his disapproval of Schaller's attacks on liberalism and the agitational methods of the Nazi storm troopers. Another teacher in Oels took issue with the neoconservatives' criticism of parliamentary democracy and called their idols in the *Tat* Circle "the intellectual carriers of German fascism." He chided Schaller and Wunsch for succumbing to the fashionable currents of cultural pessimism and to the mystical language with which the neoconservative prophets talked about the state and the *Volk*.[137] Before the national congress convened in Rostock, the chapter in Görlitz, at a meeting on 7 May 1932, adopted a resolution demanding that "the German Teachers' Association support unequivocally and resolutely the republic and democracy in the fateful conflicts of our times." Throughout 1932, left-wing liberals and Social Democrats in the Görlitz chapter sought to foster an awareness of the threat of the radical right to political freedom and tolerance by presenting lectures on the racist theories of the *völkisch* political ideologues, the proto-fascist tendencies of Germany's neoconservatives, and the changes that the Fascist dictatorship had imposed on society and the educational system in Italy.[138] Disturbed by the growth of the Nazi youth organizations and the participation of these pupils in political rallies and street demonstrations, the chapter in Breslau issued a public appeal to the parents to act as true guardians of their children. This appeal was both a protest against the indoctrination and mobilization of young people by "fanatical party leaders" and a rebuke to those Nazi elementary and secondary schoolteachers who were misusing their office and authority as educators in the service of a political party.[139]

Up to the end of 1932, Ernst Knappe faced the challenge of National Socialism with considerable courage and conviction. In December 1931, he told the executive committee that they should not allow themselves to be intimidated and to diverge from the path that they considered to be right.[140] Before the national congress in Rostock, he pleaded with teachers in Silesia to think soberly about the gravity of the threat. He pointed to the inner drive of the Nazi Party toward totalitarianism and described how such a party could take control of the teachers' association once it gained political power.[141] In the climate of political violence, which escalated with the terror campaign of the Nazi storm troopers in the cities and industrial centers of Silesia in August 1932, Knappe's admonitions could not overcome the demoralization and resignation of those teachers who thought that Germany's educators could not by themselves withstand the political parties that were indoctrinating and mobilizing the youth.[142]

The Progressivist Pedagogues and the Nazi Government

There was much apprehensiveness within the German Teachers' Association in the weeks after the formation of a new cabinet with Hitler as the Reich chancellor on 30 January 1933. Several of the editors of the association's national and regional newspapers showed immense courage in speaking out against the intimidating statements and threats made to the civil service by Hermann Göring and Bernhard Rüst in their positions as Reich commissars for the Prussian Interior and Education Ministries.[143] The discussions at the chapter meetings in Saxony in February ended with the adoption of resolutions protesting the violation of constitutional rights and the repressive police and administrative actions against the political left. The chapter in Leipzig called on the German Teachers' Association and German Civil Servants' League to join the Social Democratic trade unions in an antifascist front.[144] During the campaign for the Reichstag election on 5 March, Leo Raeppel and Max Karstedt questioned the credibility of the promises made by the Nazi Party, and quoted passages from Hitler's *Mein Kampf* and other pieces of propaganda to substantiate their warning that after the National Socialists gained control over the state, they would use political terror against their opponents. On the eve of the election, Raeppel urged the teachers not to be swept up by nationalistic fervor. He warned them of the consequences of the "total state" for the teaching profession, "the most vulnerable of all groups of civil servants," in a party dictatorship.[145]

During the tense weeks between 30 January and 5 March 1933, Artur Schilde and other members of the executive committee defended the autonomy of the Brandenburg Teachers' Association against the challenge of the National Socialists, who had planted cells in the chapters and were using the tactics of clamorous accusations and intimidation to eliminate the leadership. As a teacher in Frankfurt an der Oder stated, most of the young teachers in these cells had "not attended chapter meetings hitherto" and had "not worked positively within the chapter."[146] The chapters in the towns of Beelitz, Drebkau, and Storkow, which were dominated by Nazis, intensified their efforts to oust Karstedt from his editorial office. Schilde invited spokesmen for the three chapters to meet with the executive committee on 12 February. The association's leadership pointed out that Karstedt could not be dismissed except by a vote of the delegates' convention. They also declined to require him to publish articles written by Nazi ideologues.[147] The will to resist gave way when the passage of the Enabling Act on 23 March 1933 removed the last obstacles to the establishment of the Nazi dictatorship. Thereafter, Karstedt resigned the editorship of the newspaper.

Members of the German Teachers' Association in Berlin and Breslau also withstood the attempts of Nazi teachers to take control of their chapters in February. Kurt David came to the Breslau chapter's meeting on 21 February as a representative of the National Socialist Teachers' League. He complained about Leo Raeppel and objected specifically to articles in the *Allgemeine Deutsche Lehrerzeitung* that were critical of the Nazi governments in Thuringia and other states. He introduced a proposal that called for an immediate change in the editorship of the newspaper and for a reorientation of the German Teachers' Association in support of the Nazi government. The teachers in Breslau voted to table this motion despite David's warning that the teachers' association had to draw its resistance to a close and make a clear decision in support of National Socialism.[148] At the annual assembly of the Berlin teachers' association on 24 February, Nazi insurgents tried to place party men on the executive committee and distributed a revised ballot with the names of eight Nazi candidates before the vote was taken. The outcome of this election was a defeat for the Nazi faction. The vote for the Nazi slate brought only one of the eight candidates to the twenty-one-member executive committee.[149]

After the Reichstag election on 5 March, the Nazi government moved swiftly to liquidate the Saxon Teachers' Association. The brutal repression was widely reported in the press and had a chilling effect on the members of the German Teachers' Association. The Nazi authorities arrested Karl Trinks, the chairman of the Saxon Teachers' Association; two other officers; and Alfred Weller, the editor of the *Sächsische Schulzeitung*. The police searched the offices of the outspokenly antifascist chapter in Leipzig and arrested eight members of its executive board. The association's newspapers in Dresden and Leipzig were banned. The executive boards of the chapters as well as the state organization were forced to resign, and the leadership was handed over to people belonging to the Nazi Party and its teachers' league. These changes prepared the way for the formal decision to merge the Saxon Teachers' Association into the National Socialist Teachers' League, which was made at a delegates' convention in Leipzig on 10 April. The assembly settled this business and elected a new executive committee within one hour without any debate. Willy Hermann Potscher, a Nazi teacher in Dresden, became the new chairman by an oral vote.[150]

With similar speed and resoluteness, the Nazi authorities in Saxony purged the school administration and imposed a system of threats, controls, and ideological conformity on teachers in their schoolwork and public life.

In his new office as Saxon minister of education, Wilhelm Hartnacke suspended three school inspectors, Erler, Viehweg, and Wehner, who were Social Democrats and members of the Saxon Teachers' Association, and announced on 11 March the opening of formal procedures for their dismissal. In the following week, the purge was extended to other school inspectors. The vacancies were filled by Old Fighters in the Nazi teachers' league.[151] A sweeping decree on 14 March threatened that disciplinary measures would be taken against teachers who participated in a political party or an ideological group opposed to the government as well as teachers who acted or made statements against the Nazi Party, its leaders, and flag. An order on 24 March instructed school inspectors to examine whether the *Schulleiter* presently in office could be expected, on the basis of their previous political activities, to carry out the new government's regulations; those individuals who could not be relied upon were to be replaced immediately.[152] Hartnacke dismantled the system of collegial school governance, ordered the closing of the experimental schools, and, in a radio address, communicated his intention to suppress the new pedagogy in the schools.[153]

The new regime could not act fast enough to satisfy the impatient foes of the progressivist pedagogues. Throughout March, German Nationalist Party clubs and the Christian parents' associations demanded the dismissal of teachers with "a Marxist or freethinking orientation" and the "cleansing of the elementary schools."[154] The conservatives in the New Saxon Teachers' Association viewed the liquidation of their rival and the repression of the political parties on the left with schadenfreude. Glossing over the violations of the law and constitutional rights, Otto Arnhold stated: "The national reform should not be tripped up by these trifles. The newly elected government offers us the guarantee that our schools will be placed again on a national and Christian foundation."[155]

The Nazi dictatorship could not dissolve the professional organizations of schoolteachers immediately for legal reasons related to their registration as juridical bodies in the state and to their statutes concerning the disposal of their property and financial assets. Hans Schemm and his deputy Sablotny employed the strategy of having the membership of these organizations vote to enter the National Socialist Teachers' League as a corporate body.[156] The incorporation of the German Teachers' Association and its state branches into the Nazi teachers' league, formally executed by a vote at the delegates' conventions in May and June 1933, was merely legal window-dressing. Schemm and Sablotny carried out the dissolution of these organizations in a manner that lent the process the false appearance of a voluntary union with the league. Some of the old officers, including Georg Wolff and Heinrich Diekmann, participated in the conventions and were allowed to hold seats on the newly formed executive committees in the transition phase. The process of incorporation was controlled by agents who were appointed by the league's central leadership and assigned to the regional branches of the German Teachers' Association.

For a short time, Wolff seems to have hoped that after Raeppel's resignation on 18 March, a more cooperative relationship with the Nazi government would enable the German Teachers' Association to continue to exist as a *Berufsverein* in the Third Reich. It is doubtful that the other leaders had any illusions about this possibility; they were aware of the fascistization of the teachers' professional organizations in Mussolini's Italy and knew that the Enabling Act had given Hitler's government massive power. When Schemm presented his plan for a unified organization of German educators, they recognized it as a strategy for liquidating the long established teachers' associations by absorbing them into the Nazi teachers' league and accepted the change as "unavoidably necessary."[157] At the convention of the Prussian Teachers' Association in Schneidemühl on 11-12 April 1933, Diekmann told the delegates that there was "no other choice or alternative" for civil servants than to affirm their support for the new government. Erich Fröhlich, who led the Berlin chapter, informed the delegates that the executive board had already agreed to Schemm's guidelines, which required the teachers' associations to give up their goals and principles based on liberalism, to end their activity in cultural politics, and to place the editorial offices of their newspapers in the hands of persons who could "offer a guarantee [of political reliability] to the state powers." His remarks made it clear to them that these conditions could not be a matter for debate and a vote.[158]

Even before the state and national conventions assembled, the *Gleichschaltung*, that is, the process of bringing the professional associations of German schoolteachers under Nazi control, was started at the local and provincial levels. The Nazis took over the local chapters in an atmosphere of intimidation and political persecution and terror. The repression of the Saxon Teachers' Association and the purge of the school administration and teaching profession produced widespread insecurity and anxiety. The teachers knew that paragraph 4 of the Law for the Restoration of the Civil Service of 7 April 1933 provided for the dismissal of civil servants who did "not offer any certainty, on the basis of their previous political activity, that they [would] always support the national state without reservation." Although it is not possible to provide precise figures on the number of teachers in Germany who were penalized under this law, the available evidence suggests that elementary schoolteachers were more affected by the government's purge actions than were other civil servants.[159] Personnel changes in the elementary schools in Prussia were so extensive that the opening of the new school term in 1934 had to be postponed. The dismissal of 56 school inspectors in Prussia by October 1933 allowed functionaries of the Nazi teachers' league to fill the lower levels of the school administration and to enforce the ideological conformity of the teachers. The incidence of disciplinary measures against teachers was greater in areas where the left-wing parties were strong. In Hamburg, 98 elementary schoolteachers were dismissed in April. In Leipzig, 23 teachers were thrown out in March by a government order, and on the basis of the law of 7 April 1933 about 70 teachers lost their jobs.[160]

The *Gleichschaltung* of the teachers' associations on the local level varied according to the temperament and disposition of the local and provincial leaders of the Nazi movement. It was swift and accompanied by considerable political force in the states of Saxony, Thuringia, Hesse, and Hamburg. These precedents of brutal repression and coercion made a powerful impression on Diekmann and the other leaders of the Prussian Teachers' Association, who yielded to the necessity of accommodation.[161] Some Nazi leaders in the eastern provinces of Prussia made accommodation all the easier for the schoolteachers by employing tactics that combined threats and reassurances rather than brutal coercion.

Acting openly now as a district leader of the Nazi teachers' league in Silesia, Otto Fröhlich issued in February an admonition to teachers who had an oppositional or a distant position toward the Nazi Party. He told them bluntly that the government under Adolf Hitler would be more than a passing episode and that they had to accept the party's *völkisch* ideology and educational policies. At the same time, he made vaguely reassuring remarks about the continuation of the long established civil servants' and teachers' organizations in the Nazi state. He treated the differences between the school programs of the National Socialists and the German Teachers' Association as matters of little weight and stated that "unbridgeable differences need not exist." When Schaller reproached him for striving to build bridges instead of defining the opposing fronts sharply and fighting the "conviction liberals" in the Silesian Teachers' Association, Fröhlich was annoyed at the meddling of this neoconservative, who had not joined the Nazi Party before 1933 and was "now more papist than the pope." Fröhlich's intention was "to show colleagues who are still distant from Nazi ways of thinking that they have nothing to fear from National Socialism for their profession as well as for the German school." He defended his strategy of putting the fight between the two political camps in the past and said, "We must conciliatingly build bridges."[162]

The bridge-building strategy of the Nazi teachers' league in Silesia seems to have encouraged a disposition toward self-deception so that the *Gleichschaltung* proceeded smoothly.[163] Throughout March, representatives of the league spoke at the meetings of the chapters of the Silesian Teachers' Association. Resolutions presented by these speakers to the chapters for a vote called for the reorientation of the German Teachers' Association and the election of a new executive committee. In April and May, the chapters held their own elections and placed their leadership in Nazi hands. Gustav Geisler, a member of the Nazi teachers' league, became the chairman of the province's largest chapter in Breslau. New elections were not held in the Liegnitz chapter because its chairman had long been sympathetic to National Socialism.

The chapters in Gleiwitz and Oppeln reelected their officers since they already supported the Nazi movement.[164] In these local elections, chairmen who had been committed republicans and opponents of National Socialism were replaced by Nazi school principals and teachers in 21.5 percent of the chapters in Silesia (39 out of the 181 chapters), mostly, the larger chapters located in Breslau, Görlitz, Waldenburg, Hindenburg, and other cities.[165] Under new leadership, the chapters took the next step of voting to merge with the Nazi teachers' league.

The accounts of these meetings of schoolteachers in the eastern provinces of Prussia are very terse, but a number of reports from Brandenburg and East Prussia convey the atmosphere of anxiety and intimidation and a prevailing disposition of pragmatic adaptation. The chairman of the chapter in Potsdam opened the meeting in March by informing the members that school inspectors who were Social Democrats had been removed from their offices. He spoke of the need for adaptation to the Nazi state and added that by the very nature of this state the freedoms of democracy could not be expected. He expressed the hope that the government would not resort to a policy of revenge and massive purge.[166] In cleansing the schools in the province of Brandenburg, the National Socialists targeted the cities of Luckenwalde and Nowawes, known to them as "Red strongholds," and boastfully settled old grudges by dismissing three school principals and "quite a number of teachers."[167]

In the chapters of the teachers' association in East Prussia, the executive boards were forced to resign, and then the members were summoned to meetings to elect new officers from a slate of candidates put up by the Nazi teachers' league. At the meeting in Wehlau, a spokesman for the league delivered a bitter harangue and scolded the teachers for "joining the new movement so late."[168] Some teachers in the area of Königsberg spoke disapprovingly of Diekmann's opportunism and compliant behavior at the convention of the Prussian Teachers' Association in April 1933. Responding to their criticism that the merger with the Nazi teachers' league was "a betrayal of the cause of the association" and the liberal heritage of its forefathers, a school principal justified Diekmann's conduct: "Times have changed. It requires no special astuteness to observe that today, if one keeps in mind the development of events from 30 January up to 17 May." He reminded his colleagues that political parties no longer existed, parliamentary democracy was dead, and Germany was governed by a one-party dictatorship. "There are facts with which we as an organization have to reckon today," he said.[169]

Considerable pressure was put on elementary schoolteachers to join the Nazi teachers' league in 1933. Beginning in March and April, its membership grew by a big leap, and by December it had ballooned to 220,000.[170] This expansion of the league's membership in 1933 must be assessed with caution. Speaking at the meetings of the other professional associations, the commissars of the league did not shy away from using direct and implied threats when they urged teachers to join their organization.[171] These incidents of intimidation led the officers of the bourgeois-conservative German National Teachers' League to complain to the Nazi minister of education in Prussia on 12 May. Karl Kickhöffel, a former German Nationalist deputy in the Prussian Landtag, protested that school principals and teachers in his organization were being pressured by threats to join the Nazi teachers' league for fear of suffering harm to their livelihood and professional careers.[172]

Teachers who had joined the Nazi teachers' league in earlier years doubted the sincerity of the new converts—and with good reason. It was not too long ago that the Old Fighters had experienced difficulty penetrating the elementary school teaching profession in their areas. Otto Fröhlich noted that up to 30 January 1933, many of the league's local groups in Silesia were not able to work effectively because of their tiny membership—often as few as three or five teachers. He thought that besides the fear of losing their school positions, newcomers in the league were motivated by "careerism." Like the other Old Fighters in the league, Fröhlich was contemptuous of these "office hunters," who wanted to be "110 percent Nazi" and used any occasion to wear the insignia of the Nazi movement.[173]

The appeal of National Socialism within the elementary school teaching profession cut across generational lines. Although the majority of members of the National Socialist Teachers' League were radicalized young teachers of two age cohorts who were estranged from the profession's traditional associations and ethos, the league recruited educators from the older generations, too. Around one-third of its membership before 1933 had entered the profession during the empire.[174] Little attention in the historical literature has been given to these older teachers, apart from the observation that school principals were markedly overrepresented in the league.[175] Also ripe for the picking were refugee teachers from Poznan, West Prussia, and Upper Silesia, whose identities were shaped in the German-Polish nationality conflicts. Nationalistic and hostile to the Versailles peace settlement, they harbored a festering grievance against the republican state for mounting a "weak" defense of German nationality in the East in the postwar years. Coming out of the culture wars of the Weimar era, conservative principals and teachers in the elementary schools had an intense animosity toward German Democratic and Social Democratic reformers in their profession. The National Socialists lured these predominantly Protestant traditionalists away from the bourgeois conservative parties in 1932 by holding out to them the prospect of a counterrevolution that would abolish the changes introduced in the school system since 1918. The susceptibility of these mature educators to National Socialism suggests the degree to which professional identity had eroded during the Weimar years. Ideological struggles related to events in the political environment fractured the elementary school teaching profession more severely than did any of the rural/urban divisions of the prewar years. Blinded by these enmities and by hostility to the republican state, right-wing school principals and teachers ignored the consequences of National Socialism for the autonomy of their profession.

National Socialism increasingly penetrated the ranks of elementary school principals and teachers, especially in small towns and rural counties, and it seems safe to say that there was more support for the Nazi Party than the pre-1933 membership estimate (2.9 percent of the educators of all school types) indicates. At the same time, the small number of educators who joined the party and its affiliate before 1933 suggests the need to be cautious in drawing conclusions about the teaching profession's proclivity to National Socialism prior to January 1933 from the rush to enlist in the party after the Nazi seizure of power. The yield of the Nazi recruitment in the profession was still limited as late as March 1933, when the membership of the National Socialist Teachers' League reached 12,000 in a country with more than 300,000 teachers in all school types. The teaching profession, including all levels of the school system, was overrepresented slightly in the Nazi Party membership in relation to its proportion in the gainfully employed German population. The variation among the profession's subgroups should not be overlooked; by the beginning of 1933, there were "disproportionately more upper-school teachers" as well as principals in the party than elementary school pedagogues.[176]

Members of the German Teachers' Association who flocked into the Nazi Party after March 1933 were for the most part opportunists, motivated by careerism and the fear of losing their school offices. In view of the purge of the school administration in the German states and the swift *Gleichschaltung* of the German Teachers' Association in an atmosphere of intimidation and coercion in the spring of 1933, they saw adaptation to the Nazi state as "necessary and unavoidable."[177] Prior to the Nazi seizure of power, however, many left-wing liberals and Social Democrats in this professional association put up considerable resistance to the infiltration of National Socialism. They never underestimated the Nazi Party's grave threat to democratic government and the teaching profession, in contrast to the Secondary Schoolteachers' Association, which continued to be preoccupied with narrow career interests and whose leaders decided to maintain a neutral stance in 1932.[178] Although the educational reformers' soaring expectations in 1918–19 were not completely realized, the Weimar era brought progressive innovations to the schools and extensive freedom and self-governance to the teachers. They knew what was at stake when they repudiated National Socialism. Their defense of the democratic state and sustained criticism of the personnel policy and ideological demagoguery of office-holding National Socialists in the governments of Braunschweig, Oldenburg, and Thuringia kept the Nazi Party from making deeper inroads in the ranks of elementary schoolteachers, despite the widespread anger at Brüning's financial policies.

Notes

1. *Allgemeine Deutsche Beamten-Zeitung*, no. 6, 15 January 1931. This article was signed by "Roamer," a pseudonym for Ernst Riggert, a member of the Allgemeine Freie Lehrergewerkschaft, a socialist teachers' organization. See also Theodor Geiger, "Panik im Mittelstand," *Die Arbeit. Zeitschrift für Gewerkschaftspolitik und Wirtschaftskunde* 7 (1930): 637-59.
2. Bölling, *Volksschullehrer und Politik*, pp. 12, 202, 215; Wilfried Breyvogel, *Die soziale Lage und das politische Bewusstsein der Volksschullehrer 1927-1933* (Königstein, 1978), pp. 48, 136; Dietfrid Krause-Vilmar, "Einführung. Der aufziehende Faschismus und die Lehrerschaft in Deutschland," in *Lehrerschaft, Republik und Faschismus 1918-1933*, ed. Dietfrid Krause-Vilmar (Cologne, 1978), pp. 12-13.
3. *Nationalsozialistische Erziehung*, 25 April 1933: 130, 132; ibid., 25 June 1933: 218; *Nationalsozialistische Lehrerzeitung*, no. 7, July 1932: 16; ibid, no. 8, August 1932: 18; *Schlesische Schulzeitung*, 1 June 1933: 424-27.
4. *Westfälische Schulzeitung*, 23 July 1932: 409; *Nationalsozialistische Lehrerzeitung*, no. 7, July 1932: 16.
5. Ernst Krieck, "Die Lehrerschaft und die politische Entscheidung," *Volk im Werden* I (1933): 32-35.
6. On Chancellor Brüning's financial policies, see Hans Mommsen, *The Rise and Fall of Weimar Democracy*, trans. Elborg Forster and Larry Eugene Jones (Chapel Hill, 1996), pp. 292ff; Harold James, *The German Slump: Politics and Economics 1924-1936* (Oxford, 1986), pp. 68ff; William Patch, Jr., *Heinrich Brüning and the Dissolution of the Weimar Republic* (Cambridge, 1998).
7. Gustav Menzel, ed., *Die Bestimmungen der Reichsnotverordnungen und der Preussischen Sparverordnungen für die Volksschule und die Volksschullehrer* (Langensalza, 1932); GSA, Rep. 77, Tit. 1124, Nr. 78, report of State Secretary Lammers in the Ministry of Education to the finance minister, 30 September 1932 [copy]; report of the Prussian finance minister in 1932, quoted in *Allgemeine Deutsche Lehrerzeitung*, 24 September 1932: 709. On the impact of the cuts in public spending on the schools, see Deutscher Lehrerverein, *Umfang und Wirkungen des Volksschulabbaus. Ein Mahnruf an die Regierenden und an die Öffentlichkeit* (Berlin, 1932); SHA, Nr. 13601, and ibid, Nr. 13602, the school inspectors' reports for the school year 1931-32 sent to the Saxon Ministry of Education. See also Johannes Erger, "Lehrer und Schulpolitik in der Finanz- und Staatskrise der Weimarer Republik 1929-1933," in *Soziale Bewegung und politische Verfassung*, ed. Ulrich Engelhardt, Volker Sellin, and Horst Stuke (Stuttgart, 1976), pp. 233-59.
8. *Allgemeine Deutsche Lehrerzeitung*, 3 September 1931: 693; ibid., 17 September 1931: 725; *Schlesische Schulzeitung*, 17 September 1931: 717-19; *Lehrerzeitung für Ost- und Westpreussen*, 22 January 1932: 29-30; ibid., 29 January 1932: 39-40.
9. *Allgemeine Deutsche Lehrerzeitung*, 11 June 1931: 479-80; ibid., 18 June 1931: 485; ibid., 13 August 1931: 654; ibid., 17 September 1931: 727; *Schulblatt der Provinz Sachsen*, 15 October 1931: 363-64; *Sächsische Schulzeitung*, 14 October 1931: 697-98.
10. *Allgemeine Deutsche Lehrerzeitung*, 11 December 1930: 949-51; *Lehrerzeitung für Ost- und Westpreussen*, 9 January 1931: 15-16; *Sächsische Schulzeitung*, 14 October 1931: 698ff; ibid., 9 December 1931: 858.
11. *Allgemeine Deutsche Lehrerzeitung*, 24 September 1931: 741-43; *Schulblatt der Provinz Sachsen*, 7 January 1932: 5. See also *Schlesische Schulzeitung*, 17 September 1931: 719-21.
12. Deutscher Lehrerverein, *Verhandlungen der 40. Vertreterversammlung am 17. und 18. Mai 1932 in Rostock* (Berlin, 1932), pp. 28ff.
13. Hans Mommsen, "Staat und Bürokratie in der Ära Brüning," in *Tradition und Reform in der deutschen Politik*, ed. Gotthard Jasper (Frankfurt am Main, 1976), p. 119; Thomas Childers, *The Nazi Voter: The Social Foundations of Fascism in Germany, 1919-1933* (Chapel Hill, 1984), pp. 240-43; Jane Caplan, "Speaking the Right Language: The Nazi Party and the

Civil Service Vote in the Weimar Republic," in *The Formation of the Nazi Constituency 1919-1933*, ed. Thomas Childers (Totowa, N. J., 1986), pp. 193-98.

14. The central leadership of the German Teachers' Association in Berlin criticized the referendum campaign as an attack on the democratic state. The proposed Freedom Law in the referendum threatened cabinet ministers, who were responsible for the ratification and implementation of the Young Plan, with imprisonment for high treason. *Allgemeine Deutsche Lehrerzeitung*, 31 October 1929: 892-95; ibid., 14 November 1929: 939-40.
15. *Jahrbuch des Deutschen Lehrervereins 1931* (Berlin, 1931), pp. 102-5; *Jahrbuch des Deutschen Lehrervereins 1933* (Berlin, 1933), pp. 98-101; *Pädagogische Post*, 11 February 1932: 80-81; ibid., 13 October 1932: 515; *Katholische Schulzeitung für Norddeutschland*, 26 October 1932: 708-9.
16. In the historical literature, a meeting in 1927 is sometimes cited as the founding date of the Nazi teachers' league. Johannes Erger states (p. 215) that when this event "is seen as a stage-by-stage process," the differences in the times are "only a formalistic contradiction." Johannes Erger, "Lehrer und Nationalsozialismus. Von den traditionellen Lehrerverbänden zum Nationalsozialistischen Lehrerbund," in *Erziehung und Schulung im Dritten Reich*, ed. Manfred Heinemann (Stuttgart, 1980), Teil II, pp. 213ff; Chaim Seeligmann, "Vorläufer des nationalsozialistischen Lehrerbundes," in *Der Lehrer und seine Organisation*, ed. Heinemann, pp. 305-14; Franz Kühnel, *Hans Schemm. Gauleiter und Kultusminister* (Nuremberg, 1985), pp. 247ff.
17. Erger, "Lehrer und Nationalsozialismus," p. 223.
18. Konrad Jarausch and Gerhard Arminger, "The German Teaching Profession and Nazi Party Membership: A Demographic Logit Model," *Journal of Interdisciplinary History* 20 (1989): 197-225. In the sample of Nazi Old Fighters in the teaching profession in another study by Jarausch, 31.6 percent of the teachers who joined the Nazi Party before 1933 also belonged to the German Teachers' Association; the corresponding figure for the National Socialist Teachers' League was 26.3 percent. See table A. 17 in Jarausch, *The Unfree Professions*, p. 255. Jürgen Falter and Michael Kater, "Wähler und Mitglieder der NSDAP. Neue Forschungsergebnisse zur Soziographie des Nationalsozialismus 1925 bis 1933," *Geschichte und Gesellschaft* 19 (1993): 155-77.
19. *Sächsische Schulzeitung*, 18 November 1931: 792; ibid., 6 April 1932: 257-58. Georg Wawrzik, another Nazi agitator, contested without success his removal from the membership rolls of the Leipzig teachers' association in February 1931. See ibid., 16 May 1932: 228.
20. *Nationalsozialistische Lehrerzeitung*, no. 5, November 1930: 3.
21. Kühnel, *Hans Schemm*, pp. 27ff; Feiten, *Der nationalsozialistische Lehrerbund*, pp. 40ff.
22. On Raatz's life, see *Der Ostpreussische Erzieher. Mitteilungsblatt für die Gaufachschaften im nationalsozialistischen Lehrerbunde Ostpreussens*, 7 October 1933: 416.
23. On Knoop's life, see *Westfälische Schulzeitung*, 10 June 1933: 339.
24. *Allgemeine Deutsche Lehrerzeitung*, 27 November 1930: 917; ibid., 24 October 1930: 808.
25. *Allgemeine Deutsche Lehrerzeitung*, 27 November 1930: 917.
26. Quoted in *Allgemeine Deutsche Lehrerzeitung*, 25 December 1930: 993. On the position of the Nazis on the school question, see also Franz Sonnenberger, "Der neue 'Kulturkampf'. Die Gemeinschaftsschule und ihre historischen Voraussetzungen," in *Bayern in der NS-Zeit. Herrschaft und Gesellschaft im Konflikt*, ed. Martin Broszat et al. (Munich, 1981), vol. 3, pp. 263ff.
27. Johannes Stark, *Nationale Erziehung* (Munich, 1932), pp. 41-49.
28. Quoted in *Allgemeine Deutsche Lehrerzeitung*, 21 May 1931: 423.
29. *Nationalsozialistische Lehrerzeitung*, no. 10, November/December 1931: 10; ibid., no. 1, January 1932: 1-2. See Schemm's attack on the German Teachers' Association, also at the league's big rally in Berlin, in ibid., no. 2, February 1932: 9.
30. *Allgemeine Deutsche Lehrerzeitung*, 7 May 1932: 350; *Deutsche Lehrerzeitung*, 8 July 1932: 200.
31. Quoted in *Allgemeine Deutsche Lehrerzeitung*, 28 May 1931: 423.
32. Quoted in Klaus Scholder, *The Churches and the Third Reich*, trans. John Bowden (Philadelphia, 1988), vol. 1, pp. 191-92.

33. Quoted in Kühnel, *Hans Schemm*, pp. 257-58. On Schemm's propaganda activity among the Protestant clergy, see ibid., pp. 213ff, 226ff.
34. Pyta, *Dorfgemeinschaft und Parteipolitik*, pp. 399-400.
35. Scholder, *The Churches and the Third Reich*, vol. 1, pp. 140, 192-94; Nowak, *Evangelische Kirche und Weimarer Republik*, pp. 304-5. See also Jeremy Noakes, *The Nazi Party in Lower Saxony 1921-1933* (Oxford, 1971), p. 208.
36. *Sächsische Schulzeitung*, 21 January 1931: 41; *Allgemeine Deutsche Lehrerzeitung*, 15 January 1931: 47. See also the discussion on the credibility of the writings of Johannes Stark, Gottfried Feder, and other Nazi ideologues for assessing the policies and intentions of the Nazi Party in *Preussische Lehrerzeitung*, Beilage, 26 March 1932: 3-4.
37. Pastor Jentsch's articles were quoted in *Sächsische Schulzeitung*, 11 March 1931: 194-95; ibid., 18 March 1931: 212. On the Protestant "dialogue" with National Socialism, see Nowak, *Evangelische Kirche und Weimarer Republic*, pp. 298ff; Scholder, *The Churches and the Third Reich*, vol. 1, pp. 131ff.
38. *Pädagogische Post*, 5 March 1931: 158; ibid., 30 April 1931: 292-94. After quoting conflicting statements on the school question in the Nazi press, Peter Schumacher, its editor, stated in ibid., 12 February 1931: 111: "It is clear to anyone who reflects for a moment and remembers Hitler's support for a 'Germanic' religion that the Catholic has no friend in National Socialism but an enemy that should not be underestimated." This evidence was overlooked when Heinrich Küppers wrote that Catholic teachers misread National Socialism and that the Catholic Teachers' Association was unwilling to take a decisive stand against it until the second half of 1932. Heinrich Küppers, *Der Katholische Lehrerverband in der Übergangszeit von der Weimarer Republik zur Hitler-Diktatur* (Mainz, 1975), pp. 93-102.
39. *Pädagogische Post*, 12 November 1931: 745-46. On the Catholic bishops' admonitions against National Socialism in their pastoral letters in the spring of 1931, see Scholder, *The Churches and the Third Reich*, vol. 1, pp. 132ff; Ulrich von Hehl, *Katholische Kirche und Nationalsozialismus im Erzbistum Köln 1933-1945* (Mainz, 1977), pp. 17ff.
40. In comparison, the *Deutsche Lehrerinnenzeitung* followed more strictly the policy of political neutrality adopted by the German Women Teachers' Association. The occasional articles on National Socialism in this newspaper were confined to a mild defense of the women's movement in response to the polemics in the Nazi Party's press. See, for example, *Deutsche Lehrerinnenzeitung*, 10 May 1932: 155-57.
41. For Raeppel's response to an anti-Semitic diatribe against him, see *Allgemeine Deutsche Lehrerzeitung*, 6 March 1930: 182.
42. *Allgemeine Deutsche Lehrerzeitung*, 13 August 1931: 648; ibid., 22 October 1931: 818.
43. *Allgemeine Deutsche Lehrerzeitung*, 23 July 1932: 549-50; ibid., 30 July 1932: 561-63. See also Emil Saupe, *Die politischen Parteien und die Schule. Ein Beitrag zur Schulpolitik der Gegenwart* (Osterwieck, 1932), pp. 2-5.
44. Hilke Günther-Arndt suggests this thesis in her study of the teachers' opposition to the policies of the Nazi minister of education in Oldenburg in *Volksschullehrer und Nationalsozialismus. Oldenburgischer Landeslehrerverein und Nationalsozialistischer Lehrerbund in den Jahren der politischen und wirtschaftlichen Krise 1930-1933* (Oldenburg, 1983), pp. 9, 41-44.
45. *Allgemeine Deutsche Lehrerzeitung*, 15 May 1930: 384; ibid., 29 May 1930: 426; ibid., 19 June 1930: 495; ibid., 10 July 1930: 546-47; ibid., 17 July 1930: 565-66. Reports from the *Thüringer Lehrerzeitung* were reprinted in the newspapers of the branches of the German Teachers' Association in other states. See also Günther Neliba, "Wilhelm Frick und Thüringen als Experimentierfeld für die nationalsozialistische Machtergreifung," in *Nationalsozialismus in Thüringen*, ed. Detlev Heiden and Günther Mai (Weimar, 1995), pp. 75-96; Marie-Luise Worster-Rossbach and Monika Gühre, "Grundzüge der nationalsozialistischen Schulpolitik in Thüringen von 1930 bis 1933," in *Lehrerschaft, Republik und Faschismus*, ed. Krause-Vilmar, pp. 222ff.
46. *Allgemeine Deutsche Lehrerzeitung*, 8 October 1932: 749; ibid., 29 October 1932: 808; ibid., 21 January 1933: 51; ibid., 18 February 1933: 125-28.

47. *Allgemeine Deutsche Lehrerzeitung*, 24 October 1930: 808; ibid., 15 January 1931: 49; *Sächsische Schulzeitung*, 24 January 1931: 2; ibid., 28 January 1931: 151; ibid., 25 February 1931: 151. See also Noakes, *The Nazi Party in Lower Saxony*, p. 223.
48. *Allgemeine Deutsche Lehrerzeitung*, 7 January 1933: 8.
49. *Schlesische Schulzeitung*, 8 April 1920: 157; ibid., 5 May 1920: 189; *Lehrerzeitung für Ost- und Westpreussen*, 2 April 1921: 181.
50. On the experiences of young teachers, see *Lehrerzeitung für Ost- und Westpreussen*, 12 November 1921: 635-36; Volker Hoffmann, "Junglehrerbewegung und Gewerkschaft in den ersten Jahren der Weimarer Republik" (Ph.D. diss., Free University of Berlin, 1976); *Schulblatt der Provinz Sachsen*, 23 June 1927: 201-2; *Schlesische Schulzeitung*, 24 December 1931: 1001-2. GSA, Rep. 77, Tit. 1124, Nr. 28, Beiheft 4, Bl. 80, statistical information on the number of unemployed candidates for school offices as of 15 November 1928, prepared by the Ministry of Education for the Prussian Landtag.
51. *Der Junge Lehrer. Werkblatt des Katholischen Junglehrerbundes des Deutschen Reichs. Beilage zur Pädagogischen Post*, 12 May 1927: 66, 69-70; ibid. 26 May 1928: 73-74.
52. Max Simoneit, "Das seelische Schicksal der schulfremden Junglehrer," in *Von den Enterbten der Schule. Ein Junglehrerbrevier*, ed. Willy Hans Bannert (Berlin, 1927), pp. 25-38; Arthur Hennig, "Der Junglehrer als Typus," in ibid., pp. 16, 23-24; *Der Junge Lehrer*, 12 January 1927: 2-4.
53. Paul Kluke, "Abseits! Zum Problem der staatsbürgerlichen Geisteshaltung des schulfremden Junglehrers," in *Von den Enterbten der Schule*, ed. Bannert, pp. 78-91. See also the address given by Bernhard Bergmann to the convention of the Catholic Young Teachers' League in *Der Junge Lehrer*, 28 September 1927: 121-23.
54. *Allgemeine Deutsche Lehrerzeitung*, 2 July 1931: 544-45; *Pädagogische Post*, 29 October 1931: 701-2.
55. *Neue Sächsische Schulzeitung*, 9 March 1932: 75. On the attraction of students in the pedagogical academies to National Socialism, see Breyvogel, *Die soziale Lage*, p. 196.
56. Jarausch, *The Unfree Professions*, table A. 17, p. 255. See the discussion of the membership of *Junglehrer* in the Nazi teachers' league in *Schlesische Schulzeitung*, 2 April 1931: 563-64.
57. *Nationalsozialistische Lehrerzeitung*, no. 5, November 1930: 2; ibid., no. 10, November/December 1931: 2-5, 11; ibid., no. 1, January 1932: 6; ibid., no. 7, July 1932: 6-7.
58. Bölling, *Volksschullehrer und Politik*, p. 53.
59. *Neue Sächsische Schulzeitung*, 4 February 1931: 41; ibid., 25 November 1931: 314-15.
60. *Nationalsozialistische Lehrerzeitung*, no. 8, June 1931: 6-7; ibid., no. 6, June 1933: 10; *Neue Sächsische Schulzeitung*, 5 April 1933: 104-5, written according to the editor's note in the fall of 1932.
61. *Allgemeine Deutsche Lehrerzeitung*, 16 July 1931: 582; ibid., 30 July 1931: 610-11; ibid., 15 October 1931: 801.
62. Ernst Krieck, *Nationalpolitische Erziehung* (Leipzig, 1932), pp. 13-34, 106-7. Krieck's hostility to the Weimar Republic and sympathy for movements of the radical right were also expressed in *Grundlegende Erziehung* (Erfurt, 1930), pp. 42-45. On Krieck's ideology, see Dietrich Hoffmann, *Politische Bildung 1890-1933. Ein Beitrag zur Geschichte der pädagogischen Theorie* (Hanover, 1970), pp. 343ff; Bernd Weber, *Pädagogik und Politik vom Kaiserreich zum Faschismus. Zur Analyse politischer Optionen von Pädagogikhochschullehrern von 1914-1933* (Königstein, 1979), pp. 258ff.
63. *Evangelische Schulzeitung*, 25 November 1932: 353-55. See the articles by other members of the Protestant teachers' associations who were attracted to National Socialism in *Deutsche Lehrerzeitung. Hauptorgan des Verbandes Deutscher Evangelischer Lehrer- und Lehrerinnen-Vereine*, 8 July 1932: 299-301; ibid., 9 September 1932: 367-68; ibid., 18 November 1932: 474-76. In the early 1930s, *Die Tat* published several articles assailing the school reform movement. See Horst Grueneberg's "Schulreform mit falschem Ziel," *Die Tat* 23 (April 1931): 1-17, and idem, "Was wird aus der Schule?" *Die Tat* 23 (September 1931): 460-79. On the neoconservatives in the *Tat* Circle, see Kurt Sontheimer, "Der

Tatkreis," in *Vom Weimar zu Hitler 1930-1933*, ed. Gotthard Jasper (Cologne, 1968), pp. 197-228; Klemens von Klemperer, *Germany's New Conservatism: Its History and Dilemma in the Twentieth Century* (Princeton, 1957).

64. *Schulpflege. Zeitschrift des preussischen Rektoren-Vereins*, 30 July 1932: 338-46; 24 September 1932: 437; ibid., 17 December 1932: 587; *Neue Sächsische Schulzeitung*, 25 May 1932: 159; ibid., 6 July 1932: 207; ibid., 21 September 1932: 254. On the opposition of politically conservative educators to the new pedagogy in the late Weimar period, see also *Schulpflege*, 14 May 1932: 230-34; ibid., 3 September 1932: 393-96; ibid., 10 September 1932: 407-11; Wilhelm Höper, *Die Krise der Erziehungswissenschaft* (Osterwieck, 1932), pp. 21ff; Paul Kaltenborn, "Möglichkeiten und Grenzen der Arbeitsschule," *Die Deutsche Schule* 36 (April 1932): 172-88; K. F. Sturm, "Vor einer Wandlung des Erziehungsideals?" *Die Deutsche Schule* 36 (August 1932): 353-64.
65. See Jane Caplan's nuanced assessment of sympathy for the Nazi Party within the civil service in *Government without Administration: State and Civil Service in Weimar and Nazi Germany* (Oxford, 1988), pp. 114-16, 121-23.
66. *Neue Sächsische Schulzeitung*, 11 May 1932: 141; ibid., 26 March 1932: 91.
67. *Evangelische Schulzeitung*, 6 May 1932: 145; ibid., 27 May 1932: 170; ibid., 24 June 1932: 201-2.
68. *Deutsche Lehrerzeitung*, 28 October 1932: 443-44, 448; ibid., 9 September 1932: 367-68; *Schulpflege*, 30 July 1932: 338-46.
69. *Neue Sächsische Schulzeitung*, 4 March 1931: 41; ibid., 9 March 1932: 75-76; ibid., 24 August 1932: 214. On the high intensity of the Nazi agitation in Saxony, see Lapp, *Revolution from the Right*, pp. 188ff; Szejnmann, *Nazism in Central Germany*, pp. 55, 75-76.
70. *Deutsche Lehrerzeitung*, 24 June 1932: 282; ibid., 28 October 1932: 448.
71. *Lehrerzeitung für Ost- und Westpreussen*, 21 October 1932: 429-31.
72. *Neue Sächsische Schulzeitung*, 25 November 1931: 314-15.
73. *Westfälische Schulzeitung*, 23 July 1932: 401-7, 409.
74. See, for example, Bölling, *Volksschullehrer und Politik*, pp. 209-16. His reconstruction of the responses of the German Teachers' Association to the challenge of National Socialism in 1932 is based too heavily on the views of Georg Wolff, the chairman of the executive board. The strategy of neutrality and "dialogue" recommended by Wolff was contested and not adopted at the national congress in 1932. The teachers' association during these fateful years has a more complex history than the story of its last chairman's political myopia and opportunism. This difference in interpretation in no way diminishes the value of Bölling's careful research on this professional organization during the Weimar Republic.
75. On Wolff's thinking during these months, see *Allgemeine Deutsche Lehrerzeitung*, 27 November 1930: 926; ibid., 11 December 1930: 961-62; ibid., 22 January 1931: 59-62; *Lehrerzeitung für Ost- und Westpreussen*, 13 February 1931: 65-66.
76. *Allgemeine Deutsche Lehrerzeitung*, 2 January 1932: 1-3.
77. *Preussische Lehrerzeitung*, 27 February 1932: 3-4; ibid., 26 March 1932: 3-4; ibid., 21 April 1932: 1-2.
78. *Preussische Lehrerzeitung*, 11 February 1932: 1-2; ibid., 21 April 1932: 2-3.
79. *Preussische Lehrerzeitung*, Beilage, 26 March 1932: 2-4.
80. *Allgemeine Deutsche Lehrerzeitung*, 30 April 1932: 331. See also the article written by Ernst Müller of Dortmund in *Preussische Lehrerzeitung*, 26 March 1932: 1-3. For the objections to Wolff's strategy voiced by Karl Trinks and other members of the Saxon Teachers' Association, see *Sächsische Schulzeitung*, 3 February 1932: 77-82; ibid., 9 March 1932: 194-96; *Vertreterversammlung des Sächsischen Lehrervereins vom 21. bis 23. März 1932 in Zwickau*, pp. 62-63.
81. *Schlesische Schulzeitung*, 28 April 1932: 329.
82. *Schulblatt der Provinz Sachsen*, 11 February 1932: 56.
83. *Preussische Lehrerzeitung*, 27 February 1932: 1-2; ibid., 21 April 1932: 3-4. On Pretzel's pessimistic tendency, see Johannes Tews's observations in "C.L.A. Pretzel," *Jahrbuch des*

Deutschen Lehrervereins 1925, p. 174. At the congress of the German Teachers' Association in May 1932, Pretzel contended that it was "not the most essential task of the leadership at this time to protect the Constitution" but to ensure the unity of the association. Although he admired the democratic state ideal, he confessed openly that he did not consider the "existing form of the republic" to be the best state. Deutscher Lehrerverein, *Verhandlungen der 40. Vertreterversammlung*, pp. 91ff. On the failure of the German State Party to revitalize the liberal movement and the pessimism and resignation of left-wing liberals in these years, see Jones, *German Liberalism and the Dissolution of the Weimar System*, pp. 378ff.

84. *Brandenburgische Schulzeitung*, 12 February 1931: 64–66. The same argument was made by H. Knösel, a teacher in a rural school, evidently from his own experience as a supporter of the German Democratic Party in *Preussische Lehrerzeitung*, Beilage, 26 March 1932: 1–2; ibid., 7 July 1932: 1–2. See also Pyta, *Dorfgemeinschaft und Parteipolitik*, p. 459.
85. The *Schulwissenschaftlicher Bildungsverein* in Hamburg had a membership of 416. After the congress, this organization broke its loose ties to the German Teachers' Association. Günther's Nazi sympathies were revealed when he joined the Kampfbund für deutscher Kultur in Hamburg.
86. *Verhandlungen der 40.Vertreterversammlung*, pp. 91ff, 118–19, 122.
87. See the report of the congress in *Westfälische Schulzeitung*, 28 May 1932: 277–82.
88. *Verhandlungen der 40. Vertreterversammlung*, p. 200.
89. *Verhandlungen der 40. Vertreterversammlung*, pp. 173ff.
90. *Sächsische Schulzeitung*, 25 May 1932: 385. Wolff was sharply criticized in the report in the *Hamburger Lehrerzeitung*, reprinted in *Schlesische Schulzeitung*, 11 August 1932: 607.
91. *Schlesische Schulzeitung*, 21 July 1932: 552–54; ibid., 18 August 1932: 631.
92. Reports in the *Schulblatt für Braunschweig und Anhalt*, *Hessische Schulzeitung*, and *Badische Schulzeitung*, reprinted in *Schlesische Schulzeitung*, 11 August 1932: 606–8.
93. Traugott Kapuste's article in *Schlesische Schulzeitung*, 2 June 1932: 409–10; Albrecht Brinckmann's article in *Westfälische Schulzeitung*, 28 May 1932: 277–81; the report in the *Schleswig-Holsteinische Schulzeitung*, reprinted in *Schlesische Schulzeitung*, 11 August 1932: 606.
94. See Max Karstedt's discussion of the meaning of *parteipolitische Neutralität* in *Brandenburgische Schulzeitung*, 25 February 1933: 80–81.
95. *Jahrbuch des Deutschen Lehrervereins 1932* (Berlin, 1932), pp. 126–27.
96. *Brandenburgische Schulzeitung*, 15 January 1931: 20; ibid., 23 April 1931: 185–86.
97. *Nationalsozialistische Erziehung*, 10 August 1932: 29–30; ibid., 25 August 1932: 47–48.
98. On the expansion of the league in the province of Brandenburg, see *Nationalsozialistische Erziehung*, 10 August 1932: 31–32; ibid., 25 August 1932: 54; ibid., 10 February 1933: 43.
99. *Nationalsozialistische Erziehung*, 25 August 1932: 46; ibid., 10 October 1932: 104–5; ibid., 29 October 1932: 114–15. Polemical speeches against the educational reforms were delivered by Schemm and Heinrich Scharrelmann, a disgruntled left-wing pedagogue in Bremen who joined the Nazi movement in the early 1930s, at the rallies organized by the Nazi teachers' league in Berlin. *Nationalsozialistische Lehrerzeitung*, no. 2, February 1932: 9; ibid., no. 5, May 1932: 1–14; ibid., no. 9, September 1932: 5–8.
100. This attitude toward big-city teachers can be seen in an article by Ernst Rudolf, a rural teacher who became a National Socialist, in *Allgemeine Deutsche Lehrerzeitung*, 6 May 1933: 318–20. On the unhappiness of rural schoolteachers in their situation of social and cultural isolation, see Adolf Krönke, "Zur Psychologie des Landlehrers," ibid., 15 August 1929: 659–61; Wilhelm Schulschenk, "Der Lebensraum des Landlehrers," *Neue Preussische Lehrerzeitung*, 4 May 1932: 133–35; Hugo Hennig, *Die einklassige Schule. Eine statistische Erhebung aus dem Regierungsbezirk Gumbinnen* (Allenburg, 1929), based on a study of more than 500 teachers in the province of East Prussia.
101. Georg Arndt, *Die organisch-vereinigten Kirchen- und Schulämter in Preussen. Ihre Trennung und Vermögensauseinandersetzung* (2nd ed., Gütersloh, 1926), pp. 22ff. Before 1914, there were more than 14,100 organically connected church and school offices in the eastern provinces of Prussia. Around 10,000 of these offices remained after the loss of Poznan

and West Prussia to Poland in 1919. By January 1932, 8,193 teaching position still remained tied to church obligations. *Jahrbuch des Deutschen Lehrervereins 1933* (Berlin, 1933), p. 49.

102. *Nationalsozialistische Erziehung*, 25 September 1932: 85-86; ibid., 10 October 1932: 104-7; ibid., 11 December 1932: 167-68.

103. See Rudolf Korth, *Die preussische Schulpolitik und die polnischen Schulstreiks. Ein Beitrag zur preussischen Polenpolitik der Ära Bülow* (Würzburg, 1963); Lamberti, *State, Society, and the Elementary School*, pp. 109-53.

104. *Schlesische Schulzeitung*, 22 October 1919: 508; ibid., 26 November 1919: 562; ibid., 3 December 1919: 576; ibid., 21 January 1920: 41-42. In *Orphans of Versailles: The Germans in Western Poland 1918-1939* (Lexington, 1993), p. 35, Richard Blanke states that about 8,000 teachers took part in the exodus of Germans from the areas of Poznan and West Prussia annexed by Poland.

105. *Schlesische Schulzeitung*, 7 July 1920: 275; *Katholische Schulzeitung für Norddeutschland*, 29 April 1920: 213; ibid., 12 August 1920: 395; ibid., 26 August 1920: 416.

106. *Schlesische Schulzeitung*, 18 February 1931: 139-41; ibid., 26 February 1931: 157-60; ibid., 9 July 1931: 524-26; ibid., 23 July 1931: 564-66; ibid., 23 June 1932: 475-76; *Preussische Lehrerzeitung*, 4 August 1932: 2-4; ibid., 6 August 1932: 2-3.

107. See the report of the speech delivered in Potsdam by a teacher who was born in the Ostmark in *Brandenburgische Schulzeitung*, 8 April 1933: 154; ibid., 11 March 1933: 109; *Nationalsozialistische Erziehung*, 25 February 1933: 60.

108. *Nationalsozialistische Erziehung*, 10 August 1932: 35; ibid., 25 August 1932: 45.

109. *Brandenburgische Schulzeitung*, 27 August 1932: 356.

110. *Brandenburgische Schulzeitung*, 8 October 1932: 413-14; ibid., 12 November 1932: 463-65.

111. *Brandenburgische Schulzeitung*, 5 November 1932: 450-51, 456.

112. See the account of the early history of the Nazi teachers' league in Silesia by E. Malitius, an Old Fighter who joined the party in the 1920s, in *Schlesische Schulzeitung*, 1 June 1933: 424-27.

113. *Nationalsozialistische Lehrerzeitung*, no. 8, August 1932: 18; Jürgen Falter et al., *Wahlen und Abstimmungen in der Weimarer Republik. Materialien zum Wahlverhalten 1919-1933* (Munich, 1986), pp. 73-74.

114. *Schlesische Schulzeitung*, 30 March 1933: 246-47.

115. *Schlesische Schulzeitung*, 10 March 1932: 193. A membership record in 1921 listed 6,468 Protestants, 1,208 Catholics, and 34 Jews. See ibid., 13 April 1921: 154.

116. See the remarks of a teacher in the city of Gleiwitz in *Schlesische Schulzeitung*, 12 January 1933: 23-24; see also, ibid., 27 August 1931: 663.

117. *Schlesische Schulzeitung*, 30 September 1919: 463; ibid., 26 May 1920: 218; ibid., 16 June 1920: 245; *Katholische Schulzeitung für Norddeutschland*, 11 November 1920: 543-46. On these organizations in the plebiscite campaign, see also T. Hunt Tooley, *National Identity and Weimar Germany. Upper Silesia and the Eastern Border, 1918-1922* (Lincoln, Nebr. 1997), pp. 95, 103, 157-58.

118. *Schlesische Schulzeitung*, 9 March 1921: 98-99.

119. *Schlesische Schulzeitung*, 1 September 1920: 323; ibid., 12 January 1921: 12; *Katholische Schulzeitung für Norddeutschland*, 22 July 1920: 359; ibid., 9 September 1920: 443; ibid., 23 September 1920: 460, 466; ibid., 30 September 1920: 474; ibid., 7 October 1920: 485-86; ibid., 6 January 1921: 11; ibid., 3 February 1921: 66; ibid., 17 March 1921: 145-46. On the Polish uprising in Upper Silesia in August 1920, see Tooley, *National Identity and Weimar Germany*, pp. 188ff.

120. *Schlesische Schulzeitung*, 26 October 1921: 470-71; ibid., 21 June 1922: 268. See also ibid., 15 September 1920: 399-40; ibid., 22 September 1920: 349-50; ibid., 29 September 1920: 357-58. *Katholische Schulzeitung für Norddeutschland*, 20 October 1921: 591, 594-95; ibid., 27 October 1921: 610.

121. *Katholische Schulzeitung für Norddeutschland*, 2 August 1923: 305-7

122. On these neoconservative circles, see Schaller's account in *Schlesische Schulzeitung*, 31 August 1933: 678-80; see also ibid., 14 August 1930: 626-28; ibid., 21 August 1930: 645-50; ibid., 18 September 1930: 738-39; ibid., 12 February 1931: 131-32; ibid., 14 May 1931: 375; ibid., 10 September 1931: 711-12; ibid., 17 September 1931: 727; ibid., 15 October 1931: 805ff; ibid., 22 October 1922: 820ff.
123. *Schlesische Schulzeitung*, 10 September 1931: 712.
124. *Schlesische Schulzeitung*, 31 August 1933: 678-80; see also Schaller's comments on National Socialism in ibid., 9 March 1933: 185-86; ibid., 16 March 1933: 203-4.
125. *Schlesische Schulzeitung*, 14 April 1932: 294-95; ibid., 12 May 1932: 365-67; ibid., 21 July 1932: 552-54.
126. *Preussische Lehrerzeitung*, 9 July 1932: 3; see F. Fürle's criticism of the new pedagogy and his concept of the school that served the integral nation in the "total state" in ibid., 2 April 1932: 1-3; ibid., 5 April 1932: 1; *Schlesische Schulzeitung*, 18 August 1932: 617-19; ibid., 15 September 1932: 697-99.
127. *Schlesische Schulzeitung*, 13 April 1933: 282ff.
128. *Katholische Schulzeitung für Norddeutschland*, 19 October 1932: 699.
129. *Schlesische Schulzeitung*, 15 October 1931: 805. At the committee's meeting, this demand was deleted from the proposal, and an amended, politically innocuous version was finally adopted.
130. *Schlesische Schulzeitung*, 19 November 1931: 901-4.
131. Quoted in *Schlesische Schulzeitung*, 7 April 1932: 273.
132. *Schlesische Schulzeitung*, 11 August 1932: 610-11.
133. *Schlesische Schulzeitung*, 2 June 1932: 409-10.
134. *Schlesische Schulzeitung*, 10 November 1932: 866-67; see also ibid., 29 September 1932: 752.
135. *Schlesische Schulzeitung*, 10 November 1932: 857-59.
136. For his lecture, see *Schlesische Schulzeitung*, 30 April 1931: 325-27; ibid., 7 May 1931: 346-48.
137. *Schlesische Schulzeitung*, 7 January 1932: 6-7; ibid., 28 January 1932: 69-70; ibid., 11 February 1932: 106-7.
138. *Schlesische Schulzeitung*, 26 May 1932: 401; ibid., 10 March 1932: 181-82; ibid., 24 March 1932: 221-22; ibid., 12 May 1932: 369-70; ibid., 10 November 1932: 868; ibid., 8 December 1932: 937-39.
139. *Schlesische Schulzeitung*, 29 September 1932: 749.
140. *Schlesische Schulzeitung*, 14 January 1932: 25.
141. *Schlesische Schulzeitung*, 12 May 1932: 370.
142. *Schlesische Schulzeitung*, 18 February 1932: 125; ibid., 26 May 1932: 395-96. On the turbulent political landscape in Silesia, see Richard Bessel, *Political Violence and the Rise of Nazism: The Storm Troopers in Eastern Germany 1925-1934* (New Haven, 1984), pp. 90ff.
143. See, for example, *Allgemeine Deutsche Lehrerzeitung*, 18 February 1933: 132-33; *Sächsische Schulzeitung*, 8 February 1933: 117; ibid., 22 February 1933: 169-70; *Brandenburgische Schulzeitung*, 11 February 1933: 60-61.
144. *Sächsische Schulzeitung*, 22 February 1933: 193.
145. *Brandenburgische Schulzeitung*, 25 February 1933: 80-83; *Allgemeine Deutsche Lehrerzeitung*, 25 February 1933: 153-54; ibid., 4 March 1933: 171.
146. *Brandenburgische Schulzeitung*, 7 January 1933: 6; ibid., 21 January 1933: 29-31; ibid., 4 February 1933: 52-53.
147. *Brandenburgische Schulzeitung*, 11 March 1933: 110.
148. See the account in *Schlesische Schulzeitung*, 30 March 1933: 251.
149. See the account of this election in *Nationalsozialistische Erziehung*, 10 March 1933: 71.
150. *Allgemeine Deutsche Lehrerzeitung*, 1 April 1933: 244-45; ibid., 8 April 1933: 259-60; ibid., 6 May 1933: 327-28.
151. On the personnel changes in the school inspectorate, see *Verordnungsblatt des Sächsischen Ministeriums für Volksbildung*, 12 May 1933: 31; ibid., 12 July 1933: 50; *Neue Sächsische Schulzeitung*, 22 March 1933: 83-85; ibid., 26 April 1933: 116.

152. *Verordnungsblatt des Sächsischen Ministeriums für Volksbildung,* 20 March 1933: 15; SHA, Nr. 13858, Bl. 137.
153. *Allgemeine Deutsche Lehrerzeitung,* 8 April 1933: 258-59; ibid., 15 April 1933: 275.
154. SHA, Nr. 13858, Bl. 148 and Bl. 149, articles from the *Oetzsch-Gautzscher Nachrichten,* 3 March and 19 March 1933; ibid., Bl. 143, petition of the "Christian parents" of Löbau, Kittlitz, and Lautitz to the Ministry of Education, dated Löbau, 22 March 1933; ibid., Bl. 147, Paul Lindner to the ministry, dated Leipzig, 1 March 1933.
155. *Neue Sächsische Schulzeitung,* 22 March 1933: 82-83.
156. *Allgemeine Deutsche Lehrerzeitung,* 13 May 1933: 341-42. See also Bölling, *Volksschullehrer und Politik,* pp. 219ff.
157. *Allgemeine Deutsche Lehrerzeitung,* 25 March 1933: 213; ibid., 1 April 1933: 247.
158. Preussischer Lehrerverein, *Bericht über die Verhandlungen der ordentlichen Vertreterversammlung am 11. und 12. April 1933 in Schneidemühl* (Berlin, 1933), pp. 5, 38-39.
159. Küppers, *Der Katholische Lehrerverband,* pp. 115ff.
160. Milberg, *Schulpolitik in der pluralistischen Gesellschaft,* p. 370; Pehnke, *Sächsische Reformpädagogik,* p. 76; Feiten, *Der Nationalsozialistische Lehrerbund,* pp. 69-73; Ottwilm Ottweiler, *Die Volksschule im Nationalsozialismus* (Weinheim, 1979), pp. 47ff.
161. See the reports on the events in Thuringia and Hesse in *Allgemeine Deutsche Lehrerzeitung,* 18 March 1933: 201-2; ibid., 15 April 1933: 274-75; ibid., 13 May 1933: 345.
162. *Schlesische Schulzeitung,* 23 February 1933: 141-45; ibid., 9 March 1933: 185-86; ibid., 23 March 1933: 222.
163. See the ironical comments about the naiveté and opportunism of many teachers made by Erich Kempe, the chairman of a rural county chapter, in *Schlesische Schulzeitung,* 4 May 1933: 349.
164. *Schlesische Schulzeitung,* 30 March 1933: 251; ibid., 4 May 1933: 354.
165. See the listing of chapters and their chairmen in early January 1933 and in June 1933 in *Schlesische Schulzeitung,* 2 March 1933: 173-75; ibid., 22 June 1933: 493-95.
166. *Brandenburgische Schulzeitung,* 8 April 1933: 154.
167. *Brandenburgische Schulzeitung,* 27 May 1933: 233.
168. *Lehrerzeitung für Ost- und Westpreussen,* 12 May 1933: 206; ibid., 19 May 1933: 217; ibid., 9 June 1933: 241.
169. *Lehrerzeitung für Ost- und Westpreussen,* 26 May 1933: 221-22.
170. Feiten, *Der Nationalsozialistische Lehrerbund,* p. 63.
171. *Nationalsozialistische Erziehung,* 10 March 1933: 76; ibid., 15 April 1933: 110-12; ibid., 25 April 1933: 132.
172. *Allgemeine Deutsche Lehrerzeitung,* 20 May 1933: 359.
173. *Schlesische Schulzeitung,* 6 July 1933: 524-26.
174. See table A. 17 in Jarausch, *The Unfree Professions,* p. 255.
175. See Breyvogel's study of the league's membership in the province of Hesse-Nassau and the state of Hesse in *Die soziale Lage,* p. 201.
176. Michael Kater, *The Nazi Party: A Social Profile of Members and Leaders 1919-1945* (Cambridge, 1983), p. 69; Breyvogel, *Die soziale Lage,* pp. 199-201; Jarausch, *The Free Professions,* pp. 102-3, 109. Jarausch offers a comparison based on the subdistrict Lower Silesia. Recruiters for the Nazi teachers' league there were particularly active in the villages and small towns in the Riesengebirge region.
177. See the reports of the chapter meetings in *Brandenburgische Schulzeitung,* 8 April 1933: 154; *Lehrerzeitung für Ost- und Westpreussen,* 26 May 1933: 221. On these "1933 opportunists," see also Jarausch and Arminger, "The German Teaching Profession and Nazi Party Membership," p. 202.
178. On the Secondary Schoolteachers' Association in 1932, see Jarausch, *The Unfree Professions,* pp. 108-9; Hamburger, "Lehrer zwischen Kaiser und Führer," pp. 268-71.

Conclusion

*I*n spite of the myriad restrictions imposed on German elementary schoolteachers by the school authorities during the *Kaiserreich*, left-wing liberals in the German Teachers' Association courageously criticized the social inequalities in the educational system and fought for school reforms. After the revolution of 1918, Social Democrats and German Democrats in high state offices stood on party platforms that incorporated many of the goals of the educational reformers. The appointment of many reformers to positions in the school administration afforded them the opportunity of shaping school policy. For pedagogues who embraced the Weimar Republic enthusiastically and joined the German Democratic and Majority Social Democratic Parties, the imperative of solidifying the foundations of Germany's new democracy lent a heightened sense of purpose to the work of educational reform.

In the midst of economic distress and suffering and in the face of powerful adversaries, the progressivist pedagogues fought to realize their ideal of the common school for children of all religious and social backgrounds and a more open and democratic educational system. The slowing down of the momentum of reform in the later years of the republic should not diminish the significance of what was achieved. Most notably, the Basic School Law of 1920 abolished the special preparatory schools that required the payment of tuition fees, and made instruction in the first four years of the *Volksschule* the foundation upon which the diverse types of secondary schools stood. Members of the German Teachers' Association played a critical role in ensuring the scrupulous execution of this law. Owing to their vigilance and pressure on the Ministry of Education in Prussia to enforce it, educators in the secondary schools, who opposed the concept and social aims of a unified educational system, were defeated in their attempts to sabotage this reform. The introduction of the six-year *Aufbauschule* alongside the older types of nine-year secondary schools was an important attempt to redress the rigid practice of tracking schoolchildren at an early age and to increase the opportunities for intelligent young people who remained in the elementary school after the fourth year to enter a secondary school leading to the *Abitur*. The reluctance of successive Reich cabinets dependent on the support of the Center Party to propose a national law for teacher education, as Article 143 of the Reich Constitution promised, was a disappointment to the reformers, but five of the German states acted on their own initiative and passed laws that upgraded teacher education to a course of study pursued at the universities.

The opening of experimental public schools in many cities and the introduction of the new pedagogy in the urban schools placed Weimar Germany in the forefront of the progressive education movement. The progress of pedagogical reform during these years certainly benefited from the support of Social Democrats and German Democrats in the school administration, but official patronage alone cannot explain the expansion of the active-learning school movement. The progressivist pedagogues retained their optimistic hopes and dedication to reform throughout the troubled times of the hyperinflation. The chapters of the German Teachers' Association organized or cosponsored workshops and courses for the study of the psychology of education and the new pedagogy, and an impressive number of teachers devoted their own time and resources to upgrade their professional skills. The practice of the new methods extended beyond the ranks of Protestant teachers in the cities. Knowing that Hugo Gaudig's concept of the active-learning school was not antithetical to the place of religion in the school curriculum, many Catholic teachers were now eager to stay in stride with their Protestant colleagues.

What made the *Volksschule* become an unending issue of contention in the political battles of the ideological groups in the Weimar Republic were the issues of the relation of church and school and religious education. These questions need not have caused so much divisiveness. The reformers in the German Teachers' Association demanded the separation of church and school not out of hostility to the Christian religion, but for reasons related to their desire for autonomy in the practice of their profession and to their understanding of the purposes of public education in a modern democratic society and in a nation with a historical legacy of confessional antagonism and segregation. A minority of teachers who were Social Democrats fought for the secularization of the schools and argued that it alone would provide an unambiguous and final settlement of the old problem of church influence in the schools. Johannes Tews and other German Democratic reformers represented a more widely held view in their profession when they supported the concept of a common school in which the subject of religion would be taught as an autonomous activity of the school.

The school compromise negotiated by the three parties in the Weimar coalition in the summer of 1919 offered the possibility of settling the school question by consensus. In these negotiations Richard Seyfert and other educational reformers in the German Democratic Party fought for a model of the common school that would do justice to the concerns and sensibilities of all sides in this dispute. Convinced that the overwhelming majority of the population wanted religious education in the schools, the German Democrats argued in favor of a common school for all children (*eine für alle gemeinsame Grundschule* in the language of the Constitution of 1919 and the *Gemeinschaftsschule* in the political discourse of the 1920s), who would be separated by faith only for the instruction of religion. They thought that the dissolution of the ties between church and school need not lead to an adversarial relationship, and hoped that a division of labor in the religious education of the youth and a peaceful coexistence would follow. The teaching of religious doctrines would be left up to the churches and synagogue congregations, and the instruction of religion in the schools would be essentially the study of the Bible and would be supervised by school inspectors appointed by the state. Although the reformers in the teaching profession were unhappy with the ambiguous wording of some clauses in Article 146 of the Constitution, it is noteworthy that the deputies of the three parties in the Weimar coalition devised a politically balanced pluralist compromise for the organization of a unified system of elementary schooling for the nation. After the framing of the Constitution, however, two of the parties in the Weimar coalition did not adhere to the letter and spirit of its school articles. Responsibility for the breakdown of this agreement falls heavily on the leadership of the Center Party.

The Center Party disavowed the school compromise under the pressure of the Catholic episcopate. In uncompromising language in 1920, the Catholic bishops repudiated the provision in Article 146 that gave precedence to the common school as the *Regelschule* in the school district. They laid down maximalist demands for confessional public schools and the exercise of church influence in the school system as the condition for accepting any new school law. Center politicians and publicists of the Catholic School Organization pursued a strategy of rescuing the confessional schools through an expansive definition of the parents' right to choose a school type. They gave an interpretation to the school articles of the Constitution that was neither intended by the deputies in the German National Assembly who drafted them, nor upheld in the commentaries on the Constitution written by legal scholars in the 1920s. Catholic churchmen and politicians stubbornly clung to their conception of German society based on subcultural solidarities and envisioned school politics in the future as the competition of ideological groupings in the republican state. The intransigent stand of the Catholic bishops backed by the Center Party set a precedent that Protestant clergymen emulated when their church conference met a year later.

The success of the Catholic School Organization and Protestant Parents' League in mobilizing millions of citizens reinforced the will of the clerical defenders of confessional schooling to oppose any settlement of the school question that offered them less than their maximalist demands. The new institution of elected parents' councils introduced by the Social Democrats in 1919 gave a big boost to the growth of the parents' associations. Clergymen participated actively in the leadership and propaganda work of the Christian parents' movement and in the highly partisan election campaigns for the parents' councils. They sought to use these elections as a quasi referendum to influence the drafting of the school law. Although many Protestant and Catholic clergymen had condemned the November Revolution and were ambivalent about the republican state, they adroitly used the institutions of participatory democracy and the rhetoric of constitutional rights and democratic freedoms to advance their objectives.

The upswing of votes for the parties on the political right in the elections for the Reichstag and state parliaments in 1920 had a profound effect on school politics. The ominous decline of electoral support for the German Democrats weakened the party that had fought the hardest in the German National Assembly for the principle of unity in the school system. Because the German Democratic and Social Democratic Parties lost mandates in the Reichstag, the power of the Center Party in the formation of governing coalitions was enhanced. The Center Party used its position in Reich coalition governments to secure the passage of a school bill that would fulfill the demands of church leaders. In 1921–22 and 1927, German Democrats and Social Democrats in the German Teachers' Association took the lead in mobilizing public opinion to defeat school bills, whose concessions to church interests contained many infractions of the school articles of the Constitution. The Social Democratic Party's leadership joined the opposition reluctantly and with little gusto. Contrary to the shibboleths about the "godless" socialists in the press of the Center and right-wing parties, the Social Democratic leaders in the Reichstag and Prussian state parliament followed a moderate and inconsistent course in school politics. This pragmatic strategy made the resolute partisans of secular schooling in their own party unhappy and at the same time disappointed many liberals who demanded a scrupulous execution of the school articles of the Weimar Constitution.

The Social Democrats did not reassess their party's platform on the secularization of the schools after the Weimar Constitution was framed. Instead of endorsing the policy of the greatest possible unity in the organization of the school system, educational reformers in the Social Democratic rank and file continued to engage in propaganda work for the cause of the secular school. Richard Lohmann and Heinrich Schulz claimed that the legal recognition of the secular school—to be precise, as a *Sonderschule*—was their party's principal achievement in the drafting of Article 146. They viewed the vote of the Social Democratic delegation for the school compromise in the Constitution as a vote for the gradual realization of a secular school system in tandem with the development of political culture and the constellation of political power in the republican state. Resolutions adopted at the party's congresses in 1925 and 1927 reaffirmed the Social Democrats' commitment to the secular school and expressed the expectation that teachers who belonged to the party would give up the instruction of religion in the schools.

In 1920, advocates of the secular school in the Saxon Teachers' Association made an ill-considered attempt to hasten the attainment of this goal by exercising their constitutional right to decline to instruct the subject of religion. Like many educational reformers in the Social Democratic rank and file in 1919–20, these teachers were inclined to underestimate the influence that the Christian churches would exercise in German society after the Great War and in public life under the republic. Impressed by the strong vote for the Majority and Independent Social Democratic Parties in the state elections, they thought that political conditions following the November Revolution created the most favorable time for a definitive solution to the problematic relationship of church and school. Their defiant tactics and agitational campaign to persuade parents to register their children out of religious instruction provoked considerable anger among Protestant clergymen in Saxony. This antagonism did not abate after the Reich Court ruled in November 1920 that the provision of the Saxon school law of 1919 excluding religious instruction from the schools was unconstitutional. Surveillance of the schoolteachers became one of the prime tasks of the parents' associations. The intensity of this distrust bore little relationship to the modest results of the pedagogues' efforts to "enlighten" the parents during this year-long controversy. In 1922, only 13 percent of the pupils in the elementary schools in Saxony were exempted from religious instruction.

The Majority Social Democratic leaders in the Reichstag and Prussian parliament were more moderate in handling the issue of religion in the schools than the partisans of the secular school. They knew that religion remained an important factor in German cultural life and did not want to launch a *Kulturkampf* that would alienate working-class Catholics from their party and drive the Center Party into the arms of the antirepublicans on the right. In 1919 the Majority Social Democrats in the German National Assembly subordinated their party's school program to political considerations that were decisive for the stability of the republic and the development of parliamentary democracy. To maintain the Weimar coalition, they were willing to reach an agreement with the Center Party on the basis of mutual tolerance and freedom for the establishment of confessional and secular schools. After the Constitution designated the common school as the rule, Social Democratic politicians continued to be very conciliatory to the Center Party in *Kulturpolitik*. They did not want school legislation to divide the two big republican parties. Since the differences between them on the school question could not be reconciled, they sought to avoid conflicts that could jeopardize their collaboration. Moreover, as the lively debate on school politics at the party's congress in 1925 reveals, the Social Democratic leaders had a realistic assessment of the scant prospects of a big propaganda campaign to build up working-class support for the secular school. They did not want to invest too much political capital on this issue or to be pushed into a confrontation with the Center Party. Instead, they appealed to the Center's leadership to return to the Weimar coalition and the school compromise of 1919, and contended that a school law achieved by the Center Party in an alignment with the German Nationalists would have grave consequences for the stability of the democratic state.

In the debates over the school law, the traditionalists in the Christian churches claimed the moral high ground for themselves and accused the activists in the German Teachers' Association of being intolerant. It would be more accurate to say that the progressivist pedagogues and the defenders of the confessional school defined freedom and tolerance from opposing perspectives. What were emancipatory goals for the teachers meant the violation of the rights of religious groups for the traditionalists. The teachers defended the sovereignty of the state in the school sphere vis-à-vis the church's assertion of the primacy of parents' rights because they envisioned the state as the representative of the whole social community and as their ally in the fight for the common school and pedagogical autonomy. Clerical defenders of the confessional school contended that the establishment of an integrated school system would be a coercive act of the state and an oppression of the consciences of Christian parents.

The publicists of the Catholic School Organization disputed the premises that informed the liberals' ideal of a unified school system. They questioned whether a national culture actually existed in Germany and whether the task of nurturing a consciousness of a common cultural heritage and civic identity could be imposed on the elementary schools. The school that sought to find commonality among ideologically diverse groupings and impart shared civic and cultural values, they argued, would become a "coercive school of irreligiosity." They chided the German Democrats for ignoring the hard reality of confessional and ideological divisions within German society and attributed the school politics of the reformers to naiveté and a fanatical urge to impose uniformity. The Catholic School Organization's understanding of the consequences of cultural pluralism for public education was summed up in the motto "to each his own" and in the demand for an educational system in which the diverse types of schools would be granted full legal rights to develop and would compete with each other to become the choice of the parents in each locality.

Radical socialists in the League of Proletarian Freethinkers and the League of Free School Societies who agitated for the secular school and disaffiliation from the church in working-class areas created an impression of leftist activism that aroused anxiety in clerical circles. These fears bore no relationship to the limited results of this socialist propaganda. The perceived threat of the political left loomed large in the rhetoric of the culture wars over the schools and gave the traditionalists in the Christian churches a cover behind which they could conduct their fight to block the reforms that were advocated by pedagogues in the German Teachers' Association. Catholic churchmen and Protestant pastors, with some exceptions, could not reconcile themselves to the final school compromise made by the Weimar coalition and to a model of the common school that would alter the place of religion in elementary education. For more than a century, clergymen, as local and county school inspectors, had exercised immense influence and supervisory authority in the confessional schools and had treated religious instruction as the subject that informed the entire education of the schoolchildren and as a vital part of the church's preparation of young people for Confirmation. After the November Revolution, they could see only "hostility to religion" in the conviction of the progressivist pedagogues that the instruction of confessional doctrine and the initiation of children into the observances of their religious communities should be left up to the family and the church.

In their perceptions of *Kulturpolitik* during the republic, right-wing churchmen overestimated the influence of the partisans of the secular school within the Majority Social Democratic Party and showed an inability to distinguish between pragmatic and radical Social Democrats and between the progressivist pedagogues and left-wing ideologues. Most working-class parents had traditional views on religious education and did not withdraw their children from religious instruction in the registration for schooling as much as the clergy had feared. In the experimental schools in Saxony and in the secular schools, called *Sammelschulen*, in Prussia, the teachers repudiated the political interference of Communist parents and did not pursue partisan-political objectives. They made a clear distinction between the indoctrination of a party ideology and the civic education of future citizens of the republican state.

Clerical conservatives overreacted also in their perceptions of hostility to religion and the church within the elementary school teaching profession. An overwhelming majority of members of the German Teachers' Association were in favor of some kind of religious instruction in the schools, to a great extent without the confessional doctrines in the catechism. Teachers who supported a secular school system were a minority in the profession, and by the mid-1920s many of them perceived the secular school as a lost cause. In the debate over the Keudell school bill, Wilhelm Paulsen and other Social Democratic school reformers thought that their party should cooperate with the German Democrats in the fight for an interconfessional common school. They had come to the conclusion that it would be better to give priority to the unity of the school system over the opening of secular schools because these *Sonderschulen* would never be the choice of a large number of parents. Criticism of the church in the newspapers and meetings of the German Teachers' Association was less a matter of religious faith than resentment against the *Kulturpolitik* of the Center Party and the clergy's mobilization of the parents in the school strikes and more generally in opposition to school reforms.

Far more than a series of scattered outbursts against cultural modernity, the conflicts over school reforms in the Weimar years left in their wake deep political enmities and disaffection from the republican state. The battles between the educational reformers and the traditionalists in political life exacerbated the ideological polarization of German society and divided the parties that had formed the Weimar coalition in 1919. The traditionalists' attacks on the new pedagogy created within conservative sections of society a crisis of confidence in the modern school and its pedagogues and fed the growing malaise of cultural pessimism in the early 1930s. In their polemical attacks on the republican state, neoconservative ideologues and Nazi propagandists tapped the traditionalists' resentments, which were inflamed in the culture wars, and the vague public sensibility that "experimentation" in the schools had come too quickly and gone too far. Hans Schemm and other leaders of the National Socialist Teachers' League were quick to grasp the possibilities that opposition to the new pedagogy and the defense of the "Christian school" offered them in their propaganda against the republic and in their appeal to conservative school principals and teachers who were hostile to the German Democratic and Social Democratic reformers and longed for a counterrevolution in school politics.

BIBLIOGRAPHY

Archive Sources

Geheimes Staatsarchiv Preussischer Kulturbesitz, Berlin
   Rep. 76, Akten des Kultusministeriums
   Rep. 77, Akten des Ministeriums des Innern
Sächsisches Hauptstaatsarchiv Dresden
   Akten des Ministeriums für Volksbildung
   Nachlass Richard Seyfert
Bundesarchiv, Abteilung Potsdam
   Akten des Reichsministeriums für Wissenschaft, Erziehung, und Volksbildung

Newspapers and Periodicals

Allgemeine Deutsche Lehrerzeitung. National Organ of the Deutscher Lehrerverein.
Allgemeine Deutsche Lehrerinnenzeitung. Organ of the Allgemeiner Deutscher Lehrerinnenverein [up to 1920 published under the title of *Die Lehrerin*].
Berliner Tageblatt
Brandenburgische Schulzeitung. Organ of the Lehrerverband der Provinz Brandenburg.
Deutsche Lehrerzeitung. Organ of the Verband Deutscher Evangelischer Lehrer- und Lehrerinnen-Vereine.
Die Deutsche Schule
Evangelische Schulzeitung. Publication of the Verband Deutscher Evangelischer Lehrer- und Lehrerinnen-Vereine.
Germania
Jahrbuch des Deutschen Lehrervereins
Der Junge Lehrer. Organ of the Katholischer Junglehererbund des Deutschen Reiches [published as a supplement to the *Pädagogische Post*].
Katholische Schulzeitung für Norddeutschland. Organ of the Zweigvereine des Katholischen Lehrerverbandes Schlesien, Brandenburg-Pommern, Breslau.
Leipziger Lehrerzeitung. Organ of the Leipziger Lehrerverein.
Lehrerzeitung für Ost- und Westpreussen. Organ of the Ostpreussischer Provinzial-Lehrerverein.
Nationalsozialistische Erziehung. Combat Newspaper (*Kampfblatt*) of the Nationalsozialistischer Lehrerbund im Bereich Norddeutschland.

Nationalsozialistische Lehrerzeitung. Combat Newspaper of the Nationalsozialistischer Lehrerbund.
Die neue Erziehung. Publication of the Bund entschiedener Schulreformer.
Neue Preussische Lehrerzeitung. Organ of the Neuer Preussischer Lehrerverein.
Neue Sächsische Schulzeitung. Organ of the Neuer Sächsischer Lehrerverein.
Pädagogische Post. General Organ of the Zweigverbände des Katholischen Lehrerverbandes des Deutschen Reiches.
Pädagogische Zeitung. National Organ of the Deutscher Lehrerverein [title changed in 1919].
Preussische Jahrbücher
Preussische Lehrerzeitung. General Organ of the Preussischer Lehrerverein.
Sächsische Schulzeitung. Newspaper of the Sächsischer Lehrerverein.
Schlesische Schulzeitung. Organ of the Schlesischer Lehrerverein.
Schulblatt der Provinz Sachsen. Organ of the Lehrerverband der Provinz Sachsen.
Die Schulpflege. Newspaper of the Preussischer Rektorenverein.
Schulstatistische Blätter. Beilage zur Pädagogischen Zeitung.
Der Schulwart. Organ of the Sächsischer Erzieherbund [called *Mitteilungen des Sächsischen Erzieherbundes* from October 1920 to February 1921].
Die Tat
Vorwärts
Westdeutsche Lehrerzeitung. Organ of the Katholischer Lehrerverband des Deutschen Reiches [up to 1921].
Westfälische Schulzeitung. Organ of the Westfälischer Provinzial-Lehrerverein.
Zeitschrift für Pädagogische Psychologie und Experimentelle Pädagogik
Newspaper articles in the archive files.

Published Documents

Falter, Jürgen, et al. *Wahlen und Abstimmungen in der Weimarer Republik. Materialien zum Wahlverhalten 1919-1933.* Munich, 1986.
Fünfter Bericht über die gesamten Unterrichts- und Erziehungsanstalten im Königreiche Sachsen. Dresden, 1905.
Gesetze und Verordnungen über das Volks- und Fortbildungs-Schulwesen im Freistaate Sachsen seit 1919, 6th ed. Leipzig, 1927.
Menzel, Gustav, ed. *Die Bestimmungen der Reichsnotverordnungen und der Preussischen Sparverordnungen für die Volksschule und die Volksschullehrer.* Langensalza, 1932.
Preussische Statistik. Vol. 176: *Das gesamte niedere Schulwesen im preussischen Staate im Jahre 1901.* Berlin, 1903.
Preussische Statistik. Vol. 272: *Das Schulwesen in Preussen 1921.* Berlin, 1924.
Reichsministerium des Innern. *Reichsschulkonferenz 1920. Ihre Vorgeschichte und Vorbereitung und ihre Verhandlungen.* Berlin, 1921. Reprint, Glashütten, 1972.
Statistik des Deutschen Reichs. Vol. 438: *Das Schulwesen im Deutschen Reich. Schuljahr 1931-32.* Berlin, 1933.
Sitzungsberichte der verfassungsgebenden Preussischen Landesversammlung. Berlin, 1919-21.
Sitzungsberichte des Preussischen Landtages. Berlin, 1921-33.
Stenographische Berichte über die Verhandlungen des sächsischen Landtages. Dresden, 1920-33.

Stenographische Berichte über die Verhandlungen des sächsischen Volkskammer. Dresden, 1919-20.
Stenographische Berichte über die Verhandlungen des Reichstages. Berlin, 1920-33.
Stenographische Berichte über die Verhandlungen der verfassungsgebenden Deutschen Nationalversammlung. Berlin, 1919-20.
Vierteljahrshefte zur Statistik des Deutschen Reichs. Vol. 39: Das Schulwesen im Deutschen Reich. Schuljahr 1926-27. Berlin, 1931.
"Die Unterrichts- und Erziehungsanstalten in Sachsen. Erhebungen vom 25. März 1922." *Zeitschrift des Sächsischen Statistischen Landesamtes* 69 (1923): 78-119.
"Unterrichts- und Erziehungsanstalten in Sachsen. Erster Teil: Volksschulen. Erhebung vom 15. Mai 1931." *Zeitschrift des Sächsischen Statistischen Landesamtes* 77 (1931): 102-31.
Verordnungsblatt des Sächsischen Ministeriums für Volksbildung. Dresden, 1919-33.
Zentralblatt für die gesamte Unterrichtsverwaltung in Preussen. Berlin, 1918-33.

Other Contemporary Sources

Arndt, Georg. *Die organisch-vereinigten Kirchen- und Schulämter in Preussen. Ihre Trennung und Vermögensauseinandersetzung.* 2nd ed. Gütersloh, 1926.
Bannert, Willy Hans, ed. *Von den Enterbten der Schule. Ein Junglehrerbrevier.* Berlin, 1927.
Berger, Willy. *Wie steht's um die Volksschule? Ein Befundbericht.* Dresden, 1927.
Berliner Lehrerverband. *Lebensraum der Berliner Lehrerschaft.* Berlin, 1930.
———. *Zehn Jahre Lehrerverband Berlin 1920-1930.* Berlin, 1931.
Beyer, Ernst. *Fünfundzwanzig Jahre Sächsischer Lehrerverein. Zur Geschichte des Sächsischen Lehrervereins in den Jahren von 1898 bis 1923.* Leipzig, 1923.
Beyhl, Jakob. *Die Befreiung der Volksschullehrer aus der geistlichen Herrschaft.* Berlin, 1902.
———. *Wir fordern unser Recht! Ein Wort zur wirtschaftlichen Befreiung der Volksschullehrer.* Würzburg, 1913.
Bezirksverband der christlichen Elternvereine. *Zehn Jahre christliche Elternbewegung in Leipzig.* Leipzig, 1930.
Bierbaum, Adolf. *Schulverwaltung und Schulleitung.* Langensalza, 1919.
Boeger, Johannes. *Staatsbürgerkunde als Lehrfach der Schulen.* Berlin, 1921.
Böhler, Wilhelm. *Zum katholischen Schulideal.* Paderborn, 1922.
———. *Die katholische Schulorganisation Deutschlands.* 5th ed. Düsseldorf, 1926.
Buchenau, Artur. *Wesen und Aufgaben der Schule.* Langensalza, 1919.
Bund für Schulreform. *Erster Deutscher Kongress für Jugendbildung und Jugendkunde zu Dresden am. 6., 7., und 8. Oktober 1911.* Leipzig, 1912.
Burhenne, Heinrich. *Elternbeiräte.* Langensalza, 1920.
Cauer, Paul. *Aufbau oder Zerstörung? Eine Kritik der 'Einheitsschule'.* Münster, 1919.
Chemnitzer Lehrerverein. *Hundert Jahre Chemnitzer Lehrerverein 1831-1931.* Chemnitz, 1931.
Chemnitzer Versuchsschule. *Ein kurzer Bericht über ihre Entwicklung und ihren derzeitigen Stand.* Dresden, 1928.
Deutsche Demokratische Partei. *Bericht über die Verhandlungen des 1. Parteitages der Deutschen Demokratischen Partei abgehalten in Berlin vom 19. bis 22. Juli 1919.* Berlin, 1919.

Deutscher Lehrerverein. *Bericht über die Deutsche Lehrerversammlung in München am 4. bis 7. Juni 1906.* Leipzig, 1906.
———. *Verhandlungen der 27. Vertreterversammlung am 10.-12. Juni 1919 in Berlin.* Berlin, 1919.
———. *Verhandlungen der 29. Vertreterversammlung vom 16.-18. Mai 1921 in Stuttgart.* Berlin, 1921.
———. *Verhandlungen der 30. Vertreterversammlung am 5., 6. und 7. Juni 1922 in Hannover.* Berlin, 1922.
———. *Verhandlungen der 39. Vertreterversammlung am 26., 27. und 28. Mai 1931 zu Frankfurt am Main.* Berlin, 1931.
———. *Verhandlungen der 40. Vertreterversammlung am 17. und 18. Mai 1921 in Rostock.* Berlin, 1932.
———. *Umfang und Wirkungen des Volksschulabbaus. Ein Mahnruf an die Regierenden und an die Öffentlichkeit.* Berlin, 1932.
Dietrich, Theo., ed. *Die Pädagogische Bewegung 'Vom Kinde Aus'.* Bad Heilbrunn, 1967.
Dresdner Lehrerverein. *Die masslos heruntergewirtschaftete Volksschule.* Dresden, 1924.
Erler, Otto. *Die Volksschule im Lichte des demokratischen Staates und des Sozialismus.* Leipzig, 1919.
Evangelischer Pressverband für Deutschland. *Elternbünde. Werden und Wachsen, Aufgaben und Einrichtung.* Berlin, n.d.
Evangelischer Pressverband für Sachsen. *Wider und für die christliche Schule.* Dresden, 1921.
Fabian, Walter. *Klassenkampf um Sachsen.* Löbau, 1930; reprint, Berlin, 1972.
Ferber, Gertrud. *Berthold Ottos Pädagogisches Wollen und Wirken.* Langensalza, 1925.
Fischer, Rudolf. *Beiträge zu einer Statistik der deutschen Lehrerschaft.* Leipzig, 1916.
Föhr, Ernst. *Bekenntnis- oder Simultanschule in Baden?* Karlsruhe, 1927.
Friedrich, Theodor, et al. *Hugo Gaudig zum Gedächtnis. Worte seiner Mitarbeiter.* Leipzig, 1924.
Gansberg, Fritz. *Warum fordern wir und wie denken wir die weltliche Schule?* Bremen, 1919.
———. *Grundlinien der Schulorganisation im neuen Volksstaate.* Berlin, 1920.
Gaudig, Hugo. *Die Schule im Dienste der werdenden Persönlichkeit.* 2 vols. Leipzig, 1917.
———. *Elternhaus und Schule als Erziehungsgemeinschaft.* Leipzig, 1920.
———. *Schule und Schulleben.* Leipzig, 1923.
Geiger, Theodor. "Panik im Mittelstand." *Die Arbeit. Zeitschrift für Gewerkschaftspolitik und Wirtschaftskunde* 7 (1930): 637-54.
Gläss, Theodore, ed. *'Pädagogik vom Kinde aus.' Aufsätze Hamburger Lehrer.* Weinheim, n.d.
Gottwald, Adolf. *Zentrumspolitik in Preussen. Das Zentrum und die Lehrer.* Berlin, 1920.
Grünweller, August. *Schulreform, Volksschule und Volkswohl. Zugleich ein Protest gegen die heillose Auspowerung der Volksschule.* Berlin, 1918.
———. *Der Kampf um die Schule.* Neumünster, 1921.

———. *Richtlinien für ein verfassungsmässiges Reichsschulgesetz als Fundament einer gesunden Schulverfassung und eines gerechten Schulfriedens.* Barmen, 1927.
Haenisch, Konrad. *Kulturpolitische Aufgaben.* Berlin, 1919.
———. *Neue Bahnen der Kulturpolitik.* Stuttgart and Berlin, 1921.
Hähling, Heinrich von. *Aufruf zum Kampfe für die freie konfessionelle Schule.* Paderborn, 1922.
Hartnacke, Wilhelm. *Das Problem der Auslese der Tüchtigen. Einige Gedanken und Vorschläge zur Organisation des Schulwesens nach dem Kriege.* Leipzig, 1916.
———. *Naturgrenzen geistiger Bildung.* Leipzig, 1930.
Hennig, Hugo. *Die einklassige Schule. Eine statistische Erhebung aus dem Regierungsbezirk Gumbinnen.* Allenburg, 1929.
Henselmann, Peter. *Schule und evangelische Kirche in Preussen.* Langensalza, 1927.
Hermann, Hans. *Die Schulpolitik der Vergangenheit und das Schulprogramm der Deutschnationalen Volkspartei.* Langensalza, 1919.
Hertel, Otto. *Der Leipziger Lehrerverein in den Jahren 1896–1920.* Leipzig, 1921.
Heywang, Ernst. *Was ist Arbeitsschule? Antwort in Lehre und Beispiel.* 2nd ed. Langensalza, 1925.
Hiemann, Ewald. *Die geistigen Strömmungen der Gegenwart und die Lehrerschaft.* Leipzig, 1921.
Höper, Wilhelm. *Die Krise der Erziehungswissenschaft.* Osterwieck, 1932.
Irmer, Rudolf. *Der freie Lehrer im freien Volksstaate.* Berlin, [1919].
———. *Und wir Junglehrer ...? Grundsätzliches zur deutschen Junglehrerbewegung.* Berlin, [1919].
Kade, Franz, ed. *Stimmen zur Landschulreform.* Frankfurt am Main, 1932.
Karsen, Fritz, ed. *Die Schule der werdenden Gesellschaft.* Stuttgart, 1921.
———. *Die neuen Schulen in Deutschland.* Langensalza, 1924.
Katholische Schulorganisation. *Die nassauischen Katholiken und die Simultanschule. Ein Materialsammlung dargeboten von der Katholischen Schulorganisation der Diözese Limburg.* Düsseldorf, 1927.
———. *Das katholische Schule im Kampf der Gegenwart.* Düsseldorf, 1932.
Kerschensteiner, Georg. *Der Begriff der Arbeitsschule.* Leipzig, 1912.
Kesseler, Kurt. *Die Erhaltung des wissenschaftlich gebildeten Lehrerstandes eine Notwendigkeit.* Leipzig, 1920.
Kittel, Helmut, ed. *Die Pädagogischen Hochschulen. Dokumente ihrer Entwicklung 1920–1932.* Weinheim, 1965.
Kley, Otto. *Die deutsche Schulreform der Zukunft.* Cologne, 1917.
———. *Das Schulprogramm des Zentrums.* Langensalza, 1919.
Krieck, Ernst. *Grundlegende Erziehung.* Erfurt, 1930.
———. *Nationalpolitische Erziehung.* Leipzig, 1932.
———. "Die Lehrerschaft und die politische Entscheidung." *Volk im Werden* 1 (1933): 32–35.
Kühnel, Johannes. *Gedanken über Lehrerbildung. Eine Gegenschrift.* Leipzig, 1920.
Landé, Walter. *Die Schule in der Reichsverfassung.* Berlin, 1929.
Leipziger Lehrerverein. *Die Arbeitsschule. Beiträge aus Theorie und Praxis.* Leipzig, 1909.
Leonhardt, Erich. *50 Jahre Berliner Lehrerverein 1880–1930.* Berlin, 1930.
Lohmann, Richard. *Das Schulprogramm der Sozialdemokratie und ihre Schulpolitik.* Stuttgart, 1921.

Bibliography

Löwenstein, Kurt. *Sozialismus und Erziehung. Eine Auswahl aus den Schriften 1919–1933.* Berlin, 1976.
Meyer-Dinkgräfe, Wilhelm. *Der Lehrerstand. Berufspsychologische Erhebungen und Untersuchungen.* Göttingen, 1928.
Mittenzweg, L. *Lernschule oder Arbeitsschule? Eine kritische Betrachtung.* Langensalza, 1910.
Moog, Willy. *Grundfragen der Pädagogik der Gegenwart.* Osterwieck and Leipzig, 1923.
Mumm, Reinhard. *Das Reichsschulgesetz zur Ausführung von Artikel 146, Absatz 2 der Reichsverfassung.* Langensalza, 1922.
Muthesius, Karl. *Der Aufstieg der Begabten und die Berufslaufbahn der Volksschullehrer.* Berlin, 1916.
———. *Die Einheit des deutschen Lehrerstandes.* Berlin, 1917.
Nüchter, Friedrich. *Über schulpolitische Grundfragen der Gegenwart.* Munich, 1929.
Oestreich, Paul. *Es reut mich nicht! Schulpolitische Kämpfe zwischen Revolution und Kapp-Putsch.* Leipzig, 1923.
———. *Der deutsche Schulkampf im zwanzigsten Jahrhundert.* Frankenhausen, 1925.
Offenstein, Wilhelm. *Der Kampf um das Reichsschulgesetz.* Düsseldorf, 1925.
———. *Die Schulpolitik der Sozialdemokratie.* Düsseldorf, 1926.
———. *Der Kampf um das Reichsschulgesetz. Die Entwürfe der Jahre 1925 und 1927.* Düsseldorf, 1928.
Otto, Berthold. *Ausgewählte pädagogische Schriften.* Paderborn, 1963.
Pautsch, Otto. *Der Lehrer im Volksstaat.* Langensalza, 1919.
Poehlmann, Julie. *Der Anteil der Frauenbewegung an den Schulreformbestrebungen der Gegenwart.* Langensalza, 1925.
Popp, Walter. *Neuorientierung der Volksschule.* Langensalza, 1917.
Posselt [Dr. Eccartus]. *Die Volksschule, ein Sorgenkind. Eine Kritik des deutschen Volksschulwesens.* 3rd ed. Leipzig, 1923.
Pretzel, Carl. *Die Frage des Religionsunterrichts.* Langensalza, 1919.
———. *Geschichte des Deutschen Lehrervereins in den ersten fünfzig Jahren seines Bestehens.* Leipzig, 1921.
———. *Die Neuordnung der Lehrerbildung.* Berlin, 1920.
Preussischer Lehrerverein. *Stenographische Berichte über die Verhandlungen des Preussischen Lehrertages am 30. und 31. Mai 1919.* Magdeburg, 1919.
———. *Verhandlungen der ordentlichen Vertreterversammlung vom 9. bis 11. April 1931 in Koblenz.* Berlin, 1931
———. *Bericht über die Verhandlungen der ordentlichen Vertreterversammlung am 11. und 12. April 1933 in Schneidemühl.* Berlin, 1933.
———. *Bericht über die ausserordentliche Vertreterversammlung am 6. Juni 1933 in Magdeburg.* Berlin, 1933.
———. *Die Zukunft der Pädagogischen Akademien.* Magdeburg, 1930.
Rennert, Alfred. *Der Volksschullehrer im alten und im neuen Deutschland.* Düsseldorf, 1919.
Rissmann, Robert. *Volksschulreform, Herbartianismus, Sozialpädagogik, Persönlichkeitsbildung.* Leipzig, 1911.
Rolle, Hermann. *Bildungskrisis. Gesammelte pädagogische Aufsätze.* Habelschwerdt, 1926.
Rosin, Hermann. *Das Schulkompromiss.* Berlin, 1920.

Sächsischer Lehrerverein. *Bericht über die Vertreterversammlung und Hauptversammlung am 2. und 3. Oktober 1911 zu Leipzig.* Leipzig, n.d.
———. *Bericht über die 49. ordentliche Vertreterversammlung vom 14. bis 16. April 1924 in Bautzen.* Leipzig, 1924.
———. *Bericht über die 51. Vertreterversammlung vom 29. bis 31. März 1926 in Plauen.* Leipzig, 1926.
———. *Bericht über die 57. Vertreterversammlung vom 21. bis 23. März 1932 in Zwickau.* Dresden, n.d.
———. *Die Umgestaltung des Religionsunterrichts in den sächsischen Volksschulen.* Leipzig, 1908.
———. *Die Lehrermassregelungen in Sachsen in den Jahren 1911–1912.* Leipzig, n.d.
———. *Zum Kampf um die Volksschule.* Leipzig, 1925.
———. *Das Keudellsche Reichsschulgesetzentwurf.* Dresden, 1927.
Saupe, Emil. *Die politischen Parteien und die preussische Volksschule.* Spandau, 1913.
———. *Die Einheitsschule.* Langensalza, 1919.
———. *Die politischen Parteien und die Schule. Ein Beitrag zur Schulpolitik der Gegenwart.* Osterwieck, 1932.
Scharrelmann, Heinrich. *Erlebtes Pädagogik. Gesammelte Aufsätze und Unterrichtsproben.* Hamburg, 1912.
Scheibner, Otto. *Zwanzig Jahre Arbeitsschule in Idee und Gestaltung.* 2nd ed. Leipzig, 1930.
Scherer, Heinrich. *Deutsches Volkstum, deutsche Religion, deutscher Religionsunterricht.* Giessen, 1919.
———. *Staat und Kirche in ihrem Verhältnis zur Schule.* Berlin, 1926.
Schlemmer, Hans. *Die Schulpolitik der evangelischen Kirche Preussens.* Görlitz, 1928.
Schmidt, Ferdinand. *Das Problem der nationalen Einheitsschule.* Jena, 1916.
———. *Volksvertretung und Schulpolitik.* Berlin, 1919.
Schmidt, Otto. *Arbeitsschule und Reichsverfassung.* Berlin, 1921.
Schröteler, Joseph. *Um die Grundfrage des Schulkampfes.* Freiburg, 1928.
Schulschenk, Wilhelm. *Der Lebensraum des Landlehrers.* Magdeburg, 1932.
Schulz, Heinrich. *Die Schulreform der Sozialdemokratie.* 2nd ed. Berlin, 1919.
———. *Der Leidensweg des Reichsschulgesetzes.* Berlin, 1926.
———. *Kirchenschule oder Volksschule? Ein Kampf gegen den Reichsschulgesetzentwurf der Rechtskoalition.* Berlin, 1927.
Schulz, Otto. *Lehrerverein, Lehrergewerkschaft, Lehrerrat.* Berlin, 1921.
Schuwerack, W. G. *Der Kampf um die simultane pädagogische Akademie in Frankfurt am Main.* Düsseldorf, 1929.
Seyfert, Richard, and F. W. Foerster. *Für und wider die allgemeine Volksschule.* Leipzig, 1918.
Seyfert, Richard. *Das schulpolitische Programm der Demokratie.* Leipzig, 1919.
———. *Der Streit des Herrn Dr. Ernst Boehm gegen die akademische Lehrerbildung. Eine Abwehrschrift.* Leipzig, 1926.
Sommer, Paul. *Das deutschdemokratische Schulprogramm in seinem geschichtlichen Werden und in der Gegenwart.* Langensalza, 1919.
Sozialdemokratische Partei Deutschlands. *Protokoll des Sozialdemokratischen Parteitages 1925 in Heidelberg.* Reprint, Bonn, 1974.
———. *Protokoll des Sozialdemokratischen Parteitages 1927 in Kiel.* Reprint, Bonn, 1974.

Stark, Johannes. *Nationalsozialismus und Lehrerbildung.* Munich, 1931.
———. *Nationale Erziehung.* Munich, 1932.
Stehkämper, Hugo, ed. *Der Nachlass des Reichskanzlers Wilhelm Marx.* Cologne, 1968.
Stölze, Remigius. *Universität und Lehrerbildung.* Langensalza, 1920.
Tews, Johannes. *Der preussische Volksschullehrerstand.* Bielefeld, 1894.
———. *Die gemeinsame Elementarschule.* Bielefeld, 1896.
———. *Schulkämpfe der Gegenwart.* Leipzig, 1906.
———. *Berliner Lehrer.* Leipzig, [1907].
———. *Wer wird die Volksschule befreien?* Minden, 1908.
———. *Die deutsche Einheitsschule. Freie Bahn jedem Tüchtigen.* Leipzig, 1916.
———. *Sozialdemokratie und öffentliches Bildungswesen.* Langensalza, 1919.
———. *Die parteipolitische Spaltungen im Lehrervereinswesen.* Langensalza, 1920.
———. *Aus Arbeit und Leben. Erinnerungen und Rückblicke.* Berlin, 1921.
———. *Das Reichsschulgesetzentwurf. Seine Gefahren für Volk, Staat und Schule.* Berlin, 1921.
———. *Elternrecht und Staatsrecht auf dem Schulgebiet.* Langensalza, 1924.
———. *Zum deutschen Schulkampf. Die deutschen Reichsschulgesetzentwürfe in ihrem Verhältnis zu Staat, Kirche und Erziehung.* Frankfurt am Main, 1926.
Versuchsschule Telemannstrasse 10, 1919-1929. Ein Bericht über ihre Entwicklung und ihren gegenwärtigen Stand. Hamburg, 1929.
Viehweg, Erich. *Die sittliche Erziehung in der weltlichen Schule.* Leipzig, 1921.
Weber, Ernst. *Die Lehrerpersönlichkeit.* Leipzig, 1912.
Wegner, Konstanze, ed. *Linksliberalismus in der Weimarer Republik. Die Führungsgremien der Deutschen Demokratischen Partei und der Deutschen Staatspartei 1918-1933.* Bonn, 1980.
Weigl, Franz. *Wesen und Gestaltung der Arbeitsschule.* Paderborn, 1921.
Westfälischer Lehrerverein. *Der Westfälische Schulkampf. Materialsammlung zusammengestellt vom Geschäftsführenden Ausschuss.* Iserlohn, 1927.
Wigge, Heinrich. *Die Gefahren der Arbeitsschulbewegung.* Langensalza, 1913.
Winkler, Georg. *Aufbau des Schulwesens.* Langensalza, 1919.
Witte, Erich. *Die Elternräte.* Breslau, 1920.
———. *Die weltliche Schule.* Dortmund, 1920.
Wolff, August. *Das Prinzip der Selbsttätigkeit in der modernen Pädagogik. Ein Beitrag zur Geschichte der Arbeitsschule.* Langensalza, 1921.
Wolff, Georg. *Einführung in das Studium der Schulpolitik.* Langensalza, 1919.
———. *Die Schule in der Verfassung des Deutschen Reiches.* Langensalza, 1919.
———. *Grundschulfragen und Grundschulgegner.* Osterwieck, 1923.
———. *Das Reich und die Schule.* Berlin, 1925.

Selected Secondary Sources

Albertin, Lothar. *Liberalismus und Demokratie am Anfang der Weimarer Republik. Eine vergleichende Analyse der Deutschen Demokratischen Partei und Deutschen Volkspartei.* Düsseldorf, 1972.
Albisetti, James. *Schooling German Girls and Women: Secondary and Higher Education in the Nineteenth Century.* Princeton, 1988.
———. *Secondary School Reform in Imperial Germany.* Princeton, 1983.

Amlung, Ullrich, et al., eds. *'Die Alte Schule Überwinden.' Reformpädagogische Versuchsschulen zwischen Kaiserreich und Nationalsozialismus.* Frankfurt am Main, 1993.
Beilner, Helmut. *Die Emanzipation der bayerischen Lehrerin, aufgezeigt an der Arbeit des bayerischen Lehrerinnenvereins 1898–1933.* Munich, 1971.
Bendikat, Elfi. "'Wir müssen Demokraten sein.' Der Gesinnungsliberalismus." In Detlef Lehnert and Klaus Megerle, eds. *Politische Identität und nationale Gedenktage. Zur politischen Kultur in der Weimarer Republik,* pp. 139–80. Opladen, 1989.
Berg, Christa, ed. *Handbuch der deutschen Bildungsgeschichte.* Vol. 4: 1870–1918. Munich, 1991.
Bessel, Richard. *Germany after the First World War.* Oxford, 1993.
Blanke, Richard. *Orphans of Versailles: The Germans in Western Poland 1918–1939.* Lexington, 1993.
Böhm, Winfried. "Lehrer zwischen Kulturkritik und Gemeinschaftsutopie. Der Bund entschiedener Schulreformer." In Manfred Heinemann, ed. *Der Lehrer und seine Organisation,* pp. 191–200. Stuttgart, 1977.
Bölling, Rainer. *Volksschullehrer und Politik. Der Deutsche Lehrerverein 1918–1933.* Göttingen, 1978.
———. "Lehrerarbeitslosigkeit in Deutschland im 19. und 20. Jahrhundert." *Archiv für Sozialgeschichte* 27 (1987): 229–58.
Borg, Daniel. *The Old Prussian Church and the Weimar Republic. A Study of Political Adjustment, 1917–1927.* Hanover, 1984.
Breitgoff, Hans, Holger Erhardt, and Renate Ramb. "Theorie und Praxis der 'Arbeitsgemeinschaft sozialdemokratischer Lehrer und Lehrerinnen' 1919–1922." In Dietfrid Krause-Vilmar, ed. *Lehrerschaft, Republik und Faschismus 1918–1933,* pp. 25–78. Cologne, 1978.
Breyvogel, Wilfried. *Die soziale Lage und das politische Bewusstsein der Volksschullehrer 1927–1933.* Königstein, 1978.
Caplan, Jane. *Government without Administration: State and Civil Service in Weimar and Nazi Germany.* Oxford, 1988.
———. "Speaking the Right Language: The Nazi Party and the Civil Service Vote in the Weimar Republic." In Thomas Childers, ed. *The Formation of the Nazi Constituency 1919–1933.* Totowa, N. J., 1986.
Childers, Thomas. *The Nazi Voter: The Social Foundations of Fascism in Germany, 1919–1933.* Chapel Hill, 1984.
———. "The Social Language of Politics in Germany: The Sociology of Political Discourse in the Weimar Republic." *American Historical Review* 95 (1990): 331–58.
Cloer, Ernst. *Sozialgeschichte, Schulpolitik und Lehrerfortbildung der Katholischen Lehrerverbände im Kaiserreich und in der Weimarer Republik.* Ratingen, 1975.
Cremin, Lawrence. *The Transformation of the School: Progressivism in American Education 1876–1957.* New York, 1961.
Dachs, Herbert. *Schule und Politik. Die politische Erziehung an den österreichischen Schulen 1918 bis 1938.* Vienna, 1982.
de Lorent, Hans-Peter, and Volker Ullrich, eds. *'Der Traum von der freien Schule'. Schule und Schulpolitik in der Weimarer Republik.* Hamburg, 1988.
Depaepe, Marc. *Zum Wohl des Kindes? Pädalogie, pädagogische Psychologie und experimentelle Pädagogik in Europa und den USA, 1890–1940.* Weinheim, 1993.

Eilers, Rolf. *Die nationalsozialistische Schulpolitik. Eine Studie zur Funktion der Erziehung im totalitären Staat.* Cologne, 1963.

Erger, Johannes. "Lehrer und Schulpolitik in der Finanz- und Staatskrise der Weimarer Republik 1929-1933." In Ulrich Engelhardt et al., eds. *Soziale Bewegung und politische Verfassung*, pp. 233-59. Stuttgart, 1976.

———. "Lehrer und Nationalsozialismus. Von den traditionellen Lehrerverbänden zum Nationalsozialistischen Lehrerbundes." In Manfred Heinemann, ed. *Erziehung und Schulung im Dritten Reich*, pp. 206-31. Stuttgart, 1980.

Feinberg, Walter. *Common Schools/Uncommon Identities: National Unity and Cultural Difference.* New Haven, 1998.

Feiten, Willi. *Der Nationalsozialistische Lehrerbund. Entwicklung und Organisation. Ein Beitrag zum Aufbau und zur Organisationsstruktur des nationalsozialistischen Herrschaftssystems.* Weinheim, 1981.

Fischer, Joachim. *Die sächsische Landeskirche im Kirchenkampf 1933-1937.* Göttingen, 1972.

Führ, Christoph. *Zur Schulpolitik der Weimarer Republik.* Weinheim, 1970.

Gentsch, Dirk. *Zur Geschichte der sozialdemokratischen Schulpolitik in der Zeit der Weimarer Republik.* Frankfurt am Main, 1994.

Gordon, Frank. "The German Evangelical Churches and the Struggle for the Schools in the Weimar Republic." *Church History* 49, no. 1 (1980): 47-61.

———. "Protestantism and Socialism in the Weimar Republic." *German Studies Review* 11, no. 3 (1988): 423-46.

Götz, Margarete. *Die Heimatkunde im Spiegel der Lehrpläne der Weimarer Republik.* Frankfurt am Main, 1989.

Grünthal, Günther. *Reichsschulgesetz und Zentrumspartei in der Weimarer Republik.* Weinheim, 1970.

Günther-Arndt, Hilke. *Volksschullehrer und Nationalsozialismus. Oldenburgischer Landeslehrerverein und Nationalsozialistischer Lehrerbund in den Jahren der politischen und wirtschaftlichen Krise 1930-1933.* Oldenburg, 1983.

Gutmann, Amy. *Democratic Education.* Princeton, 1987.

Hagener, Dirk. *Radikale Schulreform zwischen Programmatik und Realität. Die schulpolitischen Kämpfe in Bremen vor dem Ersten Weltkrieg und in der Entstehungsphase der Weimarer Republik.* Bremen, 1973.

Hahn, H. J. *Education and Society in Germany.* Oxford and New York, 1998.

Hamburger, Franz. "Lehrer zwischen Kaiser und Führer. Der Deutsche Philologenverband in der Weimarer Republik." Ph.D. diss., University of Heidelberg, 1974.

Heinemann, Manfred, ed. *Sozialisation und Bildungswesen in der Weimarer Republik.* Stuttgart, 1976.

———. *Der Lehrer und seine Organisation.* Stuttgart, 1977.

Herrmann, Ulrich. "Pädagogisches Denken und Anfänge der Reformpädagogik." In Christa Berg, ed. *Handbuch der deutschen Bildungsgeschichte.* Vol. 4: *1870-1918*, pp. 147-78. Munich, 1991.

Hoffmann, Dietrich. *Politische Bildung 1890-1933. Ein Beitrag zur Geschichte der pädagogischen Theorie.* Hanover, 1970.

Hoffmann, Volker. "Junglehrerbewegung und Gewerkschaft in den ersten Jahren der Weimarer Republik." Ph.D. diss., Free University of Berlin, 1976.

Jacke, Jochen. *Kirche zwischen Monarchie und Republik. Der preussischen Protestantismus nach dem Zusammenbruch von 1918.* Hamburg, 1976.

James, Harold. *The German Slump: Politics and Economics 1924–1936*. Oxford, 1986.
Jarausch, Konrad. *The Unfree Professions: German Lawyers, Teachers, and Engineers, 1900–1950*. New York, 1990.
———. "The Decline of Liberal Professionalism: Reflections on the Social Erosion of German Liberalism, 1867–1933." In Konrad Jarausch and Larry E. Jones, eds. *In Search of a Liberal Germany: Studies in the History of German Liberalism from 1789 to the Present*, pp. 261–86. New York and Oxford, 1990.
Jarausch, Konrad, and Gerhard Arminger. "The German Teaching Profession and Nazi Party Membership: A Demographic Logit Model." *Journal of Interdisciplinary History* 20 (1989): 197–225.
Jones, Larry E. *German Liberalism and the Dissolution of the Weimar Party System 1918–1933*. Chapel Hill, 1988.
———. "German Liberalism and the Alienation of the Younger Generation in the Weimar Republic." In Konrad Jarausch and Larry E. Jones, eds. *In Search of a Liberal Germany: Studies in the History of German Liberalism from 1789 to the Present*, pp. 287–321. New York and Oxford, 1990.
Kaiser, Jochen-Christoph. *Arbeiterbewegung und organisierte Religionskritik. Proletarische Freidenkenverbände in Kaiserreich und Weimarer Republik*. Stuttgart, 1981.
Kampmann, Doris. "'Zölibat – ohne uns!' – die soziale Situation und politische Einstellung der Lehrerinnen in der Weimarer Republik." In Frauengruppe Faschismusforschung, ed. *Mutterkreuz und Arbeitsbuch. Zur Geschichte der Frauen in der Weimarer Republik und im Nationalsozialismus*, pp. 79–104. Frankfurt am Main, 1981.
Kater, Michael. *The Nazi Party: A Social Profile of Members and Leaders 1919–1945*. Cambridge, 1983.
Kehrer, Günter. "Soziale Klassen und Religion in der Weimarer Republik." In Hubert Cancik, ed. *Religions- und Geistesgeschichte der Weimarer Republik*. Düsseldorf, 1982.
Kleinau, Elke, and Claudia Opitz, eds. *Geschichte der Mädchen- und Frauenbildung*. 2 vols. Frankfurt am Main, 1996.
Klemperer, Klemens von. *Germany's New Conservatism: Its History and Dilemma in the Twentieth Century*. Princeton, 1957.
Krause-Vilmar, Dietfrid. "Einführung. Der aufziehende Faschismus und die Lehrerschaft in Deutschland." In Dietfrid Krause-Vilmar, ed. *Lehrerschaft, Republik und Faschismus 1918–1933*, pp. 7–24. Cologne, 1978.
Kühnel, Franz. *Hans Schemm. Gauleiter und Kultusminister (1891–1935)*. Nuremberg, 1985.
Kunz, Andreas. *Civil Servants and the Politics of Inflation in Germany*. Berlin and New York, 1986.
Küppers, Heinrich. *Der Katholische Lehrerverband in der Übergangszeit von der Weimarer Republik zur Hitler-Diktatur*. Mainz, 1975.
———. "Weimarer Schulpolitik in der Wirtschafts- und Staatskrise der Republik." *Vierteljahreshefte für Zeitgeschichte* 28 (1980): 20–46.
Lamberti, Marjorie. *State, Society, and the Elementary School in Imperial Germany*. New York, 1989.
———. "Elementary School Teachers and the Struggle against Social Democracy in Wilhelmine Germany." *History of Education Quarterly* 32, no. 1 (1992): 73–97.

———. "Radical Schoolteachers and the Origins of the Progressive Education Movement in Imperial Germany, 1900-1914." *History of Education Quarterly* 40, no. 1 (2000): 22-48.

———. "German Schoolteachers, National Socialism, and the Politics of Culture at the End of the Weimar Republic." *Central European History* 34, no. 1 (2001): 53-82.

Langewiesche, Dieter, and Heinz-Elmar Tenorth, eds. *Handbuch der deutschen Bildungsgeschichte*. Vol. 5: *1918-1945*. Munich, 1989.

Lapp, Benjamin. *Revolution from the Right: Politics, Class, and the Rise of Nazism in Saxony, 1919-1933*. Boston, 1997.

Lehnert, Detlef, and Klaus Megerle. "Problems of Identity and Consensus in a Fragmented Society: The Weimar Republic." In Dirk Berg-Schlosser and Ralf Rythlewski, eds. *Political Culture in Germany*, pp. 43-59. New York, 1993.

Lösche, Peter, and Franz Walter. *Die SPD. Klassenpartei – Volkspartei – Quotenpartei. Zur Entwicklung der Sozialdemokratie von Weimar bis zur deutschen Vereinigung*. Darmstadt, 1992.

Meyhöfer, Rita. *Gäste in Berlin? Jüdisches Schülerleben in der Weimarer Republik und im Nationalsozialismus*. Hamburg, 1996.

Milberg, Hildegard. *Schulpolitik in der pluralistischen Gesellschaft. Die politischen und sozialen Aspekte der Schulreform in Hamburg 1890-1935*. Hamburg, 1970.

Mommsen, Hans. "Staat und Bürokratie in der Ära Brüning." In Gotthard Jasper, ed. *Tradition und Reform in der deutschen Politik*, pp. 81-137. Frankfurt am Main, 1976.

———. *The Rise and Fall of Weimar Democracy*. Trans. by Elborg Forster and Larry E. Jones. Chapel Hill, 1996.

Morsey, Rudolf. *Die Deutsche Zentrumspartei 1917-1923*. Düsseldorf, 1966.

Neliba, Günther. "Wilhelm Frick und Thüringen als Experimentierfeld für die nationalsozialistische Machtergreifung." In Detlev Heiden and Günther Mai, eds. *Nationalsozialismus in Thüringen*, pp. 75-95. Weimar, 1995.

Noakes, Jeremy. *The Nazi Party in Lower Saxony 1921-1933*. Oxford, 1971.

Nowak, Kurt. *Evangelische Kirche und Weimarer Republik. Zum politischen Weg des deutschen Protestantismus zwischen 1918 und 1932*. Göttingen, 1981.

Oelkers, Jürgen. *Reformpädagogik. Eine kritische Dogmengeschichte*. Weinheim, 1989.

Opitz, Günther. *Der Christlich-soziale Volksdienst. Versuch einer protestantischen Partei in der Weimarer Republik*. Düsseldorf, 1969.

Orlow, Dietrich. *Weimar Prussia 1918-1925: The Unlikely Rock of Democracy*. Pittsburgh, 1986.

———. *Weimar Prussia 1925-1933: The Illusion of Strength*. Pittsburgh, 1991.

Ottweiler, Ottwilm. *Die Volksschule im Nationalsozialismus*. Weinheim, 1979.

Paris, David. *Ideology and Educational Reform: Themes and Theories in Public Education*. Boulder, 1995.

Patch, William. *Heinrich Brüning and the Dissolution of the Weimar Republic*. Cambridge, 1998.

Pehnke, Andreas. *Sächsische Reformpädagogik*. Leipzig, 1998.

Peukert, Detlev. *The Weimar Republic: The Crisis of Classical Modernity*. Trans. by Richard Deveson. London, 1991.

Poste, Burkehard. *Schulreform in Sachsen 1918-1923. Eine vergessene Tradition deutscher Schulgeschichte*. Frankfurt am Main, 1993.

Pyta, Wolfram. *Dorfgemeinschaft und Parteipolitik 1918–1933. Die Verschränkung von Milieu und Parteien in den protestantischen Landgebieten Deutschlands in der Weimarer Republik*. Düsseldorf, 1996.

Radde, Gerd, et al., eds. *Schulreform – Kontinuitäten und Brüche. Das Versuchsfeld Berlin-Neukölln*. Opladen, 1993.

Retallack, James, ed. *Saxony in German History: Culture, Society, and Politics, 1830–1933*. Ann Arbor, 2000.

Richter, Ludwig. *Kirche und Schule in den Beratungen der Weimarer Nationalversammlung*. Düsseldorf, 1996.

Ringer, Fritz. *The Decline of the German Mandarins: The German Academic Community 1890–1933*. Cambridge, 1969.

———. *Education and Society in Modern Europe*. Bloomington, 1979.

Röhrs, Hermann, and Volker Lenhart, eds. *Progressive Education across the Continents*. Frankfurt am Main, 1995.

Rudolph, Karsten. *Die sächsische Sozialdemokratie vom Kaiserreich zur Republik, 1871–1923*. Weimar, 1995.

Ruppert, Karsen. "Die Deutsche Zentrumspartei in der Mitverantwortung für die Weimarer Republik. Selbstverständnis und politische Leitideen einer konfessionellen Mittelpartei." In Winfried Becker, ed. *Die Minderheit als Mitte. Die Deutsche Zentrumspartei in der Innenpolitik des Reiches*, pp. 71–88. Paderborn, 1986.

Schäfer, Kurt. *Schulen und Schulpolitik in Frankfurt am Main 1900–1945*. Frankfurt am Main, 1994.

Schallenberger, Horst. *Untersuchungen zum Geschichtsbild der Wilhelminischen Ära und der Weimarer Zeit. Eine vergleichende Schulbuchanalyse deutscher Schulgeschichtsbücher aus der Zeit von 1888 bis 1933*. Ratingen, 1964.

Scheibe, Wolfgang. *Die Reformpädagogische Bewegung 1900–1932. Eine einführende Darstellung*. Weinheim, 1969.

Scholder, Klaus. *The Churches and the Third Reich*. Trans. by John Bowden. 2 vols. Philadelphia, 1988.

Shirley, Dennis. *The Politics of Progressive Education: The Odenwaldschule in Nazi Germany*. Cambridge, 1992.

Singer, Barnett. "From Patriots to Pacifists: The French Primary School Teachers, 1880–1940." *Journal of Contemporary History* 12 (1977): 413–34.

Sonnenberger, Franz. "Der neue 'Kulturkampf'. Die Gemeinschaftsschule und ihre historischen Voraussetzungen." In Martin Broszat et al., eds. *Bayern in der NS-Zeit. Herrschaft und Gesellschaft im Konflikt*. Vol. 3, pp. 235–327. Munich, 1981.

Sontheimer, Kurt. "Der Tatkreis." In Gotthard Jasper, ed. *Vom Weimar zu Hitler 1930–1933*, pp. 197–228. Cologne, 1968.

———. *Antidemokratisches Denken in der Weimarer Republik. Die politischen Ideen des deutschen Nationalismus zwischen 1918 und 1933*. Munich, 1978.

Steinweis, Alan. "Conservatism, National Socialism, and the Cultural Crisis of the Weimar Republic." In Larry E. Jones and James Retallack, eds. *Between Reform and Resistance: Studies in the History of German Conservatism from 1789 to 1945*, pp. 329–46. Providence and Oxford, 1993.

Stöhr, Wolfgang. *Lehrer und Arbeiterbewegung. Entstehung und Politik der ersten Gewerkschaftsorganisation der Lehrer in Deutschland von 1920 bis 1923*. Marburg, 1978.

Szejnmann, Claus-Christian. *Nazism in Central Germany: The Brownshirts in 'Red' Saxony.* New York and Oxford, 1999.

Talbott, John. *The Politics of Educational Reform in France, 1918–1940.* Princeton, 1969.

Tenorth, Heinz-Elmar. "Pädagogisches Denken." In Dieter Langewiesche and Heinz-Elmar Tenorth, eds. *Handbuch der deutschen Bildungsgeschichte.* Vol. 5: *1918–1945*, pp. 111–48. Munich, 1989.

Tilly, Gerd. *Schule und Kirche in Niedersachsen 1918–1933. Die Auseinandersetzung um das Elternrecht und das Reichsschulgesetz in der Schulpolitik der niedersächsischen Kirchen im Weimarer Staat.* Hildesheim, 1987.

Wagner-Winterhager, Luise. *Schule und Eltern in der Weimarer Republik. Untersuchungen zur Wirksamkeit der Elternbeiräte in Preussen und der Elternräte in Hamburg 1918–1922.* Weinheim, 1972.

Walk, Joseph. *Jüdische Schule und Erziehung im Dritten Reich.* Frankfurt am Main, 1991.

Weber, Bernd. *Pädagogik und Politik vom Kaiserreich zum Faschismus. Zur Analyse politischer Optionen von Pädagogikhochschullehrern von 1914–1933.* Königstein, 1979.

Weichlein, Siegfried. *Sozialmilieus und politische Kultur in der Weimarer Republik. Lebenswelt, Vereinskultur, Politik in Hessen.* Göttingen, 1996.

Winkler, Heinrich August. *Weimar 1918–1933. Die Geschichte der ersten deutschen Demokratie.* Munich, 1994.

Wittwer, Wolfgang. *Die sozialdemokratische Schulpolitik in der Weimarer Republik.* Berlin, 1980.

Worster-Rossbach, Marie-Luise, and Monika Gühne. "Grundzüge der nationalsozialistischen Schulpolitik in Thüringen von 1930 bis 1933." In Dietfrid Krause-Vilmar, ed. *Lehrerschaft, Republik und Faschismus 1918–1933*, pp. 212–55. Cologne, 1978.

Index

active-learning school. *See* progressive education
Arzt, Arthur, 26, 47, 54–55, 85, 90
Ausländer, Fritz, 79

Barth, Fritz, 172
Basic School Law of 1920, 110–11, 245
  implementation of, 116–19
  opposition to, 111–13, 115–18
Bäumer, Gertrud, 14, 174
Bavaria, 70, 163–64, 171, 201, 203
Becker, Carl, 78, 131, 133, 165–69
Beyer, Ernst, 46, 86
Boelitz, Otto, 118, 167
Böhler, Wilhelm, 71, 75, 179, 182–83
Brahn, Max, 29
Braun, Helmut, 214
Braunschweig, 207–8
Breitscheid, Rudolf, 176
Brethfeld, Max, 46, 51, 54, 62–63, 141
Brinkmann, Albrecht, 212
Brockmann, Johannes, 205
Brüning, Heinrich, 196–99
Buck, Wilhelm, 46, 88
Buttmann, Rudolf, 203

Catholic Church
  and Bavarian concordat of 1925, 163–64
  and defense of the confessional school, 22, 64, 69–70, 90–91, 97, 171, 183, 247, 250
  and National Socialism, 204–5
  and opposition to the reform of teacher education, 165–67
  and parents' rights, 90, 171
  and religious instruction in the schools, 132
  See also Catholic School Organization, Center Party, clergymen
Catholic School Organization (Katholische Schulorganisation), 71–72, 75, 163, 167, 179–80, 186, 248, 250
Catholic Teachers' Association (Katholischer Lehrerverband des Deutschen Reiches), 14, 99n.10, 133–34, 181, 201, 204–5, 224, 238n.38
Center Party, 4, 17, 22, 25, 37, 50, 75, 110, 114, 137, 186, 197, 203, 250
  and Catholic teachers, 14, 47, 50, 181
  influence in school politics, 58–60, 152, 165–66, 183–84, 246–48
  in political battles over the school law, 90, 95, 170–73, 176–77, 179–83
  See also Catholic Church
Civil Service Law of 3 April 1933, 231
Claus, Bernhard, 47, 81, 190
clergymen
  and school decrees after the November Revolution, 49–50
  political views of, 4–5, 137, 185–87, 189–90, 248, 251

clergymen (cont.)
  as school inspectors, 13–14, 17, 23, 45, 57
  See also Catholic Church, Protestant Church
common school. See school reform
confessional schools, 21–22, 95–96, 182–83.
  See also Catholic Church, Protestant Church
Constitution of 11 August 1919
  school articles in, 60–62, 69, 80–83, 88, 90–91, 183–84, 247
  and Weimar school compromise, 56–60

David, Kurt, 229
Dewey, John, 2–3, 28
Diekmann, Heinrich, 199, 230–33
Diesener, Paul, 53
Dittberner, Karl, 221

Erler, Otto, 120, 142–43, 230
experimental schools, 136–41, 187–88, 246
  opposition to, 136–37

Fleissner, Hermann, 122, 151, 160
Foerster, Friedrich Wilhelm, 112–13
France
  public school system in, 3, 109
Franzen, Anton, 206–7
Frick, Wilhelm, 206
Fröhlich, Otto, 225, 232, 234
Fröhlich, Ottomar, 138, 141, 164, 188

Gansberg, Fritz, 29, 109–10
Gaudig, Hugo, 29, 41n.54, 134–36, 224, 246
Geheeb, Paul, 29, 33, 41n.50
German Communist Party, 74, 78, 140, 188, 190, 198
German Democratic Party, 4, 57–60, 88, 95, 106–7, 117–18, 174, 214, 246, 248
  and religious education in the schools, 48, 52–54
  school program of, 47

German National People's Party, 47, 88, 110, 114, 159, 170–71, 177, 186–87, 211–12, 230, 234
  and its clerical supporters, 50–51
German People's Party, 47, 88, 117–18, 152, 181–82
German Secondary Schoolteachers' Association (Deutscher Philologenverband). See teachers in secondary schools
German Teachers' Association (Deutscher Lehrerverein), 12, 27–28, 50, 76, 158, 166, 169–70, 182–84, 237n.14
  and Bavarian concordat of 1925, 163–64
  and educational reform, 3, 11, 13–14, 18–20, 107–110, 114, 116–22, 131, 245–46
  and infiltration of the Nazis, 219–21, 223–26, 228
  membership of, 1, 13, 46, 199, 222
  and the Nazi seizure of power, 228–35
  and opposition to the Nazi movement, 7, 204–8, 212–16, 219–20, 225–29, 235, 240n.74
  in political battles over the school law, 5, 90–95, 172–74
  and the question of religious instruction, 22–27, 51–56, 97–98, 103n.113, 188, 246–47, 249, 251
  and school articles in the Weimar Constitution, 61–63, 91, 164
  school program of, 55–56, 97–98
  See also teachers in the elementary schools
German Women Teachers' Association (Deutscher Lehrerinnenverein), 12, 14, 39nn.9, 10, 65nn.11, 12
Gläser, Johannes, 28–29, 138
Gleissberg, Oskar, 62, 97, 122, 141
Gottwald, Adolf, 181
Grimme, Adolf, 154
Grünweller, August, 27, 212
Güsgens, Joseph, 205

Index

Haenisch, Konrad, 45, 57, 59, 70, 76, 106–7, 131–33, 186–87
Häntzschel, Paul, 46
Hartnacke, Wilhelm, 112–13, 155, 230
Hellmann, Carl August, 46, 58, 95
Hertel, Otto, 143
Hoffmann, Adolf, 45, 186
Holzmeier, Wilhelm, 24–25
Hübner, Oskar, 34, 53

interconfessional schools (*Simultanschulen*), 21–22, 47, 176, 179

Jewish community
  and the school system, 22, 24, 40n.31, 96, 174

Kaiser, Fritz, 151–54, 156
Kapuste, Traugott, 225
Karsen, Fritz, 119, 145
Karstedt, Max, 219, 228–29
Kerschensteiner, Georg, 31
Kesseler, Kurt, 111
Keudell, Walther von, 172
Klagges, Dietrich, 207
Knappe, Ernst, 225–28
Költzsch, Franz, 50, 80
Krieck, Ernst, 196–97, 210–12, 223–24
Kruspe, Eduard, 80–81
Küchler, Gustav, 215–16
Kühnel, Johannes, 134

Laube, Ernst, 157–58
Lauschner, Albert, 70
Law for the Protection of the Republic and teachers, 122–23
Lay, Wilhelm August, 29
League of Free School Societies (Bund der freien Schulgesellschaften Deutschlands), 76–79, 185, 187, 250
League of German Protestant Teachers' Associations, 47, 66n.15, 210–12
League of Proletarian Freethinkers (Zentralverband der proletarischen Freidenker), 187, 250

League of Resolute School Reformers (Bund entschiedener Schulreformer), 2
Leupolt, Edmund, 156–57
Lohmann, Richard, 62, 64, 71, 248
Löppelmann, Martin, 202
Löwenstein, Kurt, 138, 186

Marx, Wilhelm, 71, 90, 114, 170, 179, 182
Mausbach, Joseph, 58, 60, 69, 90
Mellmann, Paul, 115
Menzel, Gustav, 15, 37, 45–46
Meumann, Ernst, 29
Michel, Ernst, 180
Müller, Hermann, 177, 186
Mumm, Reinhard, 51, 114, 176, 189

National School Conference (Reichsschulkonferenz), 113–16
National Socialist Party (NSDAP), 6, 196, 198, 211–12, 215, 217, 221, 226, 228, 235
  and *Gleichschaltung*, 229–33
  and school question, 201–3, 252
  in state governments before 1933, 206, 219–20, 226, 235
National Socialist Teachers' League (Nationalsozialistischer Lehrerbund)
  attacks on the German Teachers' Association by, 197, 203, 210, 220, 225, 229
  founding and growth of, 200, 235, 237n.16
  leadership and members of, 200–201, 234, 237n.18
  propaganda and recruitment work of, 196–97, 209–11, 217–28, 252
  See also Schemm, Hans
neoconservatives (*Tat* Circle) 1, 190, 211, 216, 223–24, 227
New Saxon Teachers' Association, 156–57, 210–11, 230
Nüchter, Friedrich, 184

Oestreich, Paul, 2, 62

Index

parents' councils, 70–71
  elections of, 73–75, 248
parents' rights
  and school choice, 61, 64, 90–92, 174, 247
Paulsen, Wilhelm, 137–38, 176, 188
Pautsch, Otto, 15, 25
preparatory schools (*Vorschulen*), 11, 18–21, 119
Pretzel, Carl Louis, 25, 52, 55, 116, 214, 240n.83
  and the modern pedagogy, 34, 131–32
principals, 36, 88, 211–12, 234–35
  and collegial school governance, 156–57, 210, 226
progressive education (*neue Pädagogik*)
  and active-learning school, 119–20
  and civic education in the republic, 5, 119–22
  fundamental principles of, 7, 30–32
  implementation of, 35–36, 131–36, 141–45, 246
  in Germany, origins of, 8n.12, 28–35
Progressive Parties (Freisinnige Volkspartei and Freisinnige Vereinigung), 14–16, 20, 22, 38
Protestant Church
  and culture wars in Saxony, 82–86, 159–60, 252
  and defense of the confessional school, 22, 64, 70, 97
  and National Socialism, 203–4
  and opposition to school reform, 27–28, 137, 218, 241n.101
  in political battles over the school law, 93–94, 171, 177–78
  See also clergymen, parents' councils
Protestant Parents' League, 72–73, 186, 203, 248
  in Prussia (Evangelischer Elternbund), 168–70
  in Saxony (Verband der christlichen Elternvereine), 73–74, 86, 89, 159–60, 162
Prussia, 15, 22, 25, 37, 45, 74, 77, 95–96, 106, 110, 116–17, 131, 144–45, 165, 187, 199, 204, 208, 217, 232–33
Prussian School Principals' Association (Preussischer Rektorenverein), 210

Raatz, Otto, 201, 212
Raeppel, Leo, 201, 205–6, 215, 228–29
Rendtorff, Franz, 80, 85
Rheinländer, Anton, 180–81
Riggert, Ernst, 196
Röhl, Gustav, 33
Rolle, Hermann, 158–59
Romberg (school principal), 220
Rothe, Karl, 85–86, 154

Sablotny, Ewald, 217–19, 230
Saxon Teachers' Association, 74–75, 152, 154, 156, 161–62, 229–30, 240n.80
  and fight for the secular school, 78, 81–89, 188–89, 249
  and the question of religious instruction, 26, 81–82, 89, 190
  See also German Teachers' Association, progressive education
Saxony, 6, 15, 25, 29, 35–36, 45, 74, 79–89, 95, 105, 122, 142–44, 165, 187, 229–30, 232
  culture wars in, 151–62
  Transitional School Law of 1919 in, 70–71, 79, 81, 88, 106, 110
Schaller, Hermann, 223, 232
Scharrelmann, Heinrich, 29, 32–33, 140, 241n.99
Scheibner, Otto, 134–35
Schemm, Hans, 9n.17, 200–201, 203–4, 210, 217, 221, 230, 252
Scherer, Heinrich, 19, 55
Schilde, Artur, 219, 228
Schlemmer, Hans, 189
Schmidt, Ferdinand Jakob, 112
schoolchildren
  and controversy over learning achievement, 152–54, 161–62
  and postwar conditions in Saxony, 105–6, 162

and registration out of religious instruction, 57, 76-77, 79, 86, 89, 187
school law
  debate in 1921-22 on, 89-95
  debate in 1927 on, 170-82
school reforms
  and collegial school governance, 106-7
  and common school, 17, 19-21, 61, 90, 108, 246-47
  and criticism of the *Gymnasium*, 110
  in private country boarding schools, 29, 41n.50
  in secondary education, 18, 108, 118-19, 245
  in teacher education, 12, 60, 112, 115-16, 164-65
  See also experimental schools and progressive education
school strikes, 75-76, 167-69
Schröteler, Joseph, 180-81
Schulz, Heinrich, 59, 62, 64, 89, 91-92, 114, 164-65, 172, 175, 248
Schulz, Otto, 53, 163, 166, 184
Schweizer, Aegidius, 181
secular schools (*Sammelschulen*), 76-79, 187-88, 195n.122
  See also League of Free School Societies
Seyfert, Richard, 46, 57-59, 80-87, 246
Social Democratic Party, 4, 6, 88, 117-18, 137, 193n.89, 198, 227-28, 233
  and fight for secular schooling, 53-54, 64, 73-74, 80-81
  in political battles over the school law, 95, 175-77
  and school administration, 45-46, 187
  in school politics, 57-60, 62-64, 67n.49, 70-71, 164, 186, 248-49, 251
  school program of, 24, 48
  and school reform, 20-21, 38, 45, 106-7, 246
  and teachers, 24, 26, 48-49, 54, 59-60, 160-61, 164, 175, 205

Spangemacher, Heinz, 206
Spranger, Eduard, 112, 115
Stark, Johannes, 202-3
Stenzel, William, 83, 143

teacher education
  controversy over reform of, 112, 115-16
  See also school reforms
teachers in elementary schools
  and criticism of the clergy, 17, 23, 51, 55, 73-74, 76, 82, 94, 170, 184, 189
  and disaffiliation from the church, 188
  and educational reform, 1-2, 28-30, 32-35, 133-36, 138-46
  and emergency decrees of 1930-32, 197-99, 205, 209, 226, 235
  in the German-Polish conflict over Upper Silesia, 222-23
  and National Socialism, 196-97, 200, 234-35, 237n.18
  and party affiliation of, 1-2, 15, 38, 46-49, 155-56, 200, 211, 221
  and refugees from Poznan and West Prussia, 218-19, 234, 242n.104
  and the right to decline to teach religion, 61, 75, 79, 81, 88-89
  in small towns and rural localities, 133, 142-44, 215, 217-18, 222-25, 235
  social background of, 11-13
  as veterans of the world war, 55, 105, 145n.1
  and the Weimar Republic, 3, 44-45, 122-23, 162-63, 184, 199, 219, 223, 226-27, 237n.14
  and women in the profession, 12, 14, 31, 46, 65nn.11, 12
  of the younger generation, 208-9, 213
  See also Catholic Teachers' Association, Center Party, German Teachers' Association, National Socialist Teachers' League, principals, Social Democratic Party

teachers in secondary schools
  and opposition to school reform, 6, 20–21, 107, 111–18, 153, 155, 158–59, 161
  political outlook of, 16, 111, 123, 146n.18, 173, 235
teachers' seminaries (*Lehrerseminare*), 13, 164–65
Tews, Johannes
  and campaign for school reform, 16–19, 44, 107–10, 113–14, 246
  political convictions of, 15–16
  and the question of religious instruction, 24–25, 27, 37, 52, 56, 97
  in school politics during the republic, 92, 95, 172
Thiele, Fritz, 215
Thuringia, 6, 165, 206–7, 232
Tittel, Wilhelm, 123, 212, 214
Trebbin, Hermann, 215
Tribukeit (pastor in Dortmund), 170
Trinks, Karl, 212, 229, 240n.80

university professors
  in the debate over the school bill of 1927, 174
  as opponents of educational reform, 112, 115–16

Viehweg, Erich, 82, 87, 97–98, 143, 160–61, 230
Vogel, Paul, 28, 138, 141

Wächtler, Fritz, 206–7
Weber, Ernst, 34–35
Wehner, Kurt, 54, 97, 143, 230
Weigl, Franz, 14, 133–34
Weise, Martin, 120, 138, 143
Weismantel, Leo, 180
Weiss, Karl, 46, 57
Winkler, Georg, 97, 109
Wirth, Joseph, 179, 206
Wolff, Georg, 52, 62, 92, 122–23, 164, 172, 230–31, 240n.74
  and response to National Socialism, 212–14, 216
Wunsch, Kurt, 216, 223, 225
Wünsche, Alvin, 46, 85, 152, 160
Wyneken, Gustav, 29, 33

Previous Volumes in
Monographs in German History

OSTHANDEL AND OSTPOLITIK
German Foreign Trade Policies in Eastern Europe from Bismarck to Adenauer

R. M. Spaulding, University of North Carolina, Wilmington

"A monumental long-term study of a century of Germany's East European trade that demonstrates its continued response to political as well as market pressures ... of acute contemporary relevance."
—Charles Maier, Harvard University

"A long-term perspective on a topic of vital current and continuing importance, and a major contribution to the study of German-Russian relations."
—Gerald D. Feldman

Volume 1. 1997. 544 pages, 37 figs., bibliog., index
ISBN 1-57181-039-0 hardback

CITIZENS AND ALIENS
Foreigners and the Law in Britain and German States 1789–1870

A. Fahrmeir, German Historical Institute, London

"Fahrmeir's carefully argued and detailed study ... should be read by anybody who is interested in the current debate on nationality and migration."
—H-NET Reviews

"[A] pioneering study ... a genuine comparative history ... an extremely important monograph ... [and] major contribution to our understanding of the legal position of aliens in modern European history." —American Historical Review

Volume 5. 2000. 304 pages, 13 tables, bibliog., index
ISBN 1-57181-717-4 hardback

NAZISM IN CENTRAL GERMANY
The Brownshirts in 'Red' Saxony

C.-C. W. Szejnmann, Middlesex University

"Szejnmann's solid research offers, in great detail, many new and interesting insights and thus an important contribution to the history of Saxony during the National Socialist era that still needs to be written."
—Neues Archiv für Sächsische Geschichte

Volume 4. 1998. 304 pages, 12 tables, bibliog., index
ISBN 1-57181-942-8 hardback

FROM RECOVERY TO CATASTROPHE
Municipal Stabilization and Political Crisis

B. Lieberman, Fitchburg State College, MA

"A valuable book on the Weimar welfare state ... an attractive package with a full scholarly apparatus."
—German Studies Review

Volume 3. 1998. 192 pages, 13 tables, bibliog., index
ISBN 1-57181-104-4 hardback

A QUESTION OF PRIORITIES
Democratic Reform and Economic Recovery in Postwar Germany

R. Boehling, University of Maryland

"... most welcome as the first detailed analysis of political reconstruction in major postwar German cities available in English." —Choice

Volume 2. 1996. 320 pages, 12 photos, bibliog., index
ISBN 1-57181-035-8 hardback
ISBN 1-57181-159-1 paperback

www.berghahnbooks.com

New Volumes in
Monographs in German History

Volume 7
"ARYANISATION" IN HAMBURG
The Economic Exclusion of Jews and the Confiscation of Their Property in Nazi Germany

Frank Bajohr, Forschungsstelle für Zeitgeschichte in Hamburg and University of Hamburg
Translated from the German by **George Wilkes**

"This searing book about 'Aryanisation,' the process by which the Nazis robbed Jews of their economic livelihood, presents a lucid and riveting analysis of a little investigated subject. Compassionate towards the victims of the Third Reich's 'Aryanisation' program and enraged by the perpetrators, Dr. Bajohr has set a new standard for Holocaust scholarship. Integrating several narrative threads—the Nazi's economic policy, popular reactions, Jewish responses—this book is about people: people who harmed, who profited, who were robbed and exploited, who watched. Creatively conceived and meticulously documented, [this book] will become a classic work on this subject."
—**Debórah Dwork**, Center for Holocaust and Genocide Studies, Clark University

2001. 352 pages, 14 tables, bibliog., index
ISBN 1-57181-484-1 hardback
ISBN 1-57181-485-X paperback

Volume 8
POEMS IN STEEL
National Socialism and the Politics of Inventing from Weimar to Bonn

Kees Gispen, University of Mississippi

The role of National Socialism in the development of German society remains a central question of historical inquiry. This study presents original answers by examining the politics of inventing, a crucial but long ignored problem at the intersection of the history of technology and that of the law, politics, and business. The analysis of conflicts over the rights of inventors and the meaning of inventing from the 1920s to the 1950s reveals a deep chasm, reaching back to the late nineteenth century, between the forces of capital and big business on one hand and the exponents of intellectual capital—inventors, engineers, industrial scientists—on the other.

2001. 372 pages, 3 tables, 3 figs., bibliog., index
ISBN 1-57181-242-3 hardback
ISBN 1-57181-303-9 paperback

www.berghahnbooks.com

Related Titles of Interest

RETHINKING VIENNA 1900

Edited by **Steven Beller**, Washington, D.C.

"This enthralling collection of ten distinguished essays not only provides the best introduction to the subject, but is a major original contribution in its own right."
—**Tim Blanning**, Cambridge University

"Beller's excellent introduction ... clearly lays out the scope of the original argument, provides a sound review of existing scholarship and a clear summary.... [A] well-organized and focused [collection]."
—**Laura Gellott**, University of Wisconsin-Parkside

2001. 304 pages, 16 ills., bibliog., index
ISBN 1-57181-139-7 hardback
ISBN 1-57181-140-0 paperback

PRODUCTIVE MEN AND REPRODUCTIVE WOMEN
The Agrarian Household and the Emergence of Separate Spheres in the German Enlightenment

Marion W. Gray, Kansas State University

"Fascinating and original."
—Times Literary Supplement

"... suggestive, meticulous, and closely reasoned ... densely structured, highly detailed notes, comprehensive bibliography." —**Choice**

2000. 384 pages, 13 ills., bibliog., index
ISBN 1-57181-171-0 hardback
ISBN 1-57181-172-9 paperback

CREATING OUR COMMON FUTURE
Educating for Unity in Diversity

Edited by **Jack Campbell**
Published in Association with **UNESCO**

"A healthy challenge to our current priorities ... readable and thought-provoking."
—**The Friend**

The essays presented here reflect on the possibilities of a "common future" and on educational programs and projects that are aimed at transforming the vision of a more humane world into a reality.

2001. 176 pages, bibliog., index

ISBN 1-57181-279-2 hardback
ISBN 1-57181-280-6 paperback

UNIVERSITIES REMEMBERING EUROPE
Nations, Culture, and Higher Education

Edited by **Francis Crawley, Paul Smeyers, and Paul Standish**

Contents: The Idea of the European Dimension – The Challenge of Multiculturalism – The Response to the Economic Demands – Situating the Individual and Society in European Higher Education – Higher Education in a European Context: Some Recommendations and Conclusions

2000. 256 pages, bibliog., index
ISBN 1-57181-957-6 hardback

Related Titles of Interest

IMPERIAL GERMANY 1871–1914
Economy, Society, Culture and Politics

Volker R. Berghahn, Columbia University

"... not a conventional political history but a comprehensive account of German society, alive to the conflicts and contradictions in that society and attentive to broader social, economic and cultural developments."
—**New York Times Book Review**

"A comprehensive, very readable introduction to German society.... Accessible to general readers and undergraduates; recommended for all libraries."
—**Choice**

"The best comprehensive textbook on Imperial Germany available to date. [The author's] self-consciously didactic stance, his clarity of writing, his excellent cross-referencing throughout and ... the marvelous statistical appendix ... will recommend the book to undergraduates." —**History Today**

"A milestone in the historiography of the Kaiserreich ... an important and useful book both for teachers and scholars.... Students will be stimulated by the prospect of historiographic debate without being bored or turned off by its arcane twists and turns.... For now and ... for some time to come, [this book] will set the scholarly standard as well as fill a pedagogical void." —**The Historian**

1995. 372 pages, 86 tables, bibliog., index
ISBN 1-57181-013-7 hardback

GERMAN HISTORY 1789–1871
From the Holy Roman Empire to the Bismarckian Reich

Eric Dorn Brose, Drexel University

"... extraordinarily readable, compact and comprehensive coverage... a balanced presentation of the arguments for and against positions on all sides.... The reader will have a clear sense of of historical progression and major connections, while leading personalities in all fields are recognizable characters.... A fine achievement."
—**Central European History**

Studies of nineteenth-century Germany often gravitate toward Prussia or treat Germany's southern and northern regions as separate entities or else are thematically compartmentalized. This book overcomes these divisions, offering a wide-ranging account of this revolutionary century and skillfully combining narrative with analysis. Its lively style makes it very accessible and ideal for all students of nineteenth-century Germany.

1997. 392 pages, 4 maps, 11 ills., bibliog., index
ISBN 1-57181-055-2 hardback
ISBN 1-57181-056-0 paperback

www.berghahnbooks.com

Related Journal

German Politics & Society

Editor: **Andrei S. Markovits,** University of Michigan
Managing Editor: **Debi Howell-Ardila,** University of California, Berkeley

German Politics & Society is a joint publication of the University of Michigan and all North American universities featuring programs and centers of German and European studies associated with the German Academic Exchange Service (DAAD).

German Politics & Society explores the political and economic transitions in Germany from the combined perspectives of the social sciences, history, and cultural studies, and provides a forum for discussion and debate of Germany's domestic politics and role in the international community. The journal examines how film, literature, visual arts, and popular culture reflect changes and trends in German society.

Selected Forthcoming and Recent Articles:

Votes and Resources: Political Finance in Germany, *by Peter Pulzer*
Instituting Europe: Germany, the Union, and the Legacy of the Short Century, *by Michael Werz*
The PDS after Gysi: A Report from the PDS Congress in Cottbus, *by Jonathan Olsen*
(Re)constructing Community in Berlin: Turks, Jews, and German Responsibility, *by Jonathan Laurence*
Setting the Tone: A Review of German-Jewish History in Modern Times, *by Steven Beller*
Where Memory Resides: A Review of *At Memory's Edge and Munich and Memory, by Kathleen James-Chakraborty*
Ein Staatsmann mit Geschichte: Joschka Fischer's German Past, *by M. Anne Sa'adah*

ISSN 0882-7079
Vol. 20/2002, 4 issues
Institutional, Individual and Student Rates available.
journals@berghahnbooks.com

www.berghahnbooks.com

www.ingramcontent.com/pod-product-compliance
Lightning Source LLC
Chambersburg PA
CBHW052015070526
44584CB00016B/1765